Integrating Technology into Teaching

Integrating Technology into Teaching

The Technology and Learning Continuum

Art Recesso / Chandra Orrill

Learning & Performance Support Laboratory
University of Georgia

Houghton Mifflin   Boston   New York

In memory of my best friend, Captain James. J. Morris USMC.
—*Art Recesso*

I dedicate this book to the visionary educators and programmers who will push technology integration beyond anything we can imagine today.
—*Chandra Orrill*

Publisher: Patricia A. Coryell
Executive Editor: Mary Finch
Marketing Manager: Amy Whitaker
Senior Development Editor: Lisa A. Mafrici
Senior Project Editor: Aileen Mason
Senior Art and Design Coordinator: Jill Haber Atkins
Cover Design Director: Tony Saizon
Senior Photo Editor: Jennifer Meyer Dare
Composition Buyer: Chuck Dutton
New Title Project Manager: James Lonergan
Editorial Assistant: Dayna Pell
Marketing Assistant: Samantha Abrams
Editorial Assistant: Paola Moll

Cover image: © George Doyle/Getty Images

Printed in the U.S.A.

Library of Congress Control Number: 2007920366

Instructor's exam copy:
ISBN-13: 978-0-618-83328-3
ISBN-10: 0-618-83328-5

For orders, use student text ISBNs:
ISBN-13: 978-0-618-37083-2
ISBN-10: 0-618-37083-8

1 2 3 4 5 6 7 8 9-WEB-11 10 09 08 07

Brief Contents

Contents

Chapter 14 Emerging Technologies for Learning 267

Chapter 15   Integrating Technology for Diverse Learners   289

Appendixes

Features

◼ Spotlight

◼ Video Case

■ Technology in Action

■ Case Study

Preface

In our experience as instructors in educational technology courses, we have found many excellent books covering a wide array of technology tools. Too often, however, those books are not clearly centered on the needs of preservice teachers. In particular, we believe teachers need more support in developing an understanding of when and how to use technology in the current context of educational reform and high accountability.

There are many issues and ideas that preservice teachers need to know about in order to use technology in thoughtful and exciting ways to support student learning. For this book, we have drawn on our own experiences as course instructors, brought in highlights from our work as teacher collaborators, and included materials that many teachers have found useful. We have incorporated these materials in the Technology and Learning Continuum (TLC) Model, a straightforward model that guides teachers in preparing for purposeful technology integration in the classroom.

Elements of Our Approach

On the basis of our work with preservice teachers and with other teacher educators, we decided that a book grounded in learning theory and tied into a general instructional model would provide the best support and guidance for novice educational technologists. To that end, we have based this book on constructivist learning theory. We highlight ways in which technology is used in real schools by real students, and we offer a model that can work in any learning environment.

We take the idea of *integrating* technology seriously. We focus on what teachers need to think about in the way they plan instruction, configure their classrooms, and use technology to meet their learning goals.

Research About Learning

The book is grounded in theories and research about learning. As a basis for thinking about how students learn and how to create effective learning environments, we have relied on constructivist learning theory as well as the Learner-Centered Psychological Principles established by the American Psychological Association. We stress learning theory because, in our minds, the purpose of using technology is to support students as they learn. Technology should always serve learning, not vice versa.

Emphasis on Standards

This book is unique in its approach to technology integration because it assumes that all teachers work in an environment consisting of multiple and simultaneous education reform efforts. To address standards-based reform, the book is aligned with the National Educational Technology Standards (NETS) for Teachers published by the International Society for Technology in Education (ISTE).

The book approaches the NETS standards in a very explicit way. You will find excerpts from the NETS standards at the beginning of every chapter. However, we didn't stop there. We have also included highlights from a wide variety of state and national standards to help preservice teachers develop an understanding of the connection between the ideas we are talking about in this book and the requirements for classroom learning. At the end of each chapter, readers are asked to reflect on connections between the NETS and what they are studying. We hope that preservice teachers will not only learn about these standards but also make significant progress toward meeting them as they work through the course.

The TLC Model

The TLC model is an effective way to frame teachers' thinking about the planning and execution of a technology-rich learning experience. Not only does this model provide step-by-step guidance, the process is applicable to any content area or grade level. The TLC model can help preservice teachers design instruction to meet learning goals, blending instructional design with technology planning.

The TLC model is structured in a way that allows it to be assessment-driven. That is, preservice teachers begin by identifying what is to be learned and what the assessment of that learning will entail. Once they have identified those elements, teachers are better able to design instruction that caters to the goals and the assessment. This method helps create learning experiences that are focused and purposeful.

Throughout our discussion of the TLC model, we introduce many ideas for technology integration that are appropriate to the model. We consistently lean toward constructivist uses of technology, such as creating models, engaging in inquiry-based simulations, and building communities. However, to give teachers a wealth of options, we also provide more traditional suggestions, such as using word processors and the World Wide Web in the classroom and evaluating software for adoption.

Self-Assessment

Quality teaching and continuous professional growth are part of the high accountability and high expectations in today's schools. This book devotes an entire chapter to self-assessment to encourage teachers to look deeply into their own practices. We also discuss ideas for improving the way teachers study the practices of other teachers. Technology is a powerful tool for learning about what really works and what effective practice looks like in the classroom.

▰▰ A Wide Range of Technologies

This book features a wide range of technologies, presented in ways that allow preservice teachers to "see" them in action. That is, we not only introduce the tools and what they can do, but also offer vignettes of the technologies in use as well as descriptions of particular software titles that teachers may not yet know about.

We strive to include basic and standard technological tools, as well as a few more cutting-edge technologies. This approach has allowed us to discuss everything from over-the-counter software packages to freeware to innovative technologies that are just beginning to appear in schools. In the process of introducing these technologies, we have tried to incorporate important information to help preservice teachers think carefully about how technology can and should be used.

▰ Organization of the Text

The book is divided into four parts. To begin Part I: Technology and the Learning Environment, Chapter 1 establishes a vision of what technology integration can be and describes some of the innovators in educational technology research. Chapter 2 introduces the theoretical foundation of the book, presenting the Learner-Centered Psychological Principles. This chapter also helps preservice teachers think about what technology means in the context of a learning environment. Chapter 3 considers what constructivism and the Learner-Centered Psychological Principles mean for the organization of instruction and assessment. Part I ends with Chapter 4, which addresses teaching and learning standards in education. Here we encourage readers to use the standards for their own benefit and make them a meaningful part of lesson planning. Throughout Part I, we offer a variety of examples and cases to help preservice teachers understand how technology integration can function in a standards-based, constructivist learning environment.

Part II: Infusing Technology for Teaching and Learning introduces readers to the Technology and Learning Continuum one step at a time. With detailed examples, we provide opportunities for preservice teachers to understand the implications of each step for their own use of technology. In Chapter 5, we introduce the model, offer a rationale for it, and elaborate on ways to use a variety of instructional approaches. The rest of Part II is organized to address one facet of the model at a time.

In Chapter 6, we walk the preservice teacher through the *culminating performance*, the last part of a learning unit, and the appropriate goals for instruction. Why begin at the end of a learning unit? We want the preservice teacher to focus on what students will know and be able to do, so that learning units will progress continuously toward the expected outcomes.

Next, Chapter 7 supports preservice teachers in thinking about *guided learning activities*. Here, readers learn to apply powerful instructional strategies that are easily embedded in widely available technology. These are the activities that often comprise the bulk of the learning opportunities in a standards-based classroom. Chapter 8 then focuses on developing the *initiating activity*—the launching pad of the learning experience. Readers learn how critical the first learning activities are to the entire unit and how they help students relate a learning unit to prior knowledge.

Part III: Evaluate, Refine, and Extend devotes a full chapter to technology for decision making and growth. We present cutting-edge thoughts on self-assessment, encouraging teachers to use technologies to examine their own teaching practices and those of other teachers they observe. We discuss how to look for effective practice, raise real questions about classroom events, and get down to the specifics that teachers need to know.

Part IV: Technology Tools and Applications discusses a broad array of tools. The chapters, organized by tool type, include many examples of ways the tools can be used in real classrooms. Chapter 10 introduces productivity tools, including word processors, spreadsheets, databases, and presentation software. Chapter 11 focuses on development tools such as web page editors, graphics editors, and other tools students can use to make high-quality products as part of their learning. Communications tools are discussed in Chapter 12, which includes text-based, audio, and visual communications.

Chapter 13 offers an overview of the many content-area tools available for education. This chapter also includes software evaluation guidelines. Emerging tools, such as virtual reality, are the focus of Chapter 14, with particular emphasis on tools that are practical for teachers to use. We end Part IV with Chapter 15, Integrating Technology for Diverse Learners, in which we introduce some of the many cutting-edge ways that technology helps teachers engage all students in classrooms and in life.

◼ Pedagogical Features of This Book

Throughout the book we have included a number of features to help readers understand the ideas we discuss and grasp the practical applications.

Standards-related features: At the beginning of each chapter, the "Standards to Guide Your Preparation" link the chapter's ideas to the NETS standards and help readers see the relevance of these ideas for various content areas, states, and age groups. Further, each chapter ends with a "Meet the Standards" feature that offers a standards-related thought exercise. Here, prospective teachers will think about ways of applying their learning and reflect on their progress in meeting the standards. For easy reference, a complete set of the principal NETS standards for both students and teachers is included on the last page of the book and inside the back cover, respectively.

Case Studies: At the end of each chapter, a case study illustrates educational technology in a real-world situation. Questions are included to guide student reflection and classroom discussion.

 *Online Study Center*

Video Cases: To accompany this text, Houghton Mifflin has created an award-winning series of videos, the *HM Video Cases*, on major topics in education. These videos present scenes of teachers and students in real classrooms, plus interviews in which the teachers discuss important issues related to their teaching. The cases also include short bonus videos, viewing questions, a transcript of the interview with the teacher, and classroom artifacts (such as lesson plans, materials used in the lesson, and the products created by students).

In nearly every chapter we include a short feature introducing an HM Video Case that is particularly relevant to the chapter. We encourage students to view and think about the video, and we offer questions to stimulate reflection. All of these cases are readily available at the Online Study Center.

Technology in Action features: These frequent features illustrate how technology can be used in real classrooms. Like the case studies, they show prospective teachers how to translate general principles into classroom practice.

Spotlights: These short features, which occur often throughout the text, introduce a wide variety of technology tools and other topics of special interest.

Resources: Near the end of each chapter, readers will find an annotated list of resources for further exploration. The two appendixes provide dozens of additional resources on technology planning, hardware evaluation, digital libraries, learning communities, professional organizations, and more.

Marginal notes: Short phrases in the page margins help students identify and connect key ideas in the text.

Glossary: At the back of the book, the Glossary provides clear definitions for important terms.

Online Study Center and Online Teaching Center

Online Study Center

Readers of this book have access to important online resources. The Online Study Center, accessible from **http://college.hmco.com/pic/ recesso1e**, offers students links to more information on a variety of subjects. In addition to the HM Video Cases, students will discover bonus performance-based and reflection-based activities, projects connected to ISTE standards, additional web links, and helpful flashcards to review key terms in the text.

In the Online Teaching Center, which you can also reach through **http://college.hmco.com/pic/recesso1e**, instructors will find a variety of tools for teaching a course with this book as a text. For example, we provide a sample syllabus with a wide variety of activities that complement the book. A PowerPoint presentation to aid classroom instruction and expanded activities for assignment can also be found in the Online Teaching Center.

Acknowledgments

Writing a book takes a community! We are pleased to be surrounded by and networked to a fabulous group of people whose time and talents we drew on in creating this book.

First, we would like to thank the following contributors to the Spotlights and Technology in Action features: Ben Deaton, Cynthia Deaton, Sandy Geisler, and Drew Polly. These people not only provided writing support but also lent us their life experiences and creativity.

We also thank Qi Li and Marie Metzger for their technical assistance in preparing the images and securing permissions for copyrighted materials. Denise Domizi created the wolf-habitat learning activities that are used in several chapters. Gretchen Thomas, coordinator of our own technology integration course, helped us think through some of the features her students might find most useful in a book. Maureen Benicasa provided valuable editing support for early versions of the manuscript.

Finally, we thank a large group of reviewers who provided a wealth of feedback on drafts of the manuscript:

Cynthia A. Dalton Alexander, *Cerritos College*
Anne Bednar, *Eastern Michigan University*
J. Michael Blocher, *Northern Arizona University*
Teresa K. Blodgett, *Texas Tech University*
Joe P. Brasher, *Athens State University*
Pearl Chen, *California State University, Los Angeles*
Amy Coleman, *The University of Tennessee at Martin*
Michael Corry, *George Washington University*
Jane H. Eberle, *The Teachers College, Emporia State University*
Teresa J. Franklin, *Ohio University*
Lisa Harris, *Winthrop University*
Dianne Haun, *Hillsborough Community College*
John Hemphill, *Greensboro College*
Sr. Mary John Kearney, *Caldwell College*
Dennis Koutouzos, *Roosevelt University*
Mary V. Mawn, *University of Massachusetts, Amherst*
David A. McCarthy, *University of Minnesota, Duluth*
Regina Mistretta, *St. John's University*
Bob Perkins, *College of Charleston*
Charles L. Price, *University of Southern Indiana*
Glenda C. Rakes, *The University of Tennessee at Martin*
Rosemary W. Skeele, *Seton Hall University*
Barry Sponder, *Central Connecticut State University*
Neal Strudler, *University of Nevada, Las Vegas*
Guy M. Westhoff, *University of Wyoming*
Frank J. Zittle, *Cameron University*

Our work has been supported through U.S. Department of Education's Preparing Tomorrow's Teacher to Use Technology (PT3) program. A 2000 PT3 grant was awarded to Art Recesso and Martha Venn while they were at Valdosta State University (VSU) (Project # P342A000204). Very early versions of the manuscript were reviewed, used in classes and professional development, and supported by folks at VSU, including Martha Venn, Karla Hull, Catherine Price, faculty in the Instructional Technology program, and faculty in the Special Education Department. Then a 2003 PT3 grant was awarded to Art Recesso and Mike Hannafin of the Learning & Performance Support Laboratory at the University of Georgia (Project # P342A030009). We are grateful to the Department of Education, to the PT3 program, and to all the teachers, preservice teachers, and teacher educators who supported the work.

People associated with Houghton Mifflin have been very supportive, especially our development editor, Doug Gordon, who has been awesome to collaborate with. We would also like to thank Lisa Mafrici, Aileen Mason, Dayna Pell, and Paola Moll for their support through the entire editorial and production processes.

We are also lucky to have supportive colleagues and families who have provided inspiration and focus to us when we've needed it. Art would like to thank Shelby for her unending encouragement and support. She has endured years of questions about ideas and interrupted personal plans to get the manuscript together. Madelyn and Estella have been especially tolerant of Daddy's plunking on the keyboard during their favorite shows, on vacation, and everywhere in between. I can't thank the three of you enough!

Chandra would like to thank Jason, who not only helped keep her focused, but also helped her find some of the innovative technologies discussed in the book. She also thanks Stuart, who graciously allowed us to include him in Chapter 11 in the image aspect ratio example.

PART I

Technology and the Learning Environment

1

Introduction to Technology Integration

Standards to Guide Your Preparation

ISTE NETS

Teachers

▶ Demonstrate introductory knowledge, skills, and understanding of concepts related to technology.

▶ Apply current research on teaching and learning with technology when planning learning environments and experiences.

OTHER RELEVANT STANDARDS

National Council of Teachers of English (2003)

Standard 3 for teacher candidates in English Language Arts

▶ Candidates are knowledgeable about language; literature; oral, visual, and written literacy; print and nonprint media; technology; and research theory and findings.

Welcome to the world of educational technology! Technologies like the computer, various hand-held devices, and the Internet hold considerable promise as tools for both learners and teachers. In this book we introduce you to a special model (the Technology and Learning Continuum Model) and a set of technology tools that you may want to apply in ways that support your own teaching goals.

Each chapter in this book begins with "Standards to Guide Your Preparation," a list of standards for teachers' understanding and use of technology. Many of these standards are excerpts from the National Educational Technology Standards for Teachers (NETS), published by the International Society for Technology in Education (ISTE). These standards are exactly what our heading suggests—a guide for preparing to use technology in your teaching. At the end of each chapter, a section called "Meet the Standards" invites you to reflect on what you've learned and on how that learning relates to professional standards. That section also suggests an activity to deepen your knowledge.

Throughout the book we focus on technology integration from the perspective of how students learn and how technology can best be used to support that learning. In this chapter we provide a brief overview of our technology integration framework and introduce some ideas about why and how you might want to use technology in your classroom.

Why Write a Book About Technology Integration?

On the one hand, technology is a tool for classroom use in the same way that a whiteboard, an overhead projector, and graph paper are. Like any other tool, technology is only as good as the instruction that it supports and only as useful as the teacher makes it. On the other hand, technology is completely unlike other teaching and learning tools: It can do all the things that other classroom tools can do, but it also offers unparalleled interactivity.

Through the use of technology, classrooms are no longer limited to the text in a book or the confines of a particular school. Learners can go anywhere in the world on virtual field trips; they can perform scientific experiments; and they can engage in real-time research. In short, technology allows students to be actively involved in the process of constructing their own knowledge, facilitating the development of a "learner-centered" classroom (a topic that we discuss in detail later in the book). For example, we can use Virtual Solar System software to engage students in active inquiry about the solar system, phases of the moon, seasons, and other topics in astronomy. The software allows them to create models of the solar system with correct (or incorrect) physics, so that they test their knowledge and understanding of fundamental concepts. Students can demonstrate understanding not only the relative position of each planet, for example, but also how the planets influence one another, what causes seasons, and how years are defined (Barab et al., 2000).

For the teacher, technology offers not only innovative ways to teach a lesson, but also avenues to insight into the very process of teaching and

Technology and the active construction of knowledge

learning (McDonald & Naso, 1986; National Research Council [NRC], 2000). With technology, teachers can experiment, tinker, think more deeply about the process of learning, even model learning processes by acting them out to show students how to use them (Means & Olson, 1995; NRC, 2000; Office of Technology Assessment, 1995). From a more mundane perspective, technology can help teachers manage the administrative work of the classroom. A spreadsheet for attendance and grades is a vital aid. A web page that lists homework and classroom activities can help you engage parents in classroom experiences. Well-organized computer files with unit plans and instructional materials can save you time year after year as you revisit and revise lesson plans.

Technology as a teacher's aid

Goals of This Book

It is our aim in this book to give you a wide array of approaches to use in your classroom. Our model for planning instruction will allow you to tie lessons to standards, create useful assessments, and engage students in constructing their own knowledge.

Our objectives include your learning

▶ To integrate technology in ways that support diverse students' attaining high levels of learning.
▶ To integrate technology tools into various types of instruction—inquiry, investigation, and more.
▶ To write and customize learner-centered units using pedagogical approaches that support students' constructing their own knowledge.
▶ To create and organize instruction and assessments that align with current state and national learning standards, such as the National Science Education Standards and the National Educational Technology Standards.
▶ To use technology to improve your own practice.

Technology to Support Diverse Learners

There are myriad ways that technology can support the needs of all your students. In this context, we're referring to technology's capacity to (1) support the teacher in differentiating instruction for learners with diverse ability levels and (2) support learners with particular physical limitations.

Technology as an enabling tool

When technology is used to support learner-centered activity, it becomes an enabling tool. With technology, lower-achieving students have ready access to additional practice, to a glossary of information, and to a suite of tools that allow them to make abstract ideas more concrete. Many software titles, for instance, include "Hints" boxes with additional information for students who need it. And many software packages are specifically designed to create visuals that support conceptual development. For example, with Celestia software (see **http://www.shatters.net/celestia/**), students can create a model of the earth's path around the sun that features a common misconception—that the seasons are determined by

Online Study Center
See the Online Study Center for direct links to websites mentioned in the text.

the earth's rotating around the sun in an elliptical path that puts it closer to the sun at certain times of the year. When this idea is modeled and the earth is allowed to follow this path, it becomes quickly apparent that the theory is impossible. Used in this way, technology is a powerful tool for students to actually see what happens when they test their hypotheses.

Assistive technology, which we discuss later in the book, provides means to overcome physical limitations in the classroom. For some students, computers simply provide opportunities to access information in easier ways, as with text read by a computer voice generator or enlarged screen fonts. In more extreme cases, computers can become a primary means for communication. Students who are unable to talk or write can use a special keyboard or picture-coded panel with push-buttons to have the computer speak for them. In some cases, technology can allow students to stay in school who would otherwise be unable to attend. Through the use of online learning environments, for example, students have access to classroom learning even if they are housebound.

◼ Integrating an Array of Tools into Teaching and Learning

Throughout this book you will find a number of examples of ways technology can be used to support your teaching and your students' learning. You will notice that all of our guidance and examples are grounded in *how the technology is used* as much as in *what technology is used*. This marriage of the *what* and the *how* is what creates an integrated teaching and learning environment.

▰ What Technology Can Do

The many benefits of technology

Technology can improve learning and instruction, support the development of a rich learning environment, and enhance assessment. By adapting the learning environment and instruction, technology can promote students' inquiry and discovery, decrease geographic limitations, and provide opportunities to develop workplace skills. Teachers can use technology to engage the learner, support instructional strategies, deliver instruction, enhance their teaching strengths, and improve on their weaknesses. Spotlight 1.1 reviews some specific research data on technology's impact.

▰ What Technology Can't Do

Simply placing computers in the classroom will not raise test scores or improve student learning. Computer-related technology alone will not improve student learning. Technology must be *integrated* into the learning environment in ways that are aligned with standards, that address the learning goals the teacher has set, and that fit with the instructional approach being used.

SPOTLIGHT 1.1   Technology in Mathematics, Science, and Social Studies

A number of sources are beginning to present compelling evidence about the value of technology in K–12 classrooms. For example, recent scores on the National Assessment of Educational Progress (NAEP; National Center for Education Statistics [NCES], 2001, 2002a, 2002b, 2003) provide a clear indication of the power of technology. The NAEP exam is given to thousands of Americans every year in math, science, social studies, and language arts as a measure of how the educational system in this country is doing. Some of these tests include survey questions for teachers about technology use. The resulting data have been correlated with student test scores to provide some interesting results.

- *Science in 2000.* Students who used electronic probes to collect data, who downloaded data, or who used computers to analyze data monthly or more often scored higher than their counterparts who used technology for these purposes less frequently or not at all. Exchanging science information over the Internet, however, did not seem to have this effect.
- *Science in 2000.* Fourth-grade students who used computers to play learning games scored higher than their counterparts who did not. Eighth-grade students who used technology for simulations, modeling, and data analysis scored higher than those who did not.

- *Mathematics in 2000.* Eighth and twelfth graders who reported using calculators daily for classwork, homework, and tests scored higher than those who did not. However, fourth graders who used a calculator every day had lower scores.
- *Mathematics in 2000.* Eighth graders whose exposure to computers focused on demonstrating new topics or using simulations scored higher than those who used computers for drill and practice or playing math games. Even eighth graders who did not use computers at all scored higher than those who used computers merely for drill and practice and playing math games.
- *Geography in 2001.* Fourth graders who had used the Internet to a small or moderate extent to retrieve social studies information scored better than those who had not used it at all. In eighth and twelfth grades, students who had used the Internet to a moderate or large extent scored better than those students who had used it not at all or to a small extent.
- *History in 2001.* Eighth and twelfth graders who used computers to a moderate or high extent to research and write reports scored higher than those who used computers not at all or to a small extent.

Importance of how technology is used

A growing body of research is helping us understand the conditions in which technology does and does not help the teacher and learner (see Spotlight 1.1). What all of this research suggests is that *how the technology is used* is the most important aspect of its impact on student learning. Research suggests that technology benefits students most when it allows them to simulate situations, make decisions, model events and understandings, and perform other exploratory operations. Technology is least effective for learning when it is used for drill and practice.

As with nontechnology-based classroom activities, computer-based technology can't make students learn something they don't understand. It is best used when it supports the development of meaningful understanding.

■ Writing Learner-Centered Units

A primary goal of this book is to help you create learner-centered lesson plans and units. This is the single most important aspect of technology integration. With poorly planned implementation, even the best uses of technology will fail to support student learning.

An Expanded Definition of Literacy

● People in your generation enter teacher preparation courses with more knowledge of and experience with technology than any earlier generation. Clearly, you've grown up using technology in ways that affect your thinking about technology and how it can be applied to teaching and learning. Throughout the book we provide video cases linked to the book's Online Study Center, which will stimulate your thinking and suggest ways for you to apply your knowledge.

With your web browser, go to the Houghton Mifflin education site at **http://education.college.hmco.com/students.** Locate the Online Study Center for this text and bookmark it for easy access in the future. Then click on Video Cases.

For this chapter the video is called **An Expanded Definition of Literacy: Meaningful Ways to Use Technology.** What do you think the title means by "literacy"? Watch the video and read the Viewing Questions. Now consider how your experiences with technology might be compared with those of the three teachers shown in the video. How do you think your existing knowledge of technology will influence your own teaching and learning?

Two primary theories shape the instructional vision of this book:

▶ First, we rely on the American Psychological Association's **Learner-Centered Psychological Principles** (APA Work Group, 1997), which outline what research says about how people learn. These principles provide a basis for thinking carefully about how instruction should unfold to best support learners.

▶ Second, we have chosen to ground this book in the constructivist epistemology of learning. **Constructivism,** consistent with the Learner-Centered Psychological Principles, asserts that people learn by gradually making sense of their world. As they learn more about a concept or thing, they revise their mental structures representing that concept or thing.

With these two theories, we provide a model of technology integration that supports students in becoming engaged learners who persistently ask questions and participate in the processes necessary to answer those questions—regardless of the content area within which they are working.

To support you in learning how to write learning units that embody these principles, we rely on a model for technology integration that we call the **Technology and Learning Continuum Model.** You will become very familiar with this model as you work your way through the book. We also present a number of ideas about the roles of the teacher and the learners in a classroom that capitalizes on technology. We tie all of this back to fundamental ideas about how people learn and to standards-based teaching.

The Technology and Learning Continuum Model stimulates teachers to think about the process of teaching and learning based on the following assumptions:

Assumptions of the Technology and Learning Continuum Model

▶ Computer-related technology is a tool, but it is unlike any other tool for teaching and learning. (We use the term *computer-related technology* here to represent computer hardware, software, and their various components. The term *technology* here refers to all that is related to audiovisual, media, and technological items that can be used in the classroom.)

▶ Learning is a continuum.

▶ There is a progressive formalization in learning. Learners transfer knowledge from previous experiences and build on existing knowledge.

▶ High-quality instruction requires careful planning.

▶ Teachers have two critical roles in a technology-rich environment. First, they are *designers* of learning experiences, and then they become *facilitators* of learning.

■ Tying Lesson Design to Standards

All lesson design should begin with standards.

Standards provide teachers with guidance about what students should understand and be able to do. Consistent with current educational practices, this book proposes that all learning unit and subsequent lesson design should start with these standards. This means that, as a teacher, you need to know what you want students to learn before you begin identifying the tools you'll use to help them learn. Though this may seem like common sense, teachers in practice often begin planning from an activity or a computer program that they want students to use, rather than from what they want students to learn.

To help you stay focused on the standards and how they relate to your activities, we've modeled the Technology and Learning Continuum on the work of Wiggins and McTighe (2000). Their vision for good instructional design begins with the standards to be met, then asks teachers to refine those standards into smaller goals. The process continues with the teacher's identifying how students will demonstrate that they have met the goals, then the teacher's planning the activities that will help students meet the goals. This design approach helps maintain a tight connection with learning goals throughout the instructional design process.

■ Technology to Support Improvements in Your Own Practice

You've probably already thought of some teacher-oriented ways in which technology enhances your practice. Technology provides you with access to many programs that support your being organized, gives you access to a wide array of lesson ideas, and provides you with opportunities to communicate with other teachers. Technology integration is also an important aspect of a teacher's conceptual development—it can help you become a better teacher.

Technology for refining your own practice

For example, you can record your teaching practice, either by using direct evidence, such as classroom videos, or by developing a portfolio like that required for certification by the National Board for Professional Teaching Standards. By compiling evidence of your practice electronically, you can self assess your practice, refine classroom plans, share practices with other teachers or mentors for feedback or demonstration, and generally develop a richer understanding of your own teaching. This is a powerful way for teachers to engage in professional dialogues with each other, to present their work for interviews or evaluations, and to engage in purposeful professional development.

Visions of Technology Use: A Showcase of Theorists

Often teachers don't make the connection between their classroom efforts and the theories and ideas of educational technologists. To help you understand the wide variety of good ideas that exist and gain a better sense of the role of educational technology, the following pages present an introduction to several key luminaries, developers who have put theory and design together to create innovative learning environments. Some of their ideas have already had widespread influence on today's schools. Others will shape the schools of the future.

◼ Seymour Papert: Uses of Educational Technology

During the 1970s and 1980s when computers were being built for business functions and number crunching, Seymour Papert talked about children's using computers as instruments for learning and enhanced creativity. At the time there were no user-friendly interfaces, nor was there widespread use of flexible programming languages. While conducting research at the Massachusetts Institute of Technology (MIT), Papert provided children with the first opportunities to use the computer to write and to create graphics. His efforts resulted in the development of the Logo programming language.

Today Papert is considered the world's foremost expert on how technology can provide new ways to learn. He is the cofounder with Marvin Minsky of the Artificial Intelligence Lab at MIT and a founding faculty member of the MIT Media Lab, where he continues to work. Papert collaborated for many years with Jean Piaget at the University of Geneva in Switzerland.

For further inquiry, here are a few of Papert's most notable books:

Papert, S. (1993). *The children's machine: Rethinking school in the age of the computer.* New York: Basic Books.

Papert, S. (1993). *Mindstorms: Children, computers, and powerful ideas* (2nd ed.). New York: Basic Books.

Papert, S. (1996). *The connected family: Bridging the digital generation gap.* Athens, GA: Longstreet Press.

◼ Chris Dede: Virtual Reality

Chris Dede's efforts focus on the ways that technology can expand people's capacity for creating and sharing knowledge. He advocates the "use of information technology to distribute and orchestrate learning across space, time, and multiple interactive media" (Dede, 2005). Dede has made significant contributions in the areas of technology forecasting and assessment, emerging technologies for learning, and leadership in educational innovation. Recently he has been working to develop and assess learning environments based on immersive virtual reality technology and multi-user virtual environments.

Virtual reality is the simulation of realistic three-dimensional environments. For several years Dede has been training teachers to use wearable virtual reality equipment in their classrooms. His successes and findings are widely published in national and international journals.

For further inquiry, see these articles by Chris Dede:

Dede, C. (with M. Salzman, B. Loftin, & D. Sprague). (1999). Multi-sensory immersion as a modeling environment for learning complex scientific concepts. In N. Roberts, W. Feurzeig, & B. Hunter (Eds.), *Computer modeling and simulation in science education* (pp. 282–319). New York: Springer.

Dede, C. (2000). Advanced technologies and distributed learning in higher education. In D. E. Hanna & Associates, *Higher education in an era of digital competition: Choices and challenges* (pp. 71–92). Madison, WI: Atwood.

Dede, C. (2000). Emerging influences of information technology on school curriculum. *Journal of Curriculum Studies, 32*(2), 281–303.

Dede, C. (with C. Salzman, B. Loftin, & K. Ash). (2000). Using virtual reality technology to convey abstract scientific concepts. In M. J. Jacobson & R. B. Kozma (Eds.), *Learning the sciences of the 21st century: Research, design, and implementing advanced technology learning environments* (pp. 246–253). Mahwah, NJ: Erlbaum.

Dede, C. (2006). Scaling up: Evolving innovations beyond ideal settings to challenging contexts of practice. In R. K. Sawyer (Ed.), *The Cambridge handbook of the learning sciences.* New York: Cambridge University Press.

■ Michael Hannafin: Open-Ended and Resource-Based Learning Environments

Michael Hannafin is an Eminent Scholar in Technology-Enhanced Learning and Director of the Learning and Performance Support Laboratory at the University of Georgia. His research focuses on situated learning and scaffolding. He has published many articles on the psychological and pedagogical principles underlying student-centered learning and on the development of frameworks for designing and testing open-ended learning environments (OELEs) and resource-based learning environments (RBLEs).

For further inquiry, see the following sources:

Hannafin, M. J., Hill, J., & McCarthy, J. (2002). Designing resource-based learning and performance support systems. In D. Wiley (Ed.), *The instructional use of learning objects* (pp. 99–129). Bloomington, IN: Association for Educational Communications & Technology.

Hill, J., & Hannafin, M. J. (2001). Teaching and learning in digital environments: The resurgence of resource-based learning. *Educational Technology Research and Development, 49*(3), 37–52.

Land, S., & Hannafin, M. J. (2000). Student-centered learning environments. In D. H. Jonassen & S. M. Land (Eds.), *Theoretical foundations of learning environments* (pp. 1–23). Mahwah, NJ: Erlbaum.

Oliver, K., & Hannafin, M. J. (2001). Developing and refining mental models in open-ended learning environments: A case study. *Educational Technology Research and Development, 49*(4), 5–33.

■ Marcia Linn: Technology-Enhanced Learning

Marcia Linn's work centers on the use of technology to develop understanding in science. Her innovations include the use of web-based technologies to improve instruction in science, math, and engineering. Her projects funded by the National Science Foundation, such as Technology Enhanced Learning in Science (TELS) and Web Integrated Science Environment or Web-based Inquiry Science Environment (WISE), provide us with innovative ideas for effectively using technology-based learning environments. Scaffolds embedded within the systems, for example, engage users in integrating science and technology into teaching and learning.

For further inquiry, see the following web resources:

IDDEAS (Introducing Desirable Difficulties for Educational Applications in Science). Available: **http://iddeas.psych.ucla.edu/ index.html**

Marcia Linn's home page. Available: **http://tels.berkeley.edu/ ~mclinn/**

TELS (Technology Enhanced Learning in Science) Center. Available: **http://www.telscenter.org/**

WISE (Web Integrated Science Environment or Web-based Inquiry Science Environment). Available: **http://wise.berkeley.edu/**

■ David Jonassen: Designing Instruction with Technology

David Jonassen's work helps us think about computer applications as *mindtools*. He makes the distinction between learning *from* computers, learning *about* computers, and using mindtools to learn *with* computers (Jonassen, 2000).

His work is widely applied as a means for thinking about how computer-related technology—such as database and spreadsheet software, hypermedia development systems, and information communication technologies created for business functions—also serves learner needs in an educational setting. Not only are these tools of the trade in the business world, they also are effective technologies for engaging learners in "constructive, higher-order, critical thinking about the subjects they are studying" (Jonassen 2000, p. iv). Jonassen's premise is that students need tools for learning in much the same way that workers need them for productivity.

For further inquiry, see the following:

David Jonassen's home page. Available: **http://www.coe.missouri .edu/~jonassen/**

Dijkstra, S., Jonassen, D. H., & Sembill, D. (Eds.). (2001). *Multimedia learning: Results and perspectives.* New York: Peter Lang Publishing.

Jonassen, D. H. (2006). *Modeling with technology: Mindtools for conceptual change* (3rd ed.). Columbus, OH: Merrill/Prentice Hall.

SUMMARY

In this chapter we've introduced many of the key ideas of the book and presented its primary goals. We've stressed that technology itself does not improve student learning. Rather, it must be fully integrated into the learning environment. You'll appreciate this idea of "integration" better as you read later chapters. For now, keep in mind that computer-based technologies are powerful tools for both students and teachers, but they are most effective when they are used in ways that capitalize on their unique capabilities—for instance, their ability to support communication, to model and simulate situations, and to store and retrieve information.

This book will help you think about ways to integrate technology into your own classroom. We'll introduce a model—the Technology and Learning Continuum Model—that you can use as a step-by-step guide for planning instruction.

Our approach is based on the theory of constructivism and on the American Psychological Association's Learner-Centered Psychological Principles, two approaches that emphasize the need to engage learners in asking questions and building their own answers. In the next chapter you'll see, in more detail, how a learner-centered classroom functions.

RESOURCES

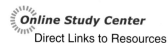
Online Study Center
    Direct Links to Resources

Design of Constructivist Learning Environments
http://www.coe.missouri.edu/~jonassen/courses/CLE/
    David Jonassen's course materials provide clear definitions of important terms in constructivist learning, as well as many links to resources.

Learner-Centered Psychological Principles: A Framework for School Reform and Redesign
http://www.apa.org/ed/cpse/LCPP.pdf

Here you can find the full text of the American Psychological Association's Learner-Centered Psychological Principles.

Technology in Education: 170 Ideas and Resources for Teachers
http://www.ael.org/rtec/ideas.htm
    This site provides a good starting point for finding useful resources. Bookmark it so that you can come back and explore it further as you read later chapters.

case
STUDY

The NECC Conference

Mr. Bustler was a third-year social studies teacher at Skylar Middle School when he decided to attend the National Educational Computing Conference (NECC), being held just a few cities away. Mr. Bustler was interested in using technology in his classroom but was unsure how to really make it work for him. After all, the science teachers had electronic probes and software simulations, and the math teachers had spreadsheets and dynamic geometry software, but he didn't know of any specific technology tools for social studies.

Mid-June arrived quickly, and Mr. Bustler eagerly drove to NECC, ready to learn. He was amazed as he drove up. There were thousands of people there! As he went through registration, he noted that there were hundreds of sessions. He flipped through the program to see what was offered. He settled first on a session called "Teaching Kids to Argue," which was being presented by a ninth-grade teacher from a nearby state. Mr. Bustler was enthusiastic about gathering ideas, so he got out his paper and pen and headed to the session. He quickly started to understand that he could create an inquiry activity in which he asked students to take sides on an issue and research that perspective on the Internet. Then his students could present their perspectives in a debate-like fashion, and the class could vote. He was excited and ready for the next session.

In the next session, he heard a fifth-grade teacher talk about an activity called "WebQuest," which allows students to work as a team to find an answer to a compelling question. He jotted down some of the question ideas the speaker presented:

▶ Examine "Cinderella" from three different cultural perspectives and use what you learn about the cultural aspects of "Cinderella" to rewrite it as if it were set in ancient Greece.
▶ Should a nearby state be allowed to use our landfill?
▶ Design a monument in honor of an important historical figure.
▶ Design a new coin or stamp for each state.
▶ Research the wonders of the world and nominate ten Human-Made Wonders.
▶ What is the role of women in history?

Elated with these ideas, Mr. Bustler took careful notes about ways to find more information about developing WebQuests, what kinds of roles students play in them, and how to assess the results. (To explore WebQuests yourself, see **http://webquest.sdsu.edu/**.)

As he stepped into another session, Mr. Bustler was amazed by the project the teacher was presenting. The teacher had asked his students to research a religious act being considered by his state's legislature. The students had used the Internet to research the actual bill and to e-mail members of the state legislature to learn their perspectives on the issues. The students had also decided to research the range of opinion at churches in their town. They created a survey and took it to a wide array of churches and temples to find out what the people in those organizations thought of the proposed legislation. Then they used spreadsheet software to analyze the data and create a series of graphs to e-mail to their state representative. Mr. Bustler was amazed. These were only seventh graders!

Mr. Bustler then attended a session in which students had used geography, history, and economics to plan a trip across Europe. Each group of students was responsible for identifying five locations to visit, each in a different county. They had to plan their itinerary, provide a rationale for the five locations they had selected, stay within a tight budget, figure out how to move between cities, and, when necessary, calculate currency conversions. The students then created websites advertising their proposed European trip to the school, and other students were allowed to vote for the one they thought was best.

After attending a few more sessions, Mr. Bustler went to the exhibit area to see some of the software and web-based products available for social studies. He found the *Decisions, Decisions* series of software from Tom Snyder Productions **(http://www.tomsnyder.com/),** which presents students with a controversial issue and a body of information, then lets them develop a decision on the issue. He took the product information and moved on. He stopped at the National Geographic booth, where he learned about the free web resource Xpeditions **(http://www.nationalgeographic .com/xpeditions/),** which houses maps, geography lesson plans, and a great deal of other information.

As he continued, he gathered information about many other social studies programs. As he left the conference, his head was reeling with new ideas for his classroom.

Questions for Reflection and Discussion

1. Did you know there is a national conference like the one described in the case?
2. Do you think it would be worthwhile for teachers to share their ideas, as the teachers in the case did? What potentially good things could come out of such sharing?
3. Can you think of three or four specific ways in which you could use technology in your content area?

Meet the Standards

Online Study Center
Standards
Go online for more resources to help you meet the standards.

In "Standards to Guide Your Preparation" at the beginning of this chapter, we listed the following key standards from the National Educational Technology Standards for Teachers (NETS), published by the International Society for Technology in Education (ISTE):

▶ Demonstrate introductory knowledge, skills, and understanding of concepts related to technology.
▶ Apply current research on teaching and learning with technology when planning learning environments and experiences.

We've aligned this chapter with those standards, and you've already begun to meet them. You'll make further progress as you read later chapters.

Here's a challenge to help develop your understanding: Think of a technology that you use in everyday life—one that isn't typically used in the classroom (for instance, a cell phone, personal digital assistant, or blog). Then consider a concept in your subject domain (social studies, English, science, whatever you plan to teach) that students often struggle to learn. Think about ways you could use that technology in your teaching and learning. Sketch out some possible ideas, using the following questions as your guide:

▶ How could you use this everyday technology to teach students the difficult concept?
▶ What would you expect students to gain from the learning experience? Would they discover new ways of applying everyday technology for their own learning?
▶ How do your ideas align with the principles you read about in this chapter?

Chapter 2

Learner-Centered Classrooms

ISTE NETS

Teachers

▶ Design developmentally appropriate learning opportunities that apply technology-enhanced instructional strategies to support the diverse needs of learners.

▶ Use technology to support learner-centered strategies that address the diverse needs of students.

▶ Apply technology to develop students' higher-order skills and creativity.

▶ Apply technology resources to enable and empower learners with diverse backgrounds, characteristics, and abilities.

OTHER RELEVANT STANDARDS

National Science Education Standards (NRC, 1996)

Teachers of science guide and facilitate learning. In doing this, teachers

▶ Focus and support inquiries.

▶ Orchestrate discourse among students about scientific ideas.

▶ Challenge students to accept and share responsibility for their own learning.

▶ Recognize and respond to student diversity and encourage all students to participate fully in science learning.

▶ Encourage and model the skills of scientific inquiry, as well as the curiosity, openness to new ideas and data, and skepticism that characterize science.

National Council for the Social Studies, Standards for the Preparation of Social Studies Teachers (2004)

Social studies teachers [should be prepared to provide] learner-centered, meaningful, integrative, value-based, challenging, and active instruction.

A critical attribute of effective teaching is establishing an environment in which all students can learn. Such a **learning environment's** elements include the physical layout of the classroom, the resources made available, and the classroom management approach. The learning environment is also defined by the kinds of learning activities in which the teacher engages the students, the academic expectations placed on the students, and the organization of instruction. In this chapter we explore these various elements that affect the learning environment.

Online Study Center

Use the Glossary Flashcards in the Online Study Center for a quick review of key terms.

What Is a Learning Environment?

As an introduction to what we mean by "learning environment," read the following "Technology in Action" features. They illustrate some of the elements that make up a learning environment, and they portray two of the numerous opportunities for creating meaningful learning experiences through and with technology. **Meaningful learning** entails students' actively developing a deep understanding of complex concepts that are central to the subject matter and to their everyday life.

Technology in Action

Computer-Aided Design

A high-school teacher decides to redesign a drafting course to use more applied learning strategies. The teacher chooses instructional strategies and learning activities that encourage students to take a more active role in their knowledge and skill development by applying the knowledge they have acquired in class. One of the strategies is to have students use computer-aided design (CAD) software to create drawings like ones they might make in the real world.

In previous years the teacher focused most class time on activities that could be accomplished in the classroom—either on the computer or with other appropriate drafting tools. However, for the new year he decides to work with a local business to expand the students' learning experience. The business owner will allow students to use a high-end plotter to print their drawings. The business also has machine parts available for students to use as models.

In this way, the learning environment expands beyond the confines of the classroom to a location outside the school. The new learning environment affords students an opportunity to apply concepts in a real setting enhanced through the use of software systems used by people employed in the field. The combination of technology and learning environment provides a simulated experience enabling the learner to demonstrate knowledge and skills in meaningful ways.

Technology in Action

Planning a City with Simulation Software

A high-school social studies teacher needs to address social studies standards focused on power, authority, and governance. She discovers simulation software that allows students to plan and run a city. She decides to create a unit, based on this simulation, about the systemic nature of government decision making.

Using her knowledge of case-based learning and of the American Psychological Association's Learner-Centered Psychological Principles, the teacher decides to create the unit in a way that allows students to divide into teams and dive right into the experience. Though she knows from the outset what the students should learn, she also determines that this is a rich experience from which many further activities might arise—activities that will motivate her students to deepen their understanding. She structures the learning opportunity to maximize the chances that her students will want to learn more. As the students build and run their cities, the teacher incorporates discussions and reflection activities that help them focus on the generalizable understandings they are developing. During the class discussions, she also captures the questions that the students are raising from their experiences in the simulation and challenges the class as a whole to make conjectures about the answers to those questions. Then, she asks them to test their conjectures the next time they are in the simulation. By using this approach, she can steer the students to the most important questions they are raising, thereby ensuring that her standards are being met.

These two "Technology in Action" scenarios highlight some of the deliberate decisions you'll need to make as you incorporate technology into your classroom. For example, you'll need to answer the following questions:

Questions to shape decisions about technology

▶ What kind of learning environment do I want to create for my students?
▶ What role can technology play in that environment?
▶ What resources do I have to help me create the learning environment?

This chapter will introduce you to some elements you may want to consider as you develop your own answers to these questions. In the following sections we explore what a learning environment is and how to support student learning through the environment you create. We also consider some of the different ways technology can be implemented in the learning environment, and we strategize ways to maximize the resources you have available.

Elements of Learning Environments

Jonassen (2000) defines the learning environment as spaces where a person or group of people interact with tools, materials, and resources in their development of knowledge and skills. The environment is essentially the context in which learning is established and supported. The environment is tightly linked to learning because it affects the way you design your learning unit—you must both respond to its limitations and use the tools available in it to enhance your students' learning opportunities.

As a teacher, part of your job will be to determine what teaching tools and resources are available, know the environment in which the learning is supposed to take place, and know the composition of that environment. Our drafting teacher, for example, determined that the learning environment would be spread across three locations: (1) the computer, using CAD software; (2) the local business, where his students would find a plotter for printing drawings, as well as machine parts to use as models; and (3) the classroom, where drafting techniques would be taught. In this case, the learning environment includes a number of elements that are authentic to the work drafters do: drafting tables, computers, and so on. All of these elements, as well as the multiple locations of the environment, allow the teacher certain opportunities in planning learning units, which would not be possible if he were confined to a traditional classroom or a computer lab.

An ideal learning environment

In the ideal setting, the learning environment supports all of the students' learning activities. This means that the ideal environment has ample resources, easy access to materials, and comfortable surroundings. As an example, imagine a science class in which students are conducting experiments related to motion. Students have a variety of tools, including electronic ones, to measure velocity and distance. They have access to the Internet and a small library where they may look up information when they have questions. They can work in small groups, and the teacher circulates among the groups, watching iterations of the experiments and asking questions about what certain results mean or why the students have designed their experiments in a certain way. Perhaps the mathematics teacher comes to the room for a math lesson that involves graphing and interpreting the data that students are collecting. The environment is designed to promote learning, and the students are engaged in hands-on activities.

Deliberate Design of Learning Environments

The Learner-Centered Psychological Principles

For our purposes, we focus on learning environments through the lens of the APA's Learner-Centered Psychological Principles (APA Work Group, 1997). These fourteen principles reflect aspects of learning and learning environments that have been found, through multiple studies over time, to be effective in promoting student learning. Though the principles are not specific guidelines for creating learning environments, they describe the kinds of opportunities and settings that are necessary for students to learn successfully. They are listed in Spotlight 2.1.

Learner-Centered Psychological Principles

As you look over this list, think about ways you might be able to address each of the principles in your own classroom—with and without technology.

Cognitive and Metacognitive Factors

1. *Nature of the learning process.* The learning of complex subject matter is most effective when it is an intentional process of constructing meaning from information and experience.
2. *Goals of the learning process.* The successful learner, over time and with support and instructional guidance, can create meaningful, coherent representations of knowledge.
3. *Construction of knowledge.* The successful learner can link new information with existing knowledge in meaningful ways.
4. *Strategic thinking.* The successful learner can create and use a repertoire of thinking and reasoning strategies to achieve complex learning goals.
5. *Thinking about thinking.* Higher order strategies for selecting and monitoring mental operations facilitate creative and critical thinking.
6. *Context of learning.* Learning is influenced by environmental factors, including culture, technology, and instructional practices.

Motivational and Affective Factors

7. *Motivational and emotional influences on learning.* What and how much is learned is influenced by the learner's motivation. Motivation to learn, in turn, is influenced by the individual's emotional states, beliefs, interests and goals, and habits of thinking.
8. *Intrinsic motivation to learn.* The learner's creativity, higher order thinking, and natural curiosity all contribute to motivation to learn. Intrinsic motivation is stimulated by tasks of optimal novelty and difficulty, relevant to personal interests, and providing for personal choice and control.
9. *Effects of motivation on effort.* Acquisition of complex knowledge and skills requires extended learner effort and guided practice. Without learners' motivation to learn, the willingness to exert this effort is unlikely without coercion.

Developmental and Social Factors

10. *Developmental influences on learning.* As individuals develop, there are different opportunities and constraints for learning. Learning is most effective when differential development within and across physical, intellectual, emotional, and social domains is taken into account.
11. *Social influences on learning.* Learning is influenced by social interactions, interpersonal relations, and communication with others.

Individual Differences

12. *Individual differences in learning.* Learners have different strategies, approaches, and capabilities for learning that are a function of prior experience and heredity.
13. *Learning and diversity.* Learning is most effective when differences in learners' linguistic, cultural, and social backgrounds are taken into account.
14. *Standards and assessment.* Setting appropriately high and challenging standards and assessing the learner as well as learning progress—including diagnostic, process, and outcome assessment—are integral parts of the learning process.

Source: APA Work Group (1997).

We encourage you to think of your students' learning environment as something that you, to a large extent, design. You may not be able to alter the shape of your classroom or its paint color, but there is much that you can control. As you make your choices, consider each of the elements described in the Learner-Centered Psychological Principles. Think about the effects of your decisions on your students' learning.

For example, if you choose to set aside a section of your classroom for silent reading, what opportunities does that afford? What if you choose to place two computers in your room? All of your decisions have

Online Study Center

Metacognition and Strategic Learning

Recall that Spotlight 2.1 included a section called "Cognitive and Metacognitive Factors." **Metacognition** refers to learners' understanding of their own thinking and learning processes. By "thinking about thinking," students can figure out how they learn best and develop strategies to maximize their learning.

To begin considering ways to develop students' metacognitive understanding, watch the HM Video Case called **Metacognition: Helping Students Become Strategic Learners.** This video, available in the Online Study Center, shows how one teacher promoted metacognition in her middle-school classroom. You can also read an interview with the teacher, Julie Craven, and see additional video clips of her students using their metacognitive skills in class.

As you watch the video, think about how you might be able to support your own students in thinking about thinking. How could you use these strategies or others in your own teaching?

New roles for the teacher

an impact on how the students interact with one another and with the content you want them to learn. In fact, the learning opportunities that you shape for your students influence not only what they can and will learn, but also the way they think about learning and school in general.

■ The Teacher's Role in a Learning Environment

Perhaps one of the most important decisions you make as a teacher is the role you'll play in your students' learning. Historically, the teacher's role has been that of *information deliverer*, in which the teacher interprets a set of material for the students, who are then responsible for practicing and retaining that material. However, as evidenced by the Learner-Centered Psychological Principles, this role isn't adequate for promoting meaningful learning. To create the learning environments that promote learning, your role as a teacher will need to be different.

For example, you'll need to see yourself as a *choreographer* of sorts, because you'll be responsible for moving students from one kind of learning activity to another. You'll also be a *questioner*, asking a lot of questions to be sure that students attend to those aspects of the learning experience reflected in student learning standards. Finally, you'll need to be a constant *assessor* of students' learning, to ensure that they are developing the kinds of understandings critical to their growth of knowledge and skills.

All of these roles become even more critical when implementing technology. In some ways, technology presents an additional challenge. For example, if you have only one computer in your classroom and twenty-five students, you'll need to think carefully about how to purposefully integrate the machine into the teaching and learning. If you have the students participating in a simulation, you'll need to ask questions to help them focus, so that the experience doesn't become just a game without educational value. Finally, you'll have to add the role of *troubleshooter.* No matter how well you plan, there are always going to be things that don't go as planned when you work with technology. This means that you'll need a backup plan, as well as some simple troubleshooting skills, to support your students' learning.

■ Characteristics of Technology in Learner-Centered Environments

Good learning environments have certain qualities that afford effective teaching and support learning. When you create your own learning environment, it should reflect these critical elements. In particular, learner-centered classrooms demonstrate strategies that are *engaging, interactive, facilitative,* and *instructionally appropriate.* You'll want to make sure these characteristics describe your classroom when you use technology.

▬▬ Engaging

For learning to take place, students must be *engaged* in a process, enabling them to acquire knowledge and meet the lesson's objectives. Refer back to the Learner-Centered Psychological Principles and notice that many of them can be addressed, in part, simply by creating an environment that piques students' interest or draws them into solving a problem. One way to create an engaging environment for your students is to create an *active* learning environment in which students are involved in hands-on activities, such as participating in a simulation, researching solutions to problems, or building and developing models.

This type of learning is sometimes known as *syntonic learning* (Papert, 1980). The word *syntonic* means "highly responsive to the environment." In this context, it suggests that students have a tangible learning experience involving more than just their mind; the learning environment also engages the senses and the emotions.

Getting students interested and involved

▬▬ Interactive

Although interactivity is highly sought after in using technology, it is a complicated construct. A high level of interactivity is a prime goal of the gaming industry—and with good reason. Children and adults alike can be captivated for hours by onslaughts of warriors and demons, by the challenges of new worlds. However, this level of interactivity in learning software can distract learners from important learning ideas. Therefore, the challenge is in finding a balance between engaging interactivity and the learning focus.

Edutainment is a buzzword describing the delivery of educational content within a gaming atmosphere. A quick walk through any store with computer software will reveal numerous titles offering to teach children a variety of topics. For the most part, edutainment games, although engaging because of their high levels of interactivity, challenge students to recite only what they already know. The teacher is still responsible for supporting students in developing their skills and in moving beyond simple recitation to deeper levels of understanding.

Promoting interactivity that is truly educational

Unfortunately, if your goal is meaningful conceptual understanding, there are very few "highly interactive" titles that represent high-quality options. Even with those titles, teachers have a tremendous responsibility to structure the learning environment in a way that supports the intended learning. This is one area in which teachers are a critical part of the technology-enhanced learning environment.

▬▬ Facilitative

Facilitative: helping students make progress

Facilitative uses of technology are those that offer students effective ways to learn content. As the teacher, your first priority in planning for technology use is to consider how technology can facilitate your students' progress toward the objectives you've set.

Think back to our drafting example. The drafting teacher can't expect to teach the students everything there is to know about technical drawing, or even about using CAD software and a high-end plotter. The students will meet some learning objectives through trial and error and by communicating with the drafting person at the local business. Nevertheless, the technology in the learning environment will facilitate the students' meeting the objectives.

▰▰▰ Instructionally Appropriate

While reading this chapter you may have sensed that instructional approaches with technology have strong ties to those without technology, but that technology can enhance and extend many approaches. That's true. Returning to the Learner-Centered Psychological Principles, instructional methods should engage students in creating meaning for themselves. They should motivate students to *want* to participate in learning, and they should capitalize on the value of student interactions as learning tools. In short, good technology-based and technology-enhanced environments need first to be good learning environments.

Which methods are appropriate for your students?

The instructional approaches available to teachers who use technology vary tremendously. A teacher might use inquiry approaches, hands-on learning approaches, or content delivery approaches. The teacher may choose to combine these with activities that involve pairs or small groups. The critical consideration is whether the instruction is *appropriate* for the students. The four-part Case Study at the end of this chapter will help you think about appropriate versus inappropriate uses of technology.

▰ Kinds of Technology-Rich Learning Environments

There are a number of different ways to divide technologies into categories. In this section we present two different categorizations: immersive versus nonimmersive and technology-enhanced versus technology-based. It's important to keep in mind that these categories are not mutually exclusive; an approach may be technology-enhanced and nonimmersive, for example. These categories are useful mainly because they give us ways of describing and understanding the various uses of technology. At the end of this section we also describe four common classroom configurations for technology-rich learning environments.

▰ Immersive Versus Nonimmersive

Immersive technologies are those in which the student essentially enters a virtual environment for learning. A military flight simulator is an example of immersive technology. The pilot enters a mock plane, completely surrounded by a virtual world and oblivious to the actual building where the machinery is housed. He or she becomes an active element of

Entering a virtual world

the simulation, acting and reacting to stimuli as they are presented. The senses are bombarded with real sounds, lights, movement, even smells. This kind of training is so effective that every military pilot and NASA astronaut spends countless hours in a simulator.

Immersive technology, though not commonplace in education today, is on the horizon for classroom use. At this time the expense of the equipment hinders widespread use in schools, but the capabilities are promising, and the implications for learning are significant.

One particular area of growing interest is **augmented reality.** In programs of this type, information is added to the learner's actual surroundings. In other words, through use of a headset or a hand-held computer, students are provided with information that enhances their experience in the location where they are physically situated. Augmented reality technologies are being developed for such settings as museums. They are also gaining widespread acceptance in military training environments, where instructors are able to provide information to learners as the learners engage in practice drills.

Nonimmersive technologies are those that do not transport the learner to a virtual place but do *simulate* another environment. The most popular simulation titles and video games (such as SimCity, The Sims, Halo, and Black & White) could be classified as nonimmersive. Nonimmersive technology provides a high level of interactivity, but the learner is not "enveloped" in the technology and is always aware of being part of a traditional classroom. Nonimmersive environments are completely housed within the computer, but the learner wears no special devices, such as gloves, goggles, or a head-mounted display; rather, he or she interacts through a computer "window" as an outsider. As you saw in the second "Technology in Action" feature at the beginning of this chapter, significant learning opportunities can be based in nonimmersive environments—opportunities that would be either impossible or uninteresting in any other format.

■ Technology-Enhanced Versus Technology-Based

Technology-enhanced learning environments use computers and related technology to augment the teaching and learning activities of the classroom. The drafting class example at the beginning of this chapter is an example of a technology-enhanced learning environment. Not all of the learning takes place using technology, and when the technology is called into play, it extends the learning already going on in the environment. The students use CAD software, a computer, and an Internet connection to apply their knowledge of drafting techniques introduced by the instructor.

As another example, you might create an activity for students to learn about earthquakes. Imagine that your classroom is located in New England, where earthquakes are uncommon and hardly ever make national headlines. Your students could use the Internet to research Southern California's San Andreas Fault. This is an example of technology used to enhance the learning environment. In this case, the Internet isn't

Technology that augments the real-world experience

Simulations

Technology to extend the learning environment

the only means by which students will learn or be engaged; rather, it's a tool for improving the teacher's capacity to provide access to timely and accurate content.

Technology-based learning environments are a much more involved use of educational technology. These environments engage students in learning *through* the computer. This isn't to say that the entire learning unit must be based in the computer; rather, noncomputer activities will draw from and build on computer activities.

Many virtual environments are considered technology based. **Virtual Reality Modeling Language (VRML),** also known as **Web3D, X3D,** or 3D modeling, provides graphical representations that allow students to interact with objects and even with other characters, called *avatars*. For example, in a chemistry simulation environment, students may practice and learn specific chemistry concepts through a VRML software package. Students use the simulation to view, interact with, and move molecules. The technology environment allows the students to see a virtual water molecule, break it apart, add it to other molecules, and learn from the reaction. As part of this technology-based learning experience, the teacher may have the students write a reflection on their learning, watch a video illustrating the molecular processes, or conduct a lab. However, if these more traditional activities all grow out of questions that were (or could have been) generated from interactions with the simulation, the environment can be seen as technology based.

Technology as the foundation of a learning environment

Common Classroom Configurations

When you enter your classroom, you may find any assortment of technology configurations in the room. In this section we consider some of the most common configurations and the benefits and challenges of each.

As you read about the different configurations, think about how they might help you or hinder you in meeting aspects of the Learner-Centered Psychological Principles. Also consider how the layouts could support students with unique needs. For example, could a visually impaired student benefit from having a computer on her desk that shows her your computer screen, only larger? Would your English-language learners benefit more from being together in a cluster or from being paired with native English speakers? Would your behaviorally challenged students work better in clusters or in pairs? Will your gifted students have adequate access to computers to explore topics more deeply?

In discussing computer configurations, we focus on full-scale computers, either desktops or laptops. For some purposes, though, handheld computing devices can also be extremely useful, as we discuss in Spotlight 2.2.

One-Computer Classroom

Though many schools have moved beyond a single computer in the classroom, there are still some where this is the norm. More often, classrooms will have multiple machines, but only one will have Internet access, or

Hand-Held Computers

One of the most promising technologies for classroom use is **hand-held computers,** also known as **personal digital assistants,** or **PDAs** (Figure 2.1). These are small computers that allow students to capture data, write or type (with a separate keyboard), calculate, and engage with a variety of special software developed for educational purposes. Hand-held computers include Windows CE devices, Palm Pilots (and later-generation Palm devices), and even some mobile phones.

Hand-held computers are appealing for education because they are inexpensive compared to their full-size counterparts, with prices starting at around $100. They are also extremely portable. Using a hand-held device, for instance, students can use scientific probes to measure temperature in a nearby pond for their physical science class, or they can track all of the foods they eat during a week as part of a nutrition inquiry.

For ideas about how to use PDAs in your classroom, see "Resources" at the end of the chapter.

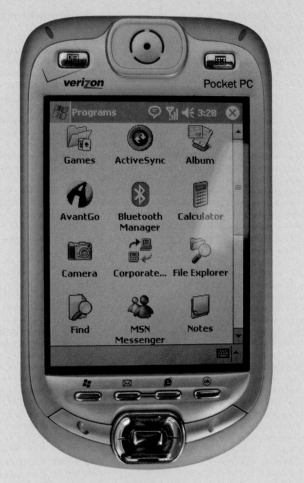

Figure 2.1 A Hand-Held Computer

only one will have projection capabilities—creating a situation similar in some respects to a one-computer classroom.

For a number of very practical reasons, the machine in a one-computer classroom often becomes the "teacher machine." After all, many schools require a significant amount of computer-based management, ranging from recording students' work in a grading program to completing online attendance reports. The teacher may also need to check e-mail or update a class web page outlining assignments and upcoming events so that students and their parents know what is expected for class each day.

Instructional uses for a single computer

However, even when the single computer houses all of the teacher's records, it can still be used for instructional purposes. The teacher may use it to model concepts or processes, show animations or videos, or work with the whole class on a simulation. There are even some software packages that have been specifically designed to manage learning in a one-computer classroom. For Tom Snyder's *Rainforest Researchers*

Table 2.1 Issues Related to Single-Computer Classrooms

Uses of a Single Computer	Drawbacks and Challenges
Concept modeling	Limited use for student practice
Process modeling (such as problem solving)	Need to have more than one activity occurring in the room at one time
Whole-class problem solving	Cannot support an inquiry method of learning
Introduction of materials	
Preparation for computer lab work	Security concerns if student records are housed on the machine
Management of a project (like the Tom Snyder software packages mentioned in the text)	Difficult to meet a wide array of learner needs without significant planning
Student presentations	Infrastructure needs such as electrical, networking wiring, and furniture

or *The Great Ocean Rescue,* students are provided with books containing the information they need to complete an inquiry-based science unit. The computer is used to record teams' responses to challenges and to guide students in their next step in the problem-solving process. In this case, the computer can provide some flexibility in the unfolding of the problem-solving process by responding to decisions students have made along the way, but the class can work on the project away from the computer.

The single-computer classroom can also provide opportunities to set up the computer as a learning center, one of a number of such centers in the classroom. Students rotate from one center to another, and eventually everyone gets a turn at the computer. This approach assumes there is appropriate software to support students as they learn on their own. Table 2.1 summarizes some of the pros and cons of a one-computer classroom.

Small Computer Cluster

A common classroom setup involves a small cluster of computers (see Figure 2.2). Typically, these clusters range from three to six computers. Depending on the school, they may or may not have Internet access.

For many teachers, clusters pose more challenges than either one computer or a room full of computers. If there are twenty-four students in a class and the teacher has six computers, she has to assign four students to a computer to do an activity. This isn't a good classroom management strategy, for two reasons. First, only one or two students will be able to see the monitor clearly, and without strong guidance only those students nearest the machine will actually use the computer. Second, because they aren't engaged in what's happening on the screen, the students who are farthest away from the computer often become distracted and cause trouble. To overcome such problems, some teachers assign students roles in the group and allow only those students whose "job" is using the computer to go near the machines. But even when the teacher remembers to rotate roles, it's a difficult model to get students to buy into.

Management strategies for computer clusters

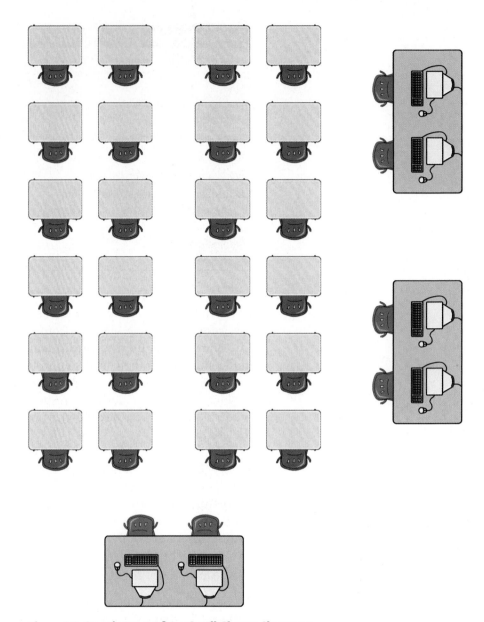

Figure 2.2 Sample Layout for a Small-Cluster Classroom

A preferred approach to maximizing the use of a computer cluster is to divide the class in half and create two activities—one on the computer and one away from it. Pair the students (or put them in groups of three) and have half the students work on each activity for half the period. Then switch groups. In our example of twenty-four students and six computers, this method means that only twelve students will be using the computers at a given time—only two students per machine. With this arrangement, everyone can benefit from the technology.

Another approach to capitalizing on the small cluster is to set up a number of learning centers and have the cluster act as one of the centers. Figure 2.3 illustrates such an arrangement. Each table

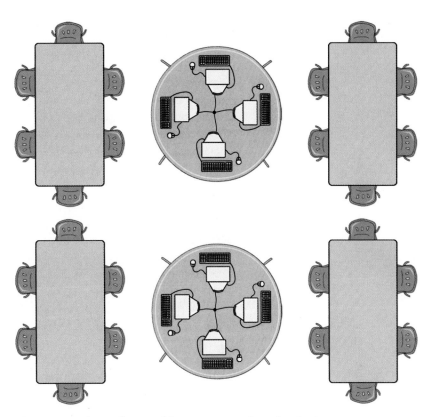

Figure 2.3 Using a Cluster of Computers as a Learning Center

Figure 2.4 A "Pod" Approach to Using a Small Number of Computers

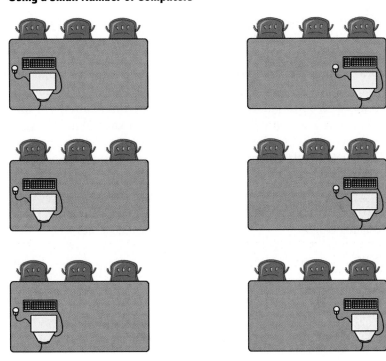

on the right and left represents a center where students engage in a certain kind of activity, and the computers in the middle form a center of their own.

A third option for working with a small number of computers is to create a set of "pods" around the room (Figure 2.4). Each pod provides table space for a group of students and one computer. In this way each group of three to five students can have easy access to technology, when they need it, throughout the school day. One pitfall of this design is that the room must be well wired to support the electrical and Internet needs of the computers, and proper furniture must be purchased to support this kind of environment. Most classroom tables are far too small or too large to support this configuration. Table 2.2 summarizes some of the uses and challenges of the small-cluster computer arrangement.

Table 2.2 Issues Related to Small Clusters of Computers

Uses of a Small Cluster	Drawbacks and Challenges
Center work	Limited use for student practice
Group work that requires only one or two members to be on the computer	Need to have more than one activity at a time in the room
Student grouping (such as heterogeneous grouping) to support diverse learners	Difficult to support simultaneous whole-class inquiry
Individual research projects as one resource for many	Cannot project screen for demonstrations
Special projects for students who need additional support	Hard to arrange students physically so that they can see the board
Special projects for advanced students	Infrastructure needs such as electrical, networking wiring, and furniture
Pods of students arranged to allow easy access to machines throughout the school day	

Computer Lab

For many teachers, the computer lab is the most comfortable place to use technology. Typically, the lab has enough computers for each student to work alone, and the software is set up on every machine. In some schools, the lab also features an additional adult who manages the lab and can help the teacher troubleshoot when things go wrong.

Planning is important with computer labs

However, the problems with labs are significant. First, there is often only one lab in a school, and class time in the lab must be scheduled in advance, which limits the teacher's flexibility. All lessons must be planned out in enough detail ahead of time for the teacher to know when to reserve the lab.

Because of the logistics involved in using the computer lab, many teachers also choose to do activities in the lab that are separate from the "normal" activities of the classroom. For example, the teacher may have students do a special "technology project" or use a program that addresses relevant content, but not in ways that are aligned with the current activities of the classroom. This isn't inherently a bad thing, but it *is* a consideration. As the teacher, you'll need to clarify your own goals for your students' use of technology, then determine the best way to meet those goals. See the summary of issues related to computer labs in Table 2.3.

Table 2.3 Issues Related to Computer Lab Configurations

Uses of a Computer Lab	Drawbacks and Challenges
Practice of concepts	Logistics of gaining access
Individual problem solving	Students have to leave the classroom—and the classroom's resources—to use computers
Individual research projects	
Writing projects	
	Often complicated when the teacher is using collaborative approaches

SPOTLIGHT
2.3 **Monitoring Software**

One kind of network software showing up in computer labs and on wireless computers is monitoring and teaching software. These programs allow the teacher to

- Broadcast one computer screen to all the computer monitors in a lab.
- Watch students' computer screens from one location.

These tools can be used in a variety of ways, ranging from behavior management to engaging learners in collaborative experiences.

Consider an elementary-school teacher who is introducing students to a tool like Kidspiration for brainstorming and concept mapping. The teacher may decide that she wants her students to understand how to create a concept map before they try to use the software themselves, so she broadcasts her own screen to every monitor in the room and walks the students through the parts of a concept map.

As another example, picture a middle-school classroom in which students are learning about force. The students find a roller coaster simulation that they're excited about. Using this simulation, the teacher may allow several groups to create different roller coasters to share with the class. Then she can broadcast each group's computer screen to everyone else while the group demonstrates its roller coaster. Because they're doing a live demonstration, the students can instantly incorporate feedback from the class into their roller coaster design to improve it. The teacher can also structure the learning experience so that the class engages in a conversation to compare successful roller coaster models and create a list of important criteria related to force. Without the broadcasting ability, it would be very difficult for the class to look at multiple models and develop a collaborative understanding of the role of force in roller coaster physics.

Finally, imagine a classroom where students are exploring a mathematical construction, such as an equilateral triangle, that could be created in several ways. By broadcasting each group's computer screen, the teacher can engage the class in a discussion of the attributes of the construction, why more than one approach works, and which construction might be "best."

Such technologies, which allow teachers to quickly demonstrate ideas or allow students to share ideas and help each other learn, offer exciting possibilities for learning that would otherwise be difficult. They also open up possibilities for students with particular disabilities; for example, students with visual impairments may be better able to view the teacher's work on their individual computer monitor than on a projection screen. Some examples of these software packages are NetOp School (http://www.netop.com/netop-8.htm) and NetSupport School (http://www.netsupportschool.com).

▬ Wireless Carts, or One-to-One, Computing

One of the currently popular solutions to technology use is rolling wireless carts, which allow a one-to-one or two-to-one student-to-computer ratio in a classroom. Typically, these carts include ten to fifteen laptop computers that use wireless technologies to link to the Internet. The teacher reserves the cart, then wheels it into the classroom and sets it up for students to use. This arrangement can provide the teacher with a tremendous amount of flexibility. If the teacher has "monitoring" software (see Spotlight 2.3), the flexibility is even greater.

Benefits of laptop carts

Laptop carts offer some benefits that traditional computer labs don't. The most important is the ability to use the machines anywhere within the wireless network. Learning isn't limited to the computer lab or the table in the back of the room. Students can work on the floor or at tables; they can even go outside to collect data.

Carts do require some of the same planning as a computer lab (the teacher must reserve them in advance), and they require a certain level of technology training to set up. Often, too, laptop carts are most appropriate

Table 2.4 Issues Related to Wireless Cart Configurations	
Uses of a Wireless Cart	Drawbacks and Challenges
Practice of concepts	Logistics of reserving, moving, and setting up the computers
Individual problem solving	
Individual research projects	Teachers have to understand how to set up the carts
Writing projects	
Student pairs	Less structured than normal classroom environment; can feel chaotic
Collaborative projects	
	Setup requires additional time and planning

for students working in pairs, because the average cart doesn't hold enough computers for each student to have one. See Table 2.4 for a list of considerations in the use of wireless computer carts.

SUMMARY

A learning environment includes all aspects of the context where learning takes place—for instance, the tools and materials that are available, the layout of the spaces, and the classroom management approach. As a teacher, you make deliberate decisions about the environment your students will experience. We hope you will create an environment that encourages meaningful learning, informed by the Learner-Centered Psychological Principles.

Technology is one aspect of the learning environment that you will design. Technology should be used in ways that are engaging and interactive, facilitate students' learning, and are instructionally appropriate.

The technology you use may be either immersive (like virtual reality) or nonimmersive. The environment may be technologically based, meaning that the entire unit draws from and builds on computer activities, or it may be just technologically enhanced.

You may be working in a single-computer classroom, or you may have computers in clusters, in a separate computer lab, or on wireless carts. Each of these configurations has certain potential benefits and certain drawbacks that you should be aware of as you plan your lessons.

As you continue reading this book, you'll have more opportunities to think about different approaches to using technology in your own classroom and your role as the teacher.

RESOURCES

Online Study Center
Direct Links to Resources

Hand-Held Computers in Education
http://m.fasfind.com/wwwtools/m/2737
.cfm?x=0&rid=2737
A collection of resources for using hand-held computers in classrooms, including ideas for projects, lists of software, and information on professional development.

Handhelds in the Classroom
http://www.education-world.com/a_tech/tech083.shtml
An *Education World* article discussing the rise in popularity of hand-held computers in classrooms, including descriptions of some schools' projects with handhelds.

Learner-Centered Psychological Principles
http://www.apa.org/ed/lcp2/lcp14.html
The APA's research-based principles for the design of instruction to meet the needs of all students.

NetOp School
http://www.netop.com/netop-8.htm
> One software option for monitoring students' computers and broadcasting a single computer screen to an entire lab.

NetSupport School
http://www.netsupportschool.com
> Another software option for monitoring students' computers and broadcasting a single computer screen to an entire lab.

Power in the Palm of Your Hand
http://kathyschrock.net/power
> Kathy Schrock's set of links to articles and websites with information about using hand-held computers in classrooms.

case
STUDY

Four Classrooms

Classroom 1   An elementary-school teacher has been given a small amount of money to purchase one mathematics software title for his classroom. He has determined that his students would benefit most from a program that allows them to develop an understanding of attributes of geometrical shapes. After checking several sources, he has narrowed his choice to two products. One allows students to try to "break" shapes, an interesting and challenging activity. But the software is complex, requiring him to spend considerable time making templates that the students could then manipulate. He'd also need to write lesson plans. The other is a drill-and-practice program with cute cartoon images. This program would take students through thirty questions that require them to name shapes and parts of shapes.

Which of these two software titles would you choose if you were the teacher? Why?

Classroom 2   A middle-school English teacher needs to have her students write a research report. She has decided that she'd like them to use the Internet as a research tool and that their topic is "Storytelling in Modern North Africa." Should she provide the students with a set of links she has selected for them, or should she let them search the entire Internet? (Her school does use blocking software to prevent students from accessing sites inappropriate for young people.) Should she provide other resources to her students as well?

Classroom 3   A high-school biology teacher has found an animation showing cellular processes. Her students normally get to see only a diagram of these processes in their textbook, and they often struggle to understand the concepts. But the teacher is unsure whether to show the animation before she lectures or during the lecture, or whether she should just provide it as enrichment material in case her students need help. How would you use an animation like this?

Classroom 4   A corporate foundation has given the four social studies teachers at Park Middle School ten computers to use for social studies instruction. The teachers are disappointed about the small number of computers, but they want to find ways to make the best use of their new technology. How might they consider arranging the computers? What implications do different arrangements have for instructional potential and for the design of the learning environment?

Questions for Reflection and Discussion

1. How does each of these scenarios relate to the issue of learning environments?
2. Which cases present questions that could be addressed with the Learner-Centered Psychological Principles?
3. Are there "right answers" to any of the situations described in the cases? If not, how can the teachers know they are making good decisions?

Meet the Standards

Online Study Center

Standards
Explore the Online Study Center for additional help in meeting the standards.

At the beginning of this chapter we listed several standards from the National Educational Technology Standards (NETS). We've aligned this chapter with these expected outcomes of your knowledge development. As a teacher, you'll be expected to

▶ Design developmentally appropriate learning opportunities that apply technology-enhanced instructional strategies to support the diverse needs of learners.
▶ Use technology to support learner-centered strategies that address the diverse needs of students.
▶ Apply technology to develop students' higher-order skills and creativity.
▶ Apply technology resources to enable and empower learners with diverse backgrounds, characteristics, and abilities.

Using what you've read in this chapter about learner-centered classrooms, think about how you might design a lesson to teach a difficult concept in your own subject area. Focus on these questions:

▶ What technologies would help?
▶ What strategies could you use?
▶ How would you structure the activity for your best student? your weakest student?
▶ Can you think of three ways technology could be used in your lessons to support higher-order thinking—that is, thinking that deals with complex ideas and relationships?

Chapter 3

Learner Needs

ISTE NETS

Teachers

▶ Design developmentally appropriate learning opportunities that apply technology-enhanced instructional strategies to support the diverse needs of learners.

▶ Apply current research on teaching and learning with technology when planning learning environments and experiences.

▶ Facilitate technology-enhanced experiences that address content standards and student technology standards.

▶ Use technology to support learner-centered strategies that address the diverse needs of students.

▶ Apply technology in assessing student learning of subject matter using a variety of assessment techniques.

OTHER RELEVANT STANDARDS

National Board for Professional Teaching Standards, Five Core Propositions (2006)

From Proposition 1. Teachers have an understanding of how students develop and learn. . . . Teachers use their understanding of individual and social learning theory . . . to form their decisions about how to teach.

From Proposition 4. [Teachers] exemplify the virtues they seek to impart to students: curiosity and a love of learning; tolerance and open-mindedness; fairness and justice; appreciation for our cultural and intellectual heritages; respect for human diversity and dignity; and such intellectual capacities as careful reasoning, the ability to take multiple perspectives, to question received wisdom, to be creative, to take risks, and to adopt an experimental and problem-solving orientation.

Regardless of the grade level or content that you teach, your job as a teacher is to support your students in learning a set of facts, processes, and concepts. Though this sounds straightforward, there are a number of different factors you need to take into account to create the best possible opportunities for learning. We address some of these in this chapter. First, we discuss what learning theory is and what it means to you as a teacher. Next, we address constructivist approaches to teaching and learning. Then we consider what it means to learn and how you, as a teacher, can measure learning. Finally, we focus on diversity in the classroom and how that influences what you do as a teacher.

All of these topics are vital to the use of technology in the classroom. Whether or not you're planning to use technology in your teaching, you should always begin your learning unit design by deciding what you want your students to learn from an experience. Once you've determined your learners' needs, it will be easier for you to design instruction that meets those needs. That's the first step toward developing your own technology-enhanced teaching and learning materials.

A Basic Introduction to Learning Theory

Learning theories are concerned with explaining how people learn. Over the last century, a wide variety of research has been conducted on learning. Though we still lack a definitive way to explain how everyone learns, many principles that are relevant to classrooms and students have been identified.

The Evolution of Learning Theory

Over time, as more research has been conducted, our understanding of how people learn has changed. In the early twentieth century, **behaviorism** was the most prominent learning theory being tested and developed. Behaviorism proposed that people learn through a series of reinforcements, whether positive or negative. For example, if a teacher wants to teach students to raise their hand before speaking out in class, she first tells them to do so. Then she provides positive reinforcement to students who follow the rule, by calling on them when they raise their hand. She also punishes misbehaving students by sending them out in the hall, having them stay after school, or requiring them to sit through a silent lunch.

Behaviorism: learning through reinforcements

One of the primary early researchers in behaviorism was B. F. Skinner. As an application of his theory, Skinner developed an instructional approach called **programmed instruction,** often considered the forerunner of many educational technologies. His teaching machines allowed learners to go through a body of information in a prescribed order, often using a fill-in-the-blanks strategy to learn the material (see Figure 3.1). Once they mastered the material, learners could move on to new topics. They could also revisit the material as many times as they needed or wanted in order to learn it.

As researchers became interested in what happens in the brain when people learn rather than just the observable outcomes of the learning,

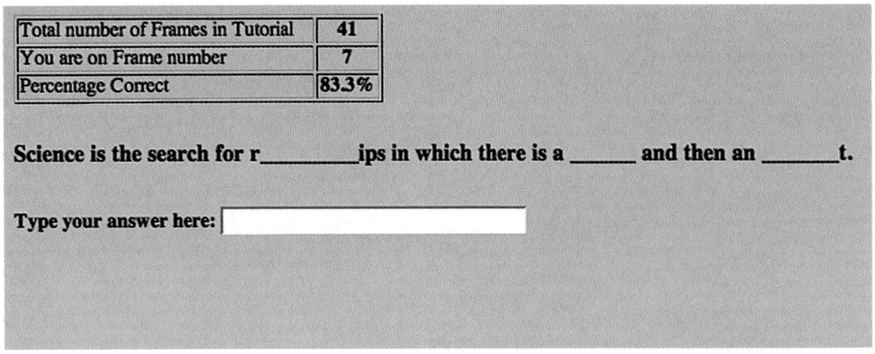

Total number of Frames in Tutorial	41
You are on Frame number	7
Percentage Correct	83.3%

Science is the search for r_____ips in which there is a _____ and then an _____t.

Type your answer here: |_____|

Figure 3.1 Sample Questions in the Style of Skinner's Programmed Instruction
Source: http://www.coedu.usf.edu/~behavior/bam/abasets/piplayer_plus.pl

behaviorism was less of a driving force in the design of instruction. It was pushed to the background by a number of different theories that attempted to explain what was happening inside the brain when individuals learned. These theories often viewed the human brain as analogous to a computer. Learning was seen as a process of getting information into and out of, and organizing it inside of, that computer. These approaches became known as information-processing theories or, more formally, **cognitive information-processing (CIP) theories.** They focused on memorizing information, a process that requires moving information from short-term memory to long-term memory. CIP theories were also concerned with supporting learners in connecting new information to old information, in much the same way that a database might link a person's name, address, and date of birth. Finally, CIP theories were concerned with retrieval of information once it is learned.

CIP theories: how the brain processes information

Traditional American classrooms have been affected significantly by information-processing theories. This is most apparent in the use of *rehearsal* strategies in classroom instruction. Teachers often introduce a concept by reminding students of what they already know. Then they introduce new material, relating it to what students know, and they follow up by assigning a certain amount of practice (rehearsal) for students to establish the material in long-term memory.

Contemporary learning theories look further into what happens inside a learner's head. Known generally as **constructivism,** these theories are concerned with how people *construct* an understanding of the world around them based on a combination of what they already know and what they experience. For example, think back to what you knew about college before you started. Now that you're a college student, your understanding has become deeper and broader.

Constructivism: how learners construct knowledge

Constructivist theories vary widely in their description of how people come to understand the world around them. All subscribe to the notion that students need to experience new ideas and processes directly in order to learn them. All of them also agree that the teacher needs to support the student in reflecting on what he or she has experienced and relating this new experience to previous experience. Where constructivist theories vary is in their views on the role of the community in the student's development.

Some constructivist theories place a heavy emphasis on the role of other people (not just teachers, but also other adults and other students) in a learner's development. Some theories don't see such a strong relationship between interpersonal relationships and student performance.

Spotlight 3.1 briefly explains some key terms used in learning theories. We explore many of these concepts in more detail later in this chapter and elsewhere in the book.

SPOTLIGHT 3.1   Key Terms in Learning Theory

Terms from Behaviorism

Behaviorism. A learning theory that focuses only on observable behaviors. To support learning in a behaviorist way, one would support the learner through a series of positive or negative reinforcements in response to the learner's observable behavior.

Conditioning. In behaviorism, this is the heart of the learning process. It is either triggered through a natural mechanism (e.g., Pavlov's experiments with dogs that showed that they salivate when they eat) or through a stimulus-response cycle in which the learner receives feedback based on his or her behavior.

Punishment. A change made to the environment to reduce the likelihood of a behavior occurring again in the future. A punishment may add something to the environment or remove something from the environment to affect the desired change.

Reinforcement. A change made to the environment to increase the likelihood of a desired behavior occurring again in the future. These can add stimuli to the environment *(positive reinforcement)* or remove stimuli from the environment *(negative reinforcement).*

Terms from Information Processing

Cognitive Information Processing (CIP). A theory of learning that views the mind as an information processing device in which information can filed away and retrieved. Learning is characterized by moving information from short-term memory to long-term memory.

Long-term memory. In information processing, this is the area of the brain for permanent storage. Information is rehearsed by the learner to be put into long-term memory. Problem-solving is approached by the learner applying organizations, called *schemata,* from their long-term memory to the situation. Information stored in long-term memory is considered permanent, and when someone "forgets" something, it is viewed as an inability to recall information rather than a loss of that information.

Short-term memory. A part of the brain that temporarily holds information but does not allow it to be added to the schemata in the brain.

Schema (plural: schemata). The organization structures of the brain that allow information to be related to each other. Learning is said to occur when these are altered through the addition or refinement of information.

Terms from Constructivism

Constructivism. A set of learning theories that asserts that each person creates their own understandings through experiences with information and/or people. Learning occurs as the learner integrates new understandings into their existing ideas about the content or context.

Scaffolding. Supports put into place to help a learner make appropriate sense of learning and to make a complex task do-able. For example, in designing a roller coaster, there are hundreds of considerations to be made, ranging from the height of the hills to the materials used. To scaffold a learning environment so that students can design a roller coaster, a teacher may choose to have students consider only height, speed, gravity, and force. As students learn more, scaffolds are slowly withdrawn.

Social negotiation. The development of one's understanding through engagement with others. In social negotiation, participants in a social structure work together to create a shared understanding of a concept or experience.

Facilitation. A teaching approach in which the instructor works to provide the student with opportunities to learn and pushes the learning through questioning strategies and introducing or reducing scaffolds, but allows the learner to engage in the hard work of learning.

Modeling. An instructional approach in which the facilitator teaches in the same way the students should be teaching or learning. For example, a facilitator may use modeling when introducing a research approach or a problem-solving approach so that the students will use that same approach for their own work.

Ill-structured. This refers to a problem that has multiple entry points and/or multiple solution tasks. It is considered ill-structured because there is no one right answer and no one right way of approaching the task. Most real-life problems are considered ill-structured. (See the example in Spotlight 3.3, later in this chapter.)

Inquiry-based learning. An instructional approach that engages students in learning content through engagement in solving problems that address "essential questions." This approach is popular in science education. Essential questions have no single right answer and offer a compelling place to begin learning. For example, "Should the U.S. change its immigration policy?" or "What would the perfect society look like?"

More knowledgeable other. A person who knows more about a particular concept, idea, or area of study than the learner. The more knowledgeable other is often a teacher or other adult, but he or she can also be a student's peer if that peer happens to know more about a topic.

General Terms

Assessment. How one measures what someone has learned. Most often, in education, this involves the use of some kind of quiz or test, though there are many other ways to successfully assess learning.

Performance assessment. A way of measuring learning by assigning an authentic task to a learner. An *authentic task* represents or closely models an activity the student might undertake in real life. Performance assessments typically require more than simply a correct answer. Instead, they ask students to combine skills, reflect on processes, and produce a "deliverable," which can range from a simple paper to a sophisticated presentation or model.

Accountability. A term often paired with *assessment.* Basically, it selects a standard to which a teacher or student will be held, then measures the degree to which the individual has met the standard. Today such standards often involve goals set by the state or school district. Also, some form of reward or penalty is often associated with accountability, such as the amount of money the school district receives and whether teachers and administrators are allowed to keep their jobs.

Learner-centered environment. An environment that attempts to meet the conditions under which people are known to learn. See our chapter "Learner-Centered Classrooms," as well as the American Psychological Association's complete discussion of Learner-Centered Psychological Principles at http://www.apa.org/ed/lcp2/lcp14.html.

Sources for further exploration: Funderstanding.com's "About Learning" section, http://www.funderstanding.com/about_learning.cfm; Wikipedia, http://en.wikipedia.org/

What Does Learning Theory Mean for Instructional Technology?

As discussed in our chapter on learner-centered classrooms, you as a teacher are the developer of a learning environment. As the developer, you're responsible for facilitating your students' learning. To this end, you plan, design, implement, and evaluate learning environments that reflect the values of your particular domain (such as science, mathematics, or English). For example, if you're a science teacher, you'll want to select technologies and instructional approaches that support inquiry, which is a crucial component of science learning. (See the discussion of inquiry-based learning in the next section.) And if you apply the principles of constructivism, you will want to select tools and activities—such as simulations, modeling tools, and research activities like collecting and analyzing data—that support your students in making sense of the world for themselves.

The primary learning theory we use throughout this book is constructivism; you'll find many examples here of uses of technology that support this kind of teaching and learning. However, we've also included examples of technologies and activities that are less constructivist—both for you to think about as a professional to determine whether they are viable and as alternatives for different kinds of learning situations.

Constructivism in the Classroom

A broad variety of classroom practices apply to constructivist environments based on the premise that learning occurs through active processes and through connections to previous knowledge and experiences (Brooks & Brooks, 1999; Jonassen, 2001; Soloway et al., 1996). In this view, instructional practices should go beyond the delivery of information; they should engage learners in the construction of knowledge leading to genuine understanding. Using a sequence of learning activities, the teacher organizes instruction in such a way that the teacher fades into the background as the learner takes center stage in the application of knowledge and skills. Here we describe two key instructional approaches that build from a constructivist foundation: inquiry-based and problem-based learning.

Inquiry-Based Learning

Inquiry-based learning is a constructivist model of instruction founded on the work of John Dewey and Jean Piaget. *Inquiry* involves making observations; posing questions; examining sources of information to see what is already known; planning investigations; reviewing what is already known in light of the student's experimental evidence; using tools to gather, analyze, and interpret data; proposing answers, explanations, and predictions; and communicating the results. It changes the focus from "what we know" to "how we come to know" (NRC, 1996, p. 23).

The essential features of inquiry-based learning include learners' (NAP, 2001)

Essential features of inquiry-based learning

▶ Engaging in questioning.
▶ Giving priority to evidence that allows them to develop and evaluate explanations.
▶ Formulating explanations from evidence in order to address questions.
▶ Communicating and justifying their explanations.

Inquiry learning projects are not unstructured, but their structure is different from traditional classroom activity. In the inquiry-based learning environment, teachers help students identify real questions and refine them into learning projects or opportunities. The students then engage in a series of learning activities to answer the questions they've posed. Throughout the process, the teacher guides the learners by listening to what they know, asking questions to challenge their thinking, providing direct guidance only as needed, and engaging them in processes that encourage them to tie what they're doing in the inquiry to what they already know. As a result of engaging in inquiries, students increase their understanding of the subject matter investigated and develop knowledge and skills needed to answer questions and investigate for greater understanding (Exline, 2003).

Technology integration is powerful enhancement to inquiry practice in the classroom. In order to perform inquiries successfully, students and teachers need access to appropriate tools for conducting investigations and communicating results (NRC, 2000). Furthermore, research demonstrates that learners develop a deeper understanding of concepts when they build and manipulate models in a context similar to a real-world setting (White & Frederiksen, 1998). Technology tools enable learners to perform and learn in far more complex ways than ever before. Standards for student learning, such as the National Science Education Standards (NSES) and the National Educational Technology Standards (NETS), clearly delineate the expectations for teachers' use of such tools in the classroom.

As an example of technology-enhanced, inquiry-based learning, a teacher could use a tool like What's the Difference from the Learning Technologies group at the National Aeronautics and Space Administration (NASA). This tool allows the teacher to use high-quality images and information from NASA's vast library to structure inquiries for students. For example, the teacher could have students compare planets closer to the sun with those that are farther away (Figure 3.2). The software allows

Integrating technology into inquiry-based learning

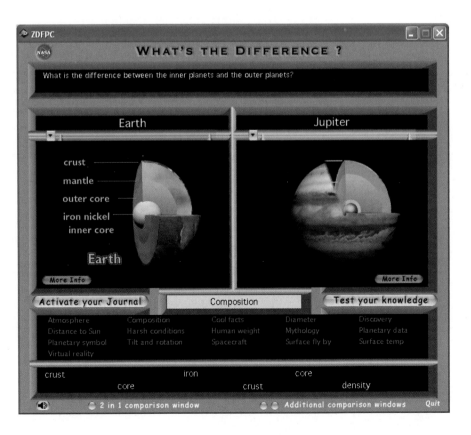

Figure 3.2 Screenshot from NASA's What's the Difference?

Though inquiry is most commonly used in science settings, there's no reason that other subjects can't be taught using inquiry-based approaches. Here are a few simple ideas and resources for other subject areas:

Inquiry in Elementary Math. In one math problem (the Wheel Problem, available as a video at **http://learner.org/resources/series32.html**), first-grade students explore what vehicles might be in a parking lot if there are twenty-four wheels total. They are provided with a wide array of tools to represent their thinking, including clay, paper, and stickers, and are encouraged to try out different combinations.

Cross-Disciplinary Unit. In Do Your Genes Drive You To Drink? (available at **http://www.sciencemuseum .org.uk**), high school students explore what's known about alcoholism from scientific, cultural, and historical perspectives.

Inquiry-Based Geography. The Xpeditions website from National Geographic (**http://www.nationalgeographic .com/xpeditions**) is home to the U.S. National Geography Standards and a variety of resources to support them. Among these resources are activities that provide students with a wide variety of experiences in using inquiry to learn about geography. For example, in the Lewis and Clark Expedition: Create Your Own Adventure inquiry, younger students are asked to plan a trip in the same way Lewis and Clark may have done. In the process, the students have to consider what to pack and how to travel, as well as make other decisions. Older students are asked to plan an "extreme adventure." Besides introducing students to an important historical event, these activities allow the students to begin to understand the size of the planet and the geography of different regions.

For more information on inquiry-based learning, see "Resources" at the end of the chapter.

students to look at detailed images and gather evidence to answer questions that the teacher has posed. Spotlight 3.2 offers examples and resources relating to inquiry-based learning in other subjects.

However, for technology to be effectively infused in instruction, it takes more than just showing hardware and software as tools. Technology must be an integral part of instruction. Helping you achieve that integration is the purpose of this book. For your own further inquiry, there are studies that support the effectiveness of professional development programs that expose teachers to technology and model its use (Becker, 2000; Bielefelt, 2001; Hasselbring et al., 2000; Means, 2000).

Problem-Based Learning

Another instructional strategy based on constructivist learning theory is the problem-based learning approach. **Problem-based learning** engages students in finding a solution to an *ill-structured problem*. In other words, the problem is complex and tied to the real world, and because of that, there are many potential solutions. Spotlight 3.3 offers an example of a high-quality problem that has been used in middle and high schools.

Learning focused on solving a problem

In problem-based learning, students do all of their learning in an effort to find a solution to the problem. This means that, when a student begins a unit like that described in Spotlight 3.3, the only information the teacher shares is the problem itself. Then the teacher takes the students through a

An Ill-Structured Problem for Science Classes, Grades 7–12

Business and community leaders in the city of Orting in Pierce County, Washington State, wish to build a new high school to accommodate and encourage the local population explosion. (Orting is only 30–40 minutes commuting time from the rapidly growing Tacoma and Seattle metropolitan areas.) However, Pierce County officials have refused permission to build the high school on county lands because they feel the location is hazardous.

Geological surveys show that both Orting and the proposed high school site are on top of solidified mudflows that originated on the slopes of nearby Mount Rainier. Based on the location of older flows around Mount Rainier and on experience gained from observing mudflows during the 1980 eruption of Mount St. Helens, county officials argue that any new mudflow coming down the valley could easily destroy the high school and anybody who happened to be in it. County officials have also passed an ordinance forbidding high-density housing (like tract-home developments) on county lands, claiming that there are not sufficient roads out of the city to allow for emergency evacuation. The ordinance has upset local developers.

City leaders counter that warnings from a system of acoustic sensors (which have not yet been built) would give students enough time to evacuate the school, if necessary. The city has tried three separate times to pass a bond issue enabling the high school to be built on city lands but has not been successful.

Representatives from both the city and the county have appealed to your company to provide them with the facts and potential risks of the situation and to recommend whether to build the high school.

Resources
Exploring the Environment Teacher Pages: Problem-Based Learning
   http://www.cotf.edu/ete/teacher/teacherout.html
Problem-Based Learning Network at the Illinois Mathematics and Science Academy
   http://www2.imsa.edu/programs/pbln
Schools of California Online Resources for Education (SCORE): Problem-Based Learning
   http://score.rims.k12.ca.us/problearn

Source: Example from NASA's Classroom of the Future: Exploring the Environment. Available: **http://www.cotf.edu/ete/modules/volcanoes/vsituations.html**.

process of identifying what they already know and what they need to find out. In this process, they also devise a plan for getting the information they need. This step is sometimes repeated throughout the problem-solving process, depending on the students and the scope of the problem. Students are also encouraged to generate possible solutions as part of the problem-solving process. The interactive cycles help students learn to test the feasibility of a solution as they gather more information.

Tools to Support Constructivist Learning

You may be wondering how teachers can support students in constructivist learning. A number of tools, both technology based and paper and pencil based, can help. For example, as you'll learn in our chapters on development and communication tools, there are many tools that support students in communicating, locating and organizing information, and collecting data.

To help you better understand how to support this kind of teaching and learning, we provide a brief overview of two common approaches here. Both fall into the general category of graphic organizers.

K What I KNOW	W What I WANT to Know	L What I LEARNED

Figure 3.3 Basic Format of a K-W-L Chart

K-W-L Charts

K-W-L charts (Figure 3.3) are three-column organizers where students fill in the information they already *know* (K), what they *want* to know in order to answer an inquiry question (W), and (at the end of the lesson) what they've *learned* (L). This organizer is a useful tool allowing students to monitor their own understanding and structure their own activities. Individual students or groups of students may keep their own charts, and the teacher may occasionally use the board to set up a chart for the class as a whole.

For example, if students are doing the problem described in Spotlight 3.3, they may start by listing the facts from the situation in the K column. In the W column they may list two or three questions that they want to start answering. As they get answers to these questions, they add them to the L column.

Sometimes K-W-L charts include an H column after the L, where students record *how* they will learn even more. For more information about K-W-L-H charts, see the "Resources" section at the end of the chapter.

Concept Maps

Concept maps are diagrams in which students connect pieces of information in a way that shows the relationships between them. For example, if students are learning about plants, they may work with such concepts as "photosynthesis," "sun," and "energy." They may create a concept map like the one in Figure 3.4 to connect these concepts. Even though it's very simple, Figure 3.4 indicates that the sun provides the energy for the plant's photosynthesis, which converts to energy that the plant can use to grow.

Concept maps are very useful for teachers to see how their students are interrelating ideas. There's often more than one way to connect ideas, but misconceptions often crop up as students try to organize their thinking.

Several software packages, including Kidspiration, Inspiration, OmniGraffle, and Belvedere, support the creation of concept maps. See "Resources" at the end of this chapter.

Students monitor their understanding and structure their activities.

Figure 3.4 Simple Example of a Concept Map

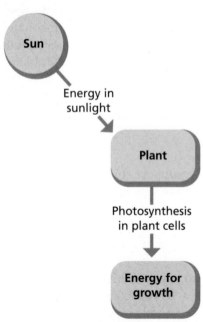

What Does It Mean to Learn?

We've introduced constructivism as the underlying theory on which this book, our model of technology use, and our primary examples are based. In this section we explore some key ideas of constructivism in greater depth. The Case Study at the end of the chapter also describes a technology-enhanced instructional approach that embodies constructivist theories of learning and instruction.

Three Levels of Learning

As you may have inferred from the previous section, different learning theories count different levels of knowledge building as learning. Even within a single learning philosophy there are multiple levels of learning. For our purposes, we consider "knowing," "knowing how to," and "understanding that" (Table 3.1).

"Knowing"

"Knowing," illustrated in the left column of Table 3.1, is a level of learning that's achieved when the learner has memorized or otherwise taken ownership of information. For example, if someone knows about the Civil War, she or he may know key dates and people, places where battles were fought, and the outcomes of key battles. People who know about the Civil War may also know something about how and why it happened—what the key issues were and so forth. This knowledge is reasonably easy to assess using written tests in various formats, such as multiple choice, fill in the blanks, and short answer.

"Knowing how to"

"Knowing how to" (the middle column of Table 3.1) is knowledge that describes what a student will be able to do at the end of the learning. For example, a student may know how to prepare a microscope slide, know how to graph a linear equation, or know how to diagram a sentence. This knowledge is also reasonably easy to assess. The skills of interest can be assessed with paper-and-pencil measures or with performance tasks that require learners to demonstrate their understanding.

Table 3.1 Examples of Three Levels of Learning

Students know . . .	Students know how to . . .	Students understand that . . .
The basic parts of a graph.	Make a graph from a table.	Graphs show changes over time.
That algebraic expressions can be used to make a graph.	Make a table from a graph.	Graphs, tables, and written descriptions can describe the same situation.
That different graphs come from different kinds of expressions.	Write a description of tabular or graphical data.	
The parts of speech.	Diagram a sentence.	Sentences are the building blocks of paragraphs.
Proper uses of words.		
The life cycle of a butterfly.	Describe the phases of a butterfly's life.	All creatures go through developmental cycles as part of their lifespan.

The third level of learning, "understanding that" (illustrated in the right-hand column of Table 3.1), is a higher level, which requires students to put together what they can do and what they know about. They begin to understand how and why certain things fit together, and they link this understanding to other things they know. For example, knowing about the Civil War can feed into an overall understanding of government; knowing how to plot a linear graph may be part of developing an understanding of functions and algebraic patterns; and knowing how to diagram a sentence is a part of understanding how to write a topical essay.

Understanding is much more difficult to assess than knowing and being able to do something. To determine the degree to which learners are developing understanding, teachers need to design activities in which students demonstrate what they know, what they can do, and how they're connecting the new concepts and skills to other understandings, concepts, and skills that they've developed. Such activities tend to be complex.

Technology can help with achieving and assessing all three levels of learning, as you'll see later in this book. For example, students can use technology to develop the deliverable that will be assessed, such as a portfolio, a presentation, a newsletter, or a brochure.

Technology in Action

Using Rainforest Researchers

In the multimedia software package called Rainforest Researchers (Tom Snyder Productions, **http://www.tomsnyder.com/**), students solve real-life problems related to the rain forest. Students work as a team, and each student has a specific role: one student is a botanist and becomes an "expert" in that role; another student is a chemist; and so on. However, the team can solve the problems embedded in the software only when each student shares the knowledge he or she has developed. In other words, each student learns one role more than others, but all students have to gain some understanding of all the roles in order to make good team decisions and solve the problems.

Because Rainforest Researchers is designed for a one-computer classroom, students have most of the materials they need in paper-based form. The computer is used to assess their answers. The computer determines whether each answer is correct, and particular events unfold in a certain order based on the quality of the decisions being made by students. For example, in an early problem, the team must decide which provisions to bring with them on their expedition. If they make unwise decisions, they're faced with challenges, such as dealing with a flat tire. Rainforest Researchers is an example of a constructivist learning environment that capitalizes on technology while attending to the limitations of many classrooms.

The Role of Others

There are multiple branches of constructivism, and each values the interactions of people. By interacting with both peers and more knowledgeable others, learners have opportunities to test their newly forming understandings in small settings and to get feedback, whether formal or informal. Further, everyone in a group will bring different understandings to the group, and those various understandings can promote a more coherent final understanding than any student might develop working alone.

Managing student groups

One important implication is that group work must be managed such that all of the participants are working together toward the same goals. In other words, grouping works only if, in the end, all the students are concentrating on the big question or problem of the unit. Too often when teachers use cooperative groups, the students divide up the work to get it done more quickly. Though they turn in a final product with all of their names on it, each worked on a part separate from the others. This isn't capitalizing on group work in the ways best suited for student-centered learning. Instead, the teacher needs to design experiences so that students work together toward a shared final outcome. The preceding "Technology in Action" presents one example of how this can be done.

Accountability and Assessment

It's important for teachers to be able to measure their students' learning. Given that we're advocating the development of learner-centered, constructivist learning environments in which students take responsibility for their learning, teachers must develop or use assessment techniques that allow them to determine their students' progress toward established benchmarks. In constructivist environments, assessment should engage students in activities in which they demonstrate their knowledge and skills. Through assessment of these activities, teachers can determine whether the students have met the learning goals. Appropriate assessment instruments may include performance tasks, written reflections about learning, and tests and quizzes. Assessment can also occur through classroom activities designed as assessments that promote students' taking responsibility for recognizing when they don't know or understand something and seeking out the answer, whether from the teacher, from other more knowledgeable people, or from written or Internet resources.

As a teacher, you'll likely rely on a variety of assessments, reflections, and project deliverables to determine a grade for your students. All of these are important because they provide an opportunity for students to demonstrate what they've learned and because they provide you with ongoing feedback about your students' understandings and misconceptions.

Preassessment

Assessing students before learning begins

One kind of assessment that you'll use in a constructivist learning environment is **preassessment,** sometimes called *diagnostic assessment*.

Preassessment, as the name implies, takes place before learning begins—either at the very beginning of a learning unit or before crucial transition points during the unit. It may be formal, such as a pretest, or more informal, such as a classroom discussion of upcoming concepts. Because they tell you what your students already know, preassessments allow you to adapt your instruction accordingly. Preassessment can involve any of the following:

▶ Diagnostic tests appropriate to the content and standards
▶ Questioning by the teacher
▶ Observation by the teacher in previous learning units or in the initial activities of the current unit

Formative Assessment

Assessments to gauge progress and adjust teaching

Next there are **formative assessments.** These kinds of assessments are undertaken periodically during the course of a unit, so that you can gauge how students are progressing in their learning of concepts and skills. The idea behind formative assessment is that you still have time for remediation or reteaching if your students aren't quite where they need to be.

Typically, formative assessment includes quizzes, team tests, and other assignments. It may also include open-ended questioning, observation, review of writing samples, and student presentations. You should always remember to include computer technologies in these assessments if your students have been using them in their work. This helps maintain a fair testing environment. For example, if you want to test students' abilities to make a graph from a table and they've done this previously using computer software, it's unfair to expect them to do it using paper and pencil. You should either ask them to use the same technology or give them opportunities to practice making graphs without the technology.

Reflection Activities

Students reflect on their learning and check their understanding.

The goal of a **reflection activity** is typically to offer students an opportunity to convey their current understanding and, through doing so, to check that understanding. In other words, by completing the reflection, students are forced to express their new understandings in words or by other means, which helps solidify their understanding and highlight areas where things aren't yet making sense.

Some teachers prefer that students write their reflections in a formal way, whereas others allow greater flexibility. In some cases, the reflection can consist of pictures or charts. Whatever the format, reflections are wonderful tools for teachers to see what students understand.

Summative Assessment

Summative assessment comes at the end of a project or learning unit and provides a "big picture" of what students have learned. Summative assessment may include evaluation of the learning unit deliverables, as well as administration of more traditional tests. The deliverables—the end result of the units you're creating for your students—may take a variety of forms, such as a presentation, a brochure, a paper, or a website.

Unlike formative assessment, which is focused on providing the teacher with insight about students' progress, the summative assessment should convey whether the students have met the objectives set forth in the learning unit. As a result, the assessment tasks, whether deliverables or tests, need to be tightly coordinated with the unit's learning objectives and with the standards the unit is intended to address. As with quizzes, technology should be used for summative assessments in ways that are consistent with the ways it was used in the learning experience. You'll read much more about assessment and learning units in Part II of this book.

Assessing whether students have met objectives

■ Grading

Determining what an assessment should measure and what form it should take is only part of the assessment task. The other portion is actually evaluating the deliverables. In the learning environments we're talking about in this book, this assessment will often be accomplished with **rubrics,** which are essentially scoring scales that you create and share with your students.

Functions of a rubric

Table 3.2 offers an example of a rubric. By using a rubric, you can align portions of the assessment with each of your learning objectives. In

Table 3.2 Example of a Rubric for a Mathematics Lesson

Task	Proficient	Somewhat Proficient	Lacks Proficiency	Points Awarded
Identifying triangles and components of triangles	The student correctly identified that all triangles have three sides and three angles. (4–5 points)	The student partially identified that all triangles have three sides and three angles. (2–3 points)	The student incorrectly identified that all triangles have three sides and three angles. (0–1 point)	
Identifying possible triangle side lengths	The student correctly identified four to five side lengths as possible or impossible. (4–5 points)	The student correctly identified two to three side lengths as possible or impossible. (2–3 points)	The student correctly identified one or no side lengths as possible or impossible. (0–1 point)	
Describing special triangles according to sides	The student correctly described three special triangles according to sides. (4–5 points)	The student correctly described two special triangles according to sides. (2–3 points)	The student correctly described one or no special triangles according to sides. (0–1 point)	
Describing special triangles according to angles	The student correctly described three special triangles according to angles. (4–5 points)	The student correctly described two special triangles according to angles. (2–3 points)	The student correctly described one or no special triangles according to angles. (0–1 point)	
Total Score				

this way the learning objectives, the assessment, and the learning tasks are all tightly tied together. The learner won't experience any ambiguity about what he or she is expected to do or about the relevance of any portion of the activities to larger learning goals.

We'll say much more about rubrics later in the book. For now, see "Resources" at the end of the chapter for further information on rubrics and other topics related to assessment.

Diverse Learners in the Constructivist Classroom

Much has been written about meeting the needs of all learners in the classroom. The constructivist learning environment can be ideal for this purpose, because it focuses on tying all learning to prior knowledge and to a variety of student-owned learning tasks. Further, constructivist learning environments allow the learner to decide how he or she will learn best, and they remove the notions that learning is linear and that certain concepts must be mastered before moving on. Instead, constructivism acknowledges that everyone learns differently and that mastery may happen in very different ways for different learners.

One important concept in discussions of diversity is the idea of **multiple intelligences,** which derives from Howard Gardner's work on human learning. Through his research Gardner deduced that people have at least nine different kinds of intelligence, as opposed to one general intelligence. Each of us possesses each kind of intelligence in differing amounts, and each kind is most important in different situations. The intelligences that Gardner (1999) identified are

Nine types of intelligence identified by Gardner

- ▶ Visual/spatial
- ▶ Musical
- ▶ Verbal
- ▶ Logical/mathematical
- ▶ Interpersonal
- ▶ Intrapersonal
- ▶ Bodily/kinesthetic
- ▶ Naturalist
- ▶ Existentialist

Gardner suggested that people should be encouraged to use their preferred intelligences in learning and to refine their dominant intelligences. He also suggested that both instructional activities and assessments should be designed to work *across* sets of intelligences so that students with various learning preferences can benefit.

It's particularly important to understand that all learners move between dominant styles depending on the situation and the learning to be done. No learner is always "visual/spatial" or "bodily/kinesthetic." Rather, every learner possesses a different level of each of the intelligences and applies them in various ways. Thus it's always important to plan learning activities that engage students in varying kinds of experiences, so that every learner has opportunities to experience the same ideas and information in different forms. In this way, learners can develop a more complex and accurate understanding of what you want them to learn.

Planning learning activities to engage various intelligences

Regardless of whether you choose to use multiple intelligences or other particular approaches to differentiating instruction, it's critical for your students' learning that you do find innovative ways to meet their needs.

Online Study Center

Multiple Intelligences in Elementary School

● To learn more about multiple intelligences, watch the HM Video Case called **Multiple Intelligences: Elementary School Instruction,** available in the Online Study Center. The video shows how one teacher, Frederick Won Park, tries to help all of his students be successful learners by including various types of intelligence in his instructional approach. The interview transcript includes Mr. Park's ideas for creating lesson plans using multiple intelligences. The bonus videos will show you how Mr. Park addressed some specific intelligences.

As you watch the videos, consider how Mr. Park's approaches are helping meet the needs of all his learners. Also think about whether any of his strategies might work in your own classroom.

Technology can help with this differentiation in the constructivist classroom. As one example, technology can allow students with significant physical limitations to participate in classroom activities, through large-screen readers or closed captioning. When used in research and inquiry projects, the Internet supports a wide range of abilities by providing materials at different reading levels, allowing more advanced students to push their knowledge further. The Internet can also supply materials in other languages for students who are learning English, and it provides materials that are not reading based for students who struggle with reading. It's up to you, as the teacher, to help your students maximize their learning, and one way to do that is to put technology to work in your classroom. "Resources" at the end of this chapter offer more information, and later chapters include many more examples.

Summary

By building your instruction on learning theory, you draw on what is known about human learning as a foundation for classroom activities. The theory of particular interest in this book is constructivism, which posits that people learn through constructing their own knowledge. A variety of activities, including reflection, helps students develop new understandings and tie them to their existing understandings.

By focusing on this particular learning theory, we emphasize learning through authentic experiences, such as solving complex, messy problems and doing research. In all cases, the learning theory and the stated learning goals shape the learning tasks. Those goals determine not only the instruction

itself, but also the assessments, including reflection, that are used to find out whether students have met the learning goals.

By using constructivist approaches, teachers can also ensure that all of their learners will have worthwhile learning experiences. Constructivism allows students to engage in a number of different learning activities, with the result that students with different mixes of intelligences can all find a way to succeed.

In today's constructivist classroom, technology plays a large role in both instruction and assessment. It helps diverse students conduct their own investigations, explore authentic problems, and create deliverables that demonstrate their understanding.

Resources

 *Online Study Center*
   Direct Links to Resources

LEARNING THEORIES

Cambridge Center for Behavioral Studies
http://www.behavior.org
   This website includes considerable information about B. F. Skinner and his theories, as well as more recent behaviorist theories.

Constructivism
http://education.indiana.edu/~p540/webcourse/construct.html
   These extensive notes on constructivism are for a course in learning theories taught by J. David Perry at Indiana University.

Funderstanding: About Learning
http://www.funderstanding.com/about_learning.cfm
   A friendly overview of a variety of learning theories.

How People Learn: Brain, Mind, Experience, and School
http://www.nap.edu/openbook/0309065577/html/index.html

> This book from the Commission on Behavioral and Social Sciences and Education is available online free of charge.

Instructional Development Timeline: Learning Theory
http://www.my-ecoach.com/idtimeline/learningtheory.html

> A timeline and brief overview of the major learning theories.

Learner-Centered Psychological Principles
http://www.apa.org/ed/lcp2/lcp14.html

> The APA's research-based principles for designing instruction to meet the needs of all students.

Learning with Technology Profile Tool
http://www.ncrtec.org/capacity/profile/profwww.htm

> A tool that will help you understand where you are in terms of creating a classroom for engaged learning and technology integration.

National Board for Professional Teaching Standards: Five Core Propositions
http://www.nbpts.org/about/coreprops.cfm

> The core beliefs of the National Board for Professional Teaching Standards.

INQUIRY-BASED LEARNING

Concept to Classroom: Inquiry-Based Learning
http://www.thirteen.org/edonline/concept2class/inquiry/index.html

> An online, self-paced minicourse to support teachers in using inquiry-based learning.

Do Your Genes Drive You to Drink?
http://www.sciencemuseum.org.uk/on%2Dline/genetics/index.asp

> An inquiry-based learning unit that focuses on science and social issues.

Exploratorium Institute for Inquiry
http://www.exploratorium.edu/IFI

> Resources on inquiry from the Exploratorium.

Inquiry: Thoughts, Views, and Strategies for the K–5 Classroom
http://www.nsf.gov/pubs/2000/nsf99148/htmstart.htm

> An online book written to support elementary-school teachers in using inquiry.

inQuiry Attic at the Franklin Institute
http://www.fi.edu/qa98/atticindex.html

> A wide array of inquiry topics for classroom use from the Franklin Institute.

Lewis and Clark Expedition: Create Your Own Adventure
http://www.nationalgeographic.com/xpeditions/activities/01/lewis.html

> An inquiry-based learning unit for geography and history.

NASA Learning Technologies: What's the Difference
http://learn.arc.nasa.gov/wtd

> An interactive, inquiry-based learning activity focusing on the planets.

Rainforest Researchers
http://www.tomsnyder.com

> An interactive, inquiry-based program that uses a model suitable for collaboration in a one-computer classroom.

The Socratic Method: Teaching by Asking Instead of by Telling
http://www.garlikov.com/Soc_Meth.html

> Rick Garlikov provides information about Socratic questioning.

The Wheel Problem
http://learner.org/resources/series32.html

> A video of first and second graders exploring combinations of vehicles that would have twenty-four wheels.

WISE (Web-Based Inquiry Science Environment)
http://wise.berkeley.edu

> A web-based, inquiry-based learning environment for middle- and high-school students.

PROBLEM-BASED LEARNING

Exploring the Environment Teacher Pages: Problem-Based Learning
http://www.cotf.edu/ete/teacher/teacherout.html

> A series of problems and resources that can be used as problem-based units in a science or social studies classroom.

North Central Regional Educational Library: K-W-L-H Technique
http://www.ncrel.org/sdrs/areas/issues/students/learning/lr1kwlh.htm

> An explanation of the K-W-L-H technique for problem solving in classrooms.

Problem-Based Learning, Especially in the Context of Large Classes
http://www.chemeng.mcmaster.ca/pbl/pbl.htm

> An article about why problem-based learning is worth using.

Problem-Based Learning Network at IMSA
http://www2.imsa.edu/programs/pbln

> A wealth of information about problem-based learning, written for teachers, from the Illinois Mathematics and Science Academy (IMSA).

CONCEPT MAPS

Belvedere
http://lilt.ics.hawaii.edu/lilt/software/belvedere/index.html

> Free software for creating concept maps.

Kidspiration and Inspiration
http://www.inspiration.com
>   Popular software for students to use in creating concept maps.

OmniGraffle
http://www.omnigroup.com/applications/omnigraffle/
>   Concept-mapping software for Macintosh computers.

ASSESSMENT

ArtsWork: Glossary of Assessment Terms
http://artswork.asu.edu/arts/teachers/assessment/glossary.htm
>   A glossary of some of the most common assessment terms that teachers need to understand.

Concept to Classroom: Assessment, Evaluation, and Curriculum Redesign
http://www.thirteen.org/edonline/concept2class/assessment/index.html
>   An online, self-paced workshop to help teachers learn about assessment.

Creating a Rubric for a Given Task
http://edweb.sdsu.edu/webquest/rubrics/rubrics.html
>   Step-by-step guidance for developing a rubric.

How to Create a Rubric from Scratch
http://intranet.cps.k12.il.us/Assessments/Ideas_and_Rubrics/Create_Rubric/create_rubric.html
>   Guidance on how to create your own rubric for any class project.

Teachers' Internet Use Guide: Assessment Strategies and Definitions
http://www.rmcdenver.com/useguide/assessme/definiti.htm
>   Brief descriptions of many different assessment techniques that you can use.

Types of Assessment
http://www.brookes.ac.uk/services/ocsd/2_learntch/types.html
>   An overview of a wide variety of assessments that you can create.

MULTIPLE INTELLIGENCES

Teacher Tap: Technology and Multiple Intelligences
http://eduscapes.com/tap/topic68.htm
>   A discussion of multiple intelligences and how you can use technology to support student learning across all the intelligences.

---

case
STUDY

The WISE Learning Environment

There are several online environments designed to support teachers in engaging students in constructivist learning activities. One of the most famous is the Web-Based Inquiry Science Environment (WISE). In this environment, students get the chance to learn science by exploring different theories and the evidence for them in order to determine which theory is most probable. Then students produce an end product; for example, one project in WISE asks students to design an energy-efficient house for the desert.

In each WISE project, students are first presented with a situation. Then they work through several steps to get the background information they need. In the desert scenario, for instance, students explore aspects of the desert climate and compare it with their own climate. This background information helps them determine what special characteristics a desert house might need.

Once they have the background information, students move into the activities of the unit. In the desert activity, after determining whether they live in a desert, students consider some potential plans for desert houses

Index of Activities   Cancel

Select an activity to jump directly to it.

1. Do you live in a desert?
2. Look at these strategies!
3. What's in a house?
4. Compare Parts of the House
5. Design a House

Figure 3.5 **Screen from the WISE Project "What's in a House?"**

and learn about key components of houses (Figure 3.5). Once they finish these steps, they make comparisons of house components and, finally, design their own desert house.

WISE provides students with opportunities to record their thinking, acquire research information, and even look for hints when they don't know what to do. One of the best things about WISE is that all the information students need is included, and the system allows them to explore the questions in depth. Because it's designed for students in middle grades, WISE offers more structure than some other environments, but it also lets students work at their own pace and gives them some flexibility in the order of their steps.

Another great feature of WISE is that its projects are varied. Students participating in them learn a scientific process in a number of settings, as well as a number of strategies for working in groups. For example, in the desert house project, students are encouraged to choose a "specialization"; each of the three students in a group selects one specialty—roofs, windows, or walls. Then they combine what they know in the final design.

You can see WISE at **http://wise.berkeley.edu.** To explore actual projects, you need to register, but there's no charge for that privilege.

Questions for Reflection and Discussion

1. How is WISE an example of a constructivist learning tool?
2. What kinds of strategies does WISE use to help students become actively engaged in their learning?
3. What features of group work are effective here?

Meet the Standards

Online Study Center

Standards
Explore the Online Study Center for additional help in meeting the standards.

Look back at "Standards to Guide Your Preparation" at the beginning of this chapter. We've aligned the chapter with the six National Educational Technology Standards (NETS) listed there.

To help yourself make progress toward meeting these standards, think about the classroom where you want to teach when you complete your degree. In your mind, where do you see the technology in that room? (Think of all the possible technologies—computers, LCD projectors, handhelds, laptop carts, and more.) How will you set up the classroom to support students in working both with technology and with one another? Ask yourself the following questions:

▶ Will the kinds of technologies you've envisioned support all of your students regardless of their learning strengths and weaknesses?
▶ Will these technologies support your students in working together?
▶ Will students have enough access to technologies to meet their learning needs?

Now think about teaching in that classroom.

▶ How will you know your students are learning what you intend them to learn?
▶ If they aren't learning what you intend, how will you address that?

Chapter 4

Using Standards

Standards to Guide Your Preparation

ISTE NETS

Teachers

- ▶ Design developmentally appropriate learning opportunities that apply technology-enhanced instructional strategies to support the diverse needs of learners.

- ▶ Facilitate technology-enhanced experiences that address content standards and student technology standards.

OTHER RELEVANT STANDARDS

ISTE Profiles for Technology-Literate Teachers: Professional Preparation Performance Profile (2000)

Prospective teachers:

- ▷ Identify the benefits of technology to maximize student learning and facilitate higher order thinking skills.

- ▷ Design and teach technology-enriched learning activities that connect content standards with student technology standards and meet the diverse needs of students.

- ▷ Design and peer teach a lesson that meets content area standards and reflects the current best practices in teaching and learning with technology.

- ▷ Integrate technology-based assessment strategies and tools into plans for evaluating specific learning activities.

55

Learning standards have become an important, and often challenging, part of today's classroom. Standards of some form or another are being used in all fifty states and across grades and subject areas. It's likely that you as a teacher will be faced with the task of making sure that your students meet certain standards. In order to do this, you'll need to understand the standards that you're expected to work toward and how your teaching materials, including technology, can help you address them.

In this chapter we provide a short overview of the standards movement, introduce you to the various kinds of standards, and provide information about the connection between technology and standards. The chapter ends with a Case Study that will allow you to apply your knowledge of standards.

A Brief History of Educational Standards

Beginnings of today's standards movement

The current standards movement in education can be traced back to the 1983 report *A Nation at Risk*. This document, prepared by the National Commission on Excellence in Education, sounded a warning about how poorly American schools were preparing students for the workforce. Ultimately, the commission argued, business and industry suffered. The report noted that students weren't receiving a rigorous, focused education and lamented the quality of teacher preparation. Concern about the report's findings led to a tidal wave of reform efforts, including the first sets of national content standards.

One of the results of *A Nation at Risk* was the formation of the Secretary's Commission on Achieving Necessary Skills (SCANS), set up by the Department of Labor. It was this commission's 1991 report, *What Work Requires of Schools*, that first brought attention to the use of technology as an essential element and a key goal of K–12 education. The SCANS report highlighted five competencies, or standards. One of the five competencies focused exclusively on technology skill development (see Table 4.1). Although the report was released in 1991, it was already evident that students would need a variety of technology skills to compete in the world of work. More interestingly, this forward-looking report seemed to acknowledge that a primary skill set for students would involve analyzing, manipulating, and retrieving information.

Table 4.1 SCANS Competencies: Technology

The SCANS competency on technology includes the following three skills for each student:

A. Selects Technology	Chooses procedures, tools or equipment including computers and related technologies.
B. Applies Technology to Task	Understands overall intent and proper procedures for setup and operation of equipment.
C. Maintains and Troubleshoots Equipment	Prevents, identifies, or solves problems with equipment, including computers and other technologies.

Source: Secretary's Commission on Achieving Necessary Skills (1991), p. 10.

The Impact of NCLB Standards

To learn more about how legislated standards and mandates can affect teachers, watch the HM Video Case called **Foundations: Aligning Instruction with Federal Legislation**, available in the Online Study Center. In this video, you'll hear teachers and other stakeholders talking specifically about the NCLB legislation and how it has affected their work. They also discuss their concerns as professionals about helping special needs children (those with individualized education plans) meet the NCLB mandates.

As you watch, think about how your own teaching will be influenced by NCLB.

- How does a mandate like NCLB affect your feelings about the standards to which you teach?
- How do you feel about having your teaching quality judged according to your students' performance?
- Do you think other kinds of legislation or mandates would be fairer to all of your students?

NCLB: a federal mandate

The SCANS report was originally intended to focus on skills that employers identified as critical for students leaving high school and entering the workforce. Later, the recommendations were expanded to include students continuing their education at either technical schools or institutions of higher education. Though the SCANS report was a landmark effort in an attempt to succinctly determine what schools should be teaching and what students should be learning, the standards were broad and lacked explanations of how to implement them in the schools.

The National Council of Teachers of Mathematics (NCTM) provided the first content standards. In 1989 NCTM's *Curriculum and Evaluation Standards for School Mathematics* provided a glimpse of what content-specific standards could be like. Since then, organizations representing every discipline taught in American K–12 schools have developed some form of content standards.

The most recent major educational move toward standards came from the federal No Child Left Behind Act (NCLB) of 2001. This legislation mandates that every state must have content standards in at least some subject areas and lays out requirements that all students—regardless of any disability or challenge—be held accountable for meeting those standards. Federal money for schools hinges on students' performance on their state's standardized tests related to the content standards. In short, NCLB has made standards critical for every student in public school in the United States.

Educational Standards Today

Today, both national organizations and states provide standards. In some cases, even local school districts have developed standards. They vary tremendously in their intent and in the specific content they include. Typically, student standards are designed to be applied to all children, regardless of race and socioeconomic status, and in many cases they were developed to ensure equality throughout multiple local school systems.

Standards serve both as guidelines that help standardize schools and as policy tools that determine funding and other school matters. In terms of student learning, the various documents address content standards, process standards, and performance standards. Increasingly, too, there are standards for teachers.

Content Standards

These are the standards most people think of when they hear about standards. **Content standards** are an attempt to define a set of concepts that students should have learned by a particular point in their learning

Sample National and State Content Standards

National Standards: Education Standards for Physical Science—Levels 5–8 (NRC, 1996)

Properties and changes of properties in matter

Motions and forces

Transfer of energy

State Standards: Science Framework for California Public Schools, Fifth Grade (2003)

1. Elements and their combinations account for all the varied types of matter in the world. As a basis for understanding this concept, students know:
   a. During chemical reactions, the atoms in the reactants rearrange to form products with different properties.
   b. All matter is made of atoms, which may combine to form molecules.
   c. Metals have properties in common, such as electrical and thermal conductivity. Some metals, such as aluminum (Al), iron (Fe), nickel (Ni), copper (Cu), silver (Ag), gold (Au), are pure elements while others, such as steel and brass, are composed of a combination of elemental metals.
   d. Each element is made of one kind of atom. These elements are organized in the Periodic Table by their chemical properties.
   e. Scientists have developed instruments that can create images of atoms and molecules showing that they are discrete and often occur in well ordered arrays.
   f. Differences in chemical and physical properties of substances are used to separate mixtures and identify compounds.

g. Properties of solid, liquid, and gaseous substances, such as sugar ($C_6H_{12}O_6$), water (H_2O), helium (He), oxygen (O_2), nitrogen (N_2), and carbon dioxide (CO_2).
h. Living organisms and most materials are composed of just a few elements.
i. Common properties of salts, such as sodium chloride (NaCl).

State Standards: Georgia Performance Standards for Science, Fifth Grade (2005)

S5P2. Students will explain the difference between a physical change and a chemical change.

a. Investigate physical changes by separating mixtures and manipulating (cutting, tearing, folding) paper to demonstrate examples of physical change.
b. Recognize that the changes in state of water (water vapor/steam, liquid, ice) are due to temperature differences and are examples of physical change.
c. Investigate the properties of a substance before, during, and after a chemical reaction to find evidence of change.

For full information on these standards, visit the following websites:

National Science Education Standards
    http://www.nap.edu/readingroom/books/nses
Science Framework for California Public Schools
    http://www.cde.ca.gov/re/pn/fd/sci-frame-dwnld.asp
Georgia's Science Performance Standards
    http://www.georgiastandards.org/science.aspx

---

career. Spotlight 4.1 provides examples of content standards at the national and state levels.

Value of content standards

From an administrative perspective, content standards are highly desirable because students can be tested quite readily to determine whether they've met them. For example, one content standard might require that students know their multiplication tables through 10. It's reasonably easy to test students' achievement of this standard using a paper-and-pencil drill or a computer-based assessment tool. For teachers, such standards are also desirable because they're concrete and easy to address through direct instruction. For instance, an elementary-school teacher can readily provide a number of different opportunities for her students to learn their multiplication tables.

SPOTLIGHT 4.2

Sample National and State Process Standards

National Process Standards: National Council of Teachers of Mathematics Standards (NCTM, 2000)

Instructional programs from prekindergarten through grade 12 should enable all students to—

- organize and consolidate their mathematical thinking through communication;
- communicate their mathematical thinking coherently and clearly to peers, teachers, and others;
- analyze and evaluate the mathematical thinking and strategies of others;
- use the language of mathematics to express mathematical ideas precisely.

State Process Standards: Pennsylvania Academic Standards for Mathematics (2005)

Pennsylvania's public schools shall teach, challenge and support every student to realize his or her maximum potential and to acquire the knowledge and skills to:

Develop a plan to analyze a problem, identify the information needed to solve the problem, carry out the plan, check whether an answer makes sense and explain how the problem was solved.

Use appropriate mathematical terms, vocabulary, language symbols and graphs to explain clearly and logically solutions to problems.

Show ideas in a variety of ways, including words, numbers, symbols, pictures, charts, graphs, tables, diagrams and models.

Connect, extend and generalize problem solutions to other concepts, problems and circumstances in mathematics.

Select, use and justify the methods, materials and strategies used to solve problems.

Use appropriate problem-solving strategies (e.g., solving a simpler problem, drawing a picture or diagram).

State Process Standards: Colorado Model Content Standards for Mathematics

Learn to communicate mathematically. The development of students' power to use mathematics involves learning the signs, symbols, and terms of mathematics. This is best accomplished in problem situations where students have an opportunity to read, write, and discuss ideas in the language of mathematics. As students communicate their ideas, they learn to clarify, refine, and consolidate their thinking.

For more information about these standards visit the following websites:

National Council of Teachers of Mathematics: Principles and Standards for School Mathematics
  http://standards.nctm.org
Pennsylvania Academic Standards
  http://www.pde.state.pa.us/stateboard_ed/cwp
Colorado K–12 Academic Standards
  http://www.cde.state.co.us/index_stnd.htm

◼ Process Standards

Process standards go beyond simply prescribing content to be learned. They attempt to define ways of thinking about a discipline. For example, a process standard may specify that students should develop an understanding of the inquiry processes in science or that students should develop problem-solving skills in mathematics. Spotlight 4.2 illustrates national and state process standards for mathematics.

Value of process standards

Process standards are critical in the sense that students need to learn about fields of study rather than just isolated skills. Further, if students are to develop transferable knowledge that helps them know when and how to use the content they've learned, process skills are essential. However, process skill development is difficult to measure. For example, the National Geography Standards state:

> Students need an understanding of why places are the way they are, because it can enrich their own sense of identity with a particular place and enable them to comprehend and appreciate both the similarities and differences in places around their own community, state, country, and planet. (National Geographic Society, 2001)

As a teacher, imagine how you might create an assessment to measure whether your students meet this portion of this standard. That would be a difficult task, and given the nature of this particular standard, it may be impossible to standardize for students across the state or the country.

Performance Standards

The Improving America's Schools Act of 1994 asserted that content standards should describe what every student should know and be able to do in the core academic content areas. In this context, we can view **performance standards** as standards that make content expectations clear. Performance standards answer the question: How good is good enough? They define how students can demonstrate their proficiency in the skills and knowledge framed by content standards. Spotlight 4.3 illustrates state performance standards in mathematics.

Performance standards:
clear and measurable

Most often, state standards focus on performance in order to clearly communicate to teachers how much their students need to know in order to succeed on various tests that are administered. Performance standards are the most measurable of the standards for three reasons:

▶ They "chunk" the content to be learned into small pieces.
▶ They define what it means to "learn" the content. For instance, should the student be able to memorize or be able to work problems?
▶ They provide clear guidance on how much content students are expected to learn at a particular level. For example, in seventh-grade biology, students need to be able to draw or describe DNA, but in high-school biology, they need to be able to explain how DNA controls cellular activities.

Standards for Teachers

In most cases, when educators and policy makers talk about standards, they are referring to standards for students—the standards that define what students need to know and be able to do. The degree to which students demonstrate mastery of these standards shapes both teacher and school evaluations.

Examples of Performance Standards

Colorado Model Standards for Mathematics (1995): Grades K–4

In grades K–4, what students know and are able to do includes

- demonstrating meanings for whole numbers, and commonly used fractions and decimals *(for example, $\frac{1}{3}$, $\frac{3}{4}$, 0.5, 0.75)*, and representing equivalent forms of the same number through the use of physical models, drawings, calculators, and computers;
- reading and writing whole numbers and knowing place-value concepts and numeration through their relationships to counting, ordering, and grouping;
- using numbers to count, to measure, to label, and to indicate location;
- developing, testing, and explaining conjectures about properties of whole numbers, and commonly-used fractions and decimals; and
- using number sense to estimate and justify the reasonableness of solutions to problems involving whole numbers, and commonly-used fractions and decimals.

Nevada Math Performance Standards

Spatial Relationships and Geometry, Grade 5. To solve problems, communicate, and make connections within and beyond the field of mathematics, students will identify, represent, verify, and apply spatial relationships and geometric properties.

Exceeds Standard

- Draw and classify angles and triangles according to given measurements.
- Identify, draw, and label circles and elements of circles, describing the relationships between the various elements.
- Identify transformations as a translation, rotation, reflection, enlargement, or reduction using the formal vocabulary for shapes that have congruence, similarity, and symmetry.
- Identify and draw shapes that have congruence, similarity, and symmetry using a wide variety of methods.
- Graph ordered pairs and identify coordinates for a given point in any quadrant. . . .

- Draw and classify angles and triangles as right, acute, or obtuse.
- Identify and draw circles and elements of circles, describing the relationships between the various elements.
- Identify a transformation as translation, rotation, reflection, enlargement, or reduction.
- Identify shapes that have congruence, similarity, and/or symmetry using a variety of methods, including transformational motions and models, drawings, and measurement tools.
- Graph ordered pairs and identify coordinates for a given point in the first quadrant. . . .

Approaches Standard

- Draw, with errors, and classify angles and triangles as right, acute, or obtuse.
- Identify and draw circles and elements of circles, displaying some understanding of the relationships between the various elements.
- Identify transformations as slides, turns, flips, larger, or smaller, with errors.
- Identify shapes that have congruence, similarity, and/or symmetry using visual comparisons.
- Graph ordered pairs and identify coordinates for a given point in the first quadrant, with inconsistent accuracy. . . .

Below Standard

- Classify angles and triangles as right, acute, or obtuse, with errors.
- Identify and draw circles and elements of circles.
- Identify transformations as slides, turns, flips, larger, or smaller, with assistance.
- Identify shapes that have congruence and symmetry, with assistance.
- Graph ordered pairs and identify coordinates for a given point in the first quadrant, with assistance. . . .

Florida's Sunshine State Standards—Grade Level Expectations in Mathematics

Number Sense, Concepts, and Operations
The fifth grade student . . .

- reads, writes, and identifies whole numbers, fractions, mixed numbers, and decimals through thousandths.

- reads, writes, and identifies common percents including 10%, 20%, 25%, 30%, 40%, 50%, 60%, 70%, 75%, 80%, 90%, and 100%.
- compares and orders whole numbers, commonly used fractions, percents, and decimals to thousandths using concrete materials, number lines, drawings, numerals, and symbols (>,<, =).
- translates problem situations into diagrams, models, and numerals using whole numbers, fractions, mixed numbers, decimals, and percents.
- knows that numbers in different forms are equivalent or nonequivalent, using whole numbers, decimals, fractions, mixed numbers, and percents.
- knows that place value relates to powers of 10.
- expresses numbers to millions or more in expanded form using powers of ten, with or without exponential notation.

- explains the similarities and differences between the decimal (base 10) number system and other number systems that do or do not use place value.

For more information on these standards, visit:

Colorado Model Standards for Mathematics
    http://www.cde.state.co.us/coloradomath

Florida Department of Education: Sunshine State Standards
    http://www.firn.edu/doe/curric/prek12/ index.html

Nevada Department of Education Math Performance Standards
    http://www.doe.nv.gov/standards/standmath/ math.html

National Board for Professional Teaching Standards

However, another set of standards is equally important for teachers to know about—standards for *teachers*. These are standards written by professional organizations that provide guidance to teachers about what it means to be a competent or expert teacher in a discipline. Perhaps the most widely recognized and highly prized are those established by the National Board for Professional Teaching Standards. These are standards in which teachers must demonstrate competence in order to achieve National Board Certification—a highly prestigious rating within the profession. The National Board standards are specialized by grade level and content area. Thus they acknowledge that a quality teacher for elementary mathematics needs to know a different kind of content and different pedagogical strategies than a high-school mathematics teacher.

Across the various standards for teachers, there's consensus that teachers need to have adequate content knowledge. In some places, this is tested with tools such as Praxis, a series of professional assessments created by the Educational Testing Service. The standards also agree that teachers need to know a variety of pedagogical strategies to support their students in learning. Further, they agree that there's a special kind of interplay between content knowledge and pedagogical strategies which allows students to learn. In other words, just knowing the content isn't enough, and neither is knowing how to manage students in groups—a quality teacher needs to know when and how to use various pedagogies to support learning of particular content.

In addition to covering content knowledge and pedagogical strategies, most standards for teachers outline certain aspects of professional practice that lead to quality teaching. These include such actions as teachers' reflecting on their practice, teachers' participation in learning communities, and teachers' pursuing higher levels of education. Spotlight 4.4 offers some resources that will help you meet these various standards.

SPOTLIGHT 4.4 Finding Help in Meeting the Standards

In addition to all the wonderful tools and resources available on the Internet for your students, there's an assortment of high-quality resources available for you as a teacher. These resources include articles, discussion boards, professional development courses, and other supports—all at little or no cost to you. To get started, check out some of the websites offered here and then use a search engine to find even more.

Discovery School
  http://school.discovery.com
  This website provides links and resources for teachers to make their classrooms run more smoothly, including lesson plans, blackline masters, and other information.

Education Reform Networks
  http://edreform.net
  Developed by the National Institute for Community Innovations, this website provides a very organized way to locate information on topics ranging from assigning homework to digital equity.

Tapped In
  http://tappedin.org
  Tapped In uses a campus metaphor to engage you in a community of teachers learning together. The website includes an array of resources, as well as real-time discussion with others.

National Versus State Standards

Features of state frameworks

Online Study Center
Review key terms online with the Glossary Flashcards.

States and national organizations take different approaches to planning, designing, and implementing learning standards. National standards are typically broader, often covering entire strands of a content area. In mathematics, for instance, a national standard might deal with "number sense." In geography, there's a group of standards for "places and regions." National standards are also typically broken into grade *bands* (such as elementary, middle, and high school) rather than individual grades. Quite often, too, national standards attempt to define how students should think about a field, as well as how they should engage in learning in that field.

In contrast, state standards, also known as *frameworks*, are often organized by individual grades. Rather than covering merely the broad goals outlined in national standards, states commonly include performance indicators for acceptable attainment of a goal. In geography, the national standard might state that students should come to see maps as a source of information about their world. The state standard might specify that students will be able to identify their home state on a map of the United States.

State standards can take a variety of forms. Some describe standards as the expected outcomes by the time a student graduates from high school. Standards in this format are known as **exit standards.** Other states have designated checkpoints along the way to determine a student's progress toward the standards. In this case, it's expected that the student will meet the learning standards to varying degrees along the continuum of education. For example, the student may be expected to achieve the same standard at an introductory, intermediate, and mastery level in fourth, eighth, and twelfth grade, respectively. In either scenario, a bar is set for all students to attain specified knowledge and skills.

Typically, state learning standards are developed by statewide committees of curriculum experts, subject area experts, leaders in business and industry, and experienced teachers in the field. The intended end result is a document to guide curriculum development, syllabi, classroom teaching, and measurement of student learning. Individual school systems become responsible for preparing students in the classroom and then documenting the degree to which students have met the standards.

In many states, statewide assessments have been created to accompany the standards. The assessments attempt to determine a student's attainment of the established learning standards and measure each school's ability to facilitate its students' progress toward these goals.

Technology Standards

NETS: defining what you should know and be able to do

Like the content-based disciplines, the area of technology and technology integration has standards to guide teachers and schools in their use of educational technologies. National organizations define what teachers should know and be able to do with technology in the classroom. The International Society for Technology in Education (ISTE) has developed the most commonly used standards related to technology integration, for both teachers and students. These are called the **National Educational Technology Standards (NETS);** you've seen selections from them at the beginning of each chapter in this book.

The Purpose of Technology Standards

Why do educational technology standards deserve emphasis? The massive influx of technology into schools has raised questions about its impact on student learning. In fact, numerous commentaries criticize large investments in technology, arguing that technologies are ill used or underused and pointing to gaps in teachers' knowledge about them. Though some of these commentaries are based on little evidence, there's compelling evidence that certain uses of technology lead to student achievement, whereas others seem not to. Further, studies have found that teachers' technical literacy and application skills are low compared to the emphasis placed on technology in schools. The NETS for teachers and for students attempt to address these problems.

Using the NETS in teacher preparation

The NETS can be used to frame objectives for teacher preparation in both undergraduate and graduate courses where technology integration is taught or incorporated into the learning process. Another expectation is that local school districts or state organizations will use the NETS (or similar standards) as a basis for teacher in-service training, as more states mandate evidence of teacher technology proficiency. As pointed out by the SCANS report in the early 1990s, quality teaching must address and capitalize on technologies.

◼ Technology to Help Students Meet Standards

For most educators, technology proficiency isn't just a goal in itself. Rather, it's a means to help students achieve content, process, and performance standards. To put it simply, technology is a tool to help students learn. But how can it best do so? That's one of the questions addressed in subsequent chapters in this book.

Thinking of technology as a tool

Too often, teachers start with a great piece of software and try to make it work for a given situation. This won't help you meet goals set by state or national organizations—or your own goals for your students. Instead, you should begin with the standards—get to know what's in them. Then identify technology tools that can help you and your students achieve these goals.

The following chapters guide you through the steps involved in integrating technology into your teaching. You'll learn how to identify appropriate tools, find ways to gain access to them, and design learning activities that give your students the best opportunities to succeed.

Summary

The standards movement has been at the forefront of educational reform since the 1980s. Content, process, and performance standards for students have been developed at both national and state levels. Teachers and schools are being held accountable for showing adequate student achievement based on these standards. There are also important standards for teachers themselves, focusing on content knowledge, pedagogical strategies, and professional practice.

ISTE has established National Educational Technology Standards (NETS) for both students and teachers. By using NETS as a framework for thinking about technology use, you can design or redesign learning units to help your students meet learning standards in any content area. In upcoming chapters, we discuss the steps you can take to reach this goal.

Resources

 *Online Study Center*
Direct Links to Resources

NATIONAL STANDARDS

Benchmarks for Science Literacy
http://www.project2061.org/tools/benchol
Standards defining what it means to be literate in science.

ISTE National Educational Technology Standards (NETS)
http://cnets.iste.org
The website for the NETS standards for technology integration.

ISTE Profiles for Technology-Literate Teachers: Professional Preparation Performance Profiles
http://cnets.iste.org/teachers/t_profiles.html

These profiles are a companion to the ISTE NETS standards, providing additional information about the skills teachers need in order to meet the NETS standards.

National Council for the Social Studies: Expectations of Excellence: Curriculum Standards for Social Studies
http://www.ncss.org/standards
The website for the national social studies standards.

National Council of Teachers of English: Standards for the English Language Arts
http://www.ncte.org/about/over/standards
The website for the national English language arts standards.

National Council of Teachers of Mathematics: Principles and Standards for School Mathematics
http://standards.nctm.org
The website for the national mathematics standards.

National Geographic Xpeditions: Geography Standards
http://www.nationalgeographic.com/xpeditions/standards/matrix.html
> The National Geography Standards and a wide array of materials to support teachers in meeting them.

National Research Council: National Science Education Standards
http://www.nap.edu/readingroom/books/nses
> The website for the national science standards.

STATE STANDARDS

StateStandards.com
http://www.statestandards.com
> A website allowing easy access to all of the state standards.

SELECTED STATE PROCESS STANDARDS

Colorado K–12 Academic Standards
http://www.cde.state.co.us/index_stnd.htm

Pennsylvania Academic Standards
http://www.pde.state.pa.us/stateboard_ed/cwp

SELECTED STATE MATHEMATICS STANDARDS

Colorado Model Standards for Mathematics
http://www.cde.state.co.us/coloradomath

Florida's Sunshine State Standards
http://www.firn.edu/doe/curric/prek12/index.html

Nevada Department of Education Math Performance Standards
http://www.doe.nv.gov/standards/standmath/math.html

SELECTED STATE SCIENCE STANDARDS

California Science Standards
http://www.cde.ca.gov/re/pn/fd/sci-frame-dwnld.asp

Georgia Science Performance Standards
http://www.georgiastandards.org/science.aspx

APPLETS TO SUPPORT STANDARDS

At the following sites you can find the online games and simulations described in the Case Study. These "applets" (small programs), which run within your web browser, demonstrate some important principles related to mathematics standards.

Number Line Bounce
http://matti.usu.edu/nlvm/nav/frames_asid_107_g_2_t_1.html
> An applet from the National Library of Virtual Manipulatives for Interactive Mathematics that allows students to use a number line representation to solve problems involving integers.

Simple Maze Game
http://www.shodor.org/interactivate/activities/pmaze/index.html
> Project Interactivate of the Shodor Education Foundation offers this applet to support students in learning to graph in quadrant 1.

Understanding Distance, Speed, and Time Relationships Using Simulation Software
http://standards.nctm.org/document/eexamples/chap5/5.2/index.htm
> An applet from the National Council of Teachers of Mathematics that allows students to compare the running rates of two children.

REPORTS ON THE STATUS OF EDUCATION

National Commission on Excellence in Education: A Nation at Risk
http://www.ed.gov/pubs/NatAtRisk/index.html
> The classic 1983 report highlighting the shortcomings of the U.S. school system is still relevant today.

What Work Requires of Schools: A SCANS Report for America 2000
http://wdr.doleta.gov/SCANS/whatwork
> A report looking at the needs of businesses as they relate to K–12 education.

case
STUDY

A Technology Mentor

Margo Sumner, a third-grade teacher at Case Elementary School, has been asked by her principal to serve as a technology mentor for her grade team. Ms. Sumner is excited by the possibility of sharing some of her successful lesson plans with her team and really wants to see instruction

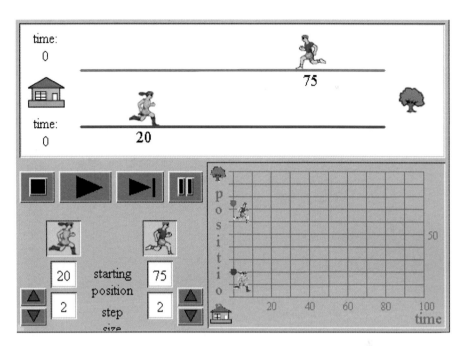

Figure 4.1 Screen from an Interactive Simulation of Two Runners

improved by technology at her school. The first week, she is visited by Lara Levitz, one of the fifth-grade teachers on her team. Ms. Levitz enters Ms. Sumner's room looking very excited and carrying some papers.

"Margo, I'm so excited about working with you on this technology thing! I know my kids need to spend more time on the computers, plus I want to get my computer lab time in before there's a long waiting list. I was out web surfing the other day and found these great websites with a lot of really great interactive programs. There's this one that has two kids on it, and it simulates how fast each of them will cross a finish line if they run at different rates. My kids like to hear stories about other kids, so I thought that might be really fun for them." (Ms. Levitz shows Ms. Sumner a printout of the screen shown in Figure 4.1.)

Ms. Levitz continues, "Another site has a program where you have to move through a minefield in a graph. I thought this one might be a lot of fun for the kids—they'll get to use computer skills and do math at the same time." Now Ms. Levitz hands her mentor the printout shown in Figure 4.2.

Ms. Levitz continues telling Ms. Sumner about the great programs she's found, concluding with a game called Number Line Bounce (Figure 4.3). She says this is the best tool of all, because her students can try out a lot of math before they have to settle on a solution to a problem. In addition, she thinks that using a number line may help students learn about coordinate graphs.

Ms. Sumner listens intently to Ms. Levitz and studies the printouts. She's very impressed with the programs Ms. Levitz has found. However, she's unsure how to support Ms. Levitz, so she decides it might help to visit Ms. Levitz's class. The two teachers agree that Ms. Sumner will watch math class the following day.

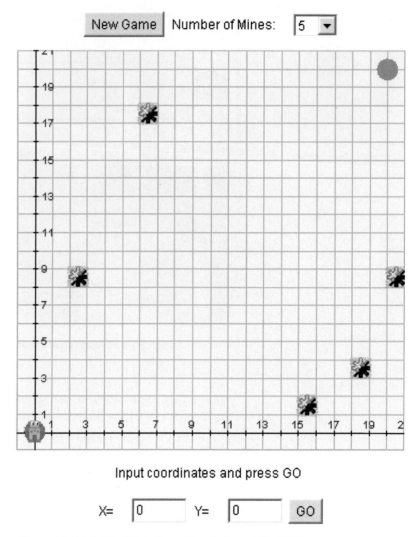

Figure 4.2 An Online Maze Game Simulating a Minefield

The next day, Ms. Sumner enters the room right as math class is getting started. She notices on the walls a recent homework assignment in which Ms. Levitz asked the students to write a description of what some graphs meant. She sees that some students were very general ("The graph starts out at medium speed, then it speeds up, then it stops for a while"), whereas other students made up scenarios for the same graph ("The bus driver was driving at medium speed while he was behind a car, but then he sped up when he got on the highway, then he had to stop for one minute to let some passengers out").

Today, students are discussing tables they've made from the same graphs. As Ms. Sumner listens, she notes that the students are indeed making progress toward understanding how to read a graph. Ms. Levitz wraps up the lesson by handing out the homework assignment, which asks the students to match some graphs to short stories about them. She reminds them that they should explain why they think a graph fits a particular story.

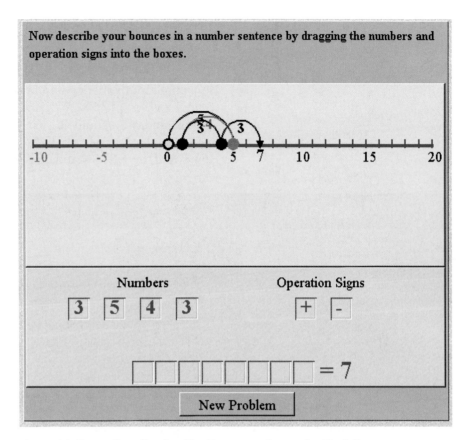

Now describe your bounces in a number sentence by dragging the numbers and operation signs into the boxes.

Numbers

3 5 4 3

Operation Signs

+ -

= 7

New Problem

Figure 4.3 Screen from Number Line Bounce, an Interactive Math Game

Ms. Sumner needs to return to her own class, so she and Ms. Levitz agree to talk after school. Later, as she prepares to meet with Ms. Levitz, Ms. Sumner mentally assesses what support she can provide. She thinks Ms. Levitz is a good teacher, with interesting activities for the students. She notes that the students seem to enjoy themselves in class, and they seem to be doing well with the graphing and stories activities. She also knows that, on last year's State Standards Test of Skills, Ms. Levitz's students scored very well on the algebra portion, with a 78 percent pass rate.

However, something is bothering Ms. Sumner. She feels she doesn't know what's coming next in the lesson sequence, and she's unsure about why and how Ms. Levitz is thinking of using each of the graphing packages she's found.

Ms. Sumner begins to make a plan. She decides to start by looking at the standards for Ms. Levitz's students, to see what they need to know about graphing and linear equations. She determines that, once she's seen the standards, she'll base her recommendation on how the technologies can help students learn the content for which they are responsible, rather than focusing merely on how good the technology activities are. Ms. Sumner knows that she's going to have to provide Ms. Levitz with some hard news: Although all of the applications Ms. Levitz has identified are very good, not all of them are appropriate for this unit in the math textbook.

Questions for Reflection and Discussion

For a moment, put yourself in Ms. Sumner's position. Write out a plan for beginning to work with Ms. Levitz.

1. How might mathematics standards help Ms. Levitz plan the use of technology?
2. Which standards should she use? (See the list of Resources for online standards publications.)
3. How could the NETS standards help guide the next steps?

Meet the Standards

Online Study Center

Standards
Go online for more help with national and state standards.

We've aligned this chapter with the "Standards to Guide Your Preparation" listed at the beginning of the chapter. Go back for a moment and reread those standards.

Now that you know more about standards and why they're important for the classroom, it's time for you to get familiar with the standards that you personally will have to address:

▶ Locate the national and state standards for the grade and content you'll be teaching (for example, eighth-grade social studies). If you're planning to teach elementary school, you might select the grade you most want to work with and either your favorite subject or one with which you feel the least familiar.

▶ Look at the standards to identify one or more standards that could be addressed through a short (for instance, one to five days' long) unit of activities.

▶ Now visit the ISTE NETS standards to see whether one or more of those is appropriate for helping you meet the content standards you've selected. If so, identify the tools, such as software or websites, that you'll be using.

▶ Now that you have the standards in mind and have selected your technology, think about how you might assess whether your students have met the standards. Will you use quizzes? tests? a performance-based task?

▶ When you've completed a sketch of your assessment plan, it's time to plan the learning activities. How will each activity address the standards you've selected? How will the activities help your students succeed on the assessment?

Once you've completed this exploration, you may want to look a grade level ahead and behind in the standards. Ask yourself whether your students will have the prerequisite skills to succeed with your unit and make sure you're preparing them for the next grade. Once you get to know them, standards provide a lot of information for teaching and learning.

PART II

Infusing Technology for Teaching and Learning

Chapter 5

A Guide for Integrating Technology

Standards to Guide Your Preparation

ISTE NETS

Teachers

▶ Design developmentally appropriate learning opportunities that apply technology-enhanced instructional strategies to support the diverse needs of learners.

Prospective teachers

▶ Plan and teach student-centered learning activities and lessons in which students apply technology tools and resources.

OTHER RELEVANT STANDARDS

National Board for Professional Teaching Standards: Early and Middle Childhood/Literacy: Reading–Language Arts Standards (2002)

Teachers are committed to fairness and equity with regard to technology use. They create learning experiences for all students that include technology tools and resources in instruction and applications.

National Council for Accreditation of Teacher Education: Unit Standards (2002)

The new professional teacher who graduates from a professionally accredited school, college, or department of education should be able to integrate technology into instruction effectively.

Part II introduces the Technology and Learning Continuum Model using a backward design process. That is, you will begin with what the students should know and be able to do—and then design a learning unit integrated with technology to meet these objectives. This chapter provides an overview for creating learner-centered, technology-infused activities. Subsequent chapters dive into the specifics of designing everyday learning activities aligned to a complete learning unit. To this end, we cross the learning continuum (how students learn) with instructional design (how we design classroom activities) to establish three broad categories of learning activities: initiating activities, guided learning activities, and culminating activities. Each set of activities focuses on what you want your students to know and be able to do at the culmination of the unit. We begin by identifying the standards we want to address, further refine those to focus on specific goals and objectives, and then create the activities to help students meet those goals and objectives.

Developing a learning unit relies on what you've learned in previous chapters. For example, what you know about learning theory will define how you teach all learners—and how you know that students learn.

We begin this chapter by describing our guide or model. The guide, essentially a blueprint for designing technology-infused learning activities, takes you through the entire process of planning instruction. The following chapters go into greater depth about each step in the process.

Developing a Learning Unit

The model as a guide to designing instruction

Figure 5.1 shows the heart of the **Technology and Learning Continuum Model**—a guide for integrating technology into your teaching and your students' learning. Developing a learner-focused and technology-infused learning unit involves planning instruction that supports learners' construction of knowledge. This instructional design process is based on what students need to know, how they will learn by using technology, and how their understanding will be measured. Notice that technology doesn't *drive* the process. Instead, decisions about technology are based on the considerations discussed in earlier chapters: learners' needs, the learning environment, and the standards that define what learners are expected to know and be able to do.

Across the top of Figure 5.1 you can see the four steps involved in designing instruction. Along the left side of the figure are the three stages of the learning continuum. The space in the middle, "Learner-Centered Activities and Technology Integration," represents what you achieve when you apply the design steps to the learning continuum. The sections that follow examine this process in detail.

The Continuum of Activities

The left side of Figure 5.1 shows the learning continuum, which we see as a progression through three sets of activities.

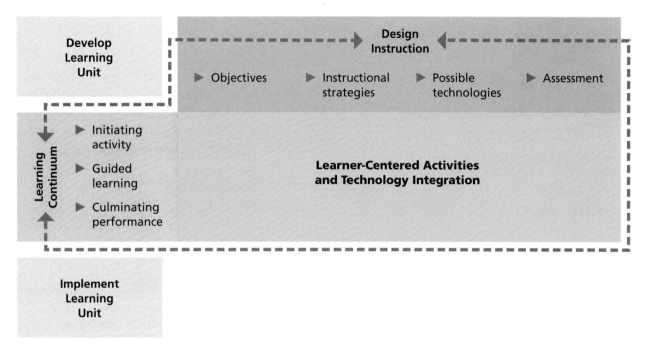

Figure 5.1 **The Technology and Learning Continuum Model** A guide for developing a technology-integrated learning unit

▶ The **initiating activity** makes a connection to prior learning and introduces students to the learning that will take place within the unit.

▶ The **guided learning** activities provide teacher- and technology-intensive support to learners as they explore and make sense of the new knowledge and skills.

▶ The **culminating performance** is the final outcome—the activity(s) where students have an opportunity to demonstrate their new knowledge and understandings.

▓ The Backward Design Process

Starting at the end—the culminating performance

Though it may seem counterintuitive, we promote a reverse, or "backward," design process. In other words, we suggest beginning the design process by focusing on the culminating performance (Wiggins & McTighe, 2001). The culminating performance embodies your goals for the learner—what you intend for the learner to know and be able to do by the end of the learning unit. From that, you work backward to the guided learning and the initiating activity. (See Spotlight 5.1 for further discussion of backward design.)

Typically, as the name suggests, the culminating activity involves students' actually "doing," or performing in ways that demonstrate their construction of knowledge and understanding of the content. Imagine, for example, that you're creating a physics unit in which students will learn key concepts by studying roller coasters. As the culminating performance, you might require your students to design their own fast, but safe, roller coaster

SPOTLIGHT 5.1   Backward Design

Backward design is a way to design your learning activities by focusing first on expected outcomes—what learners must know and be able to do by the end of the unit. Ask yourself:

- What knowledge and understanding must students have?
- How will students demonstrate this knowledge and understanding?

This process helps you avoid the inherent problems of developing activities without a clear sense of how they all link together. Both teacher and learner attain a firmer grasp of the path learning will take and how each activity is intended to improve students' ability to apply what they know.

Pragmatically, teachers like backward design because the process makes it easier to plan each learning activity. It helps them know when students understand—and when they don't.

with two hills and one loop. Their product would include an image of the coaster, as well as a scientific explanation of why it's both fast and safe.

Once you've established clear expectations for student learning through a well-designed culminating performance, you can focus the initiating activity and guided learning on building knowledge and skills that will lead to that final performance. In the roller coaster unit, the initiating activity might be one in which you demonstrate the important relationships among the concepts of friction, gravity, weight, and speed. For this purpose, you might use an online roller coaster simulation to demonstrate what can go wrong. (See the Funderstanding roller coaster simulation at **http://www.funderstanding.com/k12/coaster**.) Then, for the guided learning activities, you might engage students in a variety of miniprojects aimed at developing the necessary understanding to complete the culminating experience. For instance, you could have students use the Internet to research each of the four key physics concepts. Then you might engage them in lab activities demonstrating one or more of the concepts at a time. You might also include some direct instruction as an overview or to address confusions the students may develop. Each of these activities would include its own goals, which would build toward the culminating performance. You could administer an assessment at any point to determine whether students are making satisfactory progress.

This systematic design process provides you with well-defined daily plans for instruction. It also helps you create appropriate assessments of your students' knowledge. Let's take a closer look at the steps in the process.

Designing Instruction

Your role as a teacher is not to impart knowledge, to open learners' minds and dump everything there is to know inside. You'll quickly discover that trying to *give* students knowledge without practicing and applying fails to achieve understanding. Students need a variety of different experiences in order to learn, and simply being lectured to isn't enough for most. The design process we recommend will help you focus on what students

The Teacher's Role as a Facilitator

In the teacher-as-**facilitator** approach to instruction, the teacher acts more as a guide to learning than as a provider of knowledge. The fundamental idea is for students to be encouraged to take more control over their own learning process. As constructivist learning theory points out, students can't simply be given the information we want them to know. They must have experiences; they must link the new information or skills to things they already know; and they must take ownership of their learning.

In such a learning environment, the teacher can't be the sole provider of knowledge. Rather, the teacher guides the learner to seek out appropriate sources of information. This guidance occurs in a number of different ways; for example, the teacher can

- Ask questions that challenge students' thinking.
- Structure the classroom discussion so that students learn from one another.
- Model the behaviors of effective learning by demonstrating processes and tools.

Classroom activities then engage learners in application of the new knowledge they're forming.

Consider the following example of a teacher acting as a facilitator. In this case, the student is supposed to be developing an understanding of the attributes that should be considered when determining the shape of an object.

TEACHER: So, you have pattern blocks on your desk. Which one is a triangle?

STUDENT: [Points out triangle.]

TEACHER: How do you know that's the triangle? What do you know about triangles that helps you identify one?

STUDENT: I don't know anything about triangles.

TEACHER: Nothing at all?

STUDENT: No.

TEACHER: [picking up a square pattern block] So, is this a triangle?

STUDENT: No, it's got four sides.

TEACHER: So, a triangle can't have four sides?

STUDENT: No, it has three sides.

TEACHER: Ah—so you do know something about triangles. Now, see if you can find anything else special about a triangle.

should know and be able to do by the time they complete the culminating performance. Your instruction—the strategies, tools, and assessments you use—will *facilitate* your students' construction of knowledge, and the ability and confidence that students gain can carry over into future learning units (see Spotlight 5.2).

We suggest a four-step process for developing learning units. Look back at Figure 5.1, where the steps are listed across the top under the heading "Design Instruction." The four steps focus on

Four steps for developing learning units

▶ Objectives   ▶ Possible technologies
▶ Instructional strategies   ▶ Assessment

■ Objectives

The cornerstone of appropriate learning activities is a set of well-written learning objectives. **Objectives** are statements that explain what a student will know or be able to do as a result of a learning activity. Your selection of specific learning strategies, technologies, and assessments will be based on your objectives. To make a clear and distinct connection between your objectives and the design of learning activities, we'll dedicate some time to reviewing the objective-writing process.

Table 5.1 Examples of Standards and Topics from State Standards

State	Grade Level/ Course	Standard	Topic
California	5	The learner will be able to identify and analyze characteristics of fiction, nonfiction, poetry, and drama.	Literature analysis
California	5	The learner will be able to use conjunctions to join ideas of sentences together meaningfully.	Parts of speech
Texas	8	The learner will be able to make estimations about the end result of different genetic combinations of inherited traits.	Genetics
Texas	8	The learner will be able to use the principles of scientific inquiry in investigations.	Scientific inquiry
North Carolina	Algebra	The learner will be able to determine the difference between functions and relations.	Functions
Georgia	Government	The student will describe the legislative process, including the roles played by committees and leadership: a. explain the steps in the legislative process b. explain the function of various leadership positions within the legislature	How the government works

How to write objectives

Writing objectives involves a process called **content analysis,** which begins with a review of the content knowledge that students will learn—that is, knowledge about a particular subject or topic. In most cases, you'll begin your content analysis by visiting the standards for your grade and content area. Commonly used resources for this step are the course syllabus, state learning standards, textbooks, websites, and state syllabi for the subject area. Our chapter "Using Standards" provides a number of samples of state and national standards. Table 5.1 offers additional examples from state learning standards for various grade levels and topics.

In most cases, however, the standards are too broad to be fully met with a single learning unit. You'll need to refine the standards into specific objectives in order to create coherent and meaningful learning units. Each objective is written differently depending on the stage of the student's learning and what you expect the student to be able to do as a result of your teaching. In other words, you write objectives to clarify expectations of teaching and learning, and establish a seamless transition across all of the initiating activities, guided learning, and culminating performance (see Figure 5.2).

▬▬ Using Bloom's Taxonomy

Often, Bloom's taxonomy (Spotlight 5.3) is used to help teachers think about objectives and how to write them. In particular, Bloom's taxonomy helps you ensure that students will move beyond simple memorization to higher-level activities. If possible, you should include objectives from different levels of Bloom's taxonomy within a single learning unit. For example, in the roller coaster unit, some sample objectives might include the following:

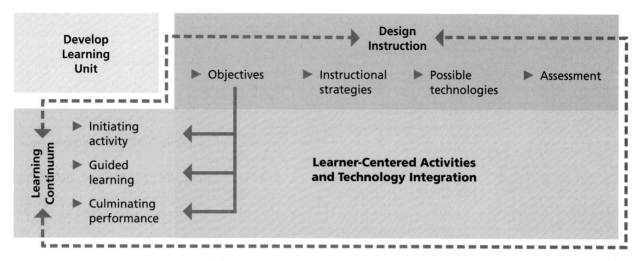

Figure 5.2 Connecting Objectives with the Learning Continuum

Sample objectives using
Bloom's taxonomy

For the initiating activity
▶ The student will be able to define relevant physics terms, including force, gravity, weight, and speed (the Knowledge level of Bloom's taxonomy).

For guided learning
▶ The student will be able to compute the speed of the roller coaster car at given points on its path (the Comprehension and Application levels of Bloom's taxonomy).

For the culminating performance
▶ The student will be able to predict whether a given roller coaster design will work (the Synthesis level of Bloom's taxonomy).
▶ The student will be able to use appropriate physics vocabulary to defend his or her roller coaster design (the Evaluation level of Bloom's taxonomy).

SPOTLIGHT 5.3 Bloom's Taxonomy

Bloom's taxonomy, developed by Benjamin Bloom, attempts to organize learning into levels according to the sophistication of mental effort necessary to meet a given goal. Bloom identified six levels of knowledge, ordered from simplest to most complex.

- *Knowledge.* The learner is able to recall such information as names, dates, or major ideas.
- *Comprehension.* The student is able to comprehend, order, compare/contrast, interpret, and/or predict consequences.

- *Application.* The learner can use the new information in a new setting and/or to solve novel problems.
- *Analysis.* The student can see patterns, organize parts, and recognize hidden meanings.
- *Synthesis.* The learner can generalize from given facts, predict and draw conclusions, and use old ideas to create new ones.
- *Evaluation.* The student can assess and value different ideas or theories, discriminate between ideas, and make reasoned choices.

Source: Adapted from Bloom et al. (1956).

Table 5.2 Key Words to Use in Writing Objectives Based on Bloom's Taxonomy

Bloom's Taxonomy Level	Selected Key Cue Words and Phrases
Knowledge	List, define, tell, describe, identify, show, label, collect, enumerate, examine, tabulate, quote, name, match, read, record, state
Comprehension	Summarize, describe, explain, paraphrase, interpret, contrast, predict, associate, distinguish, estimate, differentiate, discuss, extend, generalize, give examples
Application	Apply, demonstrate, calculate, complete, compute, illustrate, show, solve, examine, modify, relate, change, classify, experiment, discover, predict, extend
Analysis	Analyze, separate, order, explain, connect, classify, arrange, divide, compare, select, explain, diagram, focus, illustrate, infer, prioritize
Synthesis	Combine, integrate, modify, rearrange, substitute, plan, create, design, invent, compose, formulate, prepare, generalize, rewrite, model, ask "What if?"
Evaluation	Assess, decide, rank, grade, test, measure, recommend, convince, select, judge, explain, discriminate, support, conclude, compare, summarize, defend/support, reframe

Source: Adapted from University of Victoria Learning Skills Program, Bloom's Taxonomy. Available: **http://www.coun.uvic.ca/learn/program/ hndouts/bloom.html**.

Table 5.2 lists key words and phrases that can be used in your objectives at each level of the taxonomy. Referring to these can help you think of different kinds of activities that will engage your students in learning across all the levels.

▬ The Key Components of Objectives

Objectives generally have three key components:

1. A description of what the student will be able to do
2. The conditions under which the student will perform the task
3. The criteria for evaluating student performance

Each of these parts is important for both the teacher and the learner.

The first part is clear—it's a statement of what the student will know or be able to do. To understand the second part, the statement of conditions, suppose that the description of what a student will be able to do is "The student will be able to make a graph." This objective can be refined by adding a statement about the conditions under which the student will make the graph. Consider the following—and how each is a little different from the others:

▶ The student will be able to make a graph when given a table of coordinates.
▶ The student will be able to make a graph from a linear equation.
▶ The student will be able to make a graph using graphing software.
▶ The student will be able to make a graph showing a line of best fit.
▶ The student will be able to make a graph when given a written description.

The third component of a traditional objective, the criteria for evaluating performance, relates to the idea of mastery. **Mastery** is a way of thinking about learning that assumes that a student who has mastered a

Mastery

topic, idea, or concept is able to demonstrate that knowledge at least a certain amount of the time. For example, we might say that a student has mastered riding a bike when he can ride it around the block without falling down 90 percent of the time or that a student has mastered a set of vocabulary words when she gets 80 percent of them correct on a quiz.

For our purposes, we generally don't consider learning as attainment of percentages of goals. However, you may find that, for some of your objectives, this is a useful way to measure adequate growth. For example, is it adequate for your students to score 100 percent on a spelling test one time, or do they need to spell their words correctly throughout the project? These are the kinds of decisions you'll need to make as you write your objectives.

■■■ Judging the Quality of Your Objectives

How do you know you're writing high-quality, useful objectives? One good measure of an objective's appropriateness is to ask whether students' responses can be evaluated.

Writing useful objectives

Imagine that you're planning a psychology lesson that includes the concepts of stimulus and response. You may want to assess students' progress in a class question-and-answer period or on a written quiz. You write the objective as

> Know the terms *stimulus* and *response*.

But it's difficult, if not impossible, to evaluate "knowing." You must ask yourself how you'll decide whether students "know." A better way to state the objective would be as follows:

> Define the terms *stimulus* and *response*.

Only one word has changed, the verb at the beginning of the sentence, but it makes students' responses much more measurable.

As you prepare to write your own objectives, remember to keep them measurable, to focus on what you want students to learn and under what conditions. Refer to the handy checklist in Spotlight 5.4.

SPOTLIGHT 5.4

Checklist for Writing Specific Instructional Objectives

☐ Make sure that each statement meets all three of the criteria for a good learning objective.
- Description of what the student will be able to do
- The conditions under which the student will be expected to perform
- The criteria to be used for evaluation of the student's performance

☐ Begin each statement of a learning outcome with a verb that specifies a definite, observable behavior (see Table 5.2 for examples).

☐ Be sure to include complex objectives, such as appreciation and problem solving, when they are appropriate.

▬▬ Benefits of Learning Objectives

The process of writing clear learning objectives has several benefits.

1. The objectives guide you as a teacher. By being specific about what you want students to gain from instruction, you help yourself choose materials and activities.
2. Clear objectives will help drive your technology decisions. If your objectives are focused on the higher levels in Bloom's taxonomy, for instance, you'll be less likely to select lower-level technologies, such as drill-and-practice software.
3. Objectives help you develop assessments. Once you've identified what you want students to learn, you can create tests, quizzes, rubrics, and performance tasks geared to those goals.
4. Objectives help students know what they're supposed to be learning. At the beginning of a unit, you can provide your list of objectives to the students so that they can reflect on whether they're meeting them. This is another way to help learners become responsible for their own learning.

■ Instructional Strategies

Looking back at Figure 5.1 (page 75), you can see that the next step after specifying your objectives is to consider your instructional strategies. Usually your subject area will lead you to favor certain approaches to instruction. For instance, science teachers are often fluent in inquiry-based approaches, and investigation-based approaches have recently increased in popularity among mathematics teachers. Nevertheless, you should have a full range of strategies at your disposal.

The following sections (adapted from Newby et al., 2006) describe some of the common strategies in use today. As you read the text, look at the accompanying figures. Figure 5.3 shows the types of student actions associated with each instructional strategy. Figure 5.4 matches the instructional strategies to the continuum of learning activities we discussed earlier, showing which strategies are most appropriate for particular stages of the continuum.

Instructional Strategy	Read	See	Hear	Say	Do
Presentation	■	■	■		
Demonstration	■	■	■		
Discussion		■	■	■	
Inquiry	■	■	■	■	■
Problem solving	■	■	■	■	■
Cooperative learning		■	■	■	
Instructional games	■	■	■	■	■
Simulation	■	■	■	■	■

Figure 5.3 Student Actions Associated with Each Instructional Strategy

Instructional Strategy	Typical Stage in the Learning Continuum
Presentation	Initiating activity
Demonstration	Initiating activity
Discussion	Initiating activity/Guided learning
Inquiry	Guided learning/Culminating performance
Problem solving	Guided learning
Cooperative learning	Guided learning
Instructional games	Guided learning
Simulation	Guided learning/Culminating performance

Figure 5.4 **Instructional Strategies Matched with the Continuum of Learning Activities**

▬▬ Presentation

Presentation is the introduction, offering, delivering, and exhibition of information. For our purposes, it's the delivery of content knowledge for students to learn. The teacher uses this approach to prepare students for engagement in learning. Facts and information are typically given to students so that they can make use of this information in future activities. For example, you're using presentation when you introduce procedures for conducting an ethogram, an instrument for observing animal behaviors. You may use a computer, projector, and presentation software to show an actual ethogram, observation techniques, and how to code animals' movements (Nelson, 2004). Figure 5.5 shows a sample ethogram, a technique that we'll describe further in the next chapter.

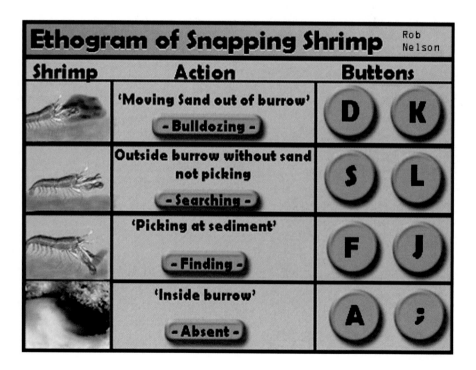

Figure 5.5 **A Sample Ethogram**

Online Study Center

Inquiry Learning in Middle-School Science

Inquiry is a core strategy for facilitating students' construction of knowledge. In fact, uses of inquiry-based instruction have evolved from science instruction to many other subject areas. In the Online Study Center, watch the HM Video Case called **Middle-School Science Instruction: Inquiry Learning.** Notice the questioning strategies the teacher uses to engage the students. How might you use inquiry in your teaching? How could you apply inquiry to other types of subject matter? Review the Classroom Artifacts and the Bonus Videos for clues.

Demonstration

Demonstration is the description or explanation of information or of a process. A demonstration usually involves examples or experiments. You might use a demonstration to illustrate how electronic probes collect data, such as temperature readings, and feed them into a computer. You'll also often use demonstration to show students how the knowledge or skills they'll be learning can be applied; for instance, you might demonstrate using a probe to understand how salinity levels affect the freezing of water (Lehigh University, 2002).

Discussion

Discussion is the examination of information by argument, comment, or debate. All subject areas use this approach. Typically, the teacher frames questions around a topic being covered in class and asks students to provide insight into it. This is a good way to conduct a preliminary and informal assessment of what students know about the topic.

Inquiry

Inquiry is the active investigation of *why* and *how.* A social studies class might be asked to investigate the causes of the Great Depression in the United States. Our chapter on learner needs describes inquiry-based learning in detail.

Problem Solving

Problem solving is the process of attempting to resolve any question or matter involving doubt, uncertainty, or difficulty. We discussed problem-solving approaches in the chapter on learner needs. Examples of this approach are found mostly in math and science, but the strategy can be applied in any subject area. Students enjoy reading about solutions to everyday problems and situations. Teachers can use a variety of stories, such as *Jack and the Beanstalk, Faithful Elephants,* or *The Old Man and the Sea,* to generate solutions to problems outlined in the stories.

Cooperative Learning

Cooperative learning is a teaching strategy in which small groups of learners (often at different ability levels) engage in a variety of activities to understand concepts. Each group member is involved in his or her own learning and in assisting the learning of others. Students may learn algebra, for example, by using real-life problems and manipulatives in a cooperative learning setting.

▬ Instructional Games

Instructional games help students gain knowledge and skills through active participation in an entertaining activity. Some instructors use Scrabble to teach vocabulary or Monopoly to teach about money. Instructors often create their own games as well, such as the well-known stock market games used in many classes. When such games use computer technology, they're often called *edutainment,* as noted in an earlier chapter.

▬ Simulation

Simulation, which we've already mentioned several times in this book, is the imitation of a process, knowledge, or skill to be learned. One example is a flight simulator, which gives novice pilots and others a chance to experience flying an airplane without leaving the ground. Other examples are software packages used to simulate frog dissection in biology classes (Henseler, 2006).

■ Possible Technologies

Choosing technology that supports students' performance

After choosing instructional strategies, your next step is to select technology. You want to choose technology that will most effectively support the students' performance of the objectives you've set for the learning unit. If you take a constructivist approach to teaching, you won't often be teaching in the presentation mode, merely lecturing and doling out factual information. Instead, you'll be engaging your students in inquiry, discussion, problem solving, and other meaningful learning activities, and your technology must support that approach.

Later chapters will give you detailed suggestions for choosing technology. As an overview, Figure 5.6 suggests how you can match instructional strategies with appropriate types of technology.

Instructional Strategy	Examples of Appropriate Technology
Presentation	Presentation software such as Microsoft PowerPoint, Visio, and Inspiration
Demonstration	LCD projector, video capture, software
Discussion	E-mail, chat, instant messaging, videoconferencing, Internet telephone
Inquiry	Probes, data collection instruments, video and audio capture
Cooperative learning	Internet, chat room, online collaboration suites
Problem solving	Software, spreadsheets, online tools
Instructional games	Sims, Carmen Sandiego, Lighthouse
Simulation	Virtual reality, computer simulations of real environments

Figure 5.6 Aligning Instructional Strategies with Appropriate Technology

■ Assessment

Assessment is one of the most overlooked details of a learning unit. Teachers often struggle to create an assessment that measures what they most want to know. But if you follow the steps outlined here, you'll be in a better position to create useful assessments. The previous three steps of designing instruction—creating objectives, choosing instructional strategies, and selecting appropriate technologies—will feed into your creation of assessment measures.

Later chapters will address assessment more specifically as it relates to designing and implementing learning activities. Here, we want you to visualize how assessment fits into the big picture of developing a learning unit and how you'll create assessments based on what you expect students to know and be able to do. Notice again that Figure 5.1 (page 75) shows assessment as the necessary final step in designing instruction for the stages of the learning continuum.

■■ Criteria for Effective Assessment

What are the criteria for a good assessment? Researchers have found that

1. Sound assessment is anchored in *authenticity* of tasks. This means assessing the way students use their skills in meaningful contexts.
2. Assessments should measure or sample a wide range of cognitive processes and abilities.
3. Assessments must provide for active, collaborative reflection by both teacher and students. Ideally, students should be active participants in designing their own assessment tasks and using assessment data to monitor and improve their own learning.
4. Assessment must be continuous. Drafts, plans, and sketches are as important a part of the big picture as final products. (Adapted from Kulieke et al., 1990, citing Valencia, 1990)

Using formative as well as summative assessment

These four points make it clear, the assessment doesn't necessarily have to come at the end of the activity. As we discussed earlier in the book, you'll want to use formative as well as summative assessments. Consider establishing checkpoints where students can demonstrate their knowledge, so that you may adjust and refine the lesson. Parts of the guided learning activity may themselves serve as effective assessments. For instance, while students are practicing problem solving, you can collect their products and evaluate their progress. The entire culminating activity also lends itself to being an effective assessment.

Your assessments should be aligned with all the other stages of the instructional design process. In other words, assessments should fully reflect the standards you're trying to meet, the objectives you've set, and the instructional strategies you've used throughout the unit. For that reason, most of your assessments should focus, not on isolated facts, but on students' application and use of their knowledge.

You may find it necessary to resort to traditional assessments for the initiating activity. At this early stage, multiple-choice questions may help you decide whether students have grasped the definitions of terms and other requisite factual knowledge. But continued reliance on such formats is unwarranted. One of the greatest pitfalls is applying constructivist theory to instruction and then using a multiple-choice or true-false assessment. Instead, use open discussions, student presentations, and other techniques that truly demonstrate what students know and are able to do.

Using Technology for Assessment

Technology is an excellent means for delivering, supporting, and providing assessment (Marzano, Pickering, & McTighe, 1993, p. 13). Technology is especially effective for

When to use technology

▶ Assessing higher-level thinking skills.
▶ Assessing application of knowledge, rather than mere memorization.
▶ Making assessment an integral part of the learning process.
▶ Accommodating multiple intelligences and special needs.

Using technology does not automatically make an activity or assessment better. A multiple choice test has the same properties and limitations whether it's on a computer or on paper. That is, the power of technology is not being tapped when it is used to do more of the same—look for the affordances of technology such as simulating environments to assess understanding instead of memory recall. Technology is also ineffective when the following conditions prevail:

When not to use technology

▶ Training students to use the technology is obtrusive or overly time consuming.
▶ Access to the technology is problematic—for instance, some students are unable to use the keyboard for a computer-based assessment.
▶ The technology greatly increases the time needed for teacher preparation.
▶ Complications with the technology can cause an assessment to be less effective, valid, or reliable.

If a particular technology doesn't provide distinct advantages to the teacher and learner, it shouldn't be used.

Assessment using technology must be appropriate for your objectives and aligned with your instructional strategies. If your instructional strategies have included inquiry and discovery, for example, then these choices should be reflected in the assessment. As one example, students might use an Internet search engine to demonstrate their inquiry and discovery processes.

The same technology you use to facilitate learning may be an effective assessment tool. If your students learn about the planets by taking a virtual reality tour of the solar system on a website, they may use the same site to demonstrate what they've learned about planetary motion. The following "Technology in Action" provides additional examples.

Incorporating Technology into Assessment Activities

Assessment can flow seamlessly from instruction, using the same kinds of technology. As one example, if you use Microsoft Excel spreadsheet software to teach students analysis, graphical representation, and problem solving with data, you can simply design time for students to demonstrate their knowledge without your assistance. Give the students a data set and ask them to use Excel to run analyses and build charts within an allotted time. You'll get immediate feedback about their progress.

Another method is to incorporate assessment into the learning activity itself. Consider this idea for using Physics Explorer, a high-school science package from Riverdeep:

> Physics Explorer provides students with a simulation environment in which there is a variety of different models, each with a large set of associated variables that can be manipulated. Students conduct experiments to determine how different variables affect each other within a physical system. For example, one task duplicates Galileo's pendulum experiments, where the problem is to figure out what variables affect the period of motion. In a second task, the student must determine what variables affect the friction acting on a body moving through a liquid. Printouts of students' work can be collected and evaluated in terms of the following traits: (1) how systematically they consider each possible independent variable, (2) whether they systematically control other variables while they test a hypothesis, and (3) whether they can formulate quantitative relationships between the independent variables and the dependent variables. (Bennett & Hawkins, 1992)

Competence	Skills Demonstrated	Technology
Knowledge	▶ Observation and recall of information ▶ Knowledge of dates, events, places ▶ Knowledge of major ideas ▶ Mastery of subject matter	▶ Word processing ▶ Spreadsheets ▶ Database software ▶ Web-page building ▶ Presentation software
Comprehension	▶ Understanding of information ▶ Grasp of meaning ▶ Translation of knowledge into new context ▶ Interpretation of facts, comparison, contrast ▶ Ordering, grouping, inferring causes ▶ Predicting consequences	Specific content area software and systems, such as ▶ Geometer's Sketchpad ▶ PASCO science applications ▶ Spreadsheet software

Figure 5.7 Bloom's Taxonomy Aligned with Technology Choices for Assessment

Competence	Skills Demonstrated	Technology
Application	▶ Using information ▶ Using methods, concepts, theories in new situations ▶ Solving problems using required skills or knowledge	▶ E-mail ▶ Web pages ▶ Educational software ▶ Learning systems
Analysis	▶ Seeing patterns ▶ Organization of parts ▶ Recognition of hidden meanings ▶ Identification of components	▶ Spreadsheet software ▶ Charting/visualization software (Inspiration, Visio) ▶ Statistical software
Synthesis	▶ Using old ideas to create new ones ▶ Generalizing from given facts ▶ Relating knowledge from several areas ▶ Predicting, drawing conclusions	▶ Presentation software ▶ Educational software ▶ Office suite software ▶ Video ▶ Portfolio
Evaluation	▶ Comparing and discriminating between ideas ▶ Assessing value of theories, presentations ▶ Making choices based on reasoned argument ▶ Verifying value of evidence ▶ Recognizing subjectivity	▶ Portfolio ▶ Video ▶ Web page ▶ Authoring software (HyperStudio, Toolkit, or Authorware)

Figure 5.7 *Continued*

As a general guideline for selecting technology for assessments, Figure 5.7 matches various types of technology to the levels in Bloom's taxonomy. Later chapters will provide specific examples of the technologies mentioned in the figure.

Summary

In the Technology and Learning Continuum Model, the learning continuum is broken into three stages: the initiating activity, guided learning, and the culminating performance. We recommend a backward design process, in which you design the last activity first and then create all the activities that precede it. As you construct each set of activities, you focus on what you want students to know and be able to do at the culmination of the unit.

The design of instruction incorporates four steps: objectives, instructional strategies, possible technologies, and assessment. Effective objectives should define what the students will be able to do,

the conditions under which they will perform the task, and the criteria for evaluating their performance. Objectives should be stated in such a way that they specify a definite, observable behavior.

Common instructional strategies include presentation, demonstration, discussion, inquiry, problem solving, cooperative learning, instructional games, and simulation. Each strategy lends itself to certain uses of technology. At the assessment stage, you should make sure that your assessments are fully aligned with your objectives, instructional strategies, and the technologies you've used.

RESOURCES

Online Study Center
Direct Links to Resources

Bloom's Taxonomy
http://www.coun.uvic.ca/learn/program/hndouts/bloom.html

Benjamin Bloom created this taxonomy to categorize the abstraction levels of questions that commonly occur in educational settings.

Bookbinders: Fusing Technology, Image, and Literature
http://www.mmischools.com

This article by Johanna Riddle offers several ideas for using problem solving and technology to enhance the study of literature in elementary school. To find this article at the MMISchools site, type the author's name in the Search box.

Design in the Classroom: Backward Design
http://ditc.missouri.edu/designProcess/designCases/backDesign.html

Grant Wiggins walks through the three stages followed by an activity designer, asking, "What are the key learning results I want students to achieve?"

InTime: Find a Video
http://www.intime.uni.edu/video.html

InTime is a Preparing Tomorrow's Teachers to Use Technology (PT3) project funded by the U.S. Department of Education. This site provides access to videos of teachers using technology in the classroom.

The Technology Applications Center for Educator Development: Assessment
http://www.tcet.unt.edu/START/assess/tools.htm

Resources for self-assessment and technology-based applications of assessment in your classroom.

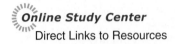

case STUDY

Building a Learning Unit

Chris is a new middle-school science teacher in a school system that's implementing new state learning standards. The new standards are more performance oriented than the old ones and are intended to provide clear expectations for assessment, instruction, and student work. They define the level of work that demonstrates achievement of the standards, enabling a teacher to know "how good is good enough." The performance standards also isolate and identify the skills students need to develop; for example, skills to problem-solve, reason, communicate, and make connections with other information.

Chris must review all the existing learning activities to make sure they're aligned with the new standards. Reflecting on previous years and looking closely at student performance data, Chris decides that the best place to begin is with the astronomy unit. Students always struggle with misconceptions about phases of the moon, seasons, and eclipses.

Chris has a large class—thirty-five students, including five with disabilities. Students' misconceptions of phases, seasons, and eclipses are well known and deeply rooted. Surveying the available resources, Chris notes that there's a science museum two hours away, a university three hours away, and an Internet connection in every classroom. Chris thinks that technology may enable the students to see and experience these concepts in new ways by helping them to overcome prior knowledge. A mobile laptop cart is available for signout, and it works well in the classroom. Chris also has three full-time computers in the classroom, as well as the usual assortment of books on astronomy and materials to teach the concepts (balls of various sizes, a flashlight, string, and so on).

But how can these resources be put to the best use? In line with the Technology and Learning Continuum Model, Chris begins to think about the four steps in designing instruction: creating objectives, selecting instructional strategies, choosing among the possible technologies, and planning for assessment.

Questions for Reflection and Discussion

1. *Objectives.* How should Chris move from the new state performance standards to specific objectives for the astronomy unit? What resources and guidelines might he draw on?
2. *Instructional strategies.* What instructional strategies are most appropriate? Why? What resources could Chris use to select one or more strategies?
3. *Possible technologies.* Considering the objectives and instructional strategies, what are the possible technologies Chris can use? What resources can help him make this decision?
4. *Assessment.* How will Chris measure learner knowledge? Where along the learning continuum would you implement assessments? How would you use technology for assessments? What resources are available to help design assessments?

Meet the Standards

Online Study Center
Standards
Additional resources are available online.

Review the items listed in "Standards to Guide Your Preparation" at the beginning of this chapter. Designing instruction may be new to you, so the key words in these standards are *plan* and *design. Teaching* itself will come later.

Using the backward design process, work through a basic plan for instructional events in your classroom. Start by thinking of a particular learning unit that you may teach and use the following questions as guides:

▶ How will you determine what your students should know and be able to do by the end of the learning unit? How will you state these expectations in a plan? Provide two or three examples of expectations, written as outcomes that you'll be able to observe when students complete the learning unit.

▶ You anticipate that it will take three lessons for students to develop their knowledge and skills sufficiently to meet the expected outcomes of the unit. Write two or three more specific objectives for each of the three activities.

▶ What instructional strategies and technologies might you use in each activity to help facilitate students' knowledge and understanding? How will you use technology to enhance the learning experiences of students from different cultures?

▶ How will you know if the students are making progress toward the unit's expected outcomes? How can technology help you determine their progress? What will you do if you find the activities are inappropriate (too hard or too easy)?

Chapter 6

The Culminating Performance

ISTE NETS

Teachers

▶ Design developmentally appropriate learning opportunities that apply technology-enhanced instructional strategies to support the diverse needs of learners.

▶ Apply technology to develop students' higher-order skills and creativity.

▶ Apply technology in assessing student learning of subject matter using a variety of assessment techniques.

OTHER RELEVANT STANDARDS

National Council for the Social Studies (2004)

Teachers in the middle grades can provide learners with experiences in making and using maps, globes, charts, models, and databases to analyze spatial distributions and properties. High school teachers can enable learners to use geographic representations and tools to analyze, explain, and solve geographic problems. They can provide learners with experiences in applying concepts and models of spatial organization to make decisions.

The National Council of Teachers of English: Initial Preparation of Teachers of Secondary English Language Arts (2003)

Help students compose and respond to film, video, graphic, and photographic, audio, and multimedia texts and use current technology to enhance their own learning and reflection on learning.

As you read in the preceding chapter, our Technology and Learning Continuum Model divides the continuum of learning into three stages of activity: the initiating activity, guided learning activities, and the culminating performance. In this and the next two chapters we explore those activities in more depth. Following our backward design approach, we begin with the last of the three—the culminating performance—because, to put it simply, you need to know where you're going before you start.

Figure 6.1 reproduces the learning continuum section of the model. If you need to remind yourself of what the entire model looks like, flip back to Figure 5.1.

What Should a Culminating Performance Look Like?

When you begin developing a learning unit, you should clearly define what the learners will know, understand, and be able to do at the end of their learning experience. The culminating performance, as the name suggests, is intended to be an opportunity for learners to conclude the learning unit with a demonstration of knowledge and skill. It is a final stage, in which learners demonstrate what they've learned through some sort of experience packaged as a performance assessment. People learn best when their knowledge is tightly linked to experience. A culminating performance provides learners with an experience to apply and build their understanding. It also provides the teacher with a rich glimpse into the students' understanding, misconceptions, and additional instructional needs.

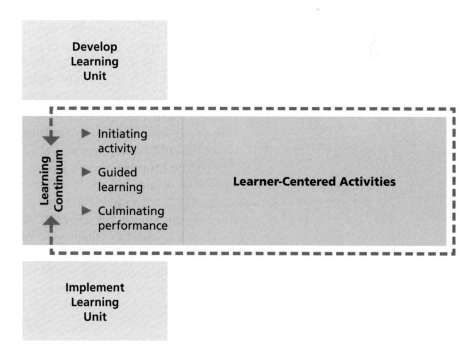

Figure 6.1 The Learning Continuum from the Technology and Learning Continuum Model

The culminating performance is an active demonstration of understanding and skill development. Hence, it should have the following attributes:

Attributes of a culminating performance

▶ Active learning: hands-on participation by the students
▶ A real or simulated environment; for instance, an actual job site or a virtual reality simulation of one
▶ Performance-based activities: doing and demonstrating
▶ Embedded, continuous assessments to measure progress, development, and improvement

A culminating performance is always an assessment approach, but often it is also a learning experience. In other words, students shouldn't stop learning just because it's time for them to demonstrate what they know. The most powerful culminating performance requires students to generalize what they've learned and apply it to new situations, particularly situations in the real world. This is called **situated learning,** or learning *in situ.*

To the greatest extent possible, the activities in the culminating performance should take place in a real-world setting. The best-case scenario is for students to demonstrate their learning in an authentic task which they might perform outside school. If the setting can't be absolutely "real," simulations can be developed.

In classrooms, authentic, real-world experiences might include doing a community-based project, presenting findings to a concerned group, creating a report to be disseminated, conducting an experiment, and other similar activities. Realistic simulations include taking a particular role in an argument or writing a letter to a fictitious character or dead person. Computer simulations also provide realistic settings for culminating experiences that could not be accomplished through real-world experiences. The key idea to keep in mind, whether using real-world experiences or using simulated ones, is that the culminating experience should be an opportunity for students to engage in complex activity to demonstrate their level of understanding as well as their basic skills.

A learning unit on wolves

To help you better understand how to design a culminating experience, we'll use an example from a curriculum on wolf habitat. Recently we collaborated with Jim Fowler to design a technology-integrated learning unit for the study of wolf habitat at his Wild Georgia wildlife park, being developed for Stone Mountain Park near Atlanta, Georgia. Fowler, known for his work on the Animal Planet television network and on such shows as *Mutual of Omaha's Wild Kingdom,* is a world-renowned conservationist. His message is simple yet powerful. If people better understood animals, they'd better understand the impact of human actions. Hence, we set out to provide a learning experience that would deliver this message and engage students in powerful learning. In our Big Bad Wolf unit, seventh graders address, in a series of three lessons, commonly held misconceptions about wolves.[1] Although the activities focus primarily on science and

---

[1] Activities for Jim Fowler's Wild Georgia, including the Big Bad Wolf, were developed with support from the BellSouth Foundation. Lead developer of the Big Bad Wolf activity was Denise Domizi.

SPOTLIGHT
6.1

Informal Learning Environments

The term **informal learning environment (ILE)** refers broadly to settings and activities outside of formal schooling, whose mission includes learning and development. Examples of such settings include after-school clubs, museums, and summer camps. Many resources are available to help you locate and effectively utilize informal learning environments. Start with these:

Association of Science-Technology Centers
   http://www.astc.org

Informal Science
   http://www.informalscience.org

Science Alliance: Informal Learning
   http://www.biotech.wisc.edu/outreach/alliance/informal.html

math, we'll use an example from English language arts. In the following sections we'll return several times to this example, which should give you a useful model to work from as you develop your own activities.

The Georgia schools' collaboration with Jim Fowler also demonstrates the importance of taking advantage of informal learning environments (see Spotlight 6.1). You, too, should look for opportunities to utilize informal learning environments as exciting places for student learning. You can turn what used to be a "field trip" into an authentic learning experience and a worthwhile expenditure of time and funds.

Designing a Culminating Performance with the Four-Step Design Process

As we pointed out in the preceding chapter, every step in the development of a unit can be accomplished through a four-step process (Figure 6.2). For the culminating performance, the four steps can be stated as follows:

The four steps in designing a culminating performance

Step 1. State the objectives (what students will know, understand, and be able to do), aligned with learning standards.

Step 2. Select instructional strategies, including the activities and products that are most appropriate for learners to (1) meet the objectives and (2) demonstrate their understanding, knowledge, and skills.

Step 3. Choose technologies as tools to support instruction and learning.

Step 4. Create assessments—rubrics to measure progress and understanding on the culminating performance.

Step 1: State Objectives

As discussed in a previous chapter, learning standards provide direction about what students should know and be able to do. Standards also help define the parameters for designing, implementing, and assessing instruction. After identifying the relevant standards, you need to translate them into focused objectives for the students' culminating performance.

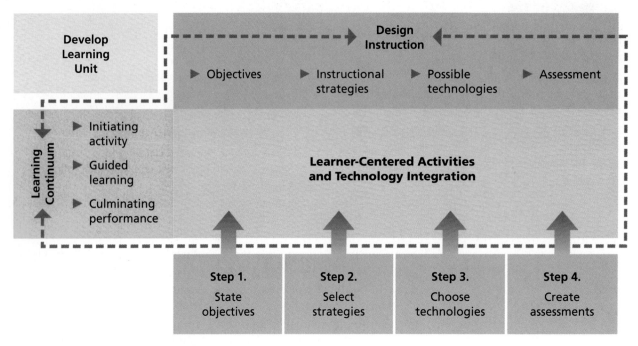

Figure 6.2 The Steps in Activity Design

▦ Identify Relevant Learning Standards

Every state has its learning standards posted online, as do the major national organizations involved in creating standards. If you're a seventh-grade English language arts teacher in Georgia, for example, you'd use a web browser to access the Georgia Standards **(http://www .georgiastandards.org).** Then you'd search the site for the appropriate grade-level and content-specific standards. Next, you may copy and paste the standards into the word processing document or template that you're using to develop your lesson plan. (See "Resources" at the end of this chapter for help in locating relevant websites.)

Many states also provide sample lesson plans and web resources linked to the standards. The Georgia Standards site, for example, provides links to a professional development center, a lesson plan builder, and samples of sequenced lesson plans. These materials are already aligned with the Georgia standards and have been implemented in the classroom by veteran teachers.

Technology is often mentioned in multiple places within states' learning standards. Technology is presented not only as a set of specific tools to be used, but also in the context of a broad expectation that teachers will integrate technology into their learning environments.

▦ Transform Standards into Objectives

Often the standards aren't in a format suitable for direct adoption in a lesson plan. You must transform them into more specific objectives. Because standards are often written in "culminating" language—expressing what learners will know and be able to do once they've met the standards—the

Table 6.1 Guide for Transforming Standards into Culminating Performance Objectives

Purposes of learning objectives	Describe what needs to happen to meet expectations.
	Focus the students' attention on what's important.
	Focus teachers' attention on what's important to include in a unit and what's important to focus on as they teach.
	Specify the knowledge, skills, and understandings on which students will be evaluated.
Three key components of learning objectives	*Description of behavior.* A description of what the student will know and be able to do
	Conditions. The conditions under which the student will perform the task
	Criteria. The criteria for evaluating student performance
Appropriate levels of Bloom's taxonomy for culminating performances	Analysis
	Synthesis
	Evaluation
Useful verbs for writing culminating performance objectives	Design, develop, formulate, judge, predict, rate, manage, organize, interpret, differentiate, support, value, generalize, model, design, invent

objectives for the culminating performance may be easier to develop than those for other parts of the lesson.

As the teacher, you'll also need to decide whether your unit will meet all aspects of a standard or whether you'll address only portions of the standard. Part of this decision rests in the scope of the standard, and part is related to your students' abilities. You want to challenge your students but not create a lesson entirely beyond their abilities.

Table 6.1 offers a handy guide for transforming standards into objectives.

▬ Writing Objectives for the Big Bad Wolf Unit

During our work on Jim Fowler's Wild Georgia project, the state performance standards were still new, and few existing curricular or instructional materials had been developed specifically to address them. In our design of the Big Bad Wolf learning unit, we began by selecting standards that would be both challenging and interesting for students. Here's one of the performance standards we chose for the area of seventh-grade English language arts:

A performance standard for the Big Bad Wolf unit

The student listens to and views various forms of text and media in order to gather and share information, persuade others, and express and understand ideas. . . . The student will select and critically analyze messages using rubrics as assessment tools.

When delivering and responding to presentations, the student:

a. Gives oral presentations or dramatic interpretations for various purposes.
b. Organizes information to achieve particular purposes and to appeal to the background and interests of the audience.
c. Shows appropriate changes in delivery (e.g., gestures, vocabulary, pace, visuals).
d. Uses language for dramatic effect.
e. Uses rubrics as assessment tools.
f. Responds to oral communications with questions, challenges, or affirmations.
g. Uses multimedia in presentations.

At Stone Mountain Park, where Wild Georgia is being developed, students can observe various animals, including wolves, interacting with their habitat and with other members of their species. Students from a visiting class can take notes on their observations and develop their own theories about the animals' behavior. With this kind of activity in mind, we translated the state performance standard into these culminating performance objectives for English language arts:

Students will:

The standard translated into objectives

▶ Extract information from their pre- and post-visit activities, and from their visit to the wolf habitat, to prepare a presentation for the class.
▶ Present their topic in an organized manner.
▶ Speak clearly, succinctly, and use appropriate technology to enhance the presentation of their topic.

■ Step 2: Select Instructional Strategies

The next step is to align your instructional strategies with the learning objectives. As you design your culminating performance, you'll want to focus on instructional approaches that engage students in demonstrating their understanding and developing further understanding through hands-on engagement.

Realistic activities

As we mentioned earlier, the ideal setting for the culminating performance is a real or closely simulated environment. For the culminating performance in our wolf unit, we wanted to provide realistic activities that a scientist would engage in as part of everyday practice. We also wanted the activities to be interdisciplinary, so that the English language arts component would connect to students' learning in life science class (see Spotlight 6.2). For these purposes, we chose problem solving as one instructional strategy: Students would choose a particular problem to investigate. One such problem might be the logging industry's impact on wolf populations. Another such problem might involve wolf social interactions: What kind of social hierarchy does the pack seem to have, and how can we tell a given wolf's status within the pack?

SPOTLIGHT 6.2   Interdisciplinary Learning Units

People's experiences in real life are seldom limited to a single domain. Given that, students should have the opportunity to cut across domains in their own learning activities—including their culminating performance. Interdisciplinary learning units are designed to interconnect learning across domains.

For example, teachers have developed learning units that link mathematics concepts (formulas for the relationship between height, speed, and acceleration), science (the role of force and gravity in car movement), and technology (building a roller coaster). By providing students with opportunities to link their knowledge as they learn, you provide them with the cognitive tools to engage in more complex culminating performances.

For more on interdisciplinary learning units, see http://olc.spsd.sk.ca/DE/PD/instr/strats/interdis

We chose to use cooperative learning as an instructional strategy. Teams of students would work together to explore the problem and develop conclusions. Each group's final presentation would include appropriate facts to support the group's arguments. To increase the similarity to real-life science, we decided that the students would share their presentations with scientists at the park. There would be time for open discussion and reflection on the merit of the students' arguments. The scientists could substantiate the students' knowledge or challenge the argument by using model habitats available at the park.

Step 3: Choose Technologies

Because of the nature of the culminating performance, it's common for it to be a unit activity that students work on as they engage in their learning. However, it's sometimes a performance assessment undertaken after the students have had an opportunity to learn the new material.

A wide range of technologies can support students in completing culminating performances. These range from word processors and page layout programs that allow students to make professional-looking products to simulations that allow the classroom to become a totally new environment, such as a roller coaster or the surface of Mars. In this section we provide examples of both and show how they can be utilized to meet objectives.

Simulations

One example of a commonly used simulation—relevant both for instruction and for the culminating performance—is the applet Net Frog **(http://curry.edschool.virginia.edu/go/frog),** which is used in schools to simulate frog dissection. Net Frog, like other frog dissection software programs, provides narration and video samples, and allows students to experience the dissection process without ever touching a frog.

Advantages of simulations

This type of software can offer teachers considerable flexibility in structuring student learning and assessment. For example, a performance assessment of students' understanding of frog physiology normally can't rely on an actual frog's presence (because of the animals' expense). Therefore, students are expected to draw organs or label illustrations as part of tests. But with a tool like the virtual dissector, students can be tested exactly the way they've learned, and they can be expected to do more than simply recall the names of parts. They can be asked to identify what organs belong within particular systems, how the systems work, and so on. Another advantage of such software is that it offers prompts and access to a wealth of information, helpful hints, and even timely intermediate assessments.

Building from the ideas underlying these kinds of simulations, some companies have developed simulations that allow students to take on professional roles. For example, LavaMind **(http://www.lavamind.com/edu.html)** makes simulations that put students in charge of different businesses (the student becomes a hotel manager or a bank manager). In these simulations, students are exposed to problems that a professional might face in the real world; they must gather data and solve the problems. These kinds of simulations can be used either for regular instruction or for culminating performances.

For science classes involved in collaboration with Wild Georgia, a simulation might involve students' interacting with a web-based function that simulates the wolf habitat. They could use applets to make decisions about the habitat. For the English language arts component, however, another type of technology seems most appropriate: videoconferencing.

■■■ Videoconferencing

Video is a powerful medium enabling the teacher to bring far-off people, places, and events right into the classroom. **Videoconferencing** (Figure 6.3) shares this advantage of ordinary video and also affords learners the opportunity to interact and participate in the remote events.

Videoconferencing technology enables synchronous communication (that is, communication in real time, at the same moment) among multiple people in multiple remote locations. Videoconferencing systems vary in functionality, capability, and quality. Many schools have access to high-end equipment that can connect multiple sites for simultaneous discussions. You also have the choice of using a simpler system, consisting of a "webcam," or video camcorder with a USB connection to your computer, and free software that allows you to establish a video link across the Internet.

A simple, low-cost videoconferencing system

The following "Technology in Action" feature describes the way we used videoconferencing for the Big Bad Wolf unit, and Spotlight 6.3 explains some terms you'll encounter in discussions of videoconferencing.

Figure 6.3 An Example of Videoconferencing

Technology in Action

Videoconferencing for the Big Bad Wolf Unit

Our wolf unit is designed to use videoconferencing so that students in local school systems hundreds of miles away can see and talk with actual scientists and curators at the wolf habitat. In fact, even the actual field trip to the wildlife park can be accomplished through the video system.

▶ First, teachers can call the park, arrange a videoconferencing link, and implement the activities from their own classroom. Students can observe events at the park through the videoconferencing cameras.

▶ Next, the students explore, build their arguments, and develop their presentations.

▶ Finally, again through the videoconferencing link, students make their presentations to scientists at the park, who listen, comment, and interactively discuss the problem being addressed by the students.

Students at multiple locations can simultaneously ask questions of the scientists and discuss the events unfolding on camera. As an added feature, teachers may collaborate with each other so that classrooms from across the state address the same problem and present their own solutions to the park scientists.

This plan assumes that videoconferencing technology is readily available and working in the teacher's building. It also assumes that the remote location—in this case, Stone Mountain Park—has videoconferencing equipment and that the two systems can be connected at little or no cost. Hence, some planning is involved in this—or any other—technology. In addition to verifying that the proper equipment is available, the teacher needs to know the equipment's location, how it works, whether technical support is needed, what capabilities to provide, how to schedule access, and whether any costs are associated with use of the equipment. Of course, it's a good idea for the teacher to practice with any technology before expecting students to use it. Most teachers prefer to have a moderate level of comfort and confidence, and they usually have a backup plan in case the technology doesn't work.

▬▬ Streaming Media

Another type of technology is **streaming media,** which delivers a continuous video (or audio) feed over the Internet or computer network. We're experiencing more applications of streaming media everyday. News agencies increasingly use the technology to push up-to-the-minute information to us. In schools, we can make use of these technologies in ways that provide quality learning opportunities for students—especially when web-based controls allow teachers and learners to access, control, and otherwise

Multiple points of presence. Multiple locations can be "present" simultaneously, so that people in each location can see and hear one another through the videoconferencing system.

Continuous presence. Each end point—that is, each place where a videoconferencing camera is located—is *continuously* connected to the other end points.

Multiconferencing unit (MCU). The MCU is a piece of hardware, installed at a central location, that enables multiple people to connect via videoconferencing.

See the Videoconferencing Cookbook (**http://www.videnet .gatech.edu/cookbook**) for an extensive glossary of terms and other information about implementing this technology in your classroom.

Learning from live events

manipulate the events. In fact, Public Broadcasting Service (PBS) stations across the country are collaborating with technology companies and local school systems to develop content that can be streamed to the classroom. In addition to hardware that meets minimum requirements, you need specific software to use this technology, but in most cases the sites themselves will prompt you to acquire the necessary software.

Streaming video often involves remotely operated cameras, which are becoming more widely accessible. These cameras provide an exciting way to connect students with a distant environment suitable for learning. Informal learning environments all over the world are installing cameras for people to observe and learn from ongoing "live" events. For example, Robert Ballard, a renowned scientist who discovered the location of the *Titanic*, operates the Institute for Exploration at Mystic Aquarium in Connecticut. Teachers and students from all over the world are able to experience and learn about marine life through streaming video technology at the associated websites (**http://www.mysticaquarium.org** and **http:// www.immersionpresents.org**). Dr. Ballard invites teachers to access live video streams to see his deep ocean expeditions and explore with him how animals live in the ocean. The tools are simple to use and provide an exciting experience for students who might otherwise never see such events or interact with people like Dr. Ballard.

In addition, remotely operated vehicles (ROVs) carrying cameras enable us to bring the student learner directly into an animal's habitat and see first-hand how it lives. This technology, among others, is used in the PBS program *Voyage of the Odyssey*, which allows visitors to track the voyage of an ocean research boat and discover marine habitats up close (**http://www.pbs.org/odyssey/odyssey/odyssey_video.html**). Many activities can be developed around such technologies.

For our project at Wild Georgia, we planned to have cameras attached to multiple wolves in the observation habitat. There would also be cameras at places where wolves tended to congregate. The streaming video from these cameras would be available both to visitors at the park itself and over the Internet to "virtual" visitors.

▬▬ Video Ethograms

Video ethograms are an exciting and effective way for students to use video to learn observation skills, compile data for reports and presentations, and construct knowledge (see Spotlight 6.4). People have developed video ethograms to study animal behavior at zoos, wildlife management areas, and parks.

The English teacher has the students develop their presentation on the basis of the data collection, analysis, and interpretation experience. In this way, the teacher not only builds on the science experience, but also extends the science learning by asking students to reflect on the process they engaged in for their ethogram research, as well as the science they learned by doing it.

Table 6.2 sums up the technology components and activities in our wildlife park experience for students who can physically visit the habitat. The plan is to make similar experiences available online for "virtual" visitors across the state.

SPOTLIGHT 6.4 — **Video Ethograms**

An ethogram is a way of coding and describing behavior patterns. Scientists utilize ethograms to observe and document animal behavior. A video ethogram combines video technology with ethogram tools to improve our ability to observe and understand events.

A typical ethogram activity provides real video footage of animals in their natural habitat. Observers (in this case, classroom teachers and learners) use actual coding schematics (or ones developed in class) as shorthand to describe what they see in the video. For example, learners may code the eating habits of animals by noting the time, location, type of food, whether the animal was alone or in a group, and whether the animal ate facing or with its back to other animals.

For examples and discussion of ethograms that you can apply to on-site observations or to video footage, see the following sites:

Behavioral Advisory Group
   http://ethograms.org/

Dolphin Communication Project
   http://www.dolphincommunicationproject.org/
   ethogram.asp

School District of Black River Falls (WI): Lesson Plan Including an Ethogram
   http://www.brf.org/curriculum/maps/agedu/files/
   vetsmallanisci.htm

Racerocks Ethology Laboratory: Sample Videos to Use with Your Ethogram
   http://www.racerocks.com/racerock/education/
   ethology/ethology.htm
   http://www.racerocks.com/racerock/jason/
   ethology/pta_ethogram.html

Racerocks.com, for example, provides a complete set of online materials allowing students to conduct video observations of animals in their habitat around Vancouver Island. Another option is to visit the local park, zoo, or wildlife habitat with teams of students armed with video camcorders and notebooks. The students can videotape the animals and habitats while on their field trip, then review the video for further details later.

For our wolf unit, video ethograms provide a low-cost and effective way to address a number of standards. We designed a video ethogram in which the video is streamed through a web page, and the ethogram is provided on the same page for completion and online data storage (Figure 6.4). The students first develop an ethogram representing the behaviors they want to code and understand in the present habitat. Then they manipulate the data collected for initial interpretations of the observations (for instance, identifying the alpha male). Finally, in the culminating performance, the science teacher has the students conduct a behavioral analysis of the animals using the video ethogram.

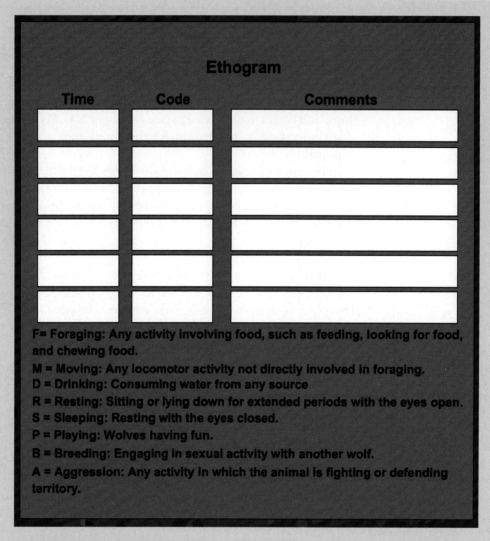

Ethogram

Time	Code	Comments

F= Foraging: Any activity involving food, such as feeding, looking for food, and chewing food.

M = Moving: Any locomotor activity not directly involved in foraging.

D = Drinking: Consuming water from any source

R = Resting: Sitting or lying down for extended periods with the eyes open.

S = Sleeping: Resting with the eyes closed.

P = Playing: Wolves having fun.

B = Breeding: Engaging in sexual activity with another wolf.

A = Aggression: Any activity in which the animal is fighting or defending territory.

Figure 6.4 **Ethogram Format for the Big Bad Wolf Unit**

Performance Assessment in a High-School English Class

Go to the Online Study Center to view the HM Video Case called **Performance Assessment: Student Presentations in a High School English Class.** Notice how the activities captured in the video vignette illustrate students fully engaged in the performance assessment to demonstrate their knowledge and understanding.

Considering the video as a model, think about how performance assessment might work in your subject area. As you ponder performance assessment, think of ways you can utilize spaces other than the classroom for students to demonstrate their knowledge.

Step 4: Create Assessments

At this point you have fully aligned objectives, instructional strategies, and technology. The next step is to fully integrate and align assessments. For your summative assessment you'll generally use one or more rubrics, which, as we noted in the chapter "Learner Needs," are scoring scales that you create and share with your students. Your rubrics should clearly describe what competence in each of the desired learning aspects will look like in the context of the culminating performance. Keep in mind, too, that students should have access to the same kinds of technologies in their assessment activities as they have in their learning activities.

Table 6.2 Technology and Instructional Activities in the Big Bad Wolf Unit

Part 1: Interdisciplinary Unit with Science Teacher	Wolves are social creatures within their pack. In order to be able to "experience" the wolves no matter where they are in their environment, the following measures will be used:
Assumptions	Each wolf will be wearing a camera. Each camera stream will be available for visitors to the habitat so they can see what the animal sees, experience the wolf's interactions with other members of the pack, and see the habitat as the wolf sees it. The video will be streamed over a wireless wide-area network and will be available online. Each wolf will also wear a global positioning system (GPS) unit. Wherever the animal is in the habitat, visitors will be able to locate it using GPS. The habitat will have "HabitatCams" located where the wolves tend to congregate the most.
Procedures	Each wolf has a GPS unit. Students will break up into two groups, and each group will go to a Yagi antenna station. The students will use the compass, antenna, and receiver to locate each wolf. Using walkie-talkies, the students at each station will communicate with each other to triangulate the location of each animal at the same time. Students will make predictions about the hierarchy and social status of the wolves in the pack. What does their proximity to the other wolves say about the social dynamics of the pack? What does their location within the habitat say about the pack's relationship to its environment? Students should think about the animals' location in the habitat (are they near water? boulders?), as well as their location in relation to the rest of the pack. Use diagrams when useful. Students will outline, organize, and construct an argument.
Part 2: Behavior Ethogram	Using the cameras the wolves carry and the cameras in the park, have the students pick one wolf (of their choice) to watch for 5 minutes. Students will complete an ethogram of their wolf's behaviors in 10-second intervals during the duration of the observation time. PocketPCs will cue the students every 10 seconds. Record all of these observations in the electronic ethogram (which is provided so that students can type data into a web interface). Students should be looking for social interactions, physical behaviors, etc. Have students make predictions about their wolf's social status in the pack. Students should feel free to take pictures with their digital cameras of anything in the habitat that they feel will help further describe their observations in their field notes.
Part 3: Field Notes and Development of Presentations	Students should have some time after visiting the wolf habitat to make entries in their field notes. Here they will use a word processor. Have them journal about their observations and their overall impressions about wolf behavior. Be sure they support their conclusions with observations. Questions to consider: How does this type of observation differ from observing in the wild? from observing a film? What frustrations might naturalists have when trying to observe wolves in the wild? Students should include a report of the season, weather, time of day, location, etc., in their field notes. Students will share their observations in small groups. Using word processing for planning, outlining, and writing, each student group will fully develop a presentation. The students will create documents that state their hypotheses, present critical elements of their arguments about wolf social interaction, and reference their sources of information. They should incorporate pictures and diagrams as appropriate.
Part 4: Videoconferencing	As a culminating performance, students will deliver their presentations to other students and, using videoconferencing, to scientists at the park.

Table 6.3 Rubric for the Culminating Performance of the Big Bad Wolf Unit				
Task	**Proficient**	**Somewhat Proficient**	**Lacks Proficiency**	**Points Awarded**
Gives oral presentations or dramatic interpretations for various purposes.	Articulates interpretations and findings in a well-structured oral presentation.	For the most part delivers well-grounded interpretations and is only at times off task.	Does not convey interpretations or provide a well-structured presentation.	
Organizes information to achieve particular purposes and to appeal to the background and interests of the audience.	Provides appropriate and highly structured information, and attends to key points of interest to engage the audience.	Provides mostly appropriate information with some structure and attends to multiple points of interest to the audience.	Lack of organization of information and inappropriate information to engage the audience.	
Shows appropriate changes in delivery (e.g., gestures, vocabulary, pace, visuals).	Able to change delivery to make specific points, key the audience to important information, and use delivery aids (visual, audio, multimedia) to deliver message.	Able at times to change delivery to make specific points; some key points are delivered using some delivery aids (visual, audio, multimedia).	Unable to change delivery to make specific points; key points are delivered without using well-developed delivery aids (visual, audio, multimedia).	
Uses language for dramatic effect.	Uses language for dramatic effect at appropriate times.	Sometimes uses language for dramatic effect.	Does not use language for dramatic effect at appropriate times.	
Uses rubrics as assessment tools.	Uses an appropriate rubric for formative and summative assessment, and to measure progress.	Uses a rubric for summative assessment, but not continuously.	Does not use an appropriate rubric.	
Responds to oral communications with questions, challenges, or affirmations.	Continuously and appropriately responds to oral communications with useful information and data.	Often responds to oral communications, for the most part with useful information and data.	Does not respond to oral communications in a meaningful way.	
Uses multimedia in presentation.	Uses multimedia to deliver information backed with data in a way that engages the audience.	Often uses multimedia to deliver some information backed with data.	Does not use multimedia in ways that engage the audience or deliver a clear, well-grounded message.	
			Total Score	

Using rubrics

Table 6.3 shows a rubric for assessing students' presentations in our Big Bad Wolf example. Think about how you might adapt this rubric for similar problem-solving activities.

In some cases, you may want to use additional assessment instruments beyond the primary performance assessment, such as quizzes and reflections to provide you with important information about your students' learning. Say, for example, that, for the primary culminating performance for the unit, students will work in groups to create a floor plan and cost estimate for

Additional assessments at the culminating stage

retiling your classroom. You may decide to supplement your assessment of the floor plans with one or two mathematical tasks that the students complete individually to demonstrate their understanding of area and perimeter.

You may also want to use some form of preassessment or diagnostic assessment before the culminating performance begins, to determine whether the students are prepared to learn through the experience. If the students aren't prepared to formulate new ideas and generalize knowledge to new situations, they will struggle.

Formative assessment may also be appropriate during the culminating performance. This would allow you to provide feedback to the students so that they can revise their work before it becomes a public artifact. The formative assessment could be as simple as your observing certain focused aspects of the students' learning; or it could be more formal, such as having students turn in a draft of their final product for feedback. By their very nature, multiday tasks, such as building an argument and planning a presentation, offer teachers the opportunity to engage in continuous feedback and adjust the instruction as needed.

Summary

The culminating performance has two critical functions. First, it's an opportunity for learners to apply their knowledge in a real or simulated environment and show that they can generalize their knowledge to new situations. Second, for the teacher, the culminating performance is a powerful assessment and feedback mechanism.

The design of a culminating performance follows the four-step process of stating learning objectives, selecting instructional strategies, choosing possible technologies, and creating assessment tools.

Objectives typically center on the higher levels of Bloom's taxonomy: analysis, synthesis, and evaluation. Instructional strategies often include simulation, problem solving, or cooperative learning. Technologies are selected to support the desired learning in meaningful and authentic ways.

Formative assessment measures may be embedded throughout the learning continuum, with a final "grading" of the culminating performance with a rubric. If the lesson is designed well, all the parts align with one another and with state or national standards, and the culminating performance itself becomes an occasion for further learning.

Resources

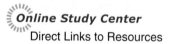
Online Study Center
    Direct Links to Resources

LEARNING STANDARDS

All state and national standards are available online.

Compendium of Standards and Benchmarks
http://www.mcrel.org/standards-benchmarks
    A good source for national standards and related resources.

Developing Educational Standards
http://edstandards.org/Standards.html
    Offers links to learning standards by state.

OBJECTIVES

Northeastern University Educational Technology Center: Learning Objectives
http://www.edtech.neu.edu/teachingsupport/assessment/general/learnob
    There are many online resources to assist with the writing of learning objectives. This one provides excellent guidance to teachers.

LEARNING THEORY

You can locate useful resources on learning theory from research labs, authors' web pages, and societies supporting the work of a particular theorist. See "Resources" in our chapter "Learner Needs." A few examples aligned with this chapter include the following:

Authentic Learning
http://chd.gse.gmu.edu/immersion/knowledgebase/strategies/constructivism/authentic.htm

> A brief summary from the Helen A. Kellar Institute at George Mason University, with links for further exploration.

Collaborative Learning Theory
http://chd.gse.gmu.edu/immersion/knowledgebase/strategies/constructivism/collaborative.htm

> Another useful site from the Kellar Institute.

How People Learn: Brain, Mind, Experience, and School
http://www.nap.edu/books/0309070368/html/

> Online text of a book from the Commission on Behavioral and Social Sciences and Education.

SIMULATIONS

To find many high-quality, free simulation resources, search online with the term "k12 simulation." Here are a few examples:

Funderstanding Roller Coaster
http://www.funderstanding.com/k12/coaster

LavaMind
http://www.lavamind.com/edu.html

Partnerships to Advance Learning in Science: Java Simulations
http://www.pals.iastate.edu/simulations

VIDEOCONFERENCING

The following projects offer interesting examples of videoconferencing that you can incorporate into the classroom:

NASA Glenn Learning Technologies Project
http://www.grc.nasa.gov/WWW/K-12

Wild Dolphin Societies
http://www.ri.net/RIGeo/rigea/earthwatch/earthwatch02/dolphinhome.html

STREAMING VIDEO

These sites provide streaming video for educational uses; also check with your local PBS station.

Georgia Public Broadcasting: Teacher Toolbox
http://www.gpb.org/public/education/toolbox/index.jsp

WGBH
http://www.wgbh.org

INTEGRATING ASSESSMENT WITH INSTRUCTION

Balanced Assessment
http://balancedassessment.concord.org

> This site provides a complete overview and useful resources for understanding the Balanced Assessment in Mathematics (BAM) program and its theoretical foundations.

Bellingham (WA) Public Schools: Seventh-Grade Research Investigation Module
http://www.bham.wednet.edu/studentgal/onlineresearch/7th/Kennewick_Man

> A useful example of a learning unit that integrates assessment into instruction.

case
STUDY

Designing a Living Room

An elementary-school teacher needs to teach her students about area and perimeter but worries that they may forget the basic number skills they've been struggling with throughout the semester. She decides to engage them in a real-world situation that will require them to design a living room for a home. The culminating performance will ask students to act as design consultants whom the homeowners have invited to bid on the job. They are given a budget and told that the living room will be an addition to the existing home. They can choose any size or shape they want, as long as they stay within budget for flooring, wallpaper or paint, and furniture.

The teacher is very excited about this project, but she also realizes that the culminating performance will be complex. The students will produce a floor plan on graph paper, a booklet that helps describe what the room will look like, and a breakdown of expenses. Given that the students haven't yet engaged in a project of this scale and that it involves considerable learning of new skills and technology, the teacher chooses a few tasks to use as intermediate assessments. For formative evaluation, she decides, she'll have students present to each other in class; then, for the final presentations, she'll invite an architect (a parent of one of the students) to come in and help discuss the plans.

In thinking about technology for the project, the teacher decides that she can have students engage in activities with spreadsheet software. There are computer applets for exploring area and perimeter, and students can also visit actual home improvement and furniture websites to determine prices.

Questions for Reflection and Discussion

1. At this stage, what's missing from this teacher's lesson plan?
2. In her rubric for this assignment, how might the teacher describe the criteria for assessing the students' performance?
3. What issues should the teacher think about in preparing to use the technology?

Meet the Standards

Online Study Center
Standards
Find more resources online to help you with standards.

We've aligned this chapter with three NETS teacher standards for designing learning opportunities and applying technology, as listed in "Standards to Guide Your Preparation" at the start of the chapter. Look back at those standards now.

The culminating performance is ideally a learning activity and a performance assessment combined in one event. Students have an opportunity to demonstrate their knowledge in an applied context, while you as the teacher assess their learning.

One way to approach designing your first culminating performance is to use an environment outside the classroom. Think of a project taking place locally: a park being built, the renovation of a downtown building—there are many possibilities. Choose one such environment and think about how you might use it for a culminating performance. Address the following questions:

▶ What kind of activity might work? Provide a brief overview.
▶ How could you engage your students in this kind of activity to demonstrate knowledge? Write four learning objectives as expected outcomes.
▶ Design the actual activity in detail. How would students demonstrate their knowledge and skill development?
▶ How would the diverse backgrounds of students be engaged in a meaningful way?
▶ How would technology play a role in supporting the activity or facilitating the students' demonstration of understanding?

Chapter 7

Guided Learning Activities

ISTE NETS

Teachers

► Plan for the management of technology resources within the context of learning activities.

► Plan strategies to manage student learning in a technology-enhanced environment.

► Apply technology to develop students' higher-order skills and creativity.

Prospective teachers

► Differentiate between appropriate and inappropriate uses of technology for teaching and learning while using electronic resources to design and implement learning activities.

OTHER RELEVANT STANDARDS

National Association for the Education of Young Children (2006)

► Children have opportunities to experience technology collaboratively with their peers, by themselves, and with a teacher or parent.

► Technology is used to extend learning within the classroom and to integrate and enrich the curriculum.

Association for Educational Communications and Technology (2000)

► *Analyzing:* process of defining what is to be learned and the context in which it is to be learned

► *Designing:* process of specifying how it is to be learned

► *Developing:* process of authoring and producing the instructional materials

► *Implementing:* actually using the materials and strategies in context

Guided learning activities provide the learner with a transitional period between the initiating activity and the culminating performance. Students are "guided" through the application and refinement of knowledge and skills that have been introduced in the initiating activity. In this period, the learner applies his or her newly developed understandings and knowledge.

Using scaffolds in guided learning

Typically, instructional strategies in the guided learning phase include discussion, problem solving, instructional games, experiments and hands-on learning, and collaborative learning. Guided learning activities also include support features called scaffolds (see Spotlight 7.1) to assist learners in developing their new understandings. Guided learning activities, regardless of the form they may take, require deliberate planning and careful control on the teacher's part so that the scaffolds provide substantial structure in the beginning and then decrease or "fade out" over time. In guided learning, scaffolds may include tools and strategies introduced by the teacher, particular kinds of questions that the teacher asks, and certain kinds of activities that students must complete as a byproduct of their learning.

As an example of the fading of structures over time, consider a typical series of laboratory experiments for middle-school students. In the first experiment, the teacher includes a good deal of structure, so that students learn safety rules and proper laboratory procedures. Over time, the teacher decreases the structure and reduces the amount of guidance, allowing for more inquiry-based lab experiences. By the end of the unit, the students aren't following a script, but instead are truly investigating a scientific hypothesis.

Assessment in the guided learning activity phase may draw from or reflect instructional strategies embedded in the learning activities.

SPOTLIGHT 7.1

Scaffolding

Scaffolding for most of us evokes images of the wood and metal frameworks that rise along the sides of structures to help contractors construct buildings. In education, scaffolding assists learners by guiding them through the learning process. Hannafin, Hill, and McCarthy (2000) provide four principal categories of scaffolds.

- *Conceptual scaffolds* help learners make decisions during their learning activities, such as which models to apply to solve a problem.
- *Metacognitive scaffolds* help learners activate prior knowledge and construct new knowledge using the learning strategies of the guided learning activity.
- *Procedural scaffolds* help learners complete tasks embedded in guided learning activities.
- *Strategic scaffolds* help learners think through and consider multiple ways to solve a problem, host a discussion, present an argument, or otherwise utilize strategies common to guided learning.

Scaffolds may be as simple as the questions in our "Meet the Standards" at the end of each chapter. These questions "scaffold" you through a performance assessment aligned with standards. Scaffolds can also be very complex, such as those embedded in software programs like TurboTax, which guide you through intricate details of the tax code with minimum difficulty.

Clearly, the assessment continues to be based on the objectives and expected outcomes of the activity as identified in the initial phases of planning the unit.

As always, the decisions about which technology to use are aligned with the instructional strategies and content of the learning activity.

Designing the Guided Learning Activity

Table 7.1 shows the key elements of a guided learning activity. To help you create these elements, we suggest the same four-step process that we described in our chapter on the culminating performance. If you follow these four steps, your end result will be a guided learning activity that is based on the standards you're trying to meet, ensures that you're helping students develop key content knowledge, integrates technology in ways that support your learning goals, and includes effectively designed and applied assessments.

As a running example in this chapter, we'll once again use the Big Bad Wolf unit, part of a series of instructional programs that we developed with Bellsouth and Jim Fowler.

Step 1: State Objectives

While designing the guided learning activity, we assume that you'll continue to identify appropriate learning standards and restate these standards as objectives, a critical process which we introduced in the preceding chapter. We also want you to think of all the learning activities as a continuum. In other words, the objectives of guided learning activities should be aligned not only with learning standards, but also with the standards and

Learning activities as a continuum

Table 7.1 Elements of a Guided Learning Activity	
Purposes of guided learning	• Teacher guides learners as they engage in scaffolded activities designed for knowledge development • Learners make progress toward application of knowledge in the culminating performance. • Learners practice skills and develop content knowledge to further their understandings
Three key components of learning objectives	1. *Behavior.* A description of what the student will know and be able to do ("Students will be able to . . . ," "Students will know . . . ," "Students will understand that . . . ") 2. *Conditions.* The conditions under which the student will perform the task 3. *Criteria.* The criteria for evaluating student performance
Appropriate levels of Bloom's taxonomy for guided learning	• Comprehension • Application • Analysis
Useful verbs for writing guided learning objectives	Summarize, describe, explain, paraphrase, interpret, contrast, predict, associate, distinguish, estimate, differentiate, discuss, extend, generalize, apply, demonstrate, calculate, complete, compute, illustrate, examine, modify, relate, change, classify, experiment, discover, predict, extend

objectives of both previous and future activities. This alignment will promote learners' smooth transition from the initiating activity to the application of knowledge in the culminating performance.

Technology should be used to enhance the instruction as well as to help move students from guided learning to self-directed learning. Our examples in this chapter begin with more structure and teacher-led learning, and move toward more student-centered activities. We present this as one typical instructional pathway, but there are certainly other pathways that don't include as many teacher-led elements. The most important goal, regardless of approach, is that learners exit this series of activities prepared for their culminating performance experiences.

■ Big Bad Wolf Lesson 1: Writing

To build from their initial understandings in meaningful ways, students should have the chance to explore their own questions about wolves in a thoughtful and data-driven manner. The first lesson activity allows students to explore topics that are personally meaningful to them and to learn about collecting and using credible information in ways that will transfer to any other topic they'd like to learn more about.

For this lesson we identified the following pertinent standards:

Standards for the Big Bad Wolf lesson 1

7th-Grade Science: Life Science. Students will examine the dependence of organisms on one another and their environments. Students

- ▶ Recognize that changes in environmental conditions can affect the survival of both individuals and entire species.
- ▶ Categorize relationships between organisms that are competitive or mutually beneficial.

7th-Grade English Language Arts: Writing. The student produces writing that establishes an appropriate organizational structure, sets a context and engages the reader, maintains a coherent focus throughout, and provides a satisfying closure. The student

- ▶ Selects a focus, an organizational structure, and a point of view based on purpose, genre expectations, audience, length, and format requirements.
- ▶ Writes texts of a length appropriate to address the topic or tell the story.
- ▶ Uses appropriate structures to ensure coherence (e.g., transition elements).
- ▶ Supports statements and claims with anecdotes, descriptions, facts and statistics, and specific examples.

7th-Grade English Language Arts: Writing. The student uses research and technology to support writing. The student

- ▶ Identifies topics, asks and evaluates questions, and develops ideas leading to inquiry, investigation, and research.
- ▶ Gives credit for both quoted and paraphrased information in a bibliography by using a consistent and sanctioned format and methodology for citations.
- ▶ Documents sources.

These standards led to the following objectives for the lesson:

Objectives for lesson 1

Students will

▶ Choose from a list of possible topics, or find a topic of their own interest, to explore in greater depth.
▶ Ask relevant questions about their topic.
▶ Identify and use information from credible sources on the Internet and computer-based software to answer their inquiries.
▶ Write a report, given time and space limitations, that expresses their point of view in an organized, structured manner and that engages the reader.
▶ Provide formative feedback to each other using a predeveloped rubric that evaluates evidence intended to support their argument.

■ Big Bad Wolf Lesson 2: The Wolf on Trial!

From early childhood, students have been taught to fear the Big Bad Wolf through stories, fairy tales, and the media. This activity puts the notion of the Big Bad Wolf on trial by giving the students a mystery to solve that challenges these early and long-held notions. Students use emergent technologies to role-play different characters and solve the mystery of who killed Farmer Brown's hens. Through collaborative learning, role-playing, inquiry, problem solving, and decision making, students discover that it's highly unlikely that the Big Bad Wolf is the culprit.

We decided that the lesson should address these performance standards:

Standards for lesson 2

7th-Grade Science: Characteristics of Science. Students will use standard safety practices for all classroom laboratory and field investigations. Students will

▶ Follow correct procedures for use of scientific apparatus.
▶ Demonstrate appropriate techniques in all laboratory situations.

7th-Grade Science: Characteristics of Science. Students will investigate the characteristics of scientific knowledge and how that knowledge is achieved. Students will apply the following to scientific concepts:

▶ As prevailing theories are challenged by new information, scientific knowledge may change.

7th-Grade English Language Arts: Listening, Speaking, Viewing. The student participates in student-to-teacher, student-to-student, and group verbal interactions. The student

▶ Asks relevant questions.
▶ Responds to questions with appropriate information.
▶ Actively solicits another person's comments or opinions.
▶ Offers own opinion forcefully without domineering.
▶ Responds appropriately to comments and questions.
▶ Gives reasons in support of opinions expressed.
▶ Clarifies, illustrates, or expands on a response when asked to do so.

▶ Employs a group decision-making technique such as brainstorming or a problem-solving sequence (e.g., recognizes problem, defines problem, identifies possible solutions, selects optimal solution, implements solution, evaluates solution).

We then translated the standards into these objectives:

Objectives for lesson 2

Students will

▶ Research the assumption that all wolves are bad.
▶ Use role-playing to learn about different aspects of life in the 1800s.
▶ Use problem-solving skills to ask relevant questions and respond to questions with appropriate information given a variety of situations and conditions.
▶ Demonstrate the extent to which their understanding of important concepts has progressed to requisite levels by communicating and collaborating with other students to solve a problem and make decisions.

Step 2: Select Instructional Strategies

In planning the culminating performance, step 2 led you to think about how learners would apply and demonstrate their knowledge. Now, as you design guided learning activities, you need to focus on how the learner will *construct* knowledge about the topic of interest. In most cases, meeting the overall goals of guided learning will take a series of activities based on a number of instructional strategies.

Choice of Strategies

Instructional strategies for guided learning activities characteristically change as the learner progresses toward the culminating performance (Newby et al., 2006). You want learners to become increasingly active and responsible for their own learning. Keeping in mind the goals of the pre-designed culminating performance, you gradually reduce the scaffolding and let students take over.

Instructional strategies change not only over time, but also according to the goals you're trying to meet. Problem solving, for example, looks very different in math than in science or language arts. Strategies also vary within subject area depending on the concepts (simple or complex) that are being learned. As an example, instructional games become increasingly complex with graduation to higher grade levels. Hence, various dimensions of the learning environment (grade level, content) may dictate the amount of structure that needs to be built into the activities in order for the learner to meet the stated objectives.

Instructional strategies for guided learning activities commonly include

Common strategies for guided learning

▶ Discussion
▶ Inquiry
▶ Problem solving
▶ Collaborative learning
▶ Instructional games

◼ Strategies for Learning About the Wolf

For the Big Bad Wolf unit, we developed a detailed series of activities that incorporates several of the instructional strategies just mentioned. See how many strategies you can identify.

Lesson 1: Writing Have students write an essay on a topic chosen from the following ideas:

► You have learned that wolves are social animals. How are the social dynamics, relationships, and community of a pack similar to those of a human family?

► How have wolves been portrayed in literature, mythology, and the media? How has this affected their treatment over the years? (*Note:* There are *very few* known cases of a wolf killing a human.)

► How has the demise of the gray wolf affected other living systems? Include a food web to represent your findings. (For example, in Yellowstone National Park, the removal of wolves has increased the elk, antelope, and deer populations, increasing the destruction of vegetation and habitat, which in turn decreases other herbivorous species, such as beaver and rabbit.)

Lesson 2: The Wolf on Trial! The teacher/facilitator will introduce the scenario: Something has been raiding Farmer Brown's hen house. For five mornings in a row, Farmer Brown has woken early to find his hen house raided and another dead hen. He suspects it is wolves. Students will work in small groups to discover the true culprit. Each student or small group of students will have a particular role. The following are examples of the roles that will be assigned:

► Farmer Brown
► The alpha wolf (a.k.a. the Big Bad Wolf)
► Other wolves in the pack
► Local hunter
► Marshal/sheriff
► Naturalist

Students will have information from the perspective of their own roles, but not information relevant to any other roles. For example, the student with the role of the alpha wolf will have information relevant to the hunting patterns of wolves (what they eat, preferred prey, and how often they eat), as well as behavior patterns (attitude towards humans, sleep patterns, social behaviors, etc.). By providing only partial information to each of the students, this activity necessitates that students work together to uncover information that will let them solve this crime. Once they have collected all the necessary evidence, they can stage a trial in the classroom.

Step 3: Choose Technologies

The best choices of technologies are those that can be used throughout the learning unit. Using the same technologies to engage learners across the continuum of activities has great advantages. One major benefit is that you don't have to invest as much class time teaching the basics of the hardware or software.

SPOTLIGHT 7.2　Technology Ideas for Guided Learning

E-mail or chat　　Students can use threaded e-mail discussions or chat to discuss, debate, journal, and keep a record of events.

Videoconferencing　　Students can use videoconferencing to see live events or speak with people in remote areas. This technology can help them share ideas or access help to solve a problem.

Probes　　Students can use electronic probes connected to laptops to collect data from local or remote locations.

Spreadsheets　　Students can use spreadsheet software to record data, make calculations using formulas, run "what ifs," and graphically represent data.

For additional ideas, see the following websites:

Awesome Library:　　http://www.awesomelibrary.org/Classroom/Technology/
Integrating Technology　　Integrating_Technology/Integrating_Technology.html
NASA Quest　　http://quest.nasa.gov
Telecollaborate!　　http://nschubert.home.mchsi.com

Using the same software for multiple purposes

If you do choose the same technology, there should be a synchronous flow of its application across the activities. For example, students may be able to use Kidspiration, concept-mapping software that allows them to combine text and pictures (see **http://www.kidspiration.com).** Initially, the software can help them capture the "facts" about wolves that they think they already know and guide their decisions about questions to be asked. In the next phase of the project, the students can use the software to capture true facts about wolves. Then they can use Kidspiration to collect data as a group and organize it to solve the mystery of the hen house raids. Spotlight 7.2 describes several other kinds of technology suitable for guided learning activities.

For the Big Bad Wolf lessons, we developed the following suggested list of technologies:

Technologies for the Big Bad Wolf lessons

Lesson 1: Writing

- ▶ Resource box
- ▶ Computer with Internet access
- ▶ Concept-mapping software to organize the report
- ▶ Internet
- ▶ Library (via online access)
- ▶ Word processing software, tablet computers, or PDAs for journaling

Lesson 2: The Wolf on Trial!

- ▶ Wolf habitat with cameras and global positioning system (GPS) units. If possible, we wanted the students to take a field trip to a habitat where they could observe wolves in the wild and collect their own data about wolf behavior.
- ▶ Concept-mapping software to organize the information that each team member is collecting

Figure 7.1 Sample Headline for the Big Bad Wolf Lesson

▶ GPS-enabled Pocket PCs or PDAs for data collection and communication. The data collected on these can be uploaded to a server that the students can then access from the classroom. PDAs can also be used to brief students on the roles they are playing: for example, one student's PDA would have information about the local hunter; another's would have information about the marshal.

▶ Laptops or PDAs for use as field notebooks

In the final lesson, students might also use simple page layout software to produce their own newspaper or broadside about the wolf on trial (Figure 7.1).

Step 4: Create Assessments

Throughout the guided learning phase, assessments are used to gauge students' understanding as they prepare to undertake the culminating performance. Numerous sources (for instance, Kulieke et al., 1990; Valencia, Heibert, & Afflerbach, 1994) provide guidance for assessing students. Experts generally agree on several points.

Guidelines for good assessment

▶ The assessments need to align clearly with stated objectives and learning strategies.

▶ The assessments should measure what students know and can do as they the develop knowledge and apply skills in authentic contexts.

Assessment in the Elementary Grades: Formal and Informal Literacy Assessment

One pitfall in using assessment measures is relegating their use to the end of a unit (summative assessment) or occasional snapshots along the way (such as quizzes). There are many more powerful ways of using assessment processes, especially formative assessment, as we described in our chapter "Learner Needs."

Now is a good time to view the HM Video Case called **Assessment in the Elementary Grades: Formal and Informal Literacy Assessment**, which you can find at the Online Study Center. The video provides insight into one teacher's use of classroom assessment to gauge student learning. How might you use similar techniques to determine whether students are making good progress toward the culminating performance of the unit?

Experimenting with simulated physical systems

▶ Assessment should be continuous, especially when used interactively as part of discussion, questioning, and performances in class.

▶ Assessments should measure cognitive processes or abilities defined in the objectives, whether formally or informally.

▶ Students should play an active role and take responsibility for using assessment data and evidence to monitor and improve their own learning.

■ Technologies for Assessment

Because technology is an important part of both instruction and assessment, we provide several brief examples and then describe at length the assessments we developed for the Big Bad Wolf unit. First, you may want to review Figure 5.7 as a refresher about how we align technology choices with assessment. Note that the following examples involve *active* assessments, avoiding the pitfall of using computers merely for passive response testing, such as multiple choice.

▰▰▰ Riverdeep Physics Explorer

Logal Physics Explorer from Riverdeep (see **http://www.riverdeep.net**) provides students with a simulation environment in which they can safely investigate and manipulate variables using a variety of models. Students develop an understanding of physical systems through experimentation. Galileo's pendulum experiments, for example, provide opportunities for students to figure out what variables affect the period of motion. Student work samples can be collected and assessed for the following qualities:

▶ How systematically students consider each possible independent variable

▶ Whether they systematically control other variables while they test a hypothesis

▶ Whether they can formulate quantitative relationships between the independent variables and the dependent variables

▰▰▰ Virtual Reality Modeling Language

Virtual Reality Modeling Language (VRML) is a viable option even for the one-computer classroom. VRML (also known as X3D or Web3D) provides three-dimensional graphical representations with which students can interact. Teachers can use predeveloped and freely available VRML modules to lead discussions on a variety of topics and determine to what extent the students know the content or have the requisite knowledge to progress to the next learning activities.

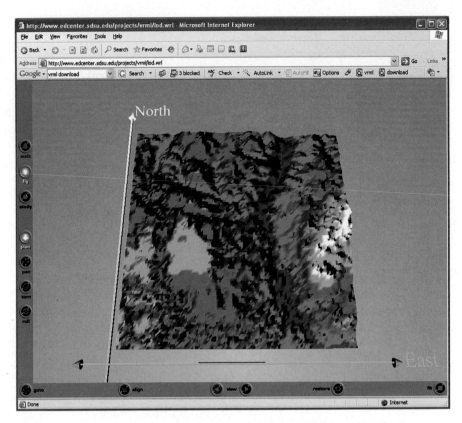

Figure 7.2 Using VRML for Teaching Maps and Legends in Elementary School Using the mouse, students can manipulate the map to show different views of the terrain.

Interactive geography learning

One strategy for using VRML in a one-computer classroom was developed by an elementary-school teacher[1] who used to teach maps and legends with a traditional large wall map. He found that his students struggled to picture the colors as a geographic representation of an area depicted on the map. He now uses a VRML website, with a predeveloped color map, to demonstrate maps and legends, and then asks a series of questions to see if his students have acquired the knowledge and can apply it when given various views of the map (see Figure 7.2).

Another elementary-school teacher[2] designed a learning activity using QuickTime Virtual Reality (QTVR) technology. Her students use the discovery method of learning to identify characteristics of biomes by using websites that are virtual sites. These sites allow students to select regions on the North American continent—taking a panoramic view of various sites—to collect information on terrain, plants, and draw conclusions about climate (see Figure 7.3).

[1] Glyn Ellis of the Valdosta City School System in Valdosta, Georgia; see **http://www.teacherresourcebank.com/VRML/LessonPlans/MapsEllis/maps.htm**

[2] Laura Williams, Colquitt County High School, Georgia; see **http://www .teacherresourcebank.com/VRML/LessonPlans/LauraWilliams/Biomes.htm**

Figure 7.3 **Portion of a Panoramic Photo Showing Biomes** Students can view the photos to collect information about plants and terrain, as well as speculate about the climate.

Students team up for a WebQuest

WebQuests

WebQuests have become a popular tool for using the Internet effectively in learning and assessment (see, for example, **http://4teachers.org)**. A **WebQuest,** to put it simply, is "a form of project-based and problem-based learning in which the resources (and often the tasks) are located on the Web" (R*TEC Teachers, 2005). One good example of a WebQuest useful for assessment is the Roaring 20s WebQuest, in which students team up to create a commemorative newspaper about the 1920s, including news articles, a feature story, a mock interview, a political cartoon, and more (see **http://projects.edtech.sandi.net/morse/roaring)**. A WebQuest site either provides the necessary resources for students or offers links to other sites where they can find the information they need.

Choosing Technology-Based Assessments

When choosing your own technology-based assessments, you may need to rely on one of two approaches. So far we've focused on developing original assessments aligned with your newly created learning activities and learning units. The other approach involves finding preexisting examples of technology used for assessment. Here you have two options:

1. You can search the Internet for websites dedicated to the topic. This approach can be frustrating because of the large number of sites

dedicated to electronic portfolios, technology, and assessment. If you choose this route, try using a quality search engine, such as Google **(http://www.google.com),** with the following search terms:

▶ learning assessment technology
▶ technology "learning assessment"
▶ assessment "learning technology"
▶ technology "learning assessment" -electronic -portfolio (The last two words are preceded by hyphens to exclude them from the search.)

To find the sites you're looking for—ones that offer specific examples of using technology for assessment—you'll need to review several sublevels of the Google search results.

2. You can search for learning activities that use technology. They're relatively easy to locate, but the challenge is determining how you can use the technology, not just for a learning activity, but for an assessment as well.

Technology in Action

Assessment for the Big Bad Wolf Unit

For the Big Bad Wolf unit, we developed the following assessment techniques:

Lesson 1: Writing

Each student's essay should thoughtfully cover a new topic that the student is interested in exploring in depth. The essay should follow an organized structure, adhere to standard writing conventions, and include information that the student has gathered from outside resources (resource box, library, Internet, and so on). The students should cite their sources and use examples, statistics, and research data to support their statements.

Possible technology choices:

▶ Computers and word processing software
▶ Internet access
▶ Access to online library catalogs and digital libraries

Lesson 2: The Wolf on Trial!

Students should work collaboratively to solve the mystery. Exemplary students will talk to other students, ask appropriate questions, and give appropriate responses when asked about their own role. Students should be able to present the information they've gathered and provide a rationale for conclusions based on this information, not on preconceptions.

Possible technology choices:

▶ Computer and note-taking software
▶ Presentation software

The preceding "Technology in Action" feature shows how we integrated technology into assessment for the Big Bad Wolf unit. Notice that we give multiple technology options for each of the three lessons.

Summary

Guided learning activities provide students with the opportunity to develop their skills and knowledge in increasingly more student-owned activities. Guided learning forms a critical transition between the initiating activity and the culminating performance.

Using a backward design approach, you begin planning guided learning activities by focusing on the goals of the culminating performance—how the learner will demonstrate knowledge through simulated settings. Hence, guided learning activities provide opportunities for increased student ownership in the learning process and a higher level of relevance as the students will see the goals they are working toward. This is accomplished through sharing knowledge (as in discussion), investigating to acquire information (inquiry), applying solutions to context-specific situations (problem solving), practicing (instructional games or simulations), and learning with others (collaborative learning).

Throughout this stage of learning, technology can improve a teacher's ability to develop interactive activities. Problem-solving software, for example, can scaffold learning by supplying mental models for approaching a problem. Productivity software, such as word processors, spreadsheets, and concept-mapping programs, helps students construct papers or presentations. These products of the learning activities can also provide opportunities for teachers to assess student learning, whether formally or informally, and the assessments then allow the teacher to make necessary changes in instruction.

Once you've developed the culminating activity and guided learning activities, you're nearly finished with your instructional design. The next step is to develop the very first activities in the sequence—those that initiate learning.

Resources

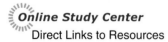
Online Study Center
Direct Links to Resources

Concept to Classroom: Inquiry-Based Learning
http://www.thirteen.org/edonline/concept2class/
inquiry/index.html
> Answers the question: What is inquiry-based learning? Also provides resources including video clips of classroom activities.

Cooperative Learning Classroom Research
http://xenia.media.mit.edu/~andyd/mindset/design/
clc_rsch.html
> Provides definitions of the classroom strategy, explains why a teacher may use it, and lists references for further inquiry on the topic.

North Central Regional Educational Laboratory: Integrating Assessment and Instruction in Ways That Support Learning
http://www.ncrel.org/sdrs/areas/issues/methods/
assment/as500.htm
> Resources on assessment compiled by one of the federally supported regional research labs.

Teacher Tap: Project, Problem, and Inquiry-Based Learning
http://eduscapes.com/tap/topic43.htm
> Provides an introduction to teaching with these three classroom strategies and explains the differences among them.

The Why Files: Science Behind the News
http://whyfiles.org
> Provides information about the science behind headline stories in the news.

case
STUDY

Geometric Transformations

As an example of different ways in which you might want to use technology to meet the goals of a lesson, consider the following sequence of lessons focused on helping young students learn about geometric transformations. The desired outcomes of the lessons are that students will know both the formal language involved and how to apply that language to their own activities. Specifically, they'll learn about translation (slides), rotation (turns), and reflection (flips). In our model, lessons 2 through 4 constitute guided learning. Lesson 1 can be considered the initiating activity, and lesson 5 is the culminating performance.

Lesson 1. The teacher wants the students to begin understanding how shapes fit together to make new shapes. Students should come to see that three basic transformations can be used to turn one shape into another. The teacher begins by having students create their own set of paper tangrams (puzzles with geometrical moving pieces), which they'll then use to solve puzzles. These initial paper-based puzzles include outlines of the shapes of all the pieces to include (see Figure 7.4).

Lesson 2. Once students have had an opportunity to use the paper-based tangrams, the teacher sets up a center in the classroom in which they can use computer-based tangrams to solve a series of puzzles (Figure 7.5). By moving the lesson to the computer, the teacher is free to provide less guidance, because the computer can provide hints to students who are stuck and has a number of puzzles that don't require copying. The teacher's job at this point is to start engaging the students in discussion about how they're solving the puzzles—are they rotating, reflecting, or translating? Do the shapes change when this happens? What changes?

Lesson 3. The teacher debriefs the students about the work they've been doing with the tangrams. They talk about how they have to rotate pieces and reflect pieces to get them to fit in the puzzles. She also has them talk about what happens when they drag the pieces. Throughout the discussion, the teacher asks them what changes about the shape when they do each of these things. She can use overhead manipulatives to test the students' theories about whether the elements that define the shape need to change. She can also have them visit the InterMath dictionary (Figure 7.6) to copy definitions and see real-world examples of transformations. Once the students seem to understand what happens when a shape is translated (slid), rotated (turned), or reflected (flipped), the teacher can move on to the next activity.

Lesson 4. Students create puzzles with their tangrams, then work with partners on the computer to solve the puzzles. The key element is that

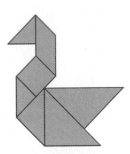

Swan

Bunny

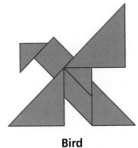

Bird

Figure 7.4 Simple Outlined Tangram Shapes
Source: Based on illustrations at http://www.enchantedlearning.com/crafts/chinesenewyear/tangram

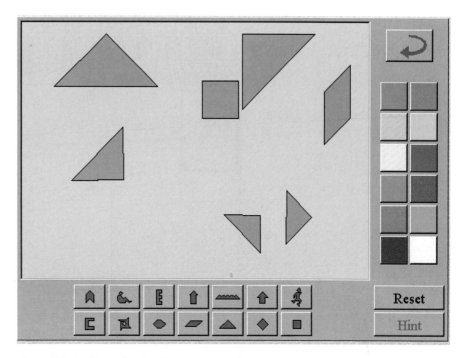

Figure 7.5 An Example of a Computer-Based Tangram Program
Source: National Library of Manipulatives for Interactive Mathematics. Available:
http://nlvm.usu.edu/en/nav/category_g_2_t_3.html

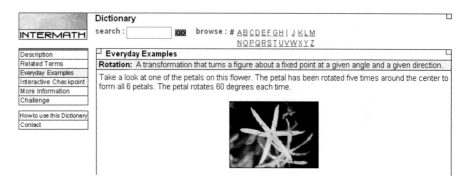

Figure 7.6 Screen from the InterMath Dictionary This online source (more formally called the Interactive Mathematics Dictionary) includes real-world examples of mathematical concepts. Explore it yourself at **http://intermath.coe.uga.edu/dictnary**
Source: Available: http://intermath.coe.uga.edu/dictnary/everyday.asp?termid=313

students can't *show* each other a puzzle; instead, they must use mathematical terminology to *describe* it. The computer is used because of its motivational aspects and because it ensures that students can't simply put down the paper with their puzzle on it and fit the pieces in. It's the teacher's job to monitor the activities and make sure students are using appropriate language.

Lesson 5. Students play the Tumbling Tetronimoes game (Figure 7.7) from Investigations in Number, Data, and Space, a curriculum developed

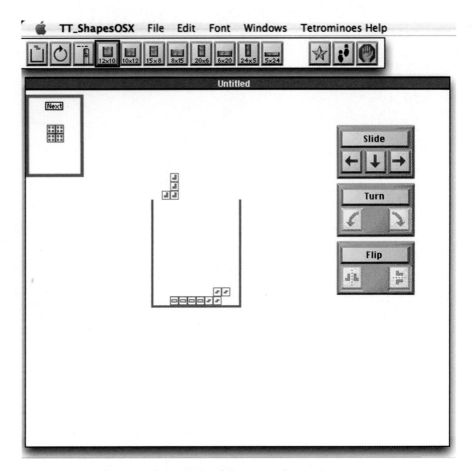

Figure 7.7 **Sample Screen from the Tumbling Tetronimoes Game**

at TERC **(http://www.terc.edu).** In this game, the students use common mathematical terms to play a video game similar to the now-classic game of Tetris. This not only serves as a culminating performance for students who've been learning about transformation, but also ties into other math concepts commonly learned at this age. Once the teacher sees that the students have a solid understanding of transformations, she can begin to ask harder questions which focus on building number sense. These might include questions about whether it's possible to get a score that isn't a multiple of four, which pieces might be easiest to fit together, and which board shapes might be easier or harder than the 12" × 10" board that the game begins with. Such questions tie geometry to number sense and area, and also engage students in making and testing conjectures. These are all important learning outcomes in elementary mathematics.

Questions for Reflection and Discussion

Throughout this guided learning experience, the teacher selects software and websites that support her goals of helping the students understand transformations and support the students in learning how to communicate mathematically. The technology includes the additional benefit of building into other concepts that the students either have already learned or will be learning. This means that the teacher can use some of these tools to tie student learning in new areas back to their previous understandings.

1. How does the teacher use these lessons to create a coherent set of experiences for the students?
2. What role do the standards play in this learning experience?
3. What role does technology play?
   a. How is technology used?
   b. What learning can or cannot occur because of the use of technology?
4. What's the teacher's role in the guided learning experience?

Meet the Standards

Online Study Center

Standards
More standards-related resources are available online.

Turn back to the opening of this chapter and review the four NETS standards with which the chapter is aligned. To spur your progress toward meeting these standards, write a brief description of a classroom activity that you believe would be appropriate for guided learning. Then think about how you might integrate technology into this activity. Here are some questions to focus your thinking:

▶ After you choose a technology that seems appropriate for the guided learning activity, search the Internet for examples of teachers' using the same technology for classroom teaching purposes. How can you determine whether or not these examples are appropriate for your purposes?

▶ How will you ensure that students' use of the technology in the classroom will match your intentions?

▶ What resources are available to help you with your decision-making process? How can you create your own resources?

▶ Describe the way you went about choosing a technology. Show that you're planning to use it appropriately and effectively.

Chapter 8

The Initiating Activity

ISTE NETS

Teachers

▶ Facilitate technology-enhanced experiences that address content standards and student technology standards.

▶ Apply technology in assessing student learning of subject matter using a variety of assessment techniques.

OTHER RELEVANT STANDARDS

International Reading Association (2003)

Classroom teacher candidates

▷ Select books, technology-based information, and nonprint materials representing multiple levels, broad interests, and cultural and linguistic backgrounds. They can articulate the research that grounds their practice.

A t this point in the book, you've "backed" your way into the first learner-centered activity of the Technology and Learning Continuum Model—the initiating activity. The initiating activity is intended as an introduction to the learning unit; from the students' point of view, it's the first in a series of activities that will lead to the culminating performance. But in your design of the learning unit, it should be the *last* step, because it's much easier to know how to get your students started if you know where you want them to end up.

To develop the initiating activity, you'll use the same four steps discussed previously: state objectives for the learning activity, select appropriate instructional strategies to facilitate learning objectives, choose technologies that support your strategies and objectives, and create assessments to measure student learning. At this point you've already determined the knowledge that your learners need in order to meet the goals of the guided learning and culminating performance activities. You've also selected the strategies to engage them and the technologies you'll use to facilitate learning. You've designed and strategically placed assessments along the continuum of activities. Now, in your design of the initiating activity, you'll focus on helping students connect the learning activities they're about to engage in with knowledge and skills that they've already developed.

The initiating activity typically employs the instructional approaches of presentation and demonstration, and discussion. The intent isn't to completely "deliver" knowledge through presentation or demonstration, but to make sure students have the requisite knowledge to begin the present unit. For example, if you want to have students make graphs to analyze data and they've never used a graph before, you know they'll need additional instruction as you embark on teaching your unit. Pressing forward without such instruction would only exacerbate their lack of knowledge, not to mention frustrate them and reduce their motivation. The initiating activity should activate their prior knowledge, make a clear connection to what they already know, and build on their strengths as they construct new knowledge. Clearly, too, your instructional strategies should be aligned with computer-related technologies, so that learners can organize and apply what they know to learn new things (NRC, 2000).

Designing the Initiating Activity

Initiating activities set the tone for your approach to teaching and learning in the classroom. Your challenge is to engage the students in such a way that they understand the expectations of the learning unit and know that they'll be active participants in their own learning. Hence, our discussion about initiating activities centers on ways to

Aims of initiating activities

1. Have students take notice of what they'll know and be able to do when completing the culminating performance.
2. Have students take an active role in their own and others' learning.

As you design the initiating activities for your learning unit, you'll continue to apply the four-step design process introduced in earlier chapters. To demonstrate this process, we'll continue to provide examples from the wolf habitat project. In this chapter we share some of the initiating activities we developed.

■ Step 1: State Objectives

Addressing the Knowledge level of Bloom's taxonomy

Objectives for the initiating activity are written to promote transference of prior knowledge and link it to the learning and application of new knowledge. In other words, you're concerned mostly with the Knowledge level of Bloom's taxonomy, at which the learner can recall such information as names, dates, and major ideas.

Initiating activities should also signify the beginning of a new unit and give foresight about what the student should know and be able to do by the end of the learning unit. Each objective should clearly lay out the path for learning and applying knowledge in the later guided learning and culminating performance activities.

As you write your objectives, continue to reference your state's learning standards, but remember that standards aren't always written in a format appropriate for developing assessments. Use the keywords in Table 8.1 to formulate objectives that are tightly aligned with the intent of your initiating activities.

For the wolf habitat initiating activity, we began by addressing existing misconceptions about wolves (prior knowledge) to set up the guided learning and culminating performance activities.

▬▬ Big Bad Wolf Initiating Activity: Recognizing Preconceptions

Many of us grew up with certain misconceptions about wolves. Many of these misconceptions came from early childhood stories, fairy tales, Hollywood, and the media in general. The first step in challenging these preconceptions and making a conceptual change is to allow students to identify their own beliefs. This also gives students a purpose for their research by highlighting specific information that they'd like to support or refute. Students usually enjoy this type of exercise because they are given an opportunity to learn about themselves and can have fun thinking about and questioning previous knowledge and misconceptions.

Table 8.1 Taxonomy Level and Keywords Appropriate for the Initiating Activity	
Bloom's Taxonomy Level	**Selected Keywords and Phrases**
Knowledge. Learner is able to recall such information as names, dates, and major ideas.	List, define, tell, describe, identify, show, label, collect, enumerate, examine, tabulate, quote, name, match, read, record, state

These are the relevant standards (drawn from state performance standards) that we identified for the first lesson on wolves:

Standards for the first lesson on wolves

7th-Grade Science: Characteristics of Science   Students will explore the importance of curiosity, honesty, openness, and skepticism in science and will exhibit these traits in their own efforts to understand how the world works.

▶ Understand the importance of—and keep—honest, clear, and accurate records in science.
▶ Understand that hypotheses can be valuable, even if they turn out not to be completely accurate.

7th-Grade Science: Characteristics of Science   Students will investigate the features of the process of scientific inquiry. Students will apply the following to inquiry learning practices:

▶ Investigations are conducted for different reasons, which include exploring new phenomena, confirming previous results, testing how well a theory predicts, and comparing competing theories.

7th-Grade English Language Arts: Listening, Speaking, Viewing
The student participates in student-to-teacher, student-to-student, and group verbal interactions. The student

▶ Initiates new topics in addition to responding to adult-initiated topics.
▶ Displays appropriate turn-taking behaviors.
▶ Actively solicits another person's comments or opinions.
▶ Offers own opinion forcefully without domineering.
▶ Volunteers contributions and responds when directly solicited by teacher or discussion leader.
▶ Gives reasons in support of opinions expressed.
▶ Clarifies, illustrates, or expands on a response when asked to do so.
▶ Employs a group decision-making technique such as brainstorming or a problem-solving sequence (e.g., recognizes problem, defines problem, identifies possible solutions, selects optimal solution, implements solution, evaluates solution).

From these standards we developed the following objectives for the first lesson:

Objectives for the first lesson on wolves

▶ Students will be able to recognize their own preconceptions and biases about wolves.
▶ Students will question and address the origins of their preconceptions.
▶ Given new knowledge and understanding about wolves, students will be able to formulate hypotheses and questions about wolf characteristics.
▶ Students will keep journals about their preconceptions, hypotheses, and questions. Assessment will be based on the content and depth of understanding presented in each student's journal.

Teachers also came up with a list of other activities or assignments for students.

▶ Around your home: Make a list of the aspects of the habitat that are necessary in order for the animals that inhabit the area to survive. If you live near a lake, a river, or the ocean, remember to include organisms that live in freshwater or saltwater environments.

▶ Research green plants, fungi (mushrooms), and animals that live in other regions of your state.

▶ Using informational resources, including maps, match animals and plants with their homes (areas in your state where they live: mountains, marsh or swamp, lakes, rivers, coast, ocean).

▶ Research the careers of women, men, and people of diverse backgrounds who study endangered animals.

▶ Develop a map of major habitats in your state. Students working in collaborative groups focusing on one animal may explain how that animal has affected the local culture.

■ Step 2: Select Instructional Strategies

Initiating activities are intended to capture learners' attention, get them interested in the unit's topics, and support the connecting of new learning to prior knowledge. Novice teachers typically frame classroom challenges in terms of what students won't or can't do. Assertions like "They don't pay attention . . . don't want to learn . . . don't listen to what I ask" blame challenges on the student. These are often characterized as classroom management or discipline problems. In fact, the problem often resides with the instructional strategies. Discipline problems, for example, disappear when a teacher enters the room and calls on the nonattentive student to read the agenda for the class period—a simple tactic that works to focus on the day's objectives. Spotlight 8.1 outlines some simple

Discipline problems often stem from instructional problems

SPOTLIGHT 8.1   Attention-Getting Strategies

It's important to consider how you will capture the students' attention to the learning. Here are a few examples of attention-getting strategies you can implement in the classroom prior to the day's lesson.

- *News or stories* from online sites can capture attention and lead students into a discussion of current events and their relationship to current learning (see Figure 8.1).
- *Lists and displays* can be used to present rank orders, choices, and varieties that can be openly discussed in class.
- *Multimedia,* with the use of sound, color schemes, and graphics, brings immediate attention to the day's topics.
- *Claims, arguments, and assertions* collected from websites can be presented by groups of students to create challenges for investigation.
- *Advice and how-to hints* for solving problems can be gathered and presented in class.

- *Questions, both rhetorical and Socratic,* projected on the wall or a screen at the beginning of class, are effective means to bring attention to the topic for the day.
- *Demonstrations* come in different varieties: step-by-step, before-and-after, side-by-side, and behind-the-scenes varieties are all effective ways of illustrating what will be accomplished through the learning unit. These demonstrations can be delivered through software, hardware, and Internet-based applications.
- *"Mythbuster"* activities are becoming increasingly available on the Internet as an entertaining way to address misconceptions.
- *Provide outlines, maps, and graphs* in a precaptured website or digital document. This helps students preview the most important information in a lesson or reading assignment.

Figure 8.1 Student-Oriented News on the Web Some websites, like this one from National Geographic, provide news stories that you can use to capture students' attention and introduce a unit.

- *Draw attention to important information* by having students practice using word processing functions to underline or highlight keywords. Use color-coding to organize key information in readings (for example, green for main idea, red for details, blue for essential information).
- *Focus on cues for important information.* Identify cues embedded in text or class lessons that students should look and listen for.
- *Cue students to upcoming transitions.* Let students know when a task is about to change and their focus will need to be adjusted.

- *Provide models of assignments and criteria for success.* Give students a clear sense of how a final product might look by showing examples and sharing exemplary products (such as model essays or drawings).

Source: Adapted from "Misunderstood Minds: Attention Responses." Available: **http://www.pbs.org/wgbh/misunderstoodminds/attentionstrats.html**

attention-getting strategies that are especially helpful when you're introducing a new unit.

We offer a word of caution at this point about "getting attention"—it can be misplaced very easily. The strategy is a means to an end—getting the students to focus in on what they will be learning in class. That is, overuse can cause the strategies to lose their impact. Be sure to use attention-getting strategies in ways that help students focus on learning. Using technology, especially multimedia, can be very powerful, but there is a fine line when it becomes a serious distraction. Learn by practicing what keeps your students' attention focused on a topic or concept.

Once you have the students' attention, you'll want to use instructional strategies and integrate technology in ways that make learning exciting and relevant. Initiating activities utilize three main instructional strategies: presentation, demonstration, and discussion. In the wolf habitat lesson, the teachers decided to use these strategies in ways like the following:

Strategies for the wolf habitat lesson

Presentation Introduce the habitats the students will learn in this unit and how each habitat is important to the lives of animals and people.

Demonstration Demonstrate how a habitat affected the growth of local culture, where people relied on the habitat for food, commerce, and culturally significant events.

Discussion Students demonstrate their emerging understandings by discussing how habitats support human and animal life. They engage in these discussions with people who live near the wolf habitat, with their group members, and then with the entire class.

These plans led to the following activities for the lesson:

Part 1: Exploring Preconceptions

Activities for the wolf habitat lesson

1. Have students work together in groups of three or four to discuss what they know (or think they know) about wolves.
2. When the groups are finished discussing, have students share their impressions while you write them on the board. The key to this exercise is not to write only answers that are true or to worry about what is true, but to record *all* impressions, mistaken or not.
3. Ask questions to prompt students to share their preconceptions. Guiding questions might include the following:
   • Are wolves dangerous?
   • What do they eat?
   • How big do they get?
   • How big is their territory?
   • Do they travel alone or in packs?
   • How big are the packs?
4. If one student says, "They get to be fifty pounds," ask if anyone thinks they get bigger or if anyone thinks they are smaller. It's perfectly okay to end up with "Weight: 25–300 pounds" on the board.
5. By the end of this session, the board should be full of different "information" (true or otherwise) about wolves.

Part 2: Journaling and Asking Questions

1. Have students journal about their (and their classmates') preconceptions about wolves. Ask them to think about the origins of their ideas about wolves.
2. Ask each student to come up with at least two questions that he or she would like to have answered about wolves, and ask students to make guesses about the answers to these questions.
3. Have students share their ideas about the origins of their preconceptions, as well as the questions they'd like to have answered, with the class.

Table 8.2 Instructional Strategies and Choices of Technology

Strategy	Possible Technologies	Application to the Wolf Habitat Unit
Presentation	PowerPoint, Visio, Inspiration	Introduce the wolf habitats that students will learn in this unit and how each habitat is important to the lives of animals and people.
Demonstration	LCD projector, videocapture, simulation, virtual reality software	Demonstrate how a wolf habitat affected the growth of local culture, where people relied on the habitat for food, commerce, and culturally significant events.
Discussion	E-mail, chat, instant messaging, videoconferencing	Have students discuss wolf habitats with people who live near them, with their group members, and then with the entire class.

▪ Step 3: Choose Technologies

Table 8.2 aligns the three instructional strategies of presentation, demonstration, and discussion with a few of the possible technology choices that would help learners to meet objectives. The table also shows some ways these technologies could be used in the wolf habitat unit.

As just one example, when students identify ideas they have about wolves, these ideas can be sorted into categories and formed into a "web" using the concept-mapping software Inspiration **(http://www.inspiration .com).** The students can then provide information for a K-W-L chart (see the chapter "Learner Needs") indicating what they already know about wolves and their habitat, followed by what they'd like to learn about the topic.

Teachers might use a companion website to introduce the topic (see Figure 8.2), and as the website is explored, students will see the goals of

Figure 8.2 Selection from a Web Page on Wolf Preconceptions Teachers can set up a simple website to introduce a unit. This page, for example, would help students explore their preconceptions about wolves. Later pages on the site would show the goals of the unit and introduce the procedures.

Online Study Center

Using Online Discussion in Middle-School Reading Instruction

Initiating activities should support students in developing an understanding of the relationship of the new learning to their prior knowledge. In the HM Video Case called **Middle School Reading Instruction: Integrating Technology,** which you can view at the Online Study Center, a middle-school teacher demonstrates his instructional strategies for connecting learning with real-life experiences. The video shows how he uses an online discussion forum to facilitate meaningful responses to the learning task.

After watching the main video, look at the section of Classroom Artifacts, which contains several examples of what students wrote in the online forum. Think about these questions:

- The teacher, Joshua Lawrence, says that, with the online forum, "every voice is heard daily." How does the forum help students with diverse backgrounds bring their unique experiences to the class in a meaningful way?
- What other technology might you use to connect this new learning unit to the students' prior learning or community-based experiences?
- In your own subject area, what uses could you make of an online forum like this one?

Using technology in meaningful ways

Formative assessment for the wolf habitat lesson

the unit. This process allows for questions and predictions to develop and be added to the K-W-L chart. Additional information might also be added to the concept web. If other computers are available in the classroom, students can explore additional websites selected by the teacher. These activities lead naturally to an in-depth study of the wolf habitat.

As you plan ways to integrate technology into an initiating activity, remember that the challenge is to harness technology's power in ways that are meaningful to learners. The message must not be lost in the medium. You don't want to overwhelm students with flashy technology that distracts them from your real purpose. The Video Case for this chapter provides a good example of appropriate technology use: seventh graders' participating in an online discussion forum that helps them make personal connections to Greek mythology, a subject that might otherwise seem remote.

■ Step 4: Create Assessments

In the initiating activity, your assessment should focus on giving learners continuous feedback about their progress and developing a general understanding for yourself of their incoming knowledge. For this purpose you'll use formative assessments, which are designed to inform both teachers and students about progress and problem areas. Here are some examples of formative assessments that teachers contributed for the wolf habitat lesson:

▶ Invite students to discuss their thinking about wolf habitats in pairs or small groups; then ask a representative to share the thinking with the larger group (a strategy called *think-pair-share*).

▶ Present several possible answers to a question about wolf habitats and then ask students to vote on them.

▶ Ask all students to write down an answer about wolf habitats, then read a select few of them aloud (strategies adapted from Boston, 2002, citing Black & Wiliam, 1998a, 1998b).

With information from assessments like these, the teacher can make adjustments to the activity content and strategies. Learners themselves can use the formative assessment information to understand where they're having trouble and what to focus on to meet objectives.

Many technologies support such formative assessment when combined with appropriate instructional strategies. The University of Minnesota Center for Teaching and Learning Services has developed some effective ways of using PowerPoint for formative assessments (Rozaitis & Baepler, 2005), but other technologies are equally useful. The following sections provide a few examples.

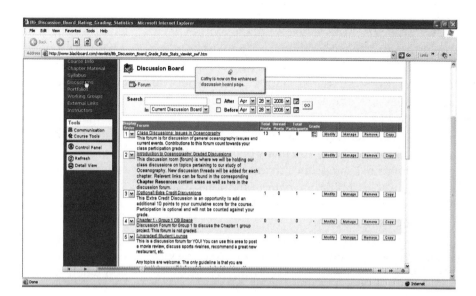

Figure 8.3 An Online Class Discussion Board The first entry represents a question posed by the teacher. The following entries are students' responses.

Discussion Boards and Online Forums

Periodically post a question to an online class discussion board or forum and ask students to respond (see Figure 8.3). This might involve the technique of *two-minute papers,* in which students are asked to write for two minutes in response to a specific question about a recent activity. Another technique, called *the muddiest point,* asks students to post an answer to a question like "What's the muddiest point from today's material?" Students are encouraged to read and respond to other students' posts.

Mind Maps

Have students create *mind maps* using concept-mapping software like Inspiration (see our chapter "Productivity Tools"). Such concept maps will chart students' progressive understanding of the content. Periodically have them update the maps to see the progress they've made and how their mental models have changed or been modified as they continue to interact with the material.

Editing Tools in Word Processing Software

Most word processing software packages incorporate tools that allow editors to track changes made to the document and to insert comments. Use these features to review drafts of students' work and suggest ways for them to make improvements.

SUMMARY

Initiating activities are the springboard to each learning unit. They launch students into a new learning venture while bringing forth existing knowledge. Initiating activities give students a preview of what's to come and explain the objectives of the new learning experience.

As a teacher, you should focus on facilitating learning with an eye toward the culminating performance, where students will actively demonstrate their knowledge and understanding in an applied context. You need, first of all, to get (and keep) your students' attention. Many strategies and a wide variety of technologies are effective in getting attention and keeping learners focused. There's a fine line, however, between capturing attention and losing the message in the medium. Too many bells and whistles become more of a hindrance than a help. Gauge for yourself how a combination of presentation software and questioning strategies, for example, engages your students in a lesson.

Instructional strategies embedded in the initiating activity are intended to transition from previous learning to the current learning unit. The teacher uses this opportunity to "set up" the unit in terms of what the students will know and be able to do when they complete the culminating performance. Strategies such as presentation, demonstration, and discussion are further enhanced by today's technology. Teachers have access to a wide range of media content that is fresh and exciting to the students—helping to bring them right into the depths of the unit without the overuse of lecture.

These last three chapters have centered on developing learner-focused activities. The next chapter introduces ways to measure your own impact and effectiveness. There we'll discuss your growth as a teacher and the support mechanisms available to you when you hit barriers.

RESOURCES

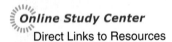
Online Study Center
Direct Links to Resources

Inspiration Software
http://www.inspiration.com
Publisher of the concept-mapping software (Inspiration and Kidspiration) that we've mentioned several times in this book.

Jon Mueller's Authentic Assessment Toolbox
http://jonathan.mueller.faculty.noctrl.edu/toolbox/index.htm
An easy-to-follow guide to authentic assessment, with plenty of examples for classroom use.

MythBusters
http://dsc.discovery.com/fansites/mythbusters/mythbusters.html
This site for the Discovery Channel TV show *MythBusters* contains quizzes and message boards that may give you ideas for helping your students explore their preconceptions.

Northwest Regional Laboratory: Assessment Toolkit
http://www.nwrel.org/assessment/toolkit98.php
Online training materials available at this site will help you construct knowledge about classroom assessment.

Plastic Mythbusters: Mythbusting Resources and Links
http://www.plasticsmythbuster.org/links.asp
Though the site is sponsored by the American Plastics Council, this page offers links to online sources about myths and "urban legends" on a wide variety of topics.

teAchnology: The Web Portal for Educators
http://www.teach-nology.com
Many useful, free resources for educators.

---

case STUDY

Eighth Graders Investigate Force, Mass, and Motion

José is in the final stage of using a backward design approach to a learning unit for his eighth-grade physical science class. He began by identifying the performance standard for this unit:

Standard: Students will investigate the relationship between force, mass, and the motion of objects.
  a. Determine the relationship between velocity and acceleration.
  b. Demonstrate the effect of balanced and unbalanced forces on an object in terms of gravity, inertia, and friction.
  c. Demonstrate the effect of simple machines (lever, inclined plane, pulley, wedge, screw, and wheel and axle) on work.

Next, José defined exactly what his students should know, understand, and be able to do when the unit is finished. Using these objectives, he identified the strategies and technologies that he'd use to help the students investigate and test their hypotheses, and designed criteria for the students to demonstrate their understanding and skill through a culminating performance. Throughout the unit he developed authentic activities for both formative and summative assessments. Now he's trying to decide how to introduce the learning unit with an appropriate initiating experience.

José believes that many students have misconceptions about the force, mass, and motion of objects. He has decided to use some examples from popular cartoons to introduce the unit, to demonstrate how these misconceptions may have arisen, and to stimulate conversation in order to discover what his students know and what misconceptions they hold. He chooses clips from Road Runner cartoons to demonstrate certain myths pertaining to gravity and physics. For example, one clip has Wile E. Coyote running straight off a cliff and remaining in midair until he realizes there's no ground beneath him, at which point he sadly waves to the viewer and drops straight down. In another clip, he's handed an anchor, at which point his free fall accelerates precipitously.

Questions for Reflection and Discussion
  1. *Step 1: State objectives.* What types of objectives might José identify for this initiating experience? What does he want his students to get out of it, and what information does José need to learn about his students' beliefs and misconceptions?
  2. *Step 2: Select instructional strategies.* What instructional strategies has José planned at this point? What other instructional strategies could he use?
  3. *Step 3: Choose technologies.* What technologies could José use to support his students' efforts, enhance communication, and allow his students to further explore the content area? Review the instructional strategies that you identified in step 2; in what ways can technology support these strategies?
  4. *Step 4: Create assessments.* Review the assessment strategies described earlier in the chapter. How could José use some of these strategies for formative assessment? What are the benefits of formative assessment at this point in the unit?

Meet the Standards

Online Study Center

Standards
Go online for additional help in understanding technology-related standards for teachers and students.

As indicated in the "Standards to Guide Your Preparation" at the beginning of this chapter, we've aligned the chapter with two fairly straightforward standards from the ISTE NETS. As a teacher, you'll be expected to:

▶ Facilitate technology-enhanced experiences that address content standards and student technology standards.

▶ Apply technology in assessing student learning of subject matter using a variety of assessment techniques.

To work on developing these abilities, imagine that you're student-teaching in a classroom that matches your grade-level and subject area preferences (eighth-grade math, third-grade language arts—whatever you choose). You've been observing the class for two weeks, during which you've seen students work through a complete learning unit. During your second week, the teacher asks you to design and implement the initiating activities for the new learning unit that will start next week.

She'd like to see you design activities capitalizing on the wide variety of technology resources available in the room. She'll provide assistance as needed, but she acknowledges that she herself isn't very familiar with technology. Assume that any technology you've read about in this book is available and think about the following questions:

▶ How will you design the initiating activity or activities? How many will there be?

▶ What technology or technologies will you choose?

▶ How will you integrate this technology into your teaching, your students' learning, and the assessments?

▶ You want the teacher to see how the technology you use in the initiating activities can be used again in the guided learning and in the culminating performance—for instruction, learning, and assessment. How will you help her understand ways to use the technology? What resources will you direct her toward?

PART III

Evaluate, Refine, and Extend

Chapter 9

Technology for Decision Making and Growth

ISTE NETS

Teachers

- ▶ Use technology resources to collect and analyze data, interpret results, and communicate findings to improve instructional practice and maximize student learning.

- ▶ Use technology resources to engage in ongoing professional development and lifelong learning.

- ▶ Continually evaluate and reflect on professional practice to make informed decisions regarding the use of technology in support of student learning.

OTHER RELEVANT STANDARDS

National Science Teachers Association (2003)
Teachers

- ▶ Reflect constantly upon their teaching and identify ways and means through which they may grow professionally.

- ▶ Use information from students, supervisors, colleagues and others to improve their teaching and facilitate their professional growth.

This chapter introduces ways to increase your capacity to look at your own and others' teaching practices. They include decision-making methods, assessment processes, and technology-based tools that will support your growth.

▶ The decision-making methods involve a four-step process for systematically thinking about your practice and clearly defining what you want to learn from others.

▶ The assessment processes will increase your capacity to understand where you are today (in terms of practice) and where you want to be (being an effective teacher).

▶ Technology-based tools can provide you with the means to capture complex environments, such as students' construction of knowledge in a very active classroom, in order to look at the teaching and learning events at your own pace. For instance, after capturing a learning episode with a video camcorder, you can review the event repeatedly and even gain more insight by showing it to an expert.

The goal is to gain the ability to think like a proficient teacher. Proficient teachers continuously assess their practices, even in the moment of teaching. They can draw from a large repertoire of strategies and make adjustments based on the classroom situation. Using the processes outlined in this chapter, you'll be emulating such teachers' thinking, and eventually this thinking about your practice will become a natural part of your own teaching. At that point you will have become a proficient teacher.

Evidence Based Decision Support

As you've worked your way through this book, you've had the opportunity to practice designing and (we hope) implementing technology-rich lessons. But how can you decide how well you're doing? Teaching and learning are very complex and fast moving—a terrible combination for those who are trying to learn and understand.

In this chapter we explore a method called **Evidence Based Decision Support (EBDS),** which will help you assess how lessons work in practice and better understand other elements of your own or someone else's teaching. EBDS encourages you, as a teacher, to collect evidence in the classroom—ranging from videotapes of teaching to samples of student work and lesson plans—and to use that evidence to better understand things that are going particularly well or that are problematic. We focus on using EBDS to analyze success in integrating technology, but you can use the same method to evaluate any other aspect of teaching.

Collecting evidence to enhance your understanding

Looking at Your Own Practices

Let's begin by looking at ways to analyze your own practices. Whether you're assessing yourself or another teacher, the EBDS process has four stages:

▶ Trigger
▶ Evidence

▶ Interpretation
▶ Action

Using the EBDS approach, you concentrate on a single attribute of the teaching and learning experience, blocking out other simultaneous events. For example, if you're interested in knowing why your students didn't understand the importance of the Lewis and Clark expedition, even after completing a WebQuest on the subject, you need to spend time reflecting on what those students did in the WebQuest and how you, as the teacher, supported their learning. In order to focus on the issues having to do with student understanding, you need to ignore (for the moment) other classroom issues, such as behavior problems or student group work.

The following sections guide you through the EBDS approach step by step.

■ Trigger Stage

Something triggers your interest in self-assessment. Assuming that you aren't self-assessing simply to meet a course requirement, you want to better understand something that has to do with your teaching or your students' learning. Like many other preservice teachers, you'll probably find that the trigger relates to one of three things.

What triggers your interest in self-assessment?

1. *Intuition.* Perhaps you sense that something about your use of technology in the classroom isn't going well (or is going much better than you'd expected). You may have seen students talking and not paying attention, for example, at the beginning of a new learning unit. At this point you're not sure if it's the way you used the technology or if something interesting was going on outside the window. You are, however, interested in determining the cause of students' not paying attention.

2. *Formal feedback.* Formal feedback includes classroom assessments, standardized tests, direct teacher observation, and other formal measures of practice and knowledge. Formative and summative assessment strategies provide powerful formal feedback. If large percentages of students get the same item wrong on a test you implemented, for example, there may be a shortcoming with the instruction.

3. *Informal feedback.* Products that students create in class and observations of student difficulties give you plenty of informal feedback. Even before assessing student learning in formal ways, you may realize that a strategy didn't work because the homework shows students struggling or because you notice consistent errors in class work. Building from these observations, you can make some assumptions that might focus your self-assessment. Keep in mind that your focus may change as you work through the process—that's to be expected.

Say that you've used software to teach a social studies lesson about the U.S. Constitution. You may have triggers like the following:

Intuition. I think the software may be too complex for the age group.
Formal feedback. The students performed poorly on the U.S. Constitution test items.
Informal feedback. Most of the students seemed to be struggling with the software.

Whatever triggers your exploration, your next step should be finding evidence to prove or refine your initial insight. This is especially true if your trigger is based on intuition or informal feedback.

■ Evidence Stage

There's evidence about your teaching and your students' learning all around you. Part of the evidence stage is determining what evidence is worth collecting. Because we're concentrating on technology integration in this textbook, we also discuss ways to use technology itself to capture your practices and to improve your capacity to think like an expert.

▬ Identifying Useful Evidence

Evidence is available in four parts of the teaching process:

Stages at which you can collect evidence

▶ *Your planning.* Lesson plans, notes, and everything else that goes into your preparation for the unit
▶ *Your enactment of practices.* The way you use your planned strategies and technology to engage students in learning
▶ *Student learning.* What and how the students actually learn
▶ *Postevent reflection.* Both formal and informal ways in which you look back on the teaching and learning events

These four parts of the teaching process are summarized in Table 9.1, along with the kinds of evidence you might collect in each. Let's examine the four parts in detail.

▬ **Planning** As Table 9.1 indicates, your search for useful evidence should extend all the way back to the planning processes you used to create the lesson. The planning stage is a good time to look for evidence concerning questions like these:

Questions you might ask about your planning

▶ How were you thinking about using technology?
▶ How did you align technology with objectives and content?
▶ How did you select technology?
▶ How did you align technology and assessment activities?

Your planning processes should also be embodied in such evidence as lesson plans, design documents, and other notes and documentation. In collecting these documents, a small scanner can be useful, because it allows you to reduce an unruly pile of papers to one neat folder on your computer. Discussions with other teachers or with students before the lesson can also be important evidence if you captured them on video.

▬ **Enactment of Practices** By *enactment* we mean the process of using instructional strategies and technology to engage the students in learning. Evidence collected from your enactment process should focus on answering questions like the following:

Questions you might ask about your use of strategies and technology

▶ How did you use technology in the classroom to facilitate learning?
▶ How did the students use technology to develop and apply their knowledge and skills?
▶ How did technology help you assess students' knowledge and skills?

Table 9.1 Evidence of Teacher Practices

Activity	Evidence	How to Collect	What It May Tell You
Planning for learning activities	1. Discussions before teaching 2. Lesson plans 3. Design documents 4. Notes or journal	1. Audio or video device 2. Collect or scan documents 3. Collect or scan documents 4. Collect or scan documents	Design of class activities (initiating, guided learning, culminating performance) Approach to selecting instructional strategies and technology
Enactment of practices	1. Instructional materials and technology used in class 2. Video of practices 3. Observation notes	1. Collect or scan documents 2. Camcorder 3. Collect or scan documents	Actual vs. perceived use of technology in the classroom Concrete evidence to address actual classroom practices
Student learning	1. Student work samples 2. In-class assessments	1. Collect or scan documents 2. Test scores, working notes, copies of actual tests	Student construction of knowledge and understanding resulting from learning activities Student progress toward goals and objectives
Postevent reflection	1. Discussion with peer or mentor 2. Notes or journal 3. Discussions with students 4. Assessment by a mentor or rater	1. Audio or video device 2. Collect or scan documents 3. Collect or scan your notes 4. Copies of written assessments	Ability to self- and collaboratively assess practices and growth

Enactment is embodied in the following evidence:

▶ *Instructional materials and resources that you used in the classroom.* These may be part of the technology, or they may be support materials that you used to facilitate students' use of the technology.

▶ *Video of classroom activities.* The video may be focused on you or the students.

▶ *Observation notes.* Notes you took while watching students work.

■■ **Student Learning**   To gauge your students' learning, you need to collect evidence representing how the student constructed or demonstrated knowledge, either as it's being developed or in a culminating performance. For this purpose, you can use a wide variety of student work samples and assessments, ranging from formal tests to working notes.

■■ **Postevent Reflection**   When a lesson is finished, you contrast your planning with the enactment in order to determine successes and deficiencies. You ask yourself which teaching and learning events went as planned, which didn't, and why.

Postevent reflection is embodied in

Examples of postevent reflection

▶ Discussions with other faculty members or with your mentor.

▶ Journal entries or notes you made while looking back on your teaching.

▶ Discussions with the students during and after class.

▶ A formal observation or assessment by a mentor or rater.

Our own student teacher collaborator is often asked to reflect on her planning and to assess her classroom practice. But discussions with her mentor often take place hours or days after the teaching event. It's hard for her to remember what happened a day or two ago, and she isn't alone. It's often difficult to remember specific events during a classroom period—especially when you were the one teaching. And once you've put a few classroom periods behind you, they begin to meld into one event. Our next section focuses on technology that can help you collect evidence to reflect thoroughly on your teaching.

Using Technology to Collect Evidence

Evidence capture devices are becoming more widely available, less expensive, and less intrusive all the time. The most complex devices are those that your school or district must buy and set up for you; but there are many simpler devices that you can supply on your own.

Video Capture

Video has proven to be a powerful tool for capturing direct evidence of classroom events. Student teachers have been bringing camcorders into the classroom to capture themselves and other teachers for more than twenty years now.

Getting consent to use video is often seen as a major challenge, but it may not be as difficult as you think. Spotlight 9.1 offers some guidelines and a sample consent form.

How the technology works. Quite simply, you can set up a camera in the back of the classroom and capture the events (see Figure 9.1). Latest improvements in even the consumer line of video camcorders allow you to zoom, adjust the quality of sound capture, and even label events. New "pro-consumer" cameras even store on a hard drive rather than on tape. You can now buy a video camcorder, such as the JVC Everio, which fits in the palm of your hand, zooms to great distances, and captures hours of video or audio on a hard drive. You don't even need a VCR for playback any longer.

Easy-to-use video cameras for recording your teaching

Typically, the camera includes software enabling you to offload the video (even if it's on tape) to a computer for playback or editing. Mid-range

---

SPOTLIGHT 9.1 Obtaining Consent to Use a Video Camera in Class

Every school system and university has different policies for recording classroom events on video, so you should become familiar with the rules and get advice from an administrator. If you intend to use the video for research or show the content publicly (in a presentation, for example), then you must follow Institutional Review Board policies set by the governing institution (e.g., your school district or your university). Typically, however, if you use the video only for professional development (for your own purposes) and don't intend to show it publicly or publish your conclusions, a less formal set of rules applies.

Even if the rules are extremely lenient, you'll want to make sure you have consent from the participants (typically, children), parents, and administrators. For our student teachers, we typically use the following consent form in multiple languages:

PARENTAL CONSENT FORM

I agree to allow my child, _____, to take part in a research study titled "Video-taping the Teacher," which is being conducted by Drs. ABC and XYZ (University of QRS) under the direction of _____ from _____ (phone: _____). The focus of this study is my child's teacher (or student teacher). I understand that my child may be videotaped in the process. I do not have to allow my child to be in this study if I do not want to. My child can stop taking part at any time without giving any reason and without penalty. I can ask to have the information related to my child returned to me, removed from the research records, or destroyed.

- The purpose of this study is to collect evidence on the actual teaching practices of student teachers. The researchers are interested in student teachers' modeling of practices that have been modeled/taught to them in their studies.
- The research does not focus on students, student learning, or student activities. My child will have no active role or expectation in this research. My child's grade will not be affected in any way. My child's activity or performance will not be evaluated by the teacher or researchers in any way.
- The research is not expected to cause any harm or discomfort. My child can quit at any time. My child's grade will not be affected if my child decides to stop taking part.
- Any information collected about my child will be held confidential unless otherwise required by law. All data will be kept in a secure location. Videos may be viewed by researchers and teachers for improvement of instructional practices. Student identities will be protected by assigning pseudonyms to school systems, school buildings, all teachers, student teachers, grade level, and course names. When possible, video will be filmed from the back of the room and focused directly on the teacher so that only a rear profile (back of head) of a limited number of students will be seen.
- The researcher will answer any questions about the research, now or during the course of the project, and can be reached by telephone at _____. I may also contact the professor supervising the research, _____ from _____ (phone: _____).
- I understand the study procedures described above. My questions have been answered to my satisfaction, and I agree to allow my child to take part in this study. I have been given a copy of this form to keep.

_____   _____   _____

Name of parent or guardian   Signature   Date

_____   _____   _____

Name of lead researcher   Signature   Date

Figure 9.1 Video Camera Capture of Small Group Discussion in a Classroom

camcorders come equipped with viewfinders so that you can watch the playback immediately after the event, without processing the video.

What the technology produces.   With a simple camcorder setup, you can record evidence of your actual classroom teaching, as well as student reactions to various parts of the lesson. You can capture your practices over multiple sessions, to see how your teaching approach is evolving, or you can single out specific events within a single lesson.

Most appropriate applications.   The camera provides an external perspective on your teaching. It can help you distinguish what really happened from what you thought was happening. For lessons in which you stand at the front of the classroom, you can also set up a camera behind yourself to capture student reactions that you may not notice while the lesson is in progress.

What the technology helps explain.   A video record can help you understand

What you can understand by analyzing a video of your own teaching

- ▶ Your actual practices rather than recollected or intended practices.
- ▶ Very specific events that occurred in the classroom.
- ▶ Your use of various strategies in class and your interactions with learners as you employed those strategies.
- ▶ Learners' responses to teaching.
- ▶ Students' interactions during classroom events.
- ▶ Students' construction of knowledge while engaged in hands-on activities.

■■ **Audio Capture** Audio capture has improved dramatically in the last five years through the invention of MP3 players and recorders. Today's digital audio-recording devices (see Figure 9.2) are small, relatively inexpensive, and able to capture high-quality sound.

Using small, unobtrusive recorders

Figure 9.2 A Typical Audio Capture Device

You can place a digital audio capture device at each work group's table. Or you can carry a device in your hand to capture your discussion and dialogue with students.

How the technology works.   Small hand-held audio devices have a built-in microphone and a tiny drive that captures the audio. The audio can be played back directly from the device or downloaded to a computer for playback.

What the technology produces.   Audio capture devices give you digital audio files that can be edited and played back, even embedded in presentations.

Most appropriate applications. With a digital audio recorder you can

▶ Capture preplanning meetings with other teachers or mentors.
▶ Capture postteaching reflection with a mentor or evaluator.
▶ Capture student discussions in the classroom when students are working in pairs or groups.
▶ Capture classroom instruction or presentations.

What the technology helps explain.   Audio recordings are most useful for understanding

▶ Actual events rather than recollections.
▶ Students' construction of knowledge through interaction in pairs or teams.

■ **Image Capture**   Like video camcorders, digital still cameras (Figure 9.3) have evolved to the point of offering high quality at a low price—meaning that most schools and teachers have easy access to them. By taking a picture, you can literally "snapshot" a moment in time for later comparison and analysis.

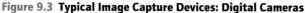

Figure 9.3 Typical Image Capture Devices: Digital Cameras

How the technology works. During class, you can simply point and click. If you have access to a printer, you can print the images—sometimes even without a computer. In most cases, the camera stores pictures to a memory stick, disc, or hard drive. All pictures can then be easily downloaded to a computer for editing, manipulation, and printing.

What the technology produces. Images of products or events as they appear during learning events are useful in many ways. You can review the images later, take them with you to share ideas with others, or even use them in a portfolio for summative assessment.

Appropriate times to take a snapshot

What might you want to photograph? Perhaps, in planning a project, students create an interesting concept map on the board. In some classrooms, you may have an electronic whiteboard that will capture an image of the students' creation (see Spotlight 9.2). If not, however, you can simply take a snapshot with your camera. You might also capture digital images of students' work in progress and again at the culmination of a project; this is especially useful if students are constructing a physical object or performing a series of steps. Or you might photograph the instructional materials, such as models or posters, that you used in the classroom.

Most appropriate applications. Still images are most useful for

- ▶ Historical documentation of your lessons.
- ▶ Evidence of events, products, and class participation.
- ▶ Documentation of events or products for portfolio assessment.

What the technology helps explain. With your digital camera you can better understand

- ▶ Visual materials that would be too large or complex to describe in words: bulletin boards, an object students designed as part of a project, and so on.
- ▶ The meaning of audio data that you've captured; for instance, one or two snapshots can help you interpret a long audio recording of a student group presentation.

■■ **Student Information Systems** Because of today's accountability requirements, it is becoming more common for schools to have some form of student information system. Student information systems not only capture class grades and scores on standardized tests; they also have the capacity to collect a wide array of data, including daily attendance, demographics, and family characteristics. Some examples are

- ▶ SASI from Pearson School Systems
  http://www.pearsonschoolsystems.com/products/sasi
- ▶ PowerSchool from Apple Education Solutions
  http://www.apple.com/education/powerschool
- ▶ MMS School Administrator Software
  http://www.cri-mms.com/

How the technology works. Data are entered individually or scanned into the system from predesigned forms, such as Scantron bubble sheets. Data are stored in the system until reports are printed. As a teacher, you can gain access to this data for your own students.

SPOTLIGHT 9.2 Whiteboard Capture Technology

Electronic whiteboards are becoming less expensive and more accessible for the classroom. This kind of tool typically involves a computer projected onto a special dry-erase-board-like surface. But it's more than a simple projection device. It's interactive, allowing teacher and students to point to items and even draw on the board with a special stylus. For example, while the class looks at the screen, one person can circle an item of interest, click a button, or change some text. At any point the device can save the work for later distribution or analysis.

Many interactive whiteboards include built-in tools that range from somewhat interactive games to shapes, icons, and colors that can be used as instructional tools. These materials are generally included for all basic content areas: science, math, language arts, geography, and so on. Leading whiteboardlike tools include the Promethean ACTIVboard **(http://www.prometheanworld.com)** and the SMART Board **(http://www.smarttech.com)**. There are similar tools that project onto regular screens but allow teacher and students to use a small tablet that can easily be passed around the classroom to highlight elements on the screen, click, and add elements.

One such tool is the InterWrite SchoolPad **(http://www.gtcocalcomp.com/interwriteschoolpad.htm)**.

Figure 9.4 shows a screen shot created by John Whalley (2004), demonstrating the utility of an electronic whiteboard for teaching nutrition. Students come to the board to drag and drop foods into the appropriate groups.

Other technologies, such as the Mimio **(http://www.mimio.com)**, enable you to capture notes, lessons, student writing samples, and drawings from existing whiteboards. You attach a device to your whiteboard and a local computer. Regular dry erase markers are inserted into the Mimio Mouse stylus like a cordless mouse that enables you to write on your existing dry erase board and have what you've written appear on the screen. This sounds like magic but actually the stylus (a casing surrounding each marker) interacts with a device suction-cupped to your dry erase board, thereby allowing everything written on the board to be shown and saved on the computer screen. The information on the board can then be printed, e-mailed, and stored electronically.

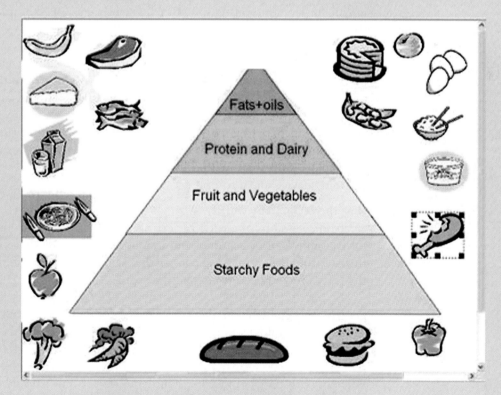

Figure 9.4 Using an Electronic Whiteboard to Teach Nutrition

What the technology produces.   Student information systems aggregate individual data at the building, system, and state levels.

Most appropriate applications.   For your purposes as a teacher, one major benefit of student information systems is that they help you understand student performance data at the classroom level. These systems have evolved from mere data capture to adding functions that enable you to analyze the data. For example, you can use your access to standardized test scores to look for patterns: On which items did the students perform well? On which items did they struggle? Through the students' answers to specific questions and types of questions, you can see which concepts they understand and which need further emphasis in class.

Analyzing standardized test scores to aid your teaching

What the technology helps explain.   By looking at groups of test questions intended to measure specific concepts (such as the concept of force in physical science), you can determine your students' success in demonstrating knowledge. Noting problem areas, you can then determine more effective teaching strategies for the next unit or the next year.

■ **Capture of Classroom Artifacts, Tools, and Resources**   Materials developed by students using such common classroom technologies as word processors and presentation software can be used as a source of evidence. Microsoft Word, for example, has Track Changes and Insert Comment functions that enable the teacher to provide feedback within a document. The electronic version of the document then becomes an artifact providing evidence not only of the student's progress, but also of the teacher's own quality and timeliness of feedback. Such documentation is useful for demonstrating assessment strategies, for example, and provides an opportunity for a mentor or evaluator to critique your work.

More often, however, artifacts of classroom teaching and learning aren't in electronic form. Sketch paper from problem solving, accompanied by the final answer given, for example, can tell you where the student's understanding breaks down. From this evidence you can attend to the learner's specific needs. Collecting and keeping track of huge quantities of classroom papers is cumbersome, though. Converting such evidence of teaching and learning into electronic form makes it easier to organize, manipulate, and share with others. For this conversion, all you need is a scanning device and a computer.

Using a scanner to make a compact electronic record

How the technology works.   Using a scanner (Figure 9.5), you can create electronic versions of a wide variety of materials. Students' journal notes, for example, can be scanned and uploaded to a computer as evidence of their writing progress. Any scanner that you buy today should come with the software you need to upload the scans.

Scanners come in a variety of types. *Flatbed scanners* have a large glass plate on which you place the paper or other object you want to scan. These devices allow you to digitize a wide variety of materials—basically anything that can be placed on the glass. *Document scanners* generally pull paper through the machine by means of an automatic feeder; they're efficient with papers but can't handle an object that isn't flat. *Hand-held scanners,* which you move across the object to be scanned, are portable and efficient with small items.

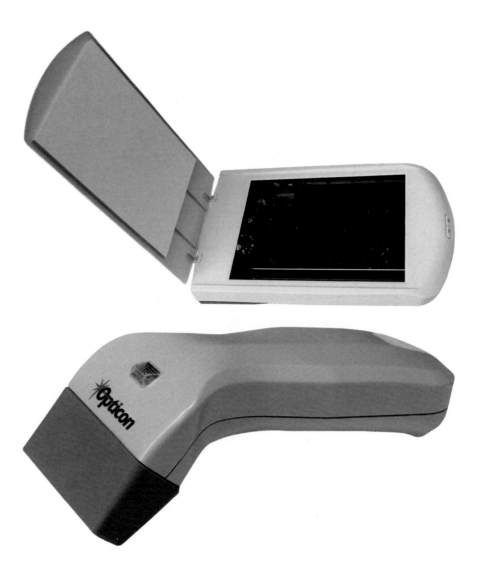

Figure 9.5 Scanning Devices

What the technology produces.   Scanners create electronic versions of materials that you no longer need or want to compile in their original format.

Most appropriate applications.   This technology is excellent for digitizing materials that are cumbersome to store or organize. Student projects can be bulky. Once you have a digital version, originals can be returned to the student and taken home. The electronic versions can also be manipulated (resized, cropped, integrated with text) to form part of a growth portfolio.

What the technology helps explain.   Actual products from the classroom help explain the relationship between teaching and learning. Digitized artifacts captured from specific points in time can be stitched together to tell a story of growth and improvement.

▆▆▆ Planning for Evidence Collection

Following the initial steps of Evidence Based Decision Support will help you focus your self-assessment. The more fine-grained the attribute of practice that you identify and document, the greater your potential for

SPOTLIGHT
9.3

Questions for Planning Your Evidence Collection

- What evidence centered on teaching practices will you collect?
- How will you collect it?

- When will you collect it? Why then?
- How will you organize it and store it for analysis?

generating clear explanations and solutions. For example, if you can focus on a particular instructional strategy, such as using software for problem solving, you can more readily look at an actual lesson and determine how it might be improved. The core idea is to focus on a defined issue that allows you to use your time as effectively as possible.

An important part of evidence collection is planning: You have to think in advance about what evidence to collect and how to collect it. Spotlight 9.3 lists some questions you can ask yourself before planning.

One of our elementary-school collaborators decided to capture video of her classroom so that she could get a closer look at what was happening. She borrowed a digital video camcorder, tripod, and digital tapes to capture science lessons. She decided to capture every day, knowing that all the evidence couldn't be reviewed, because she didn't want to take a chance on missing an important day. Once the video was collected, she marked specific days' tapes with comments; later, she focused on those that included important events, such as students' behaving particularly poorly or well. Typically, she and the supervising teacher looked at two or three of the videos each week. The videos were transferred from the camcorder onto a computer using the USB cable that came with the camera. Free software delivered with the camera was used to convert the video files into Windows Media Video (.wmv) format.

Interpretation Stage

Once you've collected and organized evidence of your teaching, you'll need to analyze it in such a way as to understand and explain the teaching events you've captured. Evidence alone can't tell the story; it only represents a complex event and allows you to look at it carefully.

Lenses for Interpretation

One way to think about the interpretation stage is to imagine a camera lens. The lens of a camera brings some attributes of what you see to the surface and pushes others into the background. A lens helps you focus on some things while eliminating others as noise or interference (Recesso et al., in press). Using a camera specialty lens for shooting fall colors in the mountains, for example, can mute the green on trees and enhance the appearance of the more colorful leaves.

Similarly, you can use a "lens" to pull to the surface fine-grained attributes of your teaching practice, making them easier to see, analyze,

An Activity for Self-Assessment of Technology Integration

The goal of this activity is to familiarize yourself with using standards as lenses for self-assessment. You may capture a mock or a real teaching activity. Follow each step.

1. Design a single learning activity (initiating activity, guided learning activities, culminating performance) integrated with technology. Select any content or concepts specific to your teaching domain; for instance, for social science you might design a lesson about the legislative branch of the U.S. government.

2. Plan how to capture evidence of the learning activity.

3. From the ISTE NETS website (http://cnets.iste.org), choose an appropriate lens for analyzing your technology integration practices. You may also choose to self-assess using national standards from your subject area.

4. Teach the learning activity. This can be done with a real class of students (most optimal), with your peers, or alone (least optimal).

5. Using your lens, compile evidence for analysis and then interpret the evidence.

6. Write a complete reflection on what you could ascertain from the events. What worked? What didn't? How do you know? What would you do differently? How would you change?

7. Collaboratively assess with a peer or mentor (faculty or teacher). What does the other person see? What successes or challenges does she or he identify? What would she or he like to see you change or do differently?

Using standards to guide your analysis

and understand. For technology integration, you can often find an appropriate lens in the standards from the ISTE NETS, like those listed at the beginning of each chapter in this book. For example, the General Preparation Performance Profile of the NETS standards for teachers indicates that teachers should "use technology tools and information resources to increase productivity, promote creativity, and facilitate academic learning." If you have a video of yourself teaching a unit in the classroom, you might analyze it with that standard in mind, asking yourself: Did I use the appropriate technology tools? Did they in fact increase students' productivity? How? Did my lesson encourage students to be creative? How well did the academic learning progress?

Spotlight 9.4 presents an activity that we often use with our preservice teachers. Notice that the final step involves collaborative assessment with a peer or mentor. We encourage you to try this activity yourself if you have the opportunity.

▬ Adapting Video Technology for Assessment and Reflection

We've talked about the benefits of recording your teaching with a simple camcorder. To make such video capture even more useful, educators have developed a number of ways to extend the technology or enhance its discussion.

▬ **Video Clubs** Dr. Miriam Sherin at Northwestern University has been refining an informal approach to teacher learning through the use of video. **Video clubs** designed by Sherin and Elizabeth van Es have opened dialogues about how teachers make sense of their mathematics teaching. Using video camcorders, teachers in local schools capture student learning in the classroom. All video is reviewed by the teacher for a postteaching event reflection. Teachers then arrive at the video club with particular video segments in mind to discuss. Together, they forge an understanding of how the students are making sense of the math through their teaching. Over time, the researchers have seen an increase in the sophistication with which the teachers talk about student learning (Sherin & Han, 2004; Sherin & van Es, 2005).

■■ **Digital Interactive Video Exploration and Reflection (DIVER)** DIVER is being developed by Dr. Roy Pea at the Stanford Center for Innovations and Learning (see **http://diver.stanford.edu).** Desktop DIVER and its web counterpart, WebDIVER, are applications that enable users to add commentary and annotations to the video. A number of teachers can comment on a single video, sharing their perspectives and discussing each other's annotations (Mills et al., 2003; Pea et al., 2004). To make this technique even more effective, Pea has utilized cutting-edge video equipment that captures the entire classroom in a 360-degree panoramic view.

■■ **Video Analysis Tool (VAT)**   Art Recesso and Michael Hannafin at the Learning and Performance Support Laboratory of the University of Georgia (see **http://lpsl.coe.uga.edu)** are developing a web-based video-capture and coding tool called the Video Analysis Tool (VAT). Their work in teacher preparation includes collaboration with the departments of Mathematics and Science Education, Elementary and Social Studies Education, and Communication Sciences and Special Education.

Classroom videos, often made with a special **Internet protocol camera** (designed to connect directly to the Internet), are uploaded to a website where users are able to analyze them. VAT has multiple applications. Preservice teachers use VAT for self-assessment of classroom practices. Faculty supervisors use the tool to remotely observe and assess preservice teacher practices. Supervising faculty use VAT to collaboratively assess preservice practices, as well as to assess their own mentoring practices.

■■ **Defining a Solution**

Defining a solution is a critical point in the self-assessment process. Evidence-based explanations of classroom events have provided a strong foundation for your decisions. Now you need to identify solutions—ways to solve the problems you've identified and to improve your teaching.

At this point the sort of collaboration shown in the "Technology in Action" case proves invaluable. The faculty supervisor and mentor helped the preservice teacher focus on questioning strategies. The effects of good questioning that should be visible in the classroom are well defined in the Teacher Reflection Tool and in existing literature. In this case there was an additional resource. The supervising teacher had been trained in Socratic questioning the previous summer. How to successfully enact the strategies in the classroom was still fresh in his mind. He also had volumes of materials from the training sessions that he could share with the preservice teacher. Their solution was to implement Socratic questioning strategies to engage the students during science learning.

In our university's teacher development program, we similarly stress collaborative analysis and sharing of insights. For example, we can

Technology in Action

Generating Explanations with the Teacher Reflection Tool

In one case we know, an elementary-school preservice teacher chose to apply a lens called the Teacher Reflection Tool (TRT). The lens was developed from a framework created by Teachers Development Group **(http://www.teachersdg.org).** The TRT lens is intended for self-assessment of practices that are common in standards-based classrooms, such as engaging students in working together, asking good questions, and using multiple approaches to solving mathematics problems.

The preservice teacher met with her supervising teacher several times each week. During three of those meetings, they analyzed classroom events together. The first week it became apparent to both of them that students weren't paying attention. Using the TRT, they decided to focus on an activity called "Understanding, Invention, and Sense Making" in the science classroom, which involved the questions listed in Table 9.2. Specifically, they focused on whether students were using a variety of approaches to answer their questions and whether those questions were genuine (showing interest in others' thinking). Before each meeting, both the preservice teacher and the mentor used video to identify clips in which they saw examples of these

Table 9.2 Teacher Reflection Tool for Understanding, Invention, and Sense Making

Does classroom activity center on scientific understanding, invention, and sense making by all students?

Specific Questions

1. Do student explanations and justifications emphasize the *meaning* of ideas and *how* and *why* the students' methods do or don't work?

2. Do students determine the correctness or sensibility of an idea or solution based on the scientific reasoning presented?

3. Are student conjectures, generalizations, scientific justifications, "what if" questions, and invented procedures the norm?

4. Do students approach problems and ideas in a variety of ways and using a variety of representations (visual, verbal, numeric, algebraic, graphic, everyday life)?

5. Do all students use models, manipulatives, and other tools to make sense of ideas, solve problems, and invent procedures, or is use of such tools limited to teacher or student demonstrations?

6. Do students use *genuine questions, statements,* and *actions* that show *genuine interest* in others' thinking, or do actions and interactions center on getting others to think in certain ways?

7. Do students listen intently and actively, and ask for clarification when they don't understand someone's methods or reasoning?

8. Is *private think time* honored and encouraged by all?

9. Do students celebrate their scientific "aha!"s and honor the difficulties that may precede such moments?

foci. Then, during their meetings, they were able to discuss their interpretations and make a plan for improving the activities in the classroom.

By using this approach, the preservice teacher began to realize that the problem wasn't simply that students were off task. Rather, they weren't engaging in authentic scientific activities. The student teacher noticed that her students approached their science activities as blank worksheets to fill out. They didn't conjecture, they didn't ask "what if" questions, and they never used any manipulatives or tools other than those that were specifically named on their lab sheets.

It was as if a light bulb had gone off—the "aha!" moment had arrived. The preservice teacher could see from the evidence, using the lens provided for her, that she was moving forward into the inquiry-based science content and activities while leaving the students using approaches that weren't inquiry based. She had an instructional strategy problem, not a class discipline problem. But what instructional strategy in particular was the problem? She talked it over with her faculty supervisor and supervising teacher. Collectively, they decided to focus on questioning strategies at the beginning of class.

Collaboratively, the preservice teacher and her mentor continued to use the TRT analysis for two more weeks, to watch for improvements in student engagement with the scientific materials. During that time they made refinements to the preservice teacher's practice which had a visible effect on her students' willingness to engage in open-ended, inquiry-oriented activities.

compare how one expert and one novice analyzed the same situation. By doing this, we open up the means for both of them to gain better understanding of what the other values. This method also allows the novice to learn more about how an expert looks at a given situation.

■ Action Stage

The final step is to implement the solution. Let's go back to our "Technology in Action" example. Assume that the supervising teacher, for example, has devised a multiweek plan to help the preservice teacher learn how to use Socratic questioning strategies in the classroom. First, the supervising teacher uses a few weekly meetings to discuss questioning strategies in general and the specific attributes of Socratic questioning. The preservice teacher begins to think about how the strategies would be effective with the science content. On two occasions the preservice teacher sets up a purposeful observation of the supervising teacher to see how he enacts Socratic questioning strategies in his own class. This isn't a typical class observation; rather, the preservice teacher has a specific lens to help her focus on the important attributes of Socratic questioning and filter out the extraneous details of day-to-day classroom events.

Next, it's the preservice teacher's turn to implement the strategies. Her initial attempts are deliberate and thoroughly planned. She regularly captures video of herself using Socratic questioning and continues to self-assess using this lens. In her regular meetings with her mentor, they look at particular video clips and discuss ideas about what's improving and what they should focus on next.

A focused approach leads to rapid improvement.

With this kind of focused, deliberate approach, you should see rapid improvement in your own teaching. In the actual case we're describing, the preservice teacher evolved within five weeks from blaming her students for a discipline problem to improving her instructional strategies. This improvement not only affected her students' learning, but also helped resolve a number of behavior problems with which she'd been dealing. Most important, the process was something she could carry with her as she became a practicing teacher.

Looking at Other Teachers' Practices

Working closely with an expert or master of a craft is a powerful way to learn. This has long been the premise of apprenticeship models, in which people learn a trade, such as carpentry, painting, or welding, from a master craftsperson. Teacher preparation and development have adopted some facets of this model. In fact, many teacher preparation programs are increasingly requiring future teachers to spend more hours in field experiences, even before they enter a teacher preparation program.

As a preservice teacher you're going to devote a lot of time to observing others. In fact, you've already done this for many years. You've been in a classroom watching a teacher since you began school. Clearly this has an impact on your perception and beliefs about what a teacher should know and be able to do. Unfortunately, some of your models may not have been exemplary, and you may need to unlearn this image of teaching. The same EBDS approach that you used to assess your own teaching can provide you with a way of looking at other teachers' practices so that you can learn more from them. Let's look at each of the four stages.

Trigger Stage: Define What You Want to Know

Begin by defining what you want to look for in your observation. For example, you may be interested in observing how spreadsheets can support data analysis in a science classroom or how a WebQuest can support high-school students in learning about the Revolutionary War.

Planning to make your observation productive

Once you've defined your desired outcome, you'll need to work with the teacher you'll be observing to be sure you see a lesson in which he or she is using technology in the ways you're interested in seeing. To make your observation as productive as possible, you'll need to plan carefully and communicate a good deal with the cooperating teacher. You should also use standards and frameworks to help you think about aspects of the experience to focus on, and you should generate a set of questions to guide your observation. With these preparations, you can have a meaningful and enlightening classroom observation that helps you really discover ways to use technology in your own teaching (see the following "Technology in Action" feature).

Technology in Action

Setting up Your Own Observation Experience

The evidence-based processes that you use to self-assess and to observe others can also help you learn from students. In fact, an opportunity to observe an exemplary teacher is also a good opportunity to see how students are engaged, construct knowledge, and apply their knowledge in the learning environment.

As an example of using the four EBDS stages, say that you'll be observing a math class. Your specific *trigger* is to better understand how students can be engaged by a culminating performance in which they demonstrate their knowledge by using web-based manipulatives. Prior to the classroom observation, arrange a time to talk with the classroom teacher. Explain your interest in seeing the use of web-based manipulatives and discuss the planning process that goes into designing the culminating performance, in which students will actually use the manipulatives to solve a problem without much guidance. Request that you be able to capture *evidence* of the students engaged in the process, demonstrating their knowledge, and creating their final products.

There are multiple ways to use technology in such a setting. You may choose to set up a video camera next to the students' computer and capture them as they work. Another option would be to use a freely available computer screen capture program to gather evidence of the student's actions, such as the particular steps they take in using the manipulatives. (For screen capture programs, go to the Tucows website listed in the "Resources" section at the end of this chapter and search for "screen capture.") Finally, you may decide just to take notes on a laptop and scan copies of the students' products that they print from the screen.

Each piece of evidence can be *analyzed* by using state learning standards or by using an assessment rubric developed by the classroom teacher. After completing the analysis, request an opportunity to review the process and your discoveries with the teacher, your faculty supervisor, or your mentor. Discuss what course of *action* you might take to use manipulatives in your own teaching.

What kinds of questions might you generate for your observation trigger? One approach is to build from the Technology and Learning Continuum Model. For example, you may be interested in seeing how a teacher plans for technology-integrated activities and then how they're implemented. In this case, you might want to visit the teacher as he or she plans, maybe even coplan the lesson with the teacher. You'd certainly want to discuss the plan with the teacher, either in person or by e-mail, before observing the classroom activity. While observing the lesson, you could look for elements of planning as they unfolded naturally in the classroom. Then you and the teacher could discuss how the plan was altered in action: What kinds of changes were made? Why were they made? How did the teacher decide what to do at key points in the lesson?

Evidence Stage: Capture Events to Study Further

The same technologies described earlier for systematically capturing evidence of your own practices are helpful when observing others. When you go into the field to observe a teacher's practices, bring along a video camera, a watch, and a notepad. It's difficult to observe and take good notes at the same time, and even more difficult to remember the critical events afterward. Hence, we suggest that you start your watch, start the camera, and note the approximate times when important events happen (you can refine the times later).

You may also find it helpful to gather artifacts from the classroom. These may include handouts that the teacher used, page numbers of activities that the students completed, URLs of websites that were used, and other relevant information that can help you re-create the lesson as you analyze it.

Gathering a variety of information

Remember that you can capture a wide array of data in classrooms, including evidence of preplanning (such as lesson plans), practice (instructional materials, teacher work samples, student work samples), and assessment (tests, quizzes, teacher reflections). By collecting a combination of data types, you'll more fully understand how an experienced teacher uses technology to enhance student learning—including the nearly invisible decisions that the teacher makes every moment while working with students in the classroom.

Interpretation Stage: Break Down the Complex Events into Smaller Units

After the observation, break down the data you've captured into smaller units for interpretation and concentrate on the evidence directly relevant to the questions you want to answer.

Focus on specific events.

For example, as you watch your video on the camera or through a TV, pay particular attention to the episodes that you noted in your observation. This process enables you to save time by focusing your interpretation on the most important events—those about which you have questions and want to understand more. Use the elements of the Technology and Learning Continuum Model or a particular standards framework (such as the ISTE standards or a framework specific to your content area) to guide your interpretation. Also review the important episodes with the teacher whom you observed or with a faculty mentor.

From this systematic review and discussion, you can draw much more from your experience than if you scan the evidence in an unfocused way.

■ Action Stage: Put Your Learning into Practice

Translating your observations into practice

As the final step, implement your own lesson based on what you saw in the other teacher's practices. For example, use what you've learned about the planning process to design your own activities that use technology to promote students' application of knowledge. Share the results with a mentor and ask for feedback. From this process you'll get a full sense of what you've learned from your classroom observation.

SUMMARY

Using technologies ranging from camcorders to Internet-based video analysis tools, you can improve your teaching through the use of technology. In the near term, these approaches will help you address classroom problems that may be preventing your students from meeting your school's goals for adequate yearly progress. In the long term, using these approaches will help you become a better teacher.

Our Evidence Based Decision Support (EBDS) approach relies on evidence extracted directly from the teaching and learning environments. It guides you through four stages in analyzing your own or others' teaching practices: the trigger stage, the evidence stage, the analysis stage, and the action stage. The intent is for you to be fully vested in setting goals and deciding how you'll reach them over time.

There are five key points to take with you from this chapter:

► Be systematic in your approach to determining what you know and need to be able to do.
► Use a variety of the most appropriate evidence; don't rely only on student achievement data, recollection, or personal interpretation.
► Self- and collaboratively assess your practices.
► When you notice problems in your own teaching, use the EBDS method to identify and implement solutions.
► Take full advantage of readily available technology to collect evidence and improve your analysis.

RESOURCES

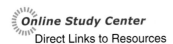
Online Study Center
Direct Links to Resources

GENERAL RESOURCES

Internet4Classrooms
http://www.internet4classrooms.com
  Offers software tutorials as well as many useful links organized by subject.

Tucows Shareware Downloads and Reviews
http://www.tucows.com
  Source for screen capture software and other useful resources.

VIDEO CAMERAS

Sites for two brands of video cameras are listed below. You can also search online for "low cost video cap-

ture," or you can go to a web shopping site and type in "video camera" to find the lowest prices on equipment or software.

Axis IP Video Cameras
http://www.axis.com
  These cameras enable you to capture and stream video from remote locations back to server storage without having to be in the room or use tapes.

JVC Everio Video Camcorders
http://www.jvc.com
  These camcorders capture all video to a hard drive, eliminating the need for tapes.

ELECTRONIC WHITEBOARDS AND SIMILAR TOOLS

The following resources serve the dual purpose of classroom teaching and assessment of practice. You can capture your instruction and evidence of students' learning (their writing on the board), as well as use these products as evidence to analyze later.

InterWrite SchoolPad
http://www.gtcocalcomp.com/interwriteschoolpad.htm

An interactive pad that allows teachers and students to add to a projected screen from anywhere in the classroom.

Mimio
http://www.mimio.com

Allows you to capture material written on a regular whiteboard.

Promethean ACTIVboard
http://www.prometheanworld.com

One of the interactive whiteboards developed for schools.

SMART Board
http://www.smarttech.com

Another interactive whiteboard developed for schools.

STUDENT INFORMATION SYSTEMS

These corporate solutions collect, store, and access data concerning students, such as gradebooks and attendance sheets.

MMS School Administrator Software
http://www.cri-mms.com

PowerSchool
http://www.apple.com/education/powerschool

SASI
http://www.pearsonschoolsystems.com/products/sasi

VIDEO ASSESSMENT TOOLS

The following tools in development enable both pre-service teachers and teacher educators to analyze video of classroom practices:

Digital Interactive Video Exploration and Reflection (DIVER)
http://diver.stanford.edu

Teachers Development Group (developer of the Teacher Reflection Tool)
http://www.teachersdg.org

Video Analysis Tool (VAT)
http://vat.uga.edu

---

case STUDY

Using Technology to Reflect on Science Teaching

When Laura Samson, a novice elementary-school teacher, heard that the Gemstone County Department of Education was hosting a summer workshop on science and reflection, she jumped at the chance to participate. She thought it would be a great way to learn science content, gather science resources, and take a closer look at her teaching strategies. Laura was also convinced that the workshop would help her feel more comfortable teaching science.

The workshop in which Laura participated was a two-week professional development course designed to provide one week of instruction and one week of practice. In addition to learning science content during the first week, Laura was introduced to the concept of reflection and a new web-based program, the Video Analysis Tool (VAT), to use for reflection on her teaching practice. During the second week, Laura was given the opportunity to test out different science activities, lesson plans, and teaching strategies on local elementary-school students. To help her examine her teaching more thoroughly, the workshop provided Laura with videotapes of her work with the elementary students. These videos were uploaded into the VAT system, and Laura was able to use the system to reflect on her science teaching.

Laura was excited about using videos to help her study certain aspects of her teaching. As she prepared to use VAT for the first time, Laura considered different triggers that she might want to pursue. One issue of utmost importance to Laura was her classroom environment. Laura knew that, through the use of video, she'd be able to look at her classroom from a different perspective. Instead of just seeing the classroom from her own position in the room, she'd be able to see it from another angle and watch herself teaching. This new viewpoint was important in helping her realize how she treated different students and how they interacted with one another. Specifically, it helped her determine whether or not she made each student feel comfortable and valued.

After viewing video of her teaching during the second week of the workshop, Laura realized that she'd been successful at making students feel comfortable and excited about learning. However, she also became aware of a few of her teaching weaknesses. Laura realized, for example, that she wasn't very good at guiding students through certain activities. She didn't always ask questions that would help them think about what they were doing and what they were learning.

One activity that Laura's students participated in centered on characteristics of trees. Laura had wanted her students to go out and identify various characteristics of trees in the schoolyard. Then she wanted them to come back inside and complete an activity in which they described and drew one of the trees they'd examined. However, not all of her students completed the activity as successfully as she'd expected. While viewing the video in the online system, Laura realized that, when her students were outside, she hadn't asked questions that encouraged them to think about the trees' characteristics. The comments she made didn't prepare them for the next phase of the activity as much as she would have liked. In this way, Laura focused her reflection on specific aspects of her teaching and began to develop a plan for improvement.

Engaging in analysis of her practice allowed Laura to identify both the strengths and the weaknesses of her teaching. These realizations helped her adjust her teaching to make use of her teaching strengths and to work on the weaknesses. Additionally, Laura was excited about using the video system during the school year to continue examining her teaching. In addition to issues that she'd identified during the summer, she planned to use VAT to analyze problems she encountered during the year.

Questions for Reflection and Discussion

Think about the way VAT allowed Laura to examine her lessons outside of the classroom and without all of the typical interferences associated with a lesson. This "out-of-the-moment" examination of her teaching provided Laura with an opportunity to recognize her teaching strengths and weaknesses.

1. What other areas of her lesson could Laura have examined through the use of videos?
2. How can videotapes of teacher practice be used to further examine the use of questioning to guide students through various activities?

3. How could Laura and other teachers use video-based evidence to show their accomplishment of national and state standards?
4. Novice teachers often need the advice and support of more experienced teachers. How could an experienced teacher use an online video system in conjunction with Laura's reflections to provide support for her teaching?

Meet the Standards

Online Study Center

Standards
Additional online material will help you prepare to meet the standards.

Look back at the "Standards to Guide Your Preparation" at the beginning of this chapter and reread the three ISTE NETS standards with which the chapter is aligned. They emphasize using technology to improve your instruction and enhance your professionalism—as well as taking the time to reflect on the way you use technology with your students.

Very often, preservice teachers are required to complete observations of classroom teachers in local schools. Typically, you'll get permission from the local teacher to observe a class and write a reflection about your experience. The journal entries are often then presented as part of your portfolio.

You may or may not need to undertake such an observation as part of your current training, but for the sake of your own professional development, consider how you'd extract the most from such an observation experience. Think about the following questions:

► How will you plan for the observation? What critical processes will guide your planning?
► How will you focus on the teacher's integration of technology in the lessons? What specifically will you look for and why?
► How will you generate good questions to ask the teacher? What are some good examples?
► What technology tools or resources will help you prepare for, conduct, and reflect on the observation?

PART IV

Technology Tools and Applications

Chapter 10

Productivity Tools

ISTE NETS

Teachers

▶ Demonstrate introductory knowledge, skills, and understanding of concepts related to technology.

▶ Identify and locate technology resources and evaluate them for accuracy and suitability.

▶ Apply technology to develop students' higher-order skills and creativity.

▶ Apply technology to increase productivity.

OTHER RELEVANT STANDARDS

California Technology Standards for Teachers (ISTE, 2006)

[Each candidate] uses a computer application to manipulate and analyze data (e.g., create, use, and report from a database; and create charts and reports from a spreadsheet).

Texas Technology Application Standards (ISTE, 2006)

The beginning teacher knows and understands:

▶ How to use appropriate computer-based productivity tools to create and modify solutions to problems.

▶ How to use technology applications to facilitate evaluation of work, including both process and product.

Tennessee Computer Technology Standards (ISTE, 2006)

▶ Students will use technology tools to enhance learning, increase productivity, and promote creativity.

▶ Students will use productivity tools to collaborate in constructing technology-enhanced models, prepare publications, and produce other creative works.

Productivity tools are probably the technologies that you'll use the most, both in your own work as a professional and with your students. These tools support a wide range of activities from writing to calculating. They are called productivity tools because they support people in doing tasks that would otherwise have to be done in a different, usually more laborious, way. For example, before we had word processors, there were typewriters. If you've ever had to correct typewritten copy—or retype it—you know one of the main advantages of a word processor.

Productivity applications are important for both you and your students; they help everyone compose, communicate, organize, and refine. In education and in business, everyone is expected to know how to use these tools.

In education, of course, the value of any technology tool lies in its ability to support high-quality instruction. Therefore, the choices you make about which, if any, productivity tools to use in a given lesson should tie directly to the goals of the lesson. Throughout this chapter and the other chapters about technology tools you'll read a number of cases illustrating different technology uses. In each case, notice how the technology ties to particular educational goals. As you read, think about ways you may want to use the tools as a teacher and how your students might use them for their own learning.

In this chapter we focus on five commonly used productivity tools: word processors, spreadsheets, databases, presentation software, and concept-mapping tools. We introduce each, discuss some typical uses in classrooms, and provide sample lessons capitalizing on the software.

Word Processors

Nearly everyone who has used a computer has used a word processor. These programs, such as Microsoft Word, AppleWorks' word processor, and WordPerfect, provide an easy way for computer users to create a wide variety of printed materials. Word processors allow the user to type in text, make multiple edits, and format in a number of ways to create an easily readable and visually appealing product.

Word processors in educational settings serve as productivity tools for both teachers and students. Teachers are able to create instructional materials, such as worksheets and tests, quickly and easily. Often, they can use the Copy and Paste features in the programs to pull together materials from multiple places or to edit tests and practice materials from publisher-provided test banks of questions. This capability allows teachers to create professional-looking materials for their students rather than the handwritten mimeographed sheets that were common only a short time ago.

Teachers can also use word processors to write letters and announcements to parents, letting them know what's happening in their classroom, announcing upcoming events, and providing other important information. Some teachers even use word processors to create simple newsletters to update parents on classroom progress and activities throughout the year.

Word processors as instructional tools

For students, word processors are an important instructional tool. First, word processors allow teachers to engage students in more authentic writing practices. Before word processors, students were often asked to write a paper one time and turn it in. The paper was either hand-written or completed on a typewriter. If any editing occurred, it required rewriting or retyping all of the text. With word processors, teachers can promote the idea that writing is a process of continual writing and refining. Editing is no longer a highly time-consuming act and can be taught from the earliest grades.

Another important aspect of word processors as instructional tools is the way they bring legibility and attractiveness to student work. It's widely believed that students will have more pride in their work if that work is professional in appearance. With word processors, any student's work can appear professional, because word processors produce legible text, can indicate misspelled words to student writers, and can even suggest more grammatically correct sentence structures.

Another strong reason for using word processors in schools is to support students in developing real-world skills that they'll use in college or the workplace. Most employers and all colleges assume that their workers and students have some level of facility with word processors. Whether students will be writing essays for classes or letters and reports in their jobs, they'll likely use word processors often and for many different purposes. The following "Technology in Action" feature discusses some of the ways word processors can be used in the classroom.

Technology in Action

Using Word Processing Creatively in the Classroom

Word processing skills are core skills that all students should have. Developing these skills can begin as early as when students begin to read. This doesn't mean that you should assign mere drill and practice on a keyboard—the typing of random words, sentences, and paragraphs. Instead, you can design projects that involve word processing programs, and you can integrate these projects into any content area.

Newspapers and Newsletters

The writing of newspapers or newsletters is a popular type of project for integrating word processing skills into learning activities. Word processing software includes easy-to-use templates, allowing students to focus on the content rather than the formatting of their work. These templates offer opportunities for students to be creative, but they can also be used simply as shells in which to insert text and graphics or photos. Either way, templates can help your students create professional-looking newsletters. Figure 10.1 shows a template from Microsoft Word.

Newspaper or newsletter projects are excellent learning tools for any curriculum area. Beyond basic grammar and writing skills, these projects

The Newslett

Instructions for creating this newsletter are included in the articles of the newsletter.↵

Fall 2004   Volume 2, Issue 3↵

↵

Schedule of Events↓
Winter 2004/2005↵

Event Date ․
Event Title. Event description with time, location, and other key information. See "The columns" for instructions on creating this sidebar․․

Event Date ․
Event Title. Event description with time, location, and other key information. See "The columns" for instructions on creating this sidebar․․

Event Date ․
Event Title. Event description with time, location, and other key information. See "The columns" for instructions on creating this sidebar․․

Event Date ․
Event Title. Event description with time, location, and other kev

This newsletter↵

Look at this newsletter in page layout view so that you see all of the pictures and text boxes. Click **Formatting Palette** so that you can easily see the formatting applied to the items on the page. Also, display nonprinting characters by selecting **Show/Hide ¶ ¶** on the toolbar.↵

The purpose of the newsletter is to demonstrate specific features rather than provide a template for your own newsletters. ↵

However, if you think the styles and other elements would be useful in your work, just save the file with another name and delete whatever you don't want to use. You could, for example, replace the newsletter banner with your own banner, delete the remainder of the document, and save it as a template for future use. ↵

The text in this newsletter is placed on the page by using columns and text boxes. For more information, see "The columns" and "'Text

unequal widths to accommodate the Schedule of Events sidebar. ↵

To set up a document with columns of unequal widths, on the **Format** menu, click **Columns**. Clear the **Equal column width** check box. If you first place your insertion point on this page and then look in the **Columns** dialog box, you'll see that the first column is 1.50" wide, and the second two columns are each 2.75" wide. ↵

Notice that the events sidebar on the left looks like a text box, but it's actually the first column on the page. It is formatted with a paragraph style that includes an orange border and a yellow fill, specified under **Borders and Shading** on the **Formatting Palette**. ↵

On subsequent pages, the columns are of equal width. You can quickly set up columns of equal width by clicking **Columns** and dragging across the number of columns you want. Whenever

Figure 10.1 A Newsletter Template in Microsoft Word Students can easily choose a preformatted template and immediately begin inserting text and graphics to suit the project.

involve students in research, analysis, summarizing, interpreting, critiquing, and clearly expressing themselves and their opinions. Newspaper-based projects also help students become more critical consumers of information in their daily life. By first analyzing the parts and purposes of a local newspaper, for example, students can begin to see the differences between news presented on the front page and information presented in the opinion or editorial sections of the paper. Through creating their own content for the newspaper, students will also begin to see the various ways that content can be presented, depending on the choices made by the author and editor. Well-chosen project topics will challenge students to think critically about and develop their own understanding of a content area.

Some topics that would lend themselves to a newspaper or newsletter format include daily activities in school, exploration of a historical event or period from multiple perspectives, and articles written from multiple perspectives about novels the students are reading. By using a newsletter or newspaper format, you can encourage your students to include editorials and factual articles, as well as cartoons and graphics that convey information.

THIS BROCHURE

Look at this brochure in page layout view (on the **View** menu) so that you can see all pictures and text boxes. Click **Formatting Palette** to easily see the formatting applied to the items on the page. Also, display nonprinting characters by making sure that **Show/Hide ¶** is selected on the toolbar.

Printing – Our design is a tri-fold brochure, laid out on two U.S. letter-sized pages with a landscape orientation (click **Page Setup** on the **File** menu). The first page includes the three outer panels of the brochure, and the second page includes the three inner ones. It should be printed double-sided and folded along the column borders.

Photo credits are listed in the Office for Mac 2004 Read Me file.

Instructions for creating this brochure are included in the body of the brochure.

SPA OPTIONS

Item	Day	Time*	Price
Mud bath			$95
Facial			$150
Personal Trainer session (1 hour)**			$70
Massage (half hour)**			$25
Dietary consultation			$30

* Requested times may be filled. To guarantee a time, please dial 0 and book your session with the concierge.

** For longer sessions, please dial 0 and reserve an extended block of time.

Order total: _____

Tax: _____

Total: _____

Name

Address or room number

Phone

Signature

Figure 10.2 A Brochure Template from Microsoft Both Microsoft Word and Microsoft Publisher have templates like this one, with which students can quickly develop a trifold brochure.

Brochures

Another excellent opportunity for incorporating word processing skills into the curriculum is having students create brochures. Again, the formatting is readily available with all word processing software and can be either rearranged to allow for student creativity or just used as a shell (see Figure 10.2). If your school has a great deal of technology, you may also find tools like Microsoft Publisher or Apple Pages to help you with designing these products.

Here are just a few of the many ideas that work well with brochures:

▶ *Trip planning.* Research a trip to a foreign country or another state, or retrace a historical trek, such as Lewis and Clark's expedition.
▶ *Marketing brochures.* Research the development and marketing of a product.
▶ *Informational brochures.* Research and write about health-related or social issues relevant to the students' peer group.

Spreadsheets

Spreadsheets are powerful mathematical and organizational tools that can be used to create a wide array of deliverables. They organize data into rows and columns as in a bookkeeping ledger, and they also offer ways to sort the data, perform calculations, and graph. Two popular spreadsheet tools are Microsoft Excel and AppleWorks' spreadsheet.

Spreadsheets as gradebooks

Spreadsheets are most commonly used by teachers as gradebooks. It's quite easy to set up a spreadsheet with one column for student names and other columns for grades on each assignment during the term. The function options in a spreadsheet can be used to calculate each student's average score. Teachers can also use spreadsheets to hold small, miscellaneous sets of information—for example, keeping track of which book number is assigned to which student.

The greatest advantages of spreadsheets come from their organizational and computing capabilities. Data can be sorted on any column or row, allowing teachers to look at student performance by grade or to view a list of students by last name. Similarly, the mathematical functions built into spreadsheets support a variety of common tasks ranging from finding averages to graphing data.

Spreadsheets as instructional tools

As instructional tools, spreadsheets are powerful devices that allow students to work with large sets of data, focus on problem solving rather than on computing, and move between different representations of the data. For example, a mathematics teacher can ask students to use a spreadsheet to solve a problem like the following:

In how many ways can nineteen coins equal exactly one dollar?

With a spreadsheet, students can quickly determine how many possible answers there are. Further, they can sort by the coins' denominations to determine whether there are any patterns in what they see (Figure 10.3). These kinds of skills are aligned with mathematical process standards, which include using technology to solve problems, using multiple representations, and engaging in mathematical reasoning (NCTM, 2000).

Pennies	Nickels	Dimes	Quarters	Number of coins	$ value
10	1	2	3	16	$1.10
10	1	4	2	17	$1.05
10	3	1	3	17	$1.10
15	2	1	1	19	$0.60
15	1	2	1	19	$0.65
15	1	1	2	19	$0.80
10	5	3	1	19	$0.90
15	0	1	3	19	$1.00
10	6	1	2	19	$1.00
10	3	5	1	19	$1.00
10	0	9	0	19	$1.00
5	12	1	1	19	$1.00
5	9	5	0	19	$1.00
0	18	1	0	19	$1.00
10	4	3	2	19	$1.10
10	1	7	1	19	$1.10
5	10	3	1	19	$1.10

Figure 10.3 Spreadsheet for the Coin Problem The coin problem spreadsheet might look like this when sorted to show the correct solutions. This problem is adapted from the InterMath website at **http://intermath.coe.uga.edu**.

If this problem were given to students without a spreadsheet, it would require considerable time to find all the possible answers, or it would need to be simplified to allow a smaller range of correct answers.

Similarly, science students might collect data on the height of a plant over time, record these data in a spreadsheet, and then convert the numbers into a graph. From the graph, they could then make predictions about how the plant's height will change over time.

The following "Technology in Action" feature about the stock market game illustrates the way spreadsheets can be integrated into a challenging activity for grades 5 and up. There are also scaled-back spreadsheet programs for younger children, such as The Cruncher and TinkerPlots.

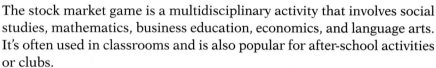

Technology in Action

The Stock Market Game

The stock market game is a multidisciplinary activity that involves social studies, mathematics, business education, economics, and language arts. It's often used in classrooms and is also popular for after-school activities or clubs.

The game sets up a simulation in which students, grades 5 though 12, are investors who explore and select which stocks they're going to buy. This open-ended problem-solving task allows students to research the various forms of business organizations, develop an understanding of how a capitalistic economy works, see the connection between market supply and demand, and gain insights into how our economy changes, as well as learn about trading on the stock market. The game requires students to make decisions, conduct research, analyze quantitative and qualitative information, and work together in teams.

There are important considerations for integrating the stock market game into the curriculum.

▶ *Adaptability.* Instruction can be as in depth as is appropriate for the content and for the students.
▶ *Scalability.* Whether there's one computer or an entire lab, the game can be tailored to fit the technology available.
▶ *Flexibility.* Instruction can be started at any time during the year and can be put on hold until time on the computers is available. Students can work daily, weekly, or only periodically.

Any spreadsheet program will enable students to track stocks over time (see Figure 10.4). With the program, students can also create charts and graphs to visually display the growth or decline in their stock choices (Figure 10.5). A number of free Internet resources provide definitions of financial terms, explanations of how the market works, links to financial resources, and a historical perspective on the market and the world economy. (See the "Resources" section at the end of this chapter.) There are even Internet versions of the game. Students or teams of students can also be challenged by a competition with other students around the world.

The Stock Market Game

Stock Symbol	Stock Name	Number Shares	Base Price	Base Value	Current Price	Current Value	Gain Loss	% Change
GPS	Gap, Inc	572.41	$17.47	$10,000.00	$19.74	$11,299.37	$1,299.37	0.13
NOC	Northrop Grum	176.55	$56.64	$10,000.00	$55.57	$9,811.09	($188.91)	(0.02)
NKE	Nike, Inc.	115.69	$86.44	$10,000.00	$89.90	$10,400.28	$400.28	0.04
DUK	Duke Energy	369.96	$27.03	$10,000.00	$31.02	$11,476.14	$1,476.14	0.15
SBUX	Starbucks Corp	313.48	$31.90	$10,000.00	$33.09	$10,373.04	$373.04	0.04
COST	Costco Wholes	202.43	$49.40	$10,000.00	$52.88	$10,704.45	$704.45	0.07
AMZN	Amazon.com	208.38	$47.99	$10,000.00	$45.99	$9,583.25	($416.75)	(0.04)
STI	SunTrust Bk	133.60	$74.85	$10,000.00	$76.57	$10,229.79	$229.79	0.02
ALA	ALCATEL	815.00	$12.27	$10,000.00	$13.45	$10,961.70	$961.70	0.10
SLE	Sara Lee Corp	556.79	$17.96	$10,000.00	$19.99	$11,130.29	$1,130.29	0.11
	Total			$100,000.00		$105,969.39	$5,969.39	0.06

Figure 10.4 Spreadsheet for the Stock Market Game This spreadsheet can be created with just a few basic formulas in Microsoft Excel or a similar program.

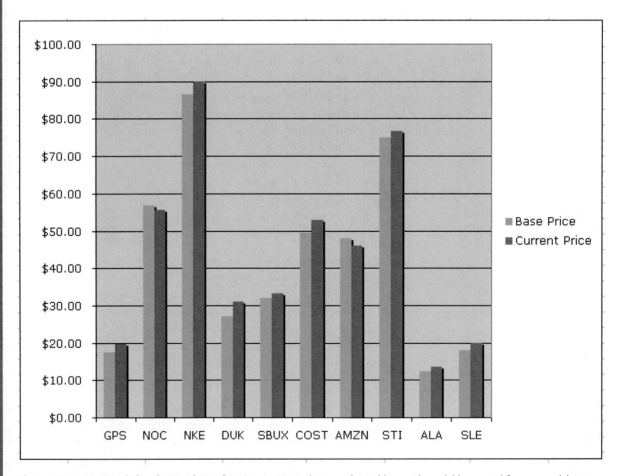

Figure 10.5 Bar Graph for the Stock Market Game Many charts and graphics can be quickly created from spreadsheet data to display the students' results in the stock market game.

Databases

Two kinds of databases

Databases are more common in businesses than in schools, largely because many database tools are complicated to use and require trained programmers to alter. However, they can be useful tools in classrooms if the correct software is available.

There are two basic kinds of databases. The simpler kind is a *tabular database* that stores all of the information together and doesn't reference other data sets. This kind of database is robust enough for many classroom activities. The more complicated databases are referred to as *relational databases*. These store data in tables that don't represent the entire data set. Instead, each table "points to" a main table that keeps everything organized. For example, think about your school library's system. The database there is a relational one, in which data about a book, such as its author and publication date, may be stored in one place, while information on its call number—which is essentially its address in the library—is stored in another place. A table links these two together by assigning the book a number and referencing that number in the other table. Then a third piece of information is tied to that book when a student checks the material out. So, a number assigned to the book that points to the book's information is also assigned to the student who currently has the book. The student's information isn't added to the book's information in the database; instead, it's only temporarily linked to it. For the purposes of this chapter, we focus on projects that can be done with the simpler kind of database.

General database tools allow the user to create fields of any kind to store data. One general database tool that's easy enough for everyday use is FileMaker. With software of this type, students in a history course can enter the names and dates of particular events as they learn about them, then search for those events by date or put them in order. Or students can record information about notable people. For example, if they're studying the early days of the United States, they'll find that certain important people show up in the historical records over and over again. The students can record every event tied to those people; then, when doing a project later in the year, they can search for a person to see everything that person did.

Dedicated databases are systems designed for collecting and organizing a particular kind of information. For example, EndNote is a dedicated program used to catalog bibliographic information about books and articles. This tool ties into a word processor, so that students can relate their citations back to the database. When their papers are completed, the students can generate their reference lists through EndNote, based on the works they've cited. EndNote does much of the formatting and organization, allowing the students to create professional-looking papers.

The following two "Technology in Action" features on databases will help you think about ways to take advantage of database software in your own teaching. One of the features illustrates a handy method of keeping track of lesson plans. The other shows that students can work with simple database software as early as the fourth grade.

Technology in Action

Database Programs to Help You Stay Organized

Database programs are most commonly used in schools to track students—for attendance, test score management, report cards, and so on. However, tools like FileMaker make it easy for you to create a management system for your lesson plan ideas and handouts, so that you don't have to keep cabinets of old handouts up to date.

Figure 10.6 shows a lesson plan database that lets you not only record information about your lessons in a way that you can easily access later by browsing topics or searching, but also assign materials to go with those lessons. Once you've entered the information you need about the objectives you're trying to meet and notes to yourself about ways to implement the lesson smoothly, you add information about how to do the lesson. Then you click on the "Materials" tab to add any worksheets,

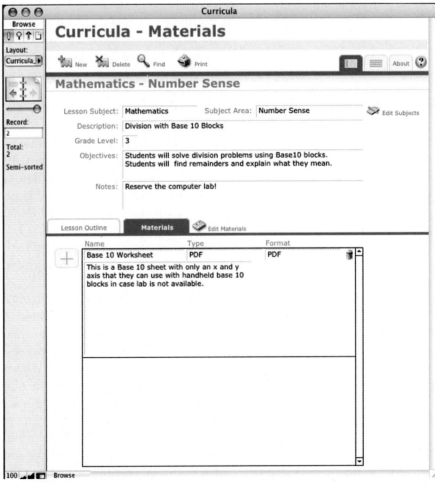

Figure 10.6 Two Screenshots from a Lesson Plan Database These screens are from an adapted version of a part of the K–12 Starter Kit from FileMaker.
Source: Software available from **http://filemaker.com**

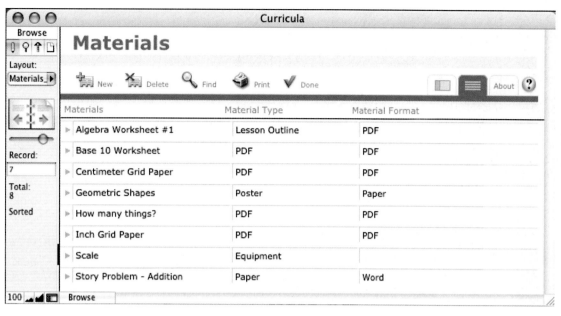

Figure 10.6 (continued)

websites, PowerPoint presentations, videos, or other materials that go with the lesson. When you add the materials, you can add information about what the material is and why you use it with this lesson plan. Because these materials are pulled in from a premade list that you create, it's easy to associate a single resource with more than one lesson plan. This makes it easier to plan year after year as your database of lesson plans and materials continues to grow.

Technology in Action

Organizing and Analyzing Data with TinkerPlots

In a fourth- or fifth-grade classroom, students can easily use a tool like TinkerPlots, Tabletop, or Fathom to analyze and organize data. For example, TinkerPlots, a data analysis tool that allows students to explore data relationships, lets them use or build a database that can be displayed in different ways. One of the data sets built into TinkerPlots is about cats. Figure 10.7 shows a portion of the cat data presented in a table.

Imagine that you want to help students understand the multiple ways in which data can be represented. You might have them organize and reorganize the cat data to explore different relationships. For example, you could ask how many cats are greater than or equal to 18 inches long and less than or equal to 10 pounds. Figure 10.8 shows one data display that students could make to answer this question. The tool allows the data to be separated or graphed and to show variation through color differences, allowing students to ask complex questions with more than two variables (for instance, "How many cats over 18 inches long and under 10 pounds are orange?").

100 Cats								
	Name	**Gender**	**Age**	**Weight**	**BodyL...**	**TailLe...**	**EyeCo...**	**PadC...**	**Tail_...**
42	Harmony	male	3.0	12	24	11	yellowish	black	0.46
43	Priscilla	female	3.0	8.5	23	11	green	mixed	0.48
44	Ralph	male	3.0	9	23	11	yellowish	black	0.48
45	Sassy	female	3.0	8	23	12	yellowish	gray	0.52
46	Saman...	female	3.0	8	27	12	blue	black	0.44
47	Shiver	male	3.0	12	23	10	yellowish	pink	0.43
48	Sparky	male	3.0	12	18	8	blue	pink	0.44
49	Taint	male	3.0	11	14	11	green	pink	0.79
50	Boo	male	3.5	10.75	19.5	11.5	yellowish	brown	0.59
51	Diva	female	3.5	11	20	12	green	pink	0.6

Figure 10.7 Sample Data Table from TinkerPlots' Cat Database

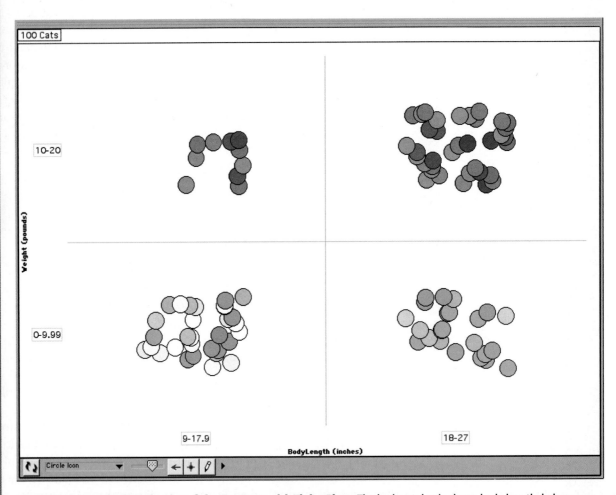

Figure 10.8 Sample Organization of the Cat Data with TinkerPlots The horizontal axis shows body length: below 18 inches (the diagrams on the left) and 18–27 inches (the diagrams on the right). The vertical axis displays weight in pounds: below 10 pounds (bottom row) and 10–20 pounds (top row).

Next, you might ask the students to consider median and mode, because those are important descriptors in data analysis. To do this by hand with more than a few pieces of data is a tedious task; however, a computer-based tool like TinkerPlots makes the analysis easy and frees students to look for patterns and make conjectures. The two images in Figure 10.9

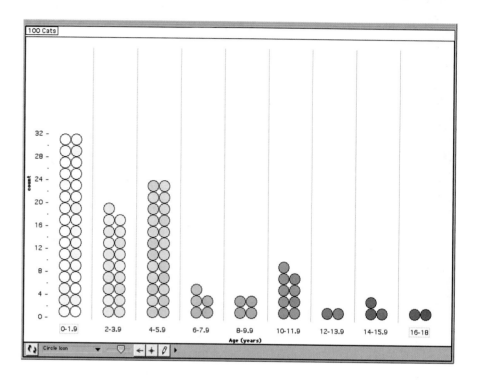

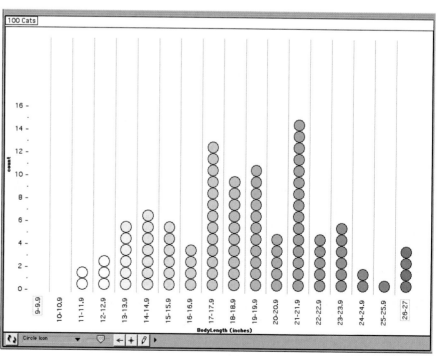

Figure 10.9 Cats Organized by Age (top) and Body Length (bottom) in TinkerPlots

were made from the same data set by simply changing the *x*-axis, which takes one click. The software also allows you to focus students' attention on where the individual pieces of data are within the data set: in displays like those in Figure 10.9, labels can be turned on to show each cat's name, age, color, or other attribute.

As students use the tool, they can draw conclusions about what kinds of graphical representations are most useful for determining mode and median or for looking at the frequency of particular sets of attributes (such as long cats under 10 pounds). Students can do authentic analyses of the data set and make inferences about the data (such as "Full-grown cats tend to be at least 17 inches long"). This kind of mathematical inference is the critical part of data analysis, and it simply isn't practical with large data sets when students have to work by hand.

Further, by using a tool like TinkerPlots, students can easily see that each point on the graph represents a piece of data. By clicking on any point, they can make the data record for that point appear next to the plot, and suddenly the data are no longer abstract ideas or numbers.

Presentation Software

Presentation tools provide users with an easy way to make a presentation that's well formatted and appealing. If your school or district is well endowed with technology, you may have some hardware, such as interactive whiteboards and tablets (see Spotlight 10.1), that can be used as a presentation tool. We focus here, however, on presentation software, which is another of the many tools that are appropriate for both students and teachers.

Slide shows

Typical presentation software programs, including Microsoft Power-Point and Apple's Keynote, create computerized slide shows. A slide show projected to the front of the class can help you pull your daily notes together for students without writing them on the board. The slides can also provide an easy way to access a number of other tools. For example,

---

SPOTLIGHT 10.1   Using Interactive Whiteboards and Tablets for Presentations

Interactive whiteboards and tablets, which we discussed in the chapter "Technology for Decision Making and Growth," allow any program to become a presentation program. In other words, if you have an interactive whiteboard like the Promethean ACTIVboard or the SMART Board, or a tablet like the InterWrite SchoolPad, you can run a program on your computer, project it on the screen, and use the stylus or tablet to interact with it.

However, like other tools discussed in this book, these are effective only when the instruction is well designed. They won't make up for a lack of planning or a poor lesson plan. They will, however, enhance good lesson plans by allowing the teacher to move freely around the room rather than being tied to a computer and by allowing students to interact both with the tool and with one another.

Elementary-School Students Use PowerPoint

To help develop your ideas about using PowerPoint in the classroom, watch the HM Video Case called **Teaching Technology Skills: An Elementary School Lesson on PowerPoint,** available in the Online Study Center. In this video, you'll see how two teachers engaged their students in presenting what they learned about the civil rights movement.

In addition to seeing an interesting project, you'll get some ideas for teaching elementary-school age students how to use technology. Check out the Bonus Videos as well, and also read transcripts of interviews with the teachers, which explain how they view technology and why they believe it's important for students to learn to use it.

Benefits of students' use of presentation software

you may have the day's objective on one slide, some key points to talk about on the next slide, and on the third slide a link to a website that you need to show students before they begin working on a project. Once the students have finished their project, you can pull up a blank summary slide and ask them to help fill it in with key ideas from the day's lesson.

The drawback of presentation software as an instructional tool is that it promotes the old-fashioned model of the teacher standing at the front of the room telling students all the information they need to know. Therefore, a teacher who chooses to use this kind of software needs to think about the instructional goals of using it and decide when it's most appropriate.

For students, presentation software is a great way to learn how to organize content for presentations. The software helps motivate them to be clear in their organization, and it encourages them to share with one another. For example, a student group may have the assignment of teaching the class about rain forests. With presentation software, they can create a presentation that includes images and movies, rather than just an oral report. Further, under the teacher's guidance, they can learn how to organize information to tell a coherent story about their topic. The software allows students to write more than if they were creating a single poster, but still forces them to be succinct in their statements. Finally, presentation software allows students to print out copies of their slides, which they can use to practice their presentation or provide as handouts in class. The following "Technology in Action" feature shows how presentation software can help students present their discoveries in a scavenger hunt.

Technology in Action

Geometry Scavenger Hunt

For the geometry scavenger hunt, students are given a list of geometric shapes to find in and around their school. Students work in small groups and use a digital camera to take pictures of the shapes on their list. With a vocabulary list (Figure 10.10) as reference, they also describe each shape and write down the examples they found. The amount of structure provided is up to the teacher and should be based on the students' age level. For younger grades, you'll probably want to have all the students go to one location, such as the playground or cafeteria. Older students may welcome the opportunity to take pictures in more than one location and even photograph shapes that aren't on their list.

Term	Brief Description	Shape
1. Line segment		
2. Angle		
3. Right angle		
4. Parallel lines or segments		

Figure 10.10 **Part of the Vocabulary List for a Scavenger Hunt**

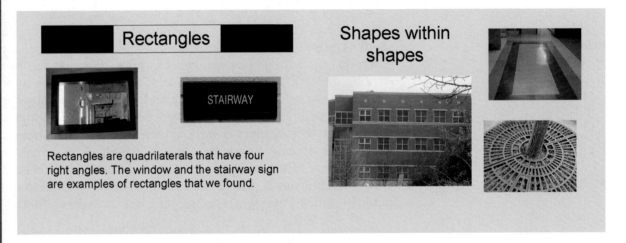

Figure 10.11 **Two Slides from a Student Presentation for a Geometry Scavenger Hunt**

After students have taken the pictures and completed the vocabulary list, the teacher and students upload the pictures into the computer. Once the photographs are in the computer, the students can use the presentation software to create the presentation. The slides in this presentation can vary in terms of content. Figure 10.11 shows two sample slides. One slide includes pictures of rectangles and a sentence describing rectangles. The second slide includes pictures of large shapes that have smaller shapes inside of them.

This activity can help students make connections between properties of geometric shapes and the world around them. By using presentation software, students have the power to include real-world pictures, in addition to pictures found on the Internet or constructed with the software's drawing tool. The software also lets students enter text to describe the shapes they've photographed.

■ Basic Screen Design for Presentations

Though it's great to be creative when preparing online presentations, there are a few key ideas that both you and your students should keep in mind to keep presentations readable and effective.

Key ideas to make presentations effective

▶ *Color.* It isn't the colors themselves, but the relationship between the colors you choose, that's important. Choose background colors and font colors that have strong contrast. Choose a dark background with white or light-colored text, or choose a light background with dark text (not red or orange text—those colors hurt readers' eyes).

▶ *Text.* Choose a sans serif font (a font that uses just the basic strokes of each character, with no short ornamental lines), such as Arial. Serif fonts, like Times New Roman, are best for printed materials. The size of the text should be large enough to be read from the back of the classroom; *test it.*

▶ *Transitions.* If using transitions between slides (nifty "fades" or "wipes" that the software makes available), choose no more than two different transition types in a given presentation. More than that will give viewers a headache and distract from the message.

▶ *Bullets.* Avoid using long paragraphs. Bulleted lists are better. Keep content points short and well spaced. Generally, no more than twenty words per slide is best.

▶ *Graphics.* Use graphics where appropriate and meaningful. Too many or unsuitable graphics can distract from the content message, but well-placed graphics are a must. If a chart or graph illustrates the point, use it.

Once all is said and done: *Test, test, test!* Always check visual presentations in advance to make sure they're clear and easily read from the back of the classroom.

Concept-Mapping Tools

In our chapter "Learner Needs," we discuss the usefulness of concept maps. Computer tools that allow the user to create such visual representations of the links among ideas are called flowcharting or **concept-mapping tools.** These are very powerful tools in classrooms because they can support students in developing outlines of their ideas and in organizing their thoughts before they begin writing or creating their own materials.

Common concept-mapping software tools

Commonly used concept-mapping tools include Inspiration and Kidspiration (for younger learners) and OmniGraffle. Many of these tools provide an easy-to-use palette of shapes that can hold concepts or ideas that the students enter (see Figure 10.12). The palettes also offer different kinds of arrows and lines to connect the ideas. The tools often also include outlining capabilities so that the computer will generate an outline from the organized ideas on the screen.

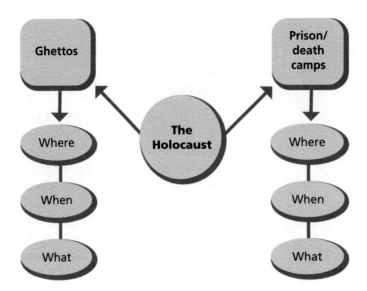

Figure 10.12 Simple Concept Map for Organizing a Paper About the Holocaust

Free Productivity Tools

Free "office" suites

Microsoft Office, comprised of multiple software programs including Word, Excel, and PowerPoint, is probably the most well known of all the productivity tool suites. However, you may find your school does not have the budget to purchase the functionality of commercial productivity tools. In this case there are a number of high-quality freeware (no cost) and shareware (low cost) titles available for you to download and use.

One example is ThinkFree Office Online **(http://www.thinkfree.com),** which offers word processing, spreadsheet, and presentation software. The best part is that it's entirely online, so you won't need to install any software on your own computer.

Another example is OpenOffice **(http://www.openoffice.org),** which will run on Macintosh, PC, and Linux-based systems. This tool includes not only word processing, spreadsheet, and presentation software, but also a drawing program and a database tool. Like ThinkFree, this tool is free.

Summary

The productivity tools highlighted in this chapter are just a few of those available. Productivity tools include word processors, spreadsheets, databases, presentation software, page-layout, and concept-mapping programs. Because they make complex tasks easier, these tools can allow students to explore subject matter in greater depth. Moreover, many of the more common productivity tools are ones that students will be expected to use in the business and academic worlds.

Productivity tools offer authentic ways for students to learn about multiple forms of communication, data manipulation, and planning strategies. With a word processor, for example, students can learn that professional writing is a process of continual writing and refining. By creating a newsletter or brochure, they gain experience in the kind of research, analysis, summarizing, and interpreting that go into real-world publications. When they use a spreadsheet or a simple database, they can focus on analyzing data and solving a genuine problem, rather than on mere calculation.

The use of these tools in classrooms requires careful planning and attention to the desired learning goals, but the rewards for your students are substantial. In addition, as we've mentioned throughout the chapter, productivity tools serve your needs as a teacher by helping you create instructional materials, communicate with parents, keep records, and present material clearly and effectively.

RESOURCES

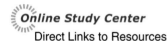
Online Study Center
Direct Links to Resources

WORD PROCESSING, SPREADSHEET, AND PAGE LAYOUT SOFTWARE

AppleWorks
http://www.apple.com/education/k12/products/appleworks
A productivity suite that includes a word processor and spreadsheet. Free on many Macintosh machines.

The Cruncher
http://www.knowledgeadventure.com
A spreadsheet program for upper-elementary students. See also the review at **http://www.thejournal.com/articles/14188** and a discussion on using The Cruncher for accessibility at **http://ncam.wgbh.org/cdrom/cruncher.html**

Microsoft Office
http://office.microsoft.com
Office includes Microsoft Word and Excel, the most common word processing and spreadsheet programs.

OpenOffice
http://www.openoffice.org
A free productivity suite that includes word processor, spreadsheet, presentation, database, and drawing products. Will run on Macintosh, Windows, and Linux systems.

ThinkFree Office Online
http://www.thinkfree.com
A free word processing, spreadsheet, and presentation software package that works from the World Wide Web so that no installation is required.

WordPerfect
http://www.corel.com
One of the early commercial word processing programs.

Adobe InDesign
http://www.adobe.com/education/products/indesign.html
Professional-grade page layout software that allows a high level of versatility.

Microsoft Publisher
http://office.microsoft.com
Included in some editions of the Microsoft Office suite, Publisher is a simple page layout program with templates for publications, such as brochures and newsletters.

STOCK MARKET GAME RESOURCES

The Stock Market Game—Lower Level
http://www.econ.org/smg
Online interactive stock market game for grades 4 and up.

The Stock Market Game—Upper Level
http://www.smgww.org
http://www.stockmarketgame.org
Students get to invest a virtual $100,000 in a portfolio to see what happens.

The Stock Market Game in Georgia
http://www.gcee.org/www/projects/smg/open.htm
Teaching materials and more for playing the Georgia version of the stock market game.

Virtual Stock Exchange
http://vse.marketwatch.com/game
An elaborate online stock-trading game environment for anyone to use.

DATABASE SOFTWARE

EndNote
http://www.endnote.com
A database program dedicated to organizing bibliographic information.

Fathom
http://keypress.com/catalog/products/software/Prod_Fathom.html
Data analysis and statistics software for middle and high school.

FileMaker
http://www.filemaker.com/solutions/k12
A user-friendly database program.

Tabletop and Tabletop Jr.
http://www.sunburst.com
>   Data organization tools developed for students. Tabletop is a spreadsheet and database; Tabletop Jr. is a graphing program.

TinkerPlots
http://keypress.com/catalog/products/software/
Prod_TinkerPlots.html
>   Data organization tool for supporting upper-elementary and middle-grades students in conducting a wide variety of analyses.

PRESENTATION SOFTWARE

Apple Keynote and Pages (parts of iWork)
http://www.apple.com/education/iwork
>   Presentation software package for Macintosh computers.

PowerPoint
http://office.microsoft.com
>   Also included in the Microsoft Office suite, PowerPoint is a very common presentation package.

CLASSROOM HARDWARE USEFUL FOR PRESENTATIONS

ACTIVboard
http://www.prometheanworld.com
>   One of the interactive whiteboards developed for schools.

InterWrite SchoolPad
http://www.gtcocalcomp.com/interwriteschoolpad.htm
>   An interactive pad that allows teachers and students to add to a projected screen from anywhere in the classroom.

SMART Board
http://www.smarttech.com
>   Another interactive whiteboard developed for schools.

Wacom Tablets
http://www.wacom.com
>   One of the most common brands of drawing tablet.

CONCEPT-MAPPING SOFTWARE

Inspiration
http://www.inspiration.com/productinfo/inspiration
>   Concept-mapping software for middle school and older.

Kidspiration
http://www.inspiration.com/productinfo/kidspiration
>   Concept-mapping software for elementary students.

OmniGraffle
http://www.omnigroup.com/applications/omnigraffle
>   Concept-mapping software for middle-school and older students.

case
STUDY

Planning How to Use New Classroom Equipment

Ms. Laramie, a seventh-grade social studies teacher, is excited because she's just received a monetary award that she wants to use to purchase equipment for her classroom. When she sits down with the school's media specialist to discuss her plans, Ms. Laramie begins talking about all the things she's eager to do. She tells the media specialist that she thinks she wants a laptop, a SMART Board, and presentation software. She explains that this hardware and software will allow her to build presentations that she can show her students.

The media specialist immediately recognizes that this approach may make the classroom less learner centered, because of the single computer and the use of the software. However, she's eager to help Ms. Laramie and likes the idea of the teacher's having access to a laptop. She asks Ms. Laramie about the goals she wants to meet and how those goals might be addressed with technology.

Together, Ms. Laramie and the media specialist decide that the best approach is for Ms. Laramie to work on developing a few lessons with her new equipment which are specifically designed to meet the applicable learning standards and to create a learner-centered environment.

Questions for Reflection and Discussion

1. On the basis of what you now know about standards-based teaching and learner-centered principles, what specific concerns do you think the media specialist may have had with Ms. Laramie's plan? (If you need to review the Learner-Centered Psychological Principles, look back at our chapter "Learner-Centered Classrooms" or go to **http://www.apa.org/ed/lcp2/lcp14.html**.)
2. Do you think Ms. Laramie can create a genuinely learner-centered environment with the tools she's selected?
3. If you had the award money Ms. Laramie received, what approach would you take in developing a plan to address standards and align your teaching with the learner-centered principles? Where would you start? What resources would you use?

Meet the Standards

Online Study Center
Standards
More standards-related resources are available online.

Take a moment to reread the NETS standards that we listed in "Standards to Guide Your Preparation" at the beginning of this chapter. How do you believe you're progressing toward meeting these standards?

To focus your reflection, think of the tools discussed in this chapter and ways in which you've already used them. Consider the following questions:

► How have productivity tools helped you be more creative? more organized? more productive?

► How does using productivity tools align with the content standards you'll be teaching?

► How can you incorporate the Learner-Centered Psychological Principles into your approaches for using these tools?

Chapter 11

Development Tools

ISTE NETS

Teachers

▶ Demonstrate introductory knowledge, skills, and understanding of concepts related to technology.

▶ Identify and locate technology resources and evaluate them for accuracy and suitability.

▶ Apply technology to develop students' higher-order skills and creativity.

▶ Manage student learning activities in a technology-enhanced environment.

OTHER RELEVANT STANDARDS

California Technology Standards for Teachers (ISTE, 2006)

Teachers will communicate through a variety of electronic media (e.g., presentations incorporating images and sound, web pages, and portfolios).

Arizona Technology Education Standards (ISTE, 2006)

Building on productivity tools, students will collaborate, publish, and interact with peers, experts, and other audiences using telecommunications and media.

Michigan Technology Curriculum Content Standards (ISTE, 2006)

Students will apply appropriate technologies to critical thinking, creative expression, and decision-making skills.

Tennessee Computer Technology Standards (ISTE, 2006)

Students will use telecommunications to collaborate, publish, and interact with peers, experts, and other audiences.

For our purposes in this book, **development tools** include those that are used to edit images, prepare web pages, and create multimedia experiences. Like productivity tools, development tools offer teachers exciting ways to promote creativity and bring authenticity to classroom tasks.

In this chapter we explore some of the tools that are commonly used in classrooms and provide you with ideas for projects and activities that align with the principles we've been discussing in this book.

Image-Editing Software

Anyone who has tried to insert photographs or clip art into a document knows the value of image-editing software, such as Photoshop, Graphic Converter, Picasa, Fireworks, and GIMP. Image-editing software ranges dramatically in complexity and price. For example, many digital cameras include simple editing software. At the other end of the scale, professional-level tools like Photoshop and Fireworks are more flexible but also more complicated to use.

Standard features of image-editing software

Some features that you can expect to find in any image-editing software include the ability to resize images, crop images, and change a color image into a grayscale one. Most of these tools also allow you to save the image in a number of different formats, including JPEG, TIFF, GIF, and PICT files—standard file types that are commonly used for web page development, presentation software, and word processing. More advanced tools include filters that allow you to dramatically change the appearance of images. For example, you can change an image to look as if it was drawn with chalk or painted with watercolors.

As a basic introduction to the power of image-editing software, consider two different cases.

1. Your students have taken a photo of the playground with your school's digital camera. They'd like to edit the photo to include in their scavenger hunt presentation. The original photo includes both a slide and a swing set, but students would like to separate the two pieces of playground equipment so that they have one photo of a slide and one of a swing set. Any image-editing software will allow them to do this.
2. You'd like to add a photograph to your class's web page. The source image you have is a 5-by-7-inch photograph that you're going to scan. This will be too big for a website, but you don't want to cut out any of the image. The software will allow you to keep the entire picture but make it smaller.

Spotlight 11.1 on image editing will give you some tips for understanding and using this type of software.

SPOTLIGHT 11.1   ## Tips for Image Editing

Here's some useful information to consider as you begin learning about image editing.

Brightness/Contrast

You can often make an image look a lot better simply by adjusting its brightness and contrast. As you increase brightness, your whites will look whiter, and your blacks will look grayer. Contrast controls how much difference there is between the whites and the blacks. As you increase contrast, your picture gains definition between the light and dark elements.

Cropping

Cropping refers to cutting out a portion of your image. Typically, cropping tools let you select the portion of the image you want to keep and discard any parts of the image that aren't in the selected area. Cropping is useful if you want to use only a portion of an image or if you're trying to save disk space. A smaller picture takes less storage space and loads more quickly if you're using it on the World Wide Web.

Resolution (DPI)

Resolution refers to the amount of detail in the image, typically measured in *dots per inch (DPI)*. The resolution you want is determined by the kind of display you'll be using. Images that will be shown only on a computer screen should be saved at 72 dpi, the limit of conventional computer monitors. By saving at this relatively low resolution, you can create a much smaller file size, which allows the image to load faster on your computer and on the World Wide Web. However, if you're going to print an image on paper, you'll want to use a higher resolution. Most of today's printers will print at least 600 dpi. If you know that you'll want to print an image, be sure to save it at a higher resolution so that the printout will provide you with a smooth image rather than a pixilated (jagged) one.

RGB/Grayscale/Black and White

Whenever you use an image editor, you have options about the colors.

- *RGB* (which stands for red, green, blue) is for full-color images. On your computer monitor, just as on a TV screen, everything is made of very tiny dots (pixels) that are either red, green, or blue. Every color you see is a combination of different intensities of these three base colors. Similarly, printers mix a small

(A)

(B)

(C)

Figure 11.1 The Importance of Aspect Ratio
(A) An original image. (B) The image resized with no attention to the aspect ratio. (C) Resizing with the aspect ratio maintained.

number of actual ink or toner colors to make up all the color tones you see in a printed image. When you print a color image, the RGB screen colors are converted into the correct ink or toner mixes for your particular printer.

- *Grayscale* images consist of varying shades of black and white. They look like what we would normally call black-and-white pictures.
- *Black and white* in image editors refers to images that are made of *only* black and white pixels. This means that there are no colors and no shades of gray. Every section of the image is either 100 percent black or 100 percent white.

In general, you'll use either RGB or grayscale. Typically, you use black and white only for something like a blackline master or a very simple line drawing.

Size

You'll want to be sure to maintain the *aspect ratio* when you resize your images. This means that all dimensions of the image change proportionally when you change its size, rather than squeezing or stretching in one direction or another. To do this, you usually just hold down the Shift key while you drag the bottom right corner of the image with your mouse.

To see the importance of maintaining image aspect ratio, look at Figure 11.1. Part A is the original image, and parts B and C were resized using a word processing program. Part B shows the effect of simply dragging the image corners—you can see that the image became distorted. Part C illustrates resizing with the Shift key held down to maintain image aspect ratio—the picture still has its proper shape.

Drawing Tools

Standard functions of drawing tools

Like image-editing tools, drawing tools allow the easy addition of graphic elements to the learning environment. Drawing tools range from the simple ones found in word processing programs to very complex and sophisticated programs like FreeHand, CorelDraw, and Illustrator. All of these tools typically include a standard set of shapes (rectangles, ovals), as well as features that allow the user to draw straight or curved lines. These tools also allow the user to add colors and patterns to a drawing.

Standalone drawing tools (those not included as part of a larger package like AppleWorks or OpenOffice) often include special functions that allow them to work particularly well with electronic drawing tablets (such as Wacom tablets; see **http://www.wacom.com**). These tools can often react to the way the user is holding the stylus and to the amount of pressure placed on the drawing tablet. This control gives users a high degree of flexibility in drawing.

Web Page Development Tools

Web pages are a great tool for instruction and for helping teachers and schools keep the community informed about things happening in the school. Creating web pages can be an entertaining activity for you and your students, and it doesn't require many special skills, as long as you keep it simple.

Some common web page creation tools are Microsoft's FrontPage and Macromedia's Dreamweaver. However, many word processors also have built-in web development tools, which are acceptable for most simple web pages. Such tools allow you to work on your web page on your own computer and to use a WYSIWYG ("what you see is what you get") interface so that you can see what your final product will look like. Many commercially available web page editors also include easy-to-use

HTML

tools that allow you to seamlessly transfer your web page from your machine to the server that will allow others to see it.

Web page development tools generally provide you with the same features as word processors but allow you to save your work in an HTML format. HTML, which stands for *hypertext markup language,* allows your page to show up on the web formatted the way you'd like it to be. In addition to including text, good web page development tools allow you to insert images and create tables. Typically, too, they provide easy ways for you to create links to other documents and web pages, as well as to customize web page colors. Spotlight 11.2 will help you understand the lingo.

Creating a web page, unlike many of the other activities suggested in this book, will require you to check with a media or instructional technology specialist at your school. You'll need this person's cooperation in order to get space on the school's web server and information about the school's policies for web pages. If your school doesn't host teacher web pages, a simple Internet search for "teacher web pages" will help you find free services to help you create a website for your class.

Web Pages for Communication with Parents

If you let parents know that you'll be posting news and homework information on the web page every day, they'll begin to use this resource. They'll check the website for important information and to make sure their children are doing the assigned work. You can also use your web page to provide additional suggestions for websites that parents can use to enhance learning at home.

SPOTLIGHT 11.2   Common Terms for Web Development

Cookie. A cookie is a file containing information saved on your computer by a server. For example, if you visit a website that requires you to specify your browser, that information will be saved in a cookie. Cookies can make your Internet experiences easier by storing information about you so that you don't have to supply it each time you log onto certain websites. Some people don't like cookies because they're put on your machine without your knowledge. However, they're generally more useful than harmful.

Firewall. A firewall is a buffer between your computer or computer network and the Internet in general. There are several kinds of firewalls, each using a different approach to protect your computer from hackers and viruses. Firewalls are, at times, problematic, because they block certain kinds of useful information from getting to your machine. It's important to know who in your school can advise you about the way firewalls

are set up for your district and what aspects can be changed to fit your needs as a teacher.

FTP (File Transfer Protocol). FTP is a means of moving files between your computer and a server, like the server that makes your classroom web page available on the Internet. There are many free and shareware software programs available to allow FTP functions. All of them ask you to find the file on your machine that you want to move and to specify the location to which you want to move it. Many web browsers now have simple FTP functions built in.

Flash. Flash is one of many programs used to create interactive web content. Flash content can include animations, movies, and interactive "applets" (small applications).

HTML (Hypertext Markup Language). Hypertext markup language is the coding used on web pages to tell the web browser how to display the content. Most robust web page editors will generate this code automatically for you but still allow you to view and modify it.

Hypertext. This is a name for all text that links to something else. On the web, the blue text links that you find on almost every page are hypertext. When you click on a hypertext link, you're taken to another part of the site or to another site entirely. Hypertext allows you to jump around in your reading, rather than reading everything linearly, as you would in a book.

Java. Java is a commonly used programming language on the Internet. Many interactive applications are written in Java.

JavaScript. JavaScript is a scripting language (rather than a programming language like Java). It allows a web page developer to insert particular functions in a web page by adding a few lines of script. For example, running heads, drop down menus that you find in manywebpages, and radio buttons or check boxes that are embedded in an online form you complete, are often done with JavaScript.

PDF (Portable Document Format). This is a common format for print documents that are stored for Internet use. PDF is powerful because it allows the user to see the document exactly as the creator of the document intended, with all the formatting intact. PDF also provides a high level of protection against plagiarism because it can't be edited easily. To view or print a PDF file, you need a program like Adobe Acrobat or the free Adobe Acrobat Reader.

Server. A server is a computer designed to deal with information requests. Servers house web files, manage e-mail routing, and store your program applications if you're on a network.

WYSIWYG. This acronym, which stands for "what you see is what you get," is used to describe programs that let you see what you're producing the same way the end user will. For example, if you're editing a web page, a WYSIWYG editor will let you see ahead of time what the web page will look like on the Internet. Most consumer programs for development use WYSIWYG interfaces.

Web Pages as Instructional Tools

Teachers can also create web pages as instructional tools. For example, a teacher using a problem-based approach may compile a list of web resources for students to reduce the amount of time they spend searching for materials. By listing all of these resources in a single web page, the teacher can keep students focused on their problem solving rather than on surfing the Internet.

Internet scavenger hunts

Similarly, you may want to create an Internet scavenger hunt to support students in learning how to locate certain kinds of information. By making the scavenger hunt web based (rather than, say, creating a worksheet for students to complete), you'll have them on the computers already and can provide some scaffolding as they learn how to find information.

WebQuests

Perhaps most powerfully, teachers can create instructional materials like WebQuests, which engage students in online problem solving, finding information with a clear goal in mind, and working together in teams. The following "Technology in Action" feature describes WebQuests in detail.

Web Pages Created by Students Themselves

Students can create web pages as products in a number of authentic learning contexts. By creating a web page, students are constructing a real product that anyone else in the world can see. This raises students' expectations for themselves and provides you with the opportunity to motivate them to do good work.

As one example, students can create a clearinghouse of rated websites on particular topics. Some teachers have had students research trips they'd like to take and post information on the Internet. Other classes have used their own student-created web pages to provide reports or newsletters on

Technology in Action

WebQuests

WebQuests are an inquiry-based instructional approach which uses the web both as a content source and as a delivery tool. WebQuests are designed to focus students' attention on using content rather than on spending time searching for it. WebQuests are a popular approach for inquiry-based learning because their fairly preset structure provides support for both teacher and students. One of the most exciting aspects of WebQuests is that they provide teachers and students with an excellent opportunity to draw from the vast resources of the Internet, creating a content-rich environment in the local classroom.

The original WebQuest model was designed by Bernie Dodge at San Diego State University in 1995. Since then, it's been used in schools all over the world. The WebQuest homepage (**http://webquest.sdsu.edu**) provides the instructional background and templates needed to develop WebQuests for any K–12 classroom. A teacher can use these tools to create a new WebQuest on a particular topic or to search through the hundreds of existing WebQuests to see whether there's already one available on the topic of interest. Though it isn't the only source of WebQuest information and examples, the WebQuest homepage provides enough information to help any teacher get started.

MARCH MADNESS

| Introduction | Task | Procedures | Resources | Evaluation | Conclusion |

INTRODUCTION

It's March Madness time˜which means, you guessed it - Basketball! Basketball is not only a sport filled with excitement, slam dunks, and unbelievable athletes; it also is full of mathematical concepts as you will find in this webquest!

TASK

In this webquest, you will look at many different areas of math found in the NCAA˜ basketball tournament. You will use the NCAA˜bracket to look at all the teams participating in the tournament. The world of math will come alive as you find fractions, decimals, and percents; probability statistics; make predictions; and look for patterns.

By the end of this webquest, you will be able to relate a variety of math facts to the NCAA˜tournament and explain the importance of Mathematics in basketball.

Figure 11.2 The First Two Components of a WebQuest
Source: http://www.madison.k12.ky.us/district/projects/WebQuest/ MarchMadness/mmwebquest.htm

WebQuests usually include six essential components for learning: introduction, task, information sources, process, guidance, and conclusion. Each component is designed to guide the student through the process to a learning outcome. Figure 11.2 illustrates the first two components, the introduction and the statement of the students' task.

WebQuests can be as simple or as complex as the content and the students' abilities allow. Typically, WebQuests involve a team of students working together in a role-play scenario—for instance, as a team of scientists, historians, or investigators. The team is charged with one or more specific tasks designed to focus the students on the learning goal. Such tasks as compiling information, solving a mystery, covering an event, creating a product or plan of action, building consensus, and analyzing information help students become immersed in the content. Figure 11.3 illustrates a WebQuest designed for a high-school history class in which students play the roles of historian, political scientist, geographer, and economist.

The process step guides students to the Internet resources that they'll use, keeping them focused. With the massive volume of resources available, carefully chosen resources are key. WebQuests also include an assessment tool to further guide students toward the learning outcome. Typically in the form of a rubric, the assessment tool specifies content objectives and describes the various gradations of individual or group performance, as shown in Figure 11.4.

The New Deal WebQuest

Scenario: In teams of four, students take on the roles of historian, political scientist, geographer, and economist. Each team is to present a comprehensive examination of the New Deal including all four perspectives. Presentations should be prepared speeches with graphic illustrations. Options include the creation of illustrative posters or (if available) electronic slide show presentations. Teachers may decide to give team awards within a class or school-wide for quality work.

Historical focus:

Background on Franklin Delano Roosevelt (These questions need to be answered.)

1. When was FDR elected to his first political office, and what was it?
2. What appointed position did he hold during Woodrow Wilson's administration?
3. What caused him to leave politics in 1920?
4. What disease did he contract in 1921, and what effect did it have on him?
5. When did FDR re-enter public office and what position was he elected to?
6. How many times was he elected President, and in what years?
7. Where and when did he die?

When did the New Deal begin and end? What do historians mean by the first and second New Deals? What problems or conditions did the New Deal address?

Political Focus

Elections and Cabinet

- How many times was FDR elected, and in what years?
- Who was in his cabinet? Why was his appointment of his Secretary of Labor significant?
- What did he promise in his First Inaugural Address?
- What does FDR say about one-third of the nation in his second inaugural?
- What do political cartoons tell us about the first 100 days of his first term?
- What do political cartoons tell us about the Supreme Court in 1937?

Figure 11.3 The New Deal WebQuest This WebQuest was developed for a high-school economic history class in which students examined the New Deal from different perspectives. The culminating activity was to prepare speeches with graphic illustrations.
Source: http://www.davison.k12.mi.us/DHS/staff/Hewitt/webquests/newdeal/NewDealquest.htm

Evaluation

Describe to the learners how their performance will be evaluated. Specify whether there will be a common grade for group work vs. individual grades.

	Beginning 1	Developing 2	Accomplished 3	Exemplary 4	Score
Stated Objective or Performance	Description of identifiable performance characteristics reflecting a beginning level of performance.	Description of identifiable performance characteristics reflecting development and movement toward mastery of performance.	Description of identifiable performance characteristics reflecting mastery of performance.	Description of identifiable performance characteristics reflecting the highest level of performance.	
Stated Objective or Performance	Description of identifiable performance characteristics reflecting a beginning level of performance.	Description of identifiable performance characteristics reflecting development and movement toward mastery of performance.	Description of identifiable performance characteristics reflecting mastery of performance.	Description of identifiable performance characteristics reflecting the highest level of performance.	
Stated Objective or Performance	Description of identifiable performance characteristics reflecting a beginning level of performance.	Description of identifiable performance characteristics reflecting development and movement toward mastery of performance.	Description of identifiable performance characteristics reflecting mastery of performance.	Description of identifiable performance characteristics reflecting the highest level of performance.	

Figure 11.4 A Simple Rubric Used to Evaluate Learning Outcomes of a WebQuest
Source: http://projects.edtech.sandi.net/staffdev/tpss99/mywebquest/index.htm

Following the constructivist model, you can provide an opportunity for students to create their own learning by having them design their own WebQuest. Creating instruction in this way allows students to analyze resources, be creative in designing how and what to present, and problem-solve real-world issues, all while learning the content.

interesting topics. Some teachers, as we mentioned in discussing Web-Quests, even have their students create WebQuests or similar instructional materials as their own deliverables.

In addition to allowing students to share their information with the world, creating web pages also allows the students to engage in multi-modal communication. They can write traditional prose or poetry, add images, add sound or voice, include video clips, or create interactive activities. They're no longer limited to either taking a test or writing a paper to demonstrate their learning. The following "Technology in Action" feature explores some specific ways in which students can create their own web pages of instructional materials.

Advantages of student-created web pages

Technology in Action

Learning About Technology Through Designing Instruction on the Internet

Students today have never known life without the Internet, just as they've never known life without cell phones or remote controls. Ideally, however, you want to encourage active as well as passive use of the Internet. To create excitement and promote students' written and visual communication skills, it's important for them not only to use the web as consumers but also to create new materials for the web.

ThinkQuest **(http://www.ThinkQuest.org)** is an international competition in which teachers and students work together to create educational websites. Students are empowered to develop their own understanding of a content area and then design instruction for other students around the world. This is an exciting way for them to construct their own learning experiences.

Teams of three to six students, along with at least one teacher-coach, compete in any of more than a dozen different categories, such as math, books and literature, history and government, and social sciences and culture. Entrants are divided by age group, ranging from age twelve and under to age nineteen and under. Thanks to the communication capabilities of the Internet, teams can include members from different places around the globe. Trips and laptop computers are awarded to winning teams. Figure 11.5 displays two sites created for the competition.

Figure 11.5 Two Websites Designed by Students for ThinkQuest Competitions
(A) A site developed by a fifteen-and-under team to teach students about genetics.
(B) An example created by a twelve-and-under team that uses a newsletter format to teach others about cows.
Source: http://library.thinkquest.org/04apr/00774 and http://library.thinkquest.org/03oct/01272

(A)

WHERE'S THE BEEF?

Click on the links in red boxes to find out!
Our sources are listed at the bottom of the pages!

February 29, 2004	Volume 1, Issue 1	MooTown, USA

COW WELCOME!

MooTown - Last night during the stormy blizzard citizens of the Mootown gathered in a townhall meeting to examine the town's most famous citizen - Daisy the Cow!!

Daisy Grazing Happily

After much debate it was determined that Daisy has four (FOUR, 4) stomachs! What a ruminant! The commission was formed to examine the moonatomy of our dearest Daisy.
To read the findings of this great commission visit the Daisy farm. Learn about the amazing four stomach and how they work. See the names of thousands of types of Daisies. Test your knowledge through a cool game of HangCow!

BEEF - IT'S WHAT'S FOR DINNER!

Very Mad Daisy

DAISY GOT MAD!

MAD FARM - Today a horrible thing happened at the farm. Three Daisies went crazy!!! They started twitching, falling, and doing weird thing. Farmers called the doctor. The doctor checked the Daisies up and said: It's a mad cow. You are all finished! We were terrified! Is this the end of our Daisy! Please help, we love those thick, juicy hamburgers. Visit this page to learn what the Mad Cow Disease does, its effect on people and economy. Read our cool interview with a research scientist.
What do you know? Take an on-line quiz!

DAISY'S FUTURE

DAISY PRODUCTS

Milky Way - What can you make of Daisy! Everything. When you think Daisy - think ice cream, milk, chocolate, yogurt, hamburger, steak, spaghetti sauce, taco, ribs, belts, boots, glue.. Glue? Yes, even the glue can be made from cow! Did that get your attention? Visit this page to find our about the other cow product.

DAISY INTERACTION

Welcome friends! Come visit with Daisy and the farmers. Have a suggestion? Maybe an opinion? Or just a want to leave the note for us? This is the place for that! So, come in, we'd love to hear from you.

(B)

Figure 11.5 *(continued)*

Teachers who have no personal experience in website creation shouldn't be discouraged from participating. Students design and develop the instructional websites; the teacher-coach's role is only to facilitate and guide the students' learning process. In fact, it's against the rules for coaches to work directly on the website.

The ThinkQuest Library hosts thousands of student-built educational websites from around the world and is available free for all to access. This content-rich resource provides useful learning opportunities for students ages nine to nineteen.

Multimedia Development Tools

The term **multimedia** in general refers to the use of more than one kind of media. In other words, multimedia projects often include sound, images, text, movies, and other elements. Most commonly, multimedia products are also interactive, allowing students to click on different things to produce different results. Chances are that you've encountered a product created by a multimedia tool in your own experiences while surfing the Internet, playing computer games, or working with edutainment titles.

Types of multimedia tools

The category of multimedia development tools can include some tools that we've already introduced, such as presentation software and web pages. The category also includes a number of tools that you've likely encountered as a user, if not as a developer, such as Flash, Director, and HyperStudio. As with the other development tools introduced in this chapter, multimedia tools are for both teachers and students to use. For all the same reasons that you'd want your students creating web pages, you'll want them to create multimedia projects.

Multimedia products can range from fairly simple, yet instructionally important, creations, such as PowerPoint games, to more elaborate tools that simulate real-world phenomena. One commonly used multimedia tool that's been popular for many years among teachers is HyperStudio. This tool allows students or teachers to create projects by developing a series of "cards" that are linked together. The concept of linked cards makes it easy for teachers and students to talk about how to develop the interactive elements and to plan carefully, using either paper cards or concept-mapping tools.

The use of multimedia learning tools provides students with virtual hands-on experiences—often working with ideas that would be difficult to simulate without technology. These experiences also provide the opportunity for nonlinear thinking, careful planning, and the development of a range of communication skills. The following two "Technology in Action" features illustrate different ways of using multimedia tools.

---

video case *Online Study Center*

Using PowerPoint in Middle-School Language Arts

● In our chapter on productivity tools we discuss the use of PowerPoint as a presentation tool. You can also think of it as a multimedia "authoring" environment, in which students can combine images, words, and other elements.

To help you develop your ideas about using PowerPoint in your classroom, watch the HM Video Case **Multimedia Literacy: Integrating Technology into the Middle School Curriculum,** which you can view in the Online Study Center. In this video, you'll see students using PowerPoint as a medium for sharing their learning about Costa Rica.

The interview transcript includes the teacher's thoughts about using technology to support students with learning disabilities. She also discusses her ideas about integrating technology with middle-school students.

Technology in Action

Making Learning Fun with Microsoft PowerPoint

Games can catch and hold the attention of students at all grade levels. With the availability of Microsoft PowerPoint software in most schools, teachers have an effective tool for creating a host of gamelike learning environments.

The real power behind the use of games in education, however, is students' ability to create their own learning by designing and building their own games. While engaged in game development, students analyze and organize content, and evaluate the content's importance. The types and complexities of learning options with PowerPoint are limited only by the teacher's imagination, and with students as game designers, this isn't typically an issue! Just by searching the Internet for "PowerPoint games," you can find countless free examples and templates ready for use. In fact, the University of Georgia has developed a website called Homemade PowerPoint Games **(http://it.coe.uga.edu/wwild/pptgames/index.html),** which houses game templates, ideas, and contributions from teachers.

A popular example is the game of Jeopardy. The teacher can develop a PowerPoint version to quiz students individually or in teams (see Figure 11.6). However, having students develop the game allows them to gain a deeper understanding of the content—and because this game is designed for the participant to view an answer and then create a question, students have to reorganize and refine the content to fit the game format. Like the Internet, recent versions of PowerPoint have hyperlinking capability,

Figure 11.6 Jeopardy Game Designed for Eighth Graders to Learn About Louisiana When the user clicks on a selected category and value (for instance, History for 200 points), the appropriate question pops up on the screen. Another click reveals the correct answer.
Source: http://www.elainefitzgerald.com/jeopardy.htm

allowing participants to move through the game in a nonlinear fashion. By clicking on a hyperlinked image, button, or word, participants are sent to any number of slide "answers" within the PowerPoint slide show.

PowerPoint's graphics tools make it easy to create unique gaming environments. By inserting graphics or images and using simple autoshapes, lines, fill colors, and text, teachers and students can design any number of stimulating ways to review course content. PowerPoint games can easily be adapted to any content for any grade level.

Technology in Action

Multimedia Tools for Hands-On Virtual Learning: The Exploratorium Website

The Exploratorium is a science museum in San Francisco. However, you don't have to travel to San Francisco to engage in hands-on science learning, thanks to the museum's multimedia website **(http://www .exploratorium.com).** On the website, the Exploratorium staff has included interactive elements, text descriptions, and opportunities to participate in a wide array of live events. Most of these resources are aimed at middle- and high-school students, though some are also appropriate for elementary learners.

As one example, in its exhibit on food science, the Exploratorium site includes a segment dedicated to bread. Here, interactive tools allow learners to understand the science of gluten and to see the bread up close (Figure 11.7). You can incorporate web pages like these into a wide variety of lesson plans. The Exploratorium's site also offers its own collection of lesson plans for you to investigate.

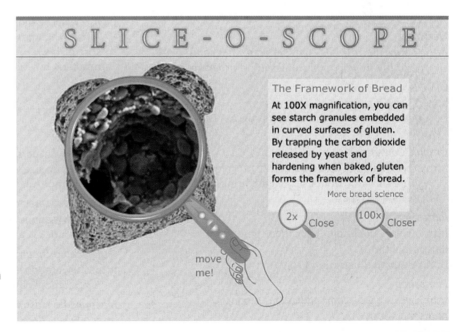

Figure 11.7 An Interactive Exhibit on the Exploratorium Website
Source: http://exploratorium.edu/cooking/bread

SUMMARY

Development tools include image-editing software, drawing tools, web page development tools, and multimedia development tools which are useful for both teachers and students. With them, teachers can create engaging lessons that support students in being creative and in making high-quality materials that can be shared with the world.

For example, if you set up a class web page, you can use it in a simple way to post news and homework information for students and their parents. Or you can design a WebQuest, in which students begin from a web page that states their task and then use various online resources to complete the task. Students can also create their own web pages to integrate and present their learning.

As with other tools, the power of development tools depends on your planning. You want to create authentic lessons that engage students in inquiry, problem solving, and other forms of exploration that call on their creativity and higher-order skills.

RESOURCES

Online Study Center
Direct Links to Resources

GRAPHICS EDITING AND DRAWING PROGRAMS

CorelDraw
http://www.corel.com
    One of the most popular drawing and illustration programs.

Fireworks
http://www.adobe.com/products/fireworks
    A program designed to help you create images for the web.

FreeHand
http://www.macromedia.com/software/freehand
    One of the most popular illustration programs.

GIMP
http://www.gimp.org
    A powerful, free image-editing program that runs on a variety of computer platforms.

Graphic Converter
http://www.graphic-converter.net
    A simple program for basic image editing and converting between file types.

Illustrator
http://www.adobe.com/education/products/illustrator.html
    A powerful illustration program.

Photoshop
http://www.adobe.com/education/products/photoshop.html
    One of the most popular and most powerful image-editing software packages.

Picasa
http://picasa.google.com
    A free PC-based program for editing images.

PRODUCTIVITY PACKAGES THAT INCLUDE DRAWING PROGRAMS

AppleWorks
http://www.apple.com/education/k12/products/appleworks
    A productivity suite that includes a painting application. Free on many Macintosh machines.

OpenOffice
http://www.openoffice.org
    A free productivity suite that includes word processing, spreadsheet, presentation, database, and drawing products for Macintosh, Windows, and Linux systems.

WEB AND MULTIMEDIA DEVELOPMENT TOOLS

HyperStudio
http://www.hyperstudio.com
    An easy-to-use tool that allows students and teachers to create multimedia projects.

Macromedia Director
http://www.adobe.com/products/director
    A multimedia authoring tool.

Macromedia Dreamweaver
http://www.adobe.com/products/dreamweaver
    A versatile web page editor and site management tool.

Macromedia Flash Basic
http://www.adobe.com/products/flash/basic
    A development tool that allows users to create animations or interactive elements for websites.

Microsoft FrontPage
http://office.microsoft.com
> A relatively easy-to-use web page editor and site management tool.

THINKQUEST INFORMATION

Human's Playground: Genetic Engineering
http://library.thinkquest.org/04apr/00774
> An example of a ThinkQuest project.

ThinkQuest
http://www.ThinkQuest.org
> The website that houses the products created as part of the ThinkQuest competition.

Where's the Beef?
http://library.thinkquest.org/03oct/01272
> Another example of a ThinkQuest project.

WEBQUESTS

March Madness
http://www.madison.k12.ky.us/district/projects/WebQuest/MarchMadness/mmwebquest.html
> A WebQuest that introduces mathematics concepts through basketball.

The New Deal WebQuest
http://www.davison.k12.mi.us/DHS/staff/Hewitt/webquests/newdeal/NewDealquest.htm
> A WebQuest that engages students in learning about the New Deal from multiple perspectives.

The WebQuest Page
http://webquest.sdsu.edu
> A comprehensive collection of materials for making WebQuests and a large collection of WebQuests made by others.

WebQuest Template
http://projects.edtech.sandi.net/staffdev/tpss99/mywebquest/index.htm
> A template for designing your own WebQuest.

POWERPOINT GAMES

Homemade PowerPoint Games
http://it.coe.uga.edu/wwild/pptgames/index.html
> Information on how to make PowerPoint games and links to some already-created games.

Jeopardy Games Created by Teachers
http://www.elainefitzgerald.com/jeopardy.htm
> Examples of PowerPoint games.

MULTIMEDIA FOR EDUCATION

The Exploratorium
http://www.exploratorium.com
> The Exploratorium in San Francisco offers a number of interactive online exhibits that use multimedia elements.

case
STUDY

Building a WebQuest

Imagine that, because of your interest in technology, your new principal has asked you to prepare a short presentation for the next faculty meeting. She wants to encourage more teachers to use the new wireless computers, and she'd like to see more current activities on the school's website. She knows that all the teachers have created their own web pages, but she's not sure whether they've allowed their students to create online materials—in fact, she says that she's not even sure whether the teachers let their students use the Internet as an instructional tool.

Excited about your presentation, you start planning. But what should you include? Think about the following questions:

Questions for Reflection and Discussion

1. What kinds of projects, tools, or activities are most likely to engage your peers in using technology in their classrooms?
2. What factors will you consider in selecting technologies and activities to include in your presentation?
3. How will you address the need to align technology with standards?

Meet the Standards

Online Study Center

Standards
See the Online Study Center for additional resources on standards for both teachers and students.

Review the NETS standards listed in "Standards to Guide Your Preparation" at the beginning of this chapter. To help yourself advance toward fulfilling these standards, reflect on these questions:

► How can the tools discussed in this chapter help you develop students' higher-order skills and creativity?
► What in particular makes these tools suitable for your classroom?
► How will you guide students in using them appropriately and effectively?

Chapter 12

Communications Tools

ISTE NETS

Teachers

▶ Design developmentally appropriate learning opportunities that apply technology-enhanced instructional strategies to support the diverse needs of learners.

▶ Use technology to support learner-centered strategies that address the diverse needs of students.

▶ Use technology resources to engage in ongoing professional development and lifelong learning.

▶ Model and teach legal and ethical practice related to technology use.

▶ Identify and use technology resources that affirm diversity.

OTHER RELEVANT STANDARDS

California Technology Standards for Teachers (ISTE, 2006)

Each candidate . . . interacts and collaborates with others using computer-based collaborative tools (e.g., threaded discussion groups, newsgroups, electronic list management applications, online chat, and audio/video conferences).

Texas Technology Application Standards (ISTE, 2006)

The beginning teacher knows and understands:

▶ How to use research skills and electronic communication to create new knowledge.

▶ How to evaluate communication in terms of both process and product.

Illinois Technology Standards for Teachers (ISTE, 2006)

The competent teacher:

▶ Will use telecommunications and information-access resources to support instruction.

▶ Knows how to access telecommunications resources to support instruction.

Massachusetts Recommended PreK–12 Instructional Technology Standards (ISTE, 2006)

[Students] demonstrate ability to use technology for research, problem-solving, and communication. Students locate, evaluate, collect, and process information from a variety of electronic sources. Students use telecommunications and other media to interact or collaborate with peers, experts, and other audiences.

ommunications tools include all those tools that allow your classroom to extend beyond its four walls. Whether by allowing your students to develop their knowledge in an online forum or by opening up your classroom to expert guests, communications tools allow new and innovative kinds of learning experiences.

For the purposes of this chapter we focus on some of the most commonly used technologies in K–12 classrooms and introduce you to some of the emerging tools that your students likely already know about. For example, we'll look at discussion boards, e-mail, websites, Internet-based telephones, chat software, and video. And we'll end with a case study that lets you think about ways a teacher can benefit from communications technologies.

The most basic way to classify communications tools is to separate them according to whether the sender and the receiver of a message are

SPOTLIGHT 12.1 Internet Jargon

Here are some explanations of key Internet-related terms that you'll need to know. Many of these definitions come from Netlingo (http://www.netlingo.com), a popular Internet dictionary that's an excellent tool for keeping up with the jargon.

Acceptable use policy (AUP). A policy established by a school or district to define how students are allowed to use the Internet. Generally, the AUP requires parents to sign a consent form and includes clear consequences for students who fail to comply with the policies.

*Blog (*short for *weblog).* A website where users can post a chronological, up-to-date e-journal of their thoughts in an open-forum communications tool. Two blog sites popular with students are Xanga (**http://www.xanga.com)** and MySpace (**http://www.myspace.com).** *Note:* Sites like these do *not* provide security for students who post personal information or photographs of themselves; many schools disapprove of their use because of concerns for student safety. But see our chapter "Content-Area Tools" for useful ways in which blogs can be used in the classroom.

Bulletin board or discussion board. A meeting or announcement system for carrying on discussions, uploading and downloading files, and so on.

Chat. A form of interactive online communication that enables users to have real-time conversations with other people who are also online.

E-mail. Mail that's electronically transmitted by a computer. E-mail sends messages instantaneously, anywhere in the world.

Internet (the Net). A system of linked computer networks, international in scope, that facilitates data transfer and communication services, such as remote login, file transfer, e-mail, newsgroups, and the World Wide Web.

Listserv. A type of automatic mailing list server developed by Eric Thomas in 1986. When e-mail is addressed to a listserv mailing list, it is automatically broadcast to everyone on the list.

Podcast. Multimedia, usually audio, that's distributed through the Internet to be played on mobile devices at a later date.

Streaming media. A general term for video or audio content that you can access on your computer with a program like QuickTime or RealPlayer, which begins playing before the file is totally downloaded. In other words, instead of waiting for a video or audio file to transfer completely to your computer, you can begin watching or listening right away.

Wiki. An interactive tool that allows multiple users to refine a single document. The most popular use of this is Wikipedia (**http://www.wikipedia.org),** an interactive encyclopedia that anyone can add information to and anyone can edit.

World Wide Web (the Web). A collection of graphical pages on the Internet that can be read and interacted with by computer. The Web exists as a global system of servers supporting specially formatted files written in a code that links them together.

operating in the same time frame. If, for example, you set up an online learning event in which all the students are logged on at the same time and can communicate with one another immediately, that's **synchronous communication.** If a message is sent at one time and received at some later time, as with e-mail, that's **asynchronous communication.** We begin with the latter category of tools because they're the ones with which students will be most familiar. As you read the chapter, you may want to refer to Spotlight 12.1, which defines some standard terms for you.

Asynchronous Communication Tools
Discussion Boards

Threaded discussions

Perhaps one of the most prevalent communications tools available to teachers is the discussion board. Such tools, also known as bulletin boards or message boards, allow students and teachers to communicate with others using simple text messages. Messages on discussion boards can be organized by the time when they were received or with a *threaded* structure that helps keep related messages together. For educational purposes, threaded discussions are probably more useful, because it's easier to follow the emergence and evolution of ideas when they're grouped by topic.

A good way to introduce yourself to discussion boards is to explore some that have been designed as professional support tools. Several websites allow teachers to turn to one another for advice and lesson plan ideas—for example, Teacher Talk Forums **(http://www.teachertalk.com)** and Teacher Focus **(http://www.teacherfocus.com).** These discussion boards can help you discuss classroom ideas, get ideas for dealing with daily struggles, or find innovative new activities for your classroom. Some such boards are project specific; others span a number of relevant topics.

Discussion boards as teaching tools

Our main focus here, though, is on discussion boards as teaching tools. Consistent with constructivist approaches to teaching, discussion boards allow students, either in the same classroom or located around the globe, to work together to explore a topic or solve a problem. Participants can read others' ideas and then post their own thoughts to add to the discussion. Because they're asynchronous, discussion boards create an environment with less pressure than live classroom discussions.

Many discussion boards are freely available on the Internet and require no specific technical skills of teachers. Two examples are Active-Board **(http://www.activeboard.com)** and DiscussionApp **(http://server .com/communityapps/discussionapp);** see "Resources" at the end of this chapter for additional examples. Other boards, often with more advanced features, are available for sale. Some discussion boards are also available as part of course tools that offer additional features, such as grade keeping, syllabus development, and a "dropbox" where students can upload files; such course tools include MyClass.Net **(http://www.myclass.net)** and Nicenet **(http://www.nicenet.org).** Many of these free tools allow people from outside your classroom to join the group. When you're looking for good tools, keep in mind who can or can't access your discussion.

The following "Technology in Action" features describe two particularly effective ways to use discussion boards with your students.

Technology in Action

Asynchronous Knowledge Building with Knowledge Forum

Asynchronous communications tools are a powerful way to conduct conversations among your students in a way that promotes careful thinking and attention to emerging understandings. Some tools are built to support this kind of thinking more than others. One example of a tool developed to support students in developing understandings is Knowledge

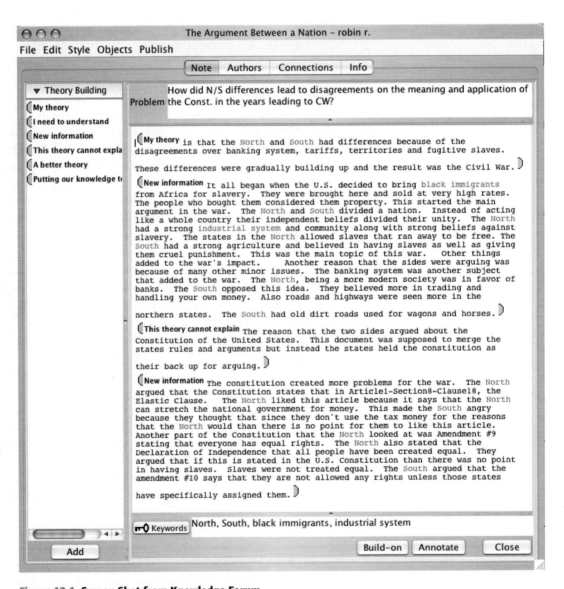

Figure 12.1 Screen Shot from Knowledge Forum
Source: All Knowledge Forum screen shots were captured from the online promotional site for K–12, **http://www.knowledgeforum .com/K-12/products.htm**

Forum, a product that emerged from a large research project called CSILE (Computer-Supported Intentional Learning Environments).

Knowledge Forum, now available as a commercial product, allows teachers to build in scaffolds that provide guidance to students in using information. Consider a high-school social studies class learning about the Civil War. Figure 12.1 shows a Knowledge Forum discussion board structure focused on a theory-building approach in which a student is prompted to state her theory, describe the information that she's finding, and consider the emerging holes in her understanding.

This kind of format allows responders to propose countertheories as well. One method for responses is the praise-question-proposal format (Figure 12.2), in which students say what they like about the original idea, ask new questions, and propose further lines of investigation.

Like other asynchronous tools, Knowledge Forum provides students and teachers with the option of looking at their discussion in either a threaded (Figure 12.3) or a nonthreaded format. But Knowledge Forum also allows students to annotate their ideas so that they can keep track of what kinds of information they got from different sources. In addition, students can easily add videos or graphics of the ideas they're discussing. Further, they can add "rise above" notes that take several separate ideas and connect them as a unified body of data to support a new theory.

More information about Knowledge Forums in a variety of educational settings is available from **http://www.knowledgeforum.com/K-12/inAction.htm**

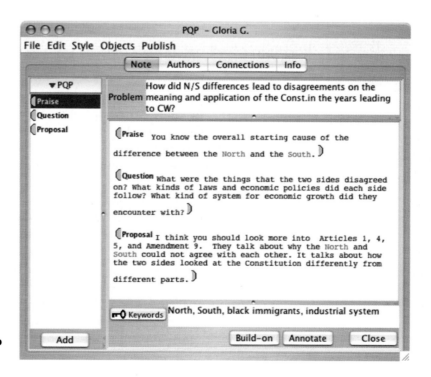

Figure 12.2 A Praise-Question-Proposal Reply to the Entry in Figure 12.1

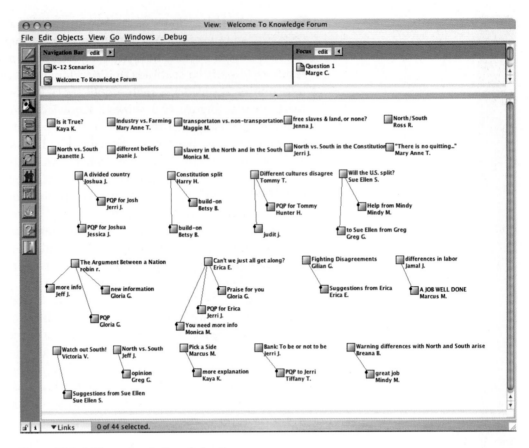

Figure 12.3 A Discussion in Knowledge Forum

Technology in Action

Using Discussion Boards to Learn Foreign Languages

Learning any foreign language requires exposure to the language in authentic contexts *and* lots of practice. Internet discussion boards are an innovative way to provide both these requirements.

For example, you could have your students plan a traditional holiday meal for one of the countries where their language is spoken. They could research the kinds of foods and activities that would occur during that meal, and do all of their planning in the foreign language on the discussion board. This would allow them to learn about the culture related to the language, as well as provide them with authentic reasons to share with one another.

Similarly, you could have them discuss a book they're reading in the foreign language, or you could have them research some aspect of the country's history and hold a debate about it. Some debate topics might be: What might have prevented the Germans from electing Hitler? or Should museums be required to return historical artifacts to countries from which they were stolen a century or more ago?

Using discussion boards as the method of communication between students provides the teacher with a vehicle to track and assess student progress. Teachers can easily monitor progress, activity, and language use, as well as provide input at any stage of the project. In addition, because students' interactions on the discussion boards are preserved, they can reflect back on their own learning and progress, as well as that of their peers.

■ E-mail

E-mail, as you already know, is one of the most powerful communications tools available today, and it's readily available to you as a teacher and to many of your students and their parents. Using e-mail, you can contact parents, participate in listservs, or receive daily or weekly newsletters with information relevant to your interests.

Listservs

Listservs are mailing lists that allow a large group of people to communicate with one another using a single e-mail address that sends a message to all the members at once. There are literally thousands of listservs available on the Internet. You can find one or more with information relevant to your interests. One place to start looking for interesting listservs is the Teacher Mailring Center **(http://teachers.net/mailrings).**

As an instructional tool, e-mail can be used for a wide variety of purposes. Here are a few examples:

Instructional uses of e-mail

▶ E-mail can allow students to communicate with an array of experts as they conduct classroom research.
▶ You can pair up with other classrooms in other parts of the country or world to have a keypal project. **Keypals** are penpals who communicate by e-mail. Keypal projects link your students with students in another classroom or school to discuss specific issues of interest. For example, many keypal projects focus on cultural similarities and differences. Communication and sharing of information between cities, states, countries, and continents happens almost immediately. A number of resources on the Internet can help you find other teachers and students with similar interests; see the "Resources" list at the end of this chapter.
▶ **Telementoring** programs use e-mail to pair a student with a mentor to explore a particular topic, as explained in the following "Technology in Action" feature.

■ Websites

In our chapter on development tools, we had much to say about web pages, including some ways to use them for communication—conveying class news and updates to parents, for instance. The discussion boards we described earlier in this chapter also operate through websites. But there are other important ways that websites provide asynchronous communication for educational purposes. In this section we discuss one application you already know about—use of the Web as an information

Telementoring

Mentoring programs are widely used to extend the classroom to include outside content expertise. Additionally, extra encouragement, academic help, and guidance can go a long way toward helping at-risk and other youths who do not have the support they need to succeed in life. Research has shown that mentoring programs improve school attendance and performance, and reduce the risk of drug or alcohol use. However, given the busy lifestyles of adults, many in-class mentoring programs struggle: It's difficult to schedule appropriate times when mentors can be available.

Nevertheless, telementoring is an alternative with a number of benefits.

1. It allows mentors to focus on the mentoring itself rather than on juggling their schedules to be in the classroom.
2. Students can e-mail their mentor whenever the need arises.
3. Telementoring eases tension for students who may initially have trouble communicating with adults.
4. Telementoring helps students develop their skills in written communication.

The teacher should set clear goals and guidelines for the mentoring project, to which both the student and the mentor agree. These may include the topics that will be discussed, whether there will be a deliverable (such as an essay) for the student to complete, and how often the student and mentor will communicate with each other.

Mentor (**http://www.mentoring.org**) and Be a Mentor (**http://www.beamentor.org**) are just two organizations that support mentoring by connecting interested adults with youths around the country. The Electronic Emissary Project at the University of Texas at Austin has published lessons and examples from its Telementoring project (**http://www.tcet.unt.edu/pubs/em/em01.pdf**). More resources are available at the U.S. Department of Education website (**http://www.ed.gov**) by searching for "mentoring." You can also search the entire web for "telementoring."

resource—and one you may not know about—use of the Web to exchange students' data and reports in collaborative research projects.

▬ The Web as an Information Source

The Web offers a vast body of information that students and teachers can access readily. A student who wants to learn about virtually any school subject—Benjamin Franklin, French grammar, polynomial equations—can find material on the Web. Countless companies and organizations use websites to communicate about their information or services to the educational world.

Using Online Source Materials

To help you develop your ideas about using the Internet and other technologies in your own classroom, watch the HM Video Case **Integrating Internet Research: High School Social Studies**, available in the Online Study Center. In this video, teacher Elizabeth Sweeney talks about how her students use online source materials. Access to the Internet, she says, "puts the assignment in the hands of the student[s]. . . . They become active learners and active participants in the lesson." In addition to the main video, check the Bonus Videos, especially Teacher Explains the Value of the Lesson. Do you agree with Ms. Sweeney's conclusions?

Teaching students to be good information consumers

One of the most important Internet skills you can teach your students, regardless of their age, is how to be good information consumers—that is, how to determine the quality and value of information they encounter on the World Wide Web or elsewhere. To help protect students from accessing inappropriate sites, many schools have set up acceptable use policies, as described in Spotlight 12.2. But there's much more you can do to help your students become users of web resources. One important step you can take in this effort is to introduce yourself and your students to website evaluation efforts.

Unlike many other tools available to you and your students, the Web has no editorial oversight. Anyone can create a web page that says absolutely anything. It may be true. It may not be. You want to ensure that you aren't misled by bad information and that your students aren't wasting their time trying to understand a web page that wasn't intended for them.

SPOTLIGHT 12.2   Acceptable Use Policies

Regardless of the communications tools you choose to use in your own classroom, you'll need to be sure that your school district supports what you're trying to do. One of the first things you need to check is your school or school district's **acceptable use policy** (AUP).

An AUP has information on how the Internet should be used and specific ways in which it can't be used by students. Typically, the AUP stresses accountability by listing responsibilities for students, teachers, and parents, and by including clear information about the consequences of failing to adhere to the rules. Most AUPs also require parents to sign a document to confirm that they approve of their child's using the Internet in school according to the policy.

One of the advantages of AUPs is that they allow students and teachers to take ownership of responsible Internet use. This is in sharp contrast to an approach that relies on simply installing strong filters and firewalls that block a large portion of the relevant content on the Web. Some communities choose to use both AUPs and filters to maximize safety for students, whereas others prefer to allow students more access to information while providing them with more responsibility to behave in acceptable ways.

For more information on AUPs, see the following sources:

Becta Schools: E-Safety Introduction
    http://schools.becta.org.uk/index.php?section=is

CyberSmart! Understand Your Acceptable Use Policy
    http://www.cybersmartcurriculum.org/lesson_plans/45_07.asp

Virginia Department of Education, Acceptable Use Policies: A Handbook
    http://www.pen.k12.va.us/go/VDOE/Technology/AUP/home.shtml

You can find a lot of great information about website evaluation at Kathy Schrock's Guide for Educators: Critical Evaluation Surveys and Resources **(http://school.discovery.com/schrockguide/eval.html)** or at WWW CyberGuides for Web Evaluation **(http://www.cyberbee.com/guides.html)**. Here, we focus on a few key ideas to keep in mind when you or your students evaluate any website. They can be divided into content issues and design issues.

■ Content Issues for Website Evaluation

► *Accuracy.* First and foremost, is the information on the website accurate? You may not always be able to tell, so you'll want to consider the other content issues listed here to provide you with some sense of the value and credibility of the information you're looking at.

► *Authority.* One way to determine the credibility of information is to determine whether the person in charge of the website is an authority on the topic. For example, if you're looking for information on weather patterns, is the web page written by a meteorologist?

Watching for bias

► *Bias.* Bias isn't inherently bad, as long as it's clear what the intent of the website is. For example, in a social studies class, you may want your students to consider a political issue from a left-wing and a right-wing perspective. In this case, sites biased toward one side of the issue might be appropriate. However, you want to beware of bias when seeking supposedly neutral websites. Bias can often be determined by looking at who sponsors the website. For example, if you're looking for information on healthy eating, you may not want to use web pages sponsored by candy makers or fast-food restaurants as your primary sources.

► *Comprehension.* Is the website written at a level your students will be able to understand? If it's written at either too high or too low a level of difficulty, your students may not gain the information they need.

► *Contact person.* A website without a contact person should raise questions in the user's mind about the credibility of the information.

► *Currency.* Many websites aren't kept up to date. Though this may not be a problem with some topics, it will be a drawback if students are researching a contemporary issue.

■ Design Issues for Website Evaluation

► *Aesthetic appeal.* Designs that aren't appealing will be less likely to engage your students. This measure, though somewhat subjective, can be summed up with a few simple criteria: whether the web page looks appropriate for the ages you're working with, whether it's well laid out and easy to read, and whether the color scheme is readable and pleasant.

► *Speed of loading.* This is a major consideration for classroom uses of the Web. You won't want your students using slow-loading websites, because they'll become bored and less likely to stick with the task at hand.

Is the site accessible for all your students?

► *Accessibility.* Well-designed websites include different elements to help people with disabilities access the information. For example, text buttons and text labels for images allow browsers that read the content aloud to the user to convey the full contents of the page.

► *Spelling and grammar.* A well-designed website shouldn't have spelling or grammatical errors. You should always be aware of spelling and grammar, because you're providing students with examples of written language, and these ought to be good examples.

► *Clarity of purpose.* How quickly can you tell the website's point of view? If the site's purpose isn't readily apparent, chances are that it isn't a good choice for classroom use.

▄▄ Tips for Searching the Web   One of the most frustrating aspects of using the Web as a research tool is trying to find appropriate content for your students—or trying to help them find appropriate content to use. There are a few searching tips that can save you time.

Framing specific queries

▶ Use quotation marks to search for particular phrases. For example "How the Civil War started" returns about 4,200 hits in Google, whereas the same phrase without quotation marks returns over 25 million.

▶ Use the plus or minus sign to be sure all of your hits include a particular word (Lincoln+Supreme+Court) or exclude particular terms (-state). This search would find all of the websites dealing with Lincoln and Supreme and Court while excluding sites that are about states.

▶ Use specific language when possible. If you're interested in Abraham Lincoln's inauguration, a search on that phrase is more likely to give you the information you want than using "Lincoln" and "inauguration" separately. Every detail you can add helps limit the number of website returns that a search engine gives you.

▶ The search engine matters. Try more than one search engine to learn which ones seem to provide you with the best information for your purposes. These engines differ because they collect information in different ways.

▄▄ Collaborative Research Projects Using the Web

Web-based inquiry projects

In the effort to promote inquiry-based learning, educators have helped set up a number of web-based projects in which students conduct their own research, gather data, and share their findings with other students and sometimes with actual scientists working in the field. One such project is GLOBE (Global Learning and Observations to Benefit the Environment), an international school-based education and science program. Based on the Web, GLOBE is funded by the U.S. Department of State and the National Science Foundation, among many other organizations, and is being implemented in partnership with over one hundred countries around the world. The following "Technology in Action" feature shows the in-depth learning opportunities that such projects offer.

Technology in Action

The GLOBE Program

Available for primary- and secondary-school classrooms, GLOBE allows students to actively participate in collecting scientifically valid measurements having to do with the atmosphere, soils, and land cover. The students participating in GLOBE periodically collect data as part of their regular classwork and submit it to a large database. They can then access both

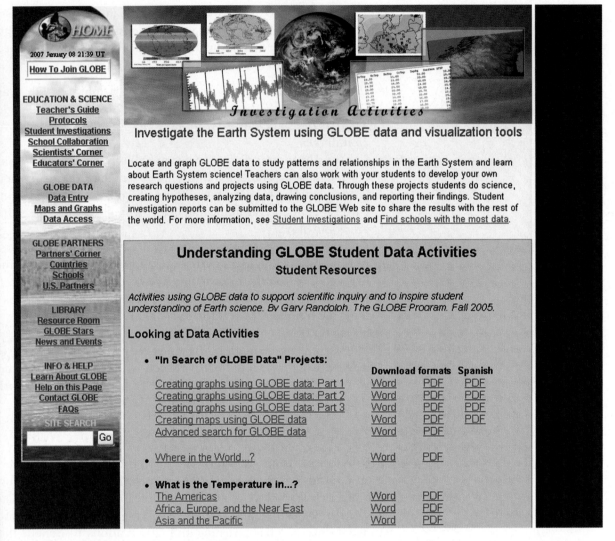

Figure 12.4 A Screen from the GLOBE Program GLOBE provides tools and activities to support environmental research for teachers and students.

Source: http://viz.globe.gov/viz-bin/show.cgi?1=en&b=g&rg=n&enc=00&nav=1&page=gallery-activity.htm

their own and other schools' data to conduct research projects. Acting as scientists, students create hypotheses, investigate environmental issues, analyze data, develop conclusions, and then report their findings. By publishing their research through the GLOBE website **(http://www.globe .gov),** students can share their information around the world.

The GLOBE project also has interactive tools (Figure 12.4) for creating maps and graphs, as well as facilities for collaborating with field scientists and other students around the world. For teachers, GLOBE provides professional development workshops, teacher's guides, and instructional videos. International networking and science facilitators are also incorporated into the program. Ongoing teacher-training workshops are scheduled in various locations around the United States.

Synchronous Communication Tools

So far in this chapter, we've looked only at asynchronous tools—tools not meant to be used simultaneously by all participants. There's another set of Internet-based communication tools intended for users to communicate with one another synchronously, in "real time." These include Internet-based telephone systems, chat tools, and video.

Internet-Based Telephone

Since the Web was started, people have tried to use it to communicate cheaply. Now, with high bandwidth and good, cheap microphones, this is feasible. Internet phone services are generally free or low in cost. With services like Skype **(http://www.skype.com),** you can call anywhere from your computer—even to regular telephones. This makes it more possible than ever to have your students talk to experts or to students at other schools. See "Resources" at the end of the chapter for a selection of Internet phone services.

One of the biggest drawbacks of these tools is that they can be blocked by the firewalls that most school districts use. So, if you're interested in using an Internet phone, you'll want to test it out before you need it in class. Another drawback is that, when network traffic is high, the quality of the connection may suffer.

Chat Tools

Chat tools allow participants to talk to one another in real time, using text and sometimes images or sound. Often, these are person-to-person tools that allow one person to communicate with another person, but not a group of people to chat together. AOL's Instant Messenger is an example of this kind of tool.

There are also chat rooms that allow many people to talk to one another at the same time. Often these are topical—devoted to a particular subject the participants want to discuss. Or they may be set up by a group of people who know one another. As an educational tool, these types of chat rooms are difficult to use because the discussion progresses in multiple strands at the same time without a lot of organization. However, they can be useful for having a "guest speaker" in your class or for helping your students brainstorm ideas for a project.

Some chat tools are specifically designed for educational uses. Complete course management systems like Blackboard **(http://www .blackboard.com)** and WebCT **(http://www.webct.com)** include a chat component. The following sections describe two other approaches to online chat for students.

Chat Rooms for Language Learners

Some websites provide a set of communications resources that are related by topic. For example, English Club (Figure 12.5) is designed to

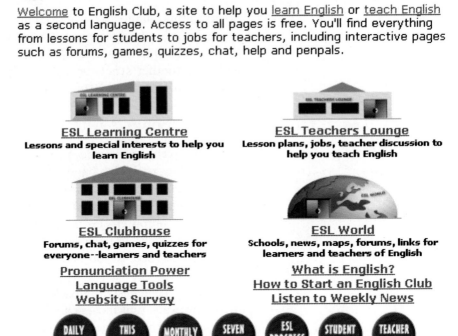

Figure 12.5 The English Club Homepage, Showing the Resources Available

Source: http://www.englishclub.com/index.htm

"Talking" online to learn a language

support English-as-a-second-language learners and their teachers. For this purpose, the website provides static materials, such as lesson plans and games. However, because learning a language is about learning to communicate, the website also includes chat rooms in which English-language learners can "talk" to one another synchronously. The website also provides additional support to teachers through asynchronous discussion boards where they can ask each other questions and share ideas. This kind of all-in-one resource provides easy ways for technology to support meaningful learning.

Building a "Virtual Campus"

With the rise of online communications tools, many different online "communities" have developed to support people in using these tools. For instance, Tapped In, a suite of communications tools and resources (located at **http://tappedin.org),** helps teachers and other educators create a "virtual campus." In each building of the "campus," there are offices, lounges, and other resources, all text based. Tapped In has become a huge community of teachers who provide help to one another. Synchronous chat is just one of the many resources available.

From the main campus map (Figure 12.6), you can choose to visit the Tapped In Center, the central point of the Tapped In campus. Once you're in the Tapped In Center, you can enter the reception area, where you'll see some of the resources available in the building (Figure 12.7). In the bottom

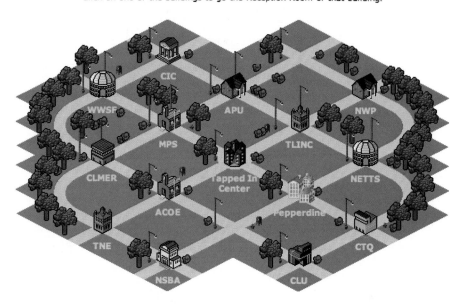

Tapped In Campus Map

Click on one of the buildings to go the Reception Room of that building.

Figure 12.6 The Tapped In Campus Map

of the window, you can watch the conversation occurring—and join the conversation yourself if you're so inclined.

Chat for educators

Being a Tapped In member allows you to chat publicly with people in the common areas—or to chat privately with one person at a time. You can also set up protected chat areas for your students. There are helpful links, as well as special interest groups where you can meet people with interests like yours.

■ Video-Based Communications

Webcams for data collection

One form of synchronous (real-time) video is webcam technology, which can also allow you to see places that you otherwise wouldn't visit. A **webcam** is any camera (usually a video rather than a still camera) that supplies images for transmission via a website. One common example is the use of webcams to broadcast traffic patterns in large cities. Your students could use such technology to do data collection about different kinds of cars or patterns in traffic.

Streaming video takes students into the field

Asynchronous one-way video communication is also available through the Web's streaming video capabilities. These technologies allow students to watch videos on the Internet just as they would watch TV or a movie in class. With more sophisticated efforts, video-based communications can be used to take your students out into the field with actual explorers or scientists, to interact with experiments as they happen. This is a far more exciting way for students to learn about the world than simply reading static materials about what these people do. The "Technology in Action" feature about the JASON Project illustrates some of the advantages that students can gain from such video technology.

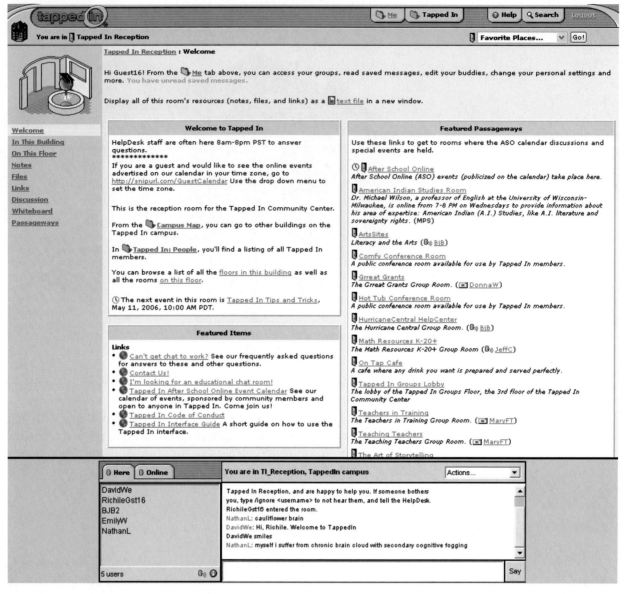

Figure 12.7 The Tapped In Center Reception Screen

Technology in Action

The JASON Project

A nonprofit subsidiary of National Geographic Society, The JASON Project creates standards-based multimedia curriculum to connect students with great explorers and great events in order to inspire and motivate them to learn science. Its new curriculum, Operation: Monster Storms, will be launched in June 2007 and will be available free online for the 2007–2008 school year (see Figure 12.8).

Operation: Monster Storms is a nine-week weather curriculum unit for middle school, although it is flexible for use at higher or lower levels.

Figure 12.8 The JASON Project website features—all free of charge online—print curricula, videos, podcasts, classroom management tools, and additional multimedia resources.

Students and teachers work with leading scientists from NASA, NOAA, and National Geographic to learn the mechanics of extreme weather events. These experts serve as role models and mentors while illustrating the core science concepts. Throughout the print and online curriculum, they are shown working side-by-side with JASON students and teachers. They also describe, in personal terms, their inspiration for becoming scientists, the courses they found valuable, and the obstacles they overcame (see Figure 12.9).

Online features include video, podcasts, digital labs (see Figure 12.10), chats, journals, bulletin boards, and teacher tools for lesson planning, alignment, assessments, reporting, and classroom management. A digital library will enable users to search JASON materials by subject, state standard, and resource type.

Each of the inquiry-based curriculum's five chapters, or missions, is led by a host researcher and contains a mission briefing, research articles, hands-on laboratory assignments, and a field assignment. Operation: Monster Storms also contains a "challenge" for all students to create and upload content for global peer review—a scientifically based video weather report. An advisory panel will review and rank the top 10 videos and JASON students will vote for the winner.

Operation: Monster Storms can be used by virtually every classroom teacher with today's technology, and most students and parents can use it at home. If teachers want to work solely from the print student and teacher editions and videos, they can still receive all the standards-based content that Operation: Monster Storms offers.

For additional information, see www.jason.org.

Figure 12.9 Mission 3: The Chase features National Geographic tornado-chaser Tim Samaras and a team of students studying thunderstorms and tornadoes.

Figure 12.10 Interactive "digital labs" use real satellite images and data to place students in the roles of scientists and decision-makers.

Videoconferencing

The power of videoconferencing is becoming increasingly accessible because of broadband Internet access and improvements in both software and hardware. Milton Chen created VSee **(http://www.vseelab.com),** for example, to overcome the limitations of traditional videoconferencing equipment. His technology provides such high compression of the data stream (video and audio) that videoconferencing is possible even in limited-bandwidth areas, such as rural schools. Using multiple computers, you can have an unlimited number of participants. The high-quality transmission resembles that of a camcorder recording.

Videoconferencing equipment and software prices continue to drop. In fact, an inexpensive USB camera (often under $50) and a free or low-cost online videoconferencing service make it possible for most schools and many homes to utilize videoconferencing technology for teaching and learning. For a comprehensive resource on videoconferencing, see the Videoconferencing Cookbook **(http://www.videnet.gatech.edu/ cookbook).** For teachers, one of the most exciting aspects of videoconferencing is that it allows your students to actually see and hear people who would otherwise not be available except through phone calls or text-based messages.

Sample applications of videoconferencing include the following:

Sample applications of videoconferencing

1. *Faculty to student teacher.* A middle-grades education professor was able to connect and communicate with her student teacher in North County Middle School. With the assistance of the school's network administration, she installed a videoconferencing system on her office desktop and was able to observe her student teacher remotely. Teacher and professor were able to communicate before and after lessons.
2. *Providing remote interpreting services.* Professor Nanci Scheetz from Valdosta State University, who works with the American Sign Language Interpreting program, uses videoconferencing to provide interpretation services for a deaf college student who is enrolled in undergraduate classes. Both the student and the interpreter have a laptop computer with videoconferencing equipment. Through this equipment the interpreter, Dr. Scheetz, is able to see both the class instructor and the deaf student. Dr. Scheetz translates the instructor's words into sign language that the student can see on her computer screen.
3. *Professional development.* Videoconferencing can open up professional development opportunities for teachers by linking a number of remote sites that include an instructor. In instances that we've seen, these opportunities allow teachers to take graduate-level courses halfway across the state, while still working with teachers in their own district. Further, the videoconferencing approach allows practicing teachers to interact with graduate students who may never have taught. This allows for interesting interactions from which both sides benefit.

SUMMARY

In this chapter you've learned about some of the different communications tools available to teachers, and you've discovered some ways those tools can be used to enhance learning for your students. A simple asynchronous tool like e-mail can be used for keypal exchanges and telementoring. The Web, besides being an excellent information source, can give you access to ambitious collaborative projects, such as the GLOBE Program.

Synchronous (real-time) tools include Internet-based telephones, chat, and videoconferencing. The JASON Project is a good example of the power of synchronous tools put to work in an inquiry-based learning environment.

The one idea that spans all of these technologies—whether synchronous or asynchronous, text based or multimedia—is that your classroom can be opened up to the world with a little bit of planning and some readily accessible tools. Contemporary technologies provide unprecedented opportunities for you and your students to work with people from anywhere in the world on virtually any kind of project.

RESOURCES

Online Study Center
Direct Links to Resources

ASYNCHRONOUS COMMUNICATION TOOLS AND IDEAS

ActiveBoard
http://www.activeboard.com
Provides a free bulletin board service.

Bedford Workshops on Teaching Writing: Strategies for Teaching with Online Tools
http://www.bedfordstmartins.com/technotes/workshops/index.htm
A brief workshop that presents ideas for using e-mail, discussion boards, and real-time discussions with students.

Cornell University Academic Technology Center: Managing Class Discussions with Technology
http://www.cit.cornell.edu/atc/materials/GS/distcomm/intro.shtml
A short workshop with tips for facilitating online discussions.

DiscussionApp
http://server.com/communityapps/discussionapp
A free threaded discussion tool.

Education World: Add Your Name to a Listserv—Today
http://www.educationworld.com/a_curr/curr062.shtml
An article about why educators should join listservs.

ePALS Classroom Exchange
http://www.epals.com
A site with tools to connect classrooms for the purposes of cultural exchange.

Intercultural E-mail Classroom Connections (IECC)
http://www.iecc.org
A service to help teachers identify partners in other cultures for classroom activities.

Knowledge Forum
http://www.knowledgeforum.com/K-12/products.htm
A knowledge-building tool designed to support students in developing understanding by helping them interact with one another to explore particular ideas.

Netlingo
http://www.netlingo.com
An online dictionary of technical terms.

Teacher Focus
http://www.teacherfocus.com
A discussion board supporting teachers on a wide range of issues.

Teacher Mailring Center
http://teachers.net/mailrings
A service that allows teachers to easily identify and sign up for a variety of listservs.

Teacher Talk Forums
http://www.teachertalk.com
An interactive discussion board for teachers.

Wikipedia
http://www.wikipedia.org
A multimedia encyclopedia, built using wiki technology, that allows anyone to add to the knowledge base.

COURSE MANAGEMENT TOOLS THAT INCLUDE COMMUNICATION TOOLS

Blackboard
http://www.blackboard.com
One of the most popular commercially available course management tools.

MyClass.Net
http://www.myclass.net
A free tool for creating a class website. With the low-cost "select service" you can create a discussion board and other interactive features.

Nicenet

http://www.nicenet.org

A free course support tool that includes a discussion tool, the ability to add links, and other common support elements.

SYNCHRONOUS TOOLS AND IDEAS FOR USING THEM

About.com Freebies: Free Internet Phone Calls

http://freebies.about.com/cs/faxphone/a/internetcalls.htm

An article reviewing the various free Internet-based phone services.

AOL Instant Messenger

http://www.aim.com

A synchronous messaging tool for person-to-person communication.

English Club

http://www.englishclub.com

A website of resources, including a discussion area, for supporting teachers who teach English as a second language.

FWD: Free World Dialup

http://www.freeworlddialup.com

A free Internet voice communication tool.

iChat

http://www.apple.com/macosx/features/ichat

A conferencing tool that allows audio, text, or video-conferencing between two or more people. Free on Macintosh computers.

Paltalk

http://www.paltalk.com

A conferencing tool that allows text-, audio-, and video-based conferencing and supports chat rooms.

Skype

http://www.skype.com

Another free Internet voice communication tool.

Tapped In

http://tappedin.org

An online resource for teachers which includes a variety of information as well as a text-based community of support.

Videoconferencing Cookbook

http://www.videnet.gatech.edu/cookbook

An online resource for creating good videoconferences, written for educators.

VSee Lab

http://www.vseelab.com

VSee allows you to see and communicate with multiple people on your computer. You can remotely edit and annotate documents, share applications and desktops, transfer files, record and share videos, and show microscope and whiteboard cameras.

ACCEPTABLE USE POLICY AND WEBSITE EVALUATION INFORMATION

Becta Schools E-Safety Introduction

http://schools.becta.org.uk/index.php?section=is

Links to guidance on writing acceptable use policies for students and teachers, as well as on developing schoolwide policies.

CyberSmart!: Understand Your Acceptable Use Policy

http://www.cybersmartcurriculum.org/lesson_plans/45_07.asp

An activity sheet for developing an acceptable use policy.

Kathy Schrock's Guide for Educators: Critical Evaluation Surveys and Resources

http://school.discovery.com/schrockguide/eval.html

Part of Kathy Schrock's rich collection of teacher's resources for using technology in the classroom.

Virginia Department of Education, Acceptable Use Policies: A Handbook

http://www.pen.k12.va.us/go/VDOE/Technology/AUP/home.shtml

A handbook on writing acceptable use policies.

WWW CyberGuides for Web Evaluation

http://www.cyberbee.com/guides.html

Tools for evaluating websites.

COMMUNICATION PROJECT IDEAS

Be a Mentor

http://www.beamentor.org

An organization that supports mentoring.

Electronic Emissary Telementoring Project

http://www.tcet.unt.edu/pubs/em/em01.pdf

A document that includes information and resources to support mentoring projects.

The GLOBE Program

http://www.globe.gov/globe_flash.html

A climate-inquiry project in which people from around the world input data that students and teachers can use to engage in authentic analysis.

The JASON Project

http://www.jasonproject.org

An interactive project that engages students in scientific inquiry by using data and video-based field experiences.

Mentor

http://www.mentoring.org

An organization to support mentoring.

U.S. Department of Education

http://www.ed.gov

The website for the U.S. Department of Education includes information on mentoring and other technology-enhanced projects funded through the department.

case STUDY

Choosing Communications Technologies

You've just transferred to a new school that has more technology than your last one because of a corporate gift from a nearby biomedical company. On the first day of preplanning, the principal holds a meeting with all the new teachers to introduce them to aspects of the school. In this introduction, he mentions that there are three wireless rolling computer carts, a wireless "umbrella" covering the campus, and six computers for the students in each classroom—all connected to the Internet.

As a new teacher, you're excited about all this technology and want to use it to help your students understand that there's a whole world out there for them to explore. You begin planning ways you might be able to use the equipment in your teaching. The principal has issued a challenge to the new teachers to impress him with their efforts. What will you do to impress the principal and meet your learning goals?

Questions for Reflection and Discussion

1. What kinds of communications technologies will you include in your plans?
   a. What kinds of learning goals will these help you to meet?
   b. How will you use the technologies?
2. How will you find out about possible uses of communications technologies for your own particular field?
3. What are some ways you can go about figuring out which communications tools are right for you and your students?

Meet the Standards

Online Study Center

Standards
Go online for more resources on standards.

Take a moment to reread "Standards to Guide Your Preparation" at the beginning of this chapter. We've presented a number of communications technologies to help you reach outside your immediate surroundings both for personal growth and for instructional purposes.

▶ How can you use these technologies to help yourself create better learning opportunities for your students?

▶ How can you use them to help yourself continue to develop as a teacher throughout your career?

▶ What are the benefits of using the communications tools described in this chapter? What are the dangers?

▶ How can communication technology help you reach out to all of your students, regardless of their race, gender, or economic status?

Chapter 13

Content-Area Tools

Standards to Guide Your Preparation

ISTE NETS

Teachers

► Demonstrate introductory knowledge, skills, and understanding of concepts related to technology.

► Identify and locate technology resources and evaluate them for accuracy and suitability.

► Facilitate technology-enhanced experiences that address content standards and student technology standards.

► Use technology to support learner-centered strategies that address the diverse needs of students.

► Apply technology to develop students' higher-order skills and creativity.

► Apply technology to increase productivity.

OTHER RELEVANT STANDARDS

National Social Studies Standards (ISTE, 2006)

The skills that should be promoted in an excellent social studies program include the following:

► acquiring information and manipulating data;

► developing and presenting policies, arguments, and stories;

► constructing new knowledge; and

► participating in groups.

National English Language Arts Standards (ISTE, 2006)

Students use a variety of technological and information resources (e.g., libraries, databases, computer networks, and video) to gather and synthesize information and to create and communicate knowledge.

National Science Standards (ISTE, 2006)

Science as Inquiry (K–4): Fundamental abilities and concepts that underlie this standard include:

► Ask a question about objects, organisms, and events in the environment.

► Plan and conduct a simple investigation.

► Employ simple equipment and tools to gather data and extend the senses.

► Use data to construct a reasonable explanation.

► Communicate investigations and explanations.

National Mathematics Standards (ISTE, 2006)

Technology is essential in teaching and learning mathematics; it influences the mathematics that is taught and enhances students' learning. Calculators and computers are reshaping the mathematical landscape, and school mathematics should reflect those changes. Students can learn more mathematics more deeply with the appropriate and responsible use of technology. They can make and test conjectures. They can work at higher levels of generalization or abstraction. In the mathematics classrooms envisioned in [the standards], every student has access to technology to facilitate his or her mathematics learning.

We've looked at a variety of software programs and Internet applications so far in this section of the book. Now we consider how different kinds of software can enhance each of the content areas. In this chapter we first talk about how to evaluate software. Then we introduce a vision of how technology can be used in each of the content areas and describe some different classes of software that might be useful. This isn't a comprehensive survey of all possible content-area software, but an overview of some different ideas for using software in your classroom. We assume that you've been thinking about how the technologies described in previous chapters relate to your content area.

Software Evaluation

One of the most important aspects of using technology in your classroom is making good decisions about which technologies to use. Just because you have access to a piece of software doesn't mean that it's a good choice for meeting your instructional goals.

Software evaluation occurs at two points: first, when the software package is purchased and, second, when it's selected for use in a learning environment. As a teacher, you'll often select software for your learning environment, but you'll also have occasional opportunities to help purchase software. Therefore, it's important to consider the kinds of questions you'll want to ask at each of these two levels.

Purchasing Software

When you're looking at a piece of software to determine whether to buy it, chances are that you don't have a specific instructional goal in mind. Rather, you have a general idea of the kinds of tools that would be helpful. In this situation, it's sometimes difficult to select software that will turn out to be relevant and useful. However, there are a few key elements that will increase your likelihood of selecting good software.

Key elements to look for in software

Quality of the Content
- ▶ Is there enough content?
- ▶ Is it interactive?
- ▶ Is it written accurately?
- ▶ Is it current?
- ▶ Is it free of gender, ethnic, and racial bias?
- ▶ Does it provide learning opportunities that are consistent with the instructional approaches you use in your school? (For example, if your school uses a whole language approach to reading, you may not want to purchase software focused on phonics.)

Ease of Use for Students
- ▶ Can students easily navigate within the program?
- ▶ Can students use the program without a lot of guidance?
- ▶ Are the directions explicit?

> ▶ Is there a help section—and is it actually helpful?
> ▶ Does the software seem engaging?

Management Aspects

> ▶ Does the software make it easy for teachers to keep student records?
> ▶ Is it possible—better yet, easy—to set difficulty levels for students?
> ▶ Does the software allow differentiation of instruction, so that students with different needs can receive different kinds of guidance?
> ▶ In what settings will the software work best (learning centers, whole class activities, small groups)?

Clearly, these questions don't all have the same impact. Together, however, they'll help you gain an overall picture of the software's value.

Evaluation forms

Often, schools create evaluation forms that ask raters to assign scores to software using these kinds of categories. The score sheets typically include a section for notes about what the rater liked best and least about the software, as well as a place for a short description. The "Case Study" near the end of this chapter contains a software evaluation form that you may find useful. You can also find a number of such forms on the Internet; see "Resources" before the "Case Study."

As you think about purchasing software, remember that many useful applications are available free of charge. Spotlight 13.1 discusses open-source software that can perform some of the same functions as commercial products.

■ Choosing Software for Your Lessons

The next phase of software evaluation comes in your own classroom planning. When you're planning a lesson and want to include technology in it, there are some important elements to think about.

SPOTLIGHT 13.1   **Open-Source Software**

A growing movement in the software world is *open-source software (OSS)*, software developed in such a way that it can be altered by programmers anywhere. In other words, the source code for the software is available, and the licenses under which it is released allow anyone to alter it. Even if you aren't a programmer, you can access these tools as a user.

This can be a good thing for education, because many high-quality programs are available at no charge. For example, Edubuntu (http://www.edubuntu.org) is a Linux-based operating system built just for students. It includes many built-in word processing and drawing programs, as well as

tools to support content learning, such as the periodic table. Mozilla Firefox (http://www.mozilla.com/firefox) is a commonly used web browser that is OSS. Firefox allows fast, free web surfing. Some other tools mentioned previously in this book are also OSS; for example, GIMP (http://gimp.org) and OpenOffice (http://www.openoffice.org).

It's likely that, even if you haven't used one of these programs before, you have benefited from them. Often, network managers will use OSS for server-based applications, such as mail routers or firewalls. OSS often offers flexibility and security that are either impossible or extremely expensive through commercial means.

SPOTLIGHT 13.2 — Edutainment and Technotainment

Too often, school media centers and store shelves are lined with software that's designed mainly to be entertaining. Often these titles look like they're also educational. For example, a rocket blasts off into space, and it's your job to shoot aliens by providing correct answers to math problems; or the voice in the software reads a story, and your students can click on elements in the picture to make things happen. But how much do students actually *learn* from such experiences?

There's nothing wrong with children using software for entertainment purposes, but you want to take steps to ensure the technology helps them meet standards and goals you've set for them. Most of the time, "edutainment" or "technotainment" titles won't help students meet educational goals.

An important element for you to consider when evaluating different software titles is whether the software is educational or just entertaining. A few key questions can help you find out (adapted from McKenzie, 2000).

1. Does the activity or software tie technology use to your stated goals?
2. Does the software require students to engage in higher levels of understanding, or simply rely on memorized facts?
3. Do the activities go into the appropriate depth for your students, or just skim the surface?
4. Is too much time spent on movies and animations, rather than on learning activities?
5. Does the software "grow" with your students, allowing them to engage in more complex thinking and problem solving as they progress?

Students love cartoons and action, but they can be equally captivated by good problems to solve and good stories. Test edutainment software for yourself and read reviews—look for a clear sense that there is learning taking place alongside the fun.

Important questions to ask

▶ What is the goal of your lesson, and how will this piece of software help you meet that goal?
▶ Will the software help you meet the standards you've selected?
▶ How will you use the software: in small groups, in a learning center, with the whole class, or as a tutorial?
▶ How well does the software align with the instructional approach you use in your teaching? For example, if you teach mathematics using an exploration-oriented, hands-on approach, drill-and-practice software wouldn't be helpful. However, a dynamic geometry software package would be.

Online Study Center
See the online resources for direct links to the software evaluation forms and reviews listed at the end of this chapter.

Published reviews of software packages can help you answer these questions. The "Resources" at the end of this chapter include links to a number of software review sites where you can find useful information. See also Spotlight 13.2, which discusses ways to tell whether a software package's primary use is entertainment rather than education.

You may find it useful to have a tool for keeping track of your answers to instructional questions. One approach that we've used is the "Software Evaluation for Mathematics" tool shown in Table 13.1. Notice how this tool keeps everything focused on the instructional goals rather than on the technology.

Table 13.1 Software Evaluation for Mathematics

Question	Your Response
What problem are you trying to address?	
What is your goal for this lesson?	
Which standards are you planning to address?	
Technology selected	
Brief description of plan (What will you do? What will students do?)	
How will this plan address your problem? How will it help you meet your goal?	
How does this software package/Internet application support meeting the goals you have set?	

Software in the Content Areas

Though we've focused on a variety of generic technologies in this book, it's also very important for you to be familiar with the kinds of software available specifically for your classroom. These range from Internet-based applets to CD-ROM titles. Software for the classrooms can be very specific (for example, teaching about the ear to young students) or comprehensive (software designed to support content learning across several grades). It can also be free or expensive. In this section we provide a snapshot of the kinds of tools available, and the "Resources" at the end of the chapter offer a sampling of the many titles available.

As discussed elsewhere in this book, different kinds of technologies have certain benefits and drawbacks. It will be up to you as the teacher to decide the important factors for your own students. Table 13.2 gives a brief overview of some generic benefits and drawbacks of different software types.

Social Studies

According to the Curriculum Standards for Social Studies adopted by the National Council for the Social Studies **(http://www.socialstudies.org/standards/introduction),** social studies in grades K–12 is designed to promote civic competence—the knowledge, skills, and attitudes needed to make decisions about the public good. Social studies integrates such diverse disciplines as history, geography, political science, sociology, and geography, as well as language arts.

Working from these goals, we can identify three clear uses for software in the social studies classroom: fact resources, decision-making and problem-solving applications, and organizational resources.

Table 13.2 Overview of Software Benefits and Drawbacks

Software Type	Benefits	Drawbacks
Drill and practice	• Easy to use • Often provides immediate feedback • Generally focused on one or a small set of concepts • Good way to practice rote information	• Data indicate this isn't always effective. • Doesn't allow connections between and among ideas • Inappropriate for conceptual understanding
Simulation	• Engaging • Allows students to experience complex problem solving and application of knowledge	• Students need additional guidance to understand what's important.
Tutorial	• Focused guidance • Infinite patience • Available as a just-in-time tool for supporting learners when they have a specific need	• Limited to a particular content focus • Often provides information without application or practice
Game	• Engaging and fun • Allows students to solve complex, applied problems	• Sometimes game play is separate from content focus, making the game irrelevant. • Requires scaffolding to ensure that students are learning intended concepts
Modeling	• Great communication tool for supporting students' sense making and for helping teachers understand students' thinking • Can be used to demonstrate complex processes	• Often hard to learn • Maximum value comes from students' using the tool, which means that all students need access to computers.
Reference	• Easy, searchable access to large bodies of information • Incorporation of multimedia elements	• Depends on teacher to create worthwhile activities for using them

▬ Fact Resources

Digital encyclopedias

There are many products available for fact finding in social studies. The most obvious of these are the various encyclopedia CD-ROMs and DVDs. Nearly every book-based encyclopedia publisher (for instance, Britannica, World Book, and Grolier) also offers a digital version. These resources provide easy access to a great deal of factual information for students to work with in their research. Internet encyclopedias are also available; one of them, Wikipedia, even offers students a chance to contribute their own knowledge (see Spotlight 13.3).

Electronic encyclopedias are more easily searchable than traditional print versions. They also provide a degree of interactivity that makes the research more interesting and can help students better understand events or phenomena. For example, in Wikipedia, terms are hyperlinked when they refer to a relevant entry. In the Finland example in Figure 13.1, the terms *Finnish, Swedish,* and *Nordic countries* all link to entries on these subjects. This allows faster access to relevant topics, so that students can do deeper and more meaningful research.

Other fact-oriented resources

There are also fact-oriented CD-ROMs featuring particular aspects of history or government, such as the Facts On File products that include *American Government on File* and *American Historical Images.* All of these resources can be valuable for student research and the development of high-quality reports.

Wikipedia

The online encyclopedia Wikipedia (**http://www.wikipedia .org**) uses so-called wiki technology to put the world at students' fingertips free of charge. Figure 13.1 shows a sample entry. All the content is in the public domain and can be used at no charge. In addition, Wikipedia is set up to invite readers to contribute to it; anyone can submit an article or changes to an existing article. Because of these advantages, the site is being developed in 200 languages.

The downside to this approach, of course, is that, in some cases, people may have posted wrong information or even "vandalized" Wikipedia. As with any other Internet resource, it's important for you and your students to consider the information carefully before using it. Of course, because there are so many people accessing Wikipedia every day, misinformation tends to be corrected quite quickly.

The upside is that your junior-high or high-school students can publish material that they've written for you. This means that they'll have access to a real audience and can be part of a worldwide effort to create an important body of knowledge. One important thing to remember is that the writing needs to be consistent with that in other Wikipedia entries.

Finland

From Wikipedia, the free encyclopedia

Finland (Finnish: *Suomi*, Swedish: *Finland*), officially the **Republic of Finland** (Finnish: *Suomen tasavalta*, Swedish: *Republiken Finland*), is one of the Nordic countries. It is situated in northern Europe, bounded by the Baltic Sea with the Gulf of Finland to the south and the Gulf of Bothnia to the west. Finland has land frontiers with Sweden in the west, Norway in the north and Russia in the east. The Åland Islands, off the south-western coast, are under Finnish sovereignty while enjoying extensive autonomy.

Finland has a population of five million people spread over more than 330,000 square kilometres (127,000 sq. mi) making it one of the most sparsely populated countries in the world (see List of countries by population density).

Finland is ranked thirteenth on the 2005 United Nations Human Development Index.

Contents [hide]

1 History
2 Etymology
3 Politics
4 Subdivisions
5 Geography
6 Education
   6.1 PISA Test Results:

Suomen tasavalta
Republiken Finland
Republic of Finland

Flag   Coat of arms

Motto: none

Anthem: *Maamme* (Finnish) / *Vårt land* (Swedish)
("Our Land" in English)

Capital   Helsinki
              60°10′ N 24°56′ E

Largest city   Helsinki

Figure 13.1 Screen Shot from Wikipedia

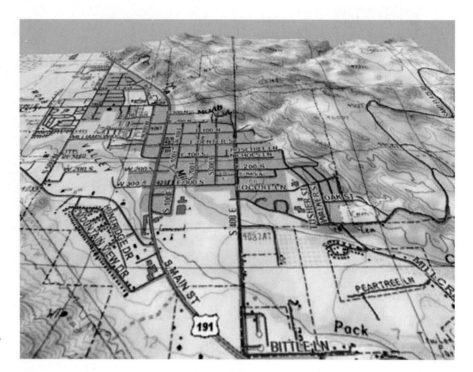

Figure 13.2 Screen Shot of a Topographical Map from National Geographic's TOPO! Software
Source: http://maps.nationalgeographic.com/topo/streets.cfm

Other types of factual resources include map programs like those from National Geographic and Street Atlas USA. These allow users to do three-dimensional "fly-bys" or to view a topographical image (see Figure 13.2). With GPS technology, as explained in the following "Technology in Action" feature, you can make geography projects even more exciting and interactive.

Technology in Action

GPS in Classrooms

Global positioning systems (GPS) are a reasonably priced technology that you can use in your social studies classroom for a variety of purposes related to maps and geography. GPS systems work by communicating with a network of twenty-seven satellites that orbit the earth sending back a variety of data. These satellites were originally sent into orbit to support military navigation. Now, however, you can buy a small GPS receiver for your car, home, or classroom. Every time your GPS receives data, it's coming from four of the satellites simultaneously.

There are several different projects in which classroom teachers can participate with GPS technology. Project ATLAS **(http://cfa-www.harvard .edu/space_geodesy/ATLAS),** funded by the Smithsonian Institution, provides lesson plan ideas that help integrate science and social studies in interesting ways. For example, in one activity students are asked to map their neighborhood using GPS data, selecting certain landmarks to include in their map.

Another lesson idea is to have a student create a map of another student's journey. For this activity, developed by the CHICOS project at the California Institute of Technology, the first student creates a path using GPS readings. Then the second student must determine where the first student went, which direction she or he turned, and so on. More information is available at **http://www.chicos.caltech.edu/classroom/GPS/GPSActivity1.html.**

A third lesson idea allows students to study states by following the travels of their own "travel bug." (The "bug," typically a small device shaped like a dog tag, is described in detail at **http://www.geocaching.com/track/faq.aspx.)** Students can use GPS information to track the bug, then create a travel brochure that highlights the places where their bug went. More information is available at **http://www.uen.org/Lessonplan/preview.cgi?tid=93902&LPid=12855.**

Decision-Making and Problem-Solving Software

Software that asks students to solve a problem or make a decision

A number of software titles engage students in learning about aspects of social studies through problem presentation, research, and debate. These titles typically center on a single problem or issue and provide students with the information they need to make a grounded decision. Titles in this group include Decisions, Decisions from Tom Snyder Productions, a series that engages students in debate about social studies issues ranging from the Revolutionary War to violence in the media (Figure 13.3). Another Tom Snyder title, Community Construction Kit, asks students to create a neighborhood authentic to a particular time period.

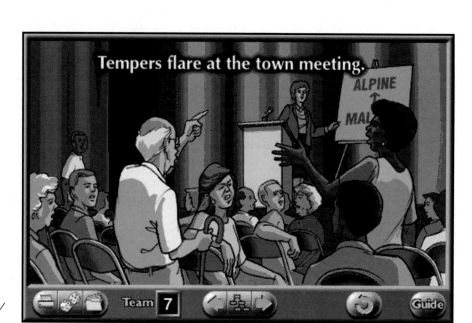

Figure 13.3 Screen Shot from Decisions, Decisions: Town Government
Source: http://www.tomsnyder.com/products/product.asp?SKU=DECTOG

The Oregon Trail, from Riverdeep, is one of the oldest and most widely used titles in this category. In The Oregon Trail, students engage in a simulation of the trip west on the Oregon Trail in the nineteenth century. They have to make a variety of decisions about supplies and routes as they go. Moving to the twenty-first century, the popular SimCity from Maxis has students design and populate their own city—and try to make it function. This title provides many learning opportunities, ranging from understanding the economic implications of city layouts to developing an understanding of how terrain affects land value.

Organizational Resources

Another popular category of software for social studies is organizational software. This is software that organizes information and events so that students can re-create an event in history.

Software for timelines

One example is Tom Snyder's TimeLiner, which helps students create timelines and similar arrangements of data. It allows students to organize information and flag it according to type. There are also free online tools that work similarly, such as HyperHistory **(http://www.hyperhistory.com/ online_n2/History_n2/a.html).** As discussed in our chapter on productivity tools, database programs are also appropriate for organizing information and creating links in ways that allow students to make sense of a large body of data for their own historical research.

Language Arts

The underlying vision of *Standards for the English Language Arts* (NCTE, 1996) is that language arts will provide students with opportunities to develop reading, writing, and other communication abilities. This general literacy extends from students' having exposure to a wide variety of literature from various periods throughout history to students' engaging in communication through written and spoken language. Clearly, comprehension plays an important role throughout the standards. The standards even suggest that part of the English language arts curriculum should include students' learning to synthesize a wide array of information in order to create new knowledge.

A number of software titles are available to meet a variety of goals in language arts. These range from titles focused on reading and grammar to packages that attempt to support students in becoming better writers. As you consider the various software options, you'll want to be aware of the edutainment-versus-education tensions discussed earlier. Many titles for language arts lean toward edutainment.

Reading Comprehension

Software for assessing reading comprehension

Software designed to support reading comprehension generally focuses on one of two approaches. In titles like Accelerated Reader (Renaissance Learning) and Scholastic Reading Inventory (Scholastic, Inc.), students are asked to read paper-based books, then use the computer as an assessment tool to determine whether their comprehension skills are progressing.

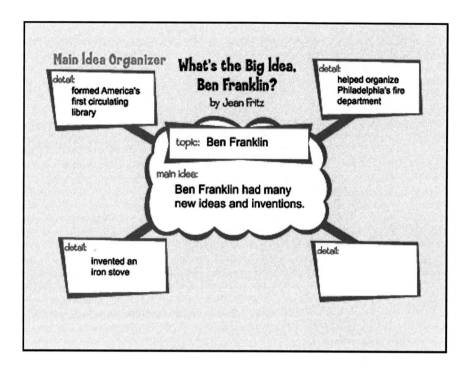

Figure 13.4 Screen Shot from Reading for Meaning
Source: http://www.tomsnyder.com/products/product.asp?SKU=RFMROM&Subject=LanguageArts

These programs also provide guidance to the teacher and the student about the reading level at which the student should be working.

Other reading comprehension titles include activities and exercises that support students' development of key reading skills, such as identifying the main idea of a story, determining cause and effect, learning to paraphrase and summarize, and using graphic organizers as comprehension tools. These titles range from Reading for Meaning (Figure 13.4) and Thinking Reader from Tom Snyder software to Destination Reading from Riverdeep. Though most of these titles are aimed at elementary levels, programs that aim to improve student reading comprehension are available through high-school level.

▬ Interactive Books

A variety of interactive books are available for young readers and for readers learning a different language. These tend to include a narrated story, often with text that follows along, and certain interactive components. The better titles include interactivity that ensures that students are comprehending the story by asking them to select particular options based on the story. The "Resources" at the end of this chapter include information on several titles, as well as links to reviews of many more.

▬ Phonics

Related to other reading comprehension software are several titles that rely specifically on a phonics-based approach to learning to read. When selecting any of these titles, it's very important to consider the approach to reading that your schools use. Phonics titles focus on helping students learn what certain letter combinations sound like alone and together.

ESL and Foreign-Language Learning with Software

Some software titles have been developed specifically for nonnative English speakers to learn English. Similarly, other titles are available to help native English speakers learn other languages.

These titles range from drill-and-practice to game-based approaches. Some even claim to offer an "immersive" opportunity for language learning. Though software alone is likely not enough support for learning a second language, it can provide students with a variety of interactive opportunities to apply their newly developing skills. The following resources offer a starting place for locating useful software titles:

Elementary Education: Foreign Language Resources
http://www.pitt.edu/~poole/eledforeign.html

ESL: Games
http://iteslj.org/links/ESL/Games

ESL.net: ESL Software for Public or Private Schools
http://www.esl.net/software_schools.html

Some, like Fonty, even capitalize on voice recognition software to ensure that students learn about the sounds.

Spelling

A number of games attempt to make rote activities, such as learning to spell, more interesting for students. Some allow teachers to customize word lists. Titles in this category include I LOVE Spelling (Riverdeep), Tenth Planet: Consonant Blends and Digraphs (Sunburst), and Stickybear's Spelling (Optimum Resource).

Grammar

The wide array of grammar titles available are appropriate for elementary- and middle-school students, as well as some second-language English learners. (For software designed particularly for learners of English as a second language [ESL], see Spotlight 13.4.) These focus on helping users learn which word forms and tenses to use, how to identify the parts of a sentence, and other similar grammatical challenges. Like reading titles, however, many of these software packages are packed with animations and interactions that are irrelevant to the learning activities. However, some do offer high-quality experiences for students who need practice.

Interactions and animations—sometimes relevant to learning, sometimes not

Writing Support

Many language education classrooms are becoming more writer centered through the use of **weblogs** (also called **blogs**) to help students organize their thinking and allow students and teachers to provide each other with feedback. See Spotlight 13.5 for a brief discussion of ways to use blogs in the classroom.

A large number of more traditional tools also support writing across all phases of student development. As mentioned in an earlier chapter, productivity tools like Inspiration and Kidspiration, as well as page layout programs, provide excellent opportunities to support student writing.

SPOTLIGHT 13.5 — Blogs for Improving Writing

Blogs are quite simple to use (no special hardware or software is needed) and freely available online. Currently, teachers use blogs to update parents and community members about class events. This is a very easy way for teachers to communicate. However, a more powerful use of blogs is for students to use them as a writing tool. In using a public environment in which other people will read their writing, students learn how to organize their ideas and write clearly. With commenting features built into blogging software, the teacher can provide feedback directly to each student. Students can also read each other's blogs as a way of providing feedback to each other. Because of the format, it's easy for students to engage in daily or weekly postings, making writing a regular part of their everyday life.

There are security and safety issues, however. Everything students write will be public, unless you select a tool like Live-Journal, which allows for private posting. If you want your students to create blogs, you need to identify an appropriate blogging tool and provide the students with clear guidelines. See "Resources" at the end of the chapter for further information about educational uses of blogging.

Software specifically designed to support writing

If you're looking for even more focused guidance for students' writing, consider tools designed specifically to support writing. Some software titles, such as Storybook Weaver (Riverdeep), provide stems to write from and aim to make the process more fun by allowing easy animation and illustration. Others, such as Write It Right (Merit Software), are designed to analyze student writing and help the writer correct errors. Some error correction programs, such as StyleWriter, provide not only feedback and support, but also guidance designed to make your students better writers.

The following "Technology in Action" features describe two particularly innovative approaches. The first discusses a way to integrate Inspiration with video in a challenging and highly motivating writing assignment. The second focuses on a newer type of writing software—applications designed for collaborative writing.

Technology in Action

Making Movies in Language Arts

Technology can be used to create lessons for your students that are both educational and consistent with constructivist principles. One example of this is in middle-grades language arts.

> *In your group, choose a famous fable or short story. Rewrite it to fit into today's culture. You'll rewrite the fable and then make a video between three to five minutes in length, in which your group acts out the fable or story.*

After students identify the fable or story that they're going to rewrite, they'll need to plan their modifications. Using Inspiration or other concept-mapping software, students can graphically brainstorm their

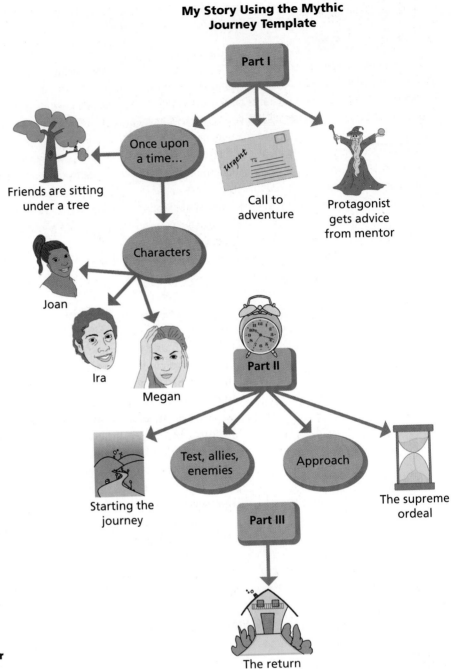

Figure 13.5 Concept Map for Rewriting a Fable

ideas about the fable they're modifying. Once they have a concept map like the one in Figure 13.5, they can readily generate an outline and write their movie script with a word processor.

The movie can then be recorded with a digital video camera that connects directly to a computer. Software like iMovie **(http://www.apple .com/ilife/imovie)** or other video-editing software will allow students to cut, combine, and edit their movie clips into a finished video.

Technology in Action

Collaborative Writing Software

Among the new language arts technologies is collaborative writing software. Using this kind of software, any number of people can work on a single document, making changes, adding comments, even comparing versions of the piece they're working on together. One place you can access this technology free of charge is at Writeboard (**http://writeboard.com**).

Say that a teacher gives a group of students a writing assignment. Using Writeboard, each student can add to and edit the document as he or she finds additional information. The teacher and group members can easily track which student added which materials, and there are ways to retrieve older versions if the students decide they've made a mistake. Further, the piece can be exported as either a text document or HTML to put on the Web.

◾ Science

The National Science Education Standards (NRC, 1996) describe a vision of science education at all levels that strives to place students in the role of actual scientists, allowing them to learn about the world and the work of scientists through inquiry-based activities and authentic exploration. The use of educational technologies in the science classroom allows students to participate in activities that might not otherwise be available; that is, technology allows students to collect, organize, and share data in ways that noncomputerized tools can't. As with all other content areas, science also benefits from complex scenarios that can be developed by experts and engaged in by students. Here we focus on a few key categories of software for science: inquiry-based and problem-solving approaches, virtual labs and simulations, models and demonstrations, and science software for young learners.

▬ Inquiry-Based and Problem-Solving Approaches

Engaging students in investigations

Using a variety of pedagogical models, software titles in this category engage students in investigating a situation or problem. The software includes a variety of information for students to consider and asks them to make one or more decisions based on the information they've been provided. These titles often have students using either debate techniques (such as the Science Court Explorations series from Tom Snyder) or jigsaw strategies that ask each student to become "expert" in one particular area, then work in a group with several other experts to make a decision (such as Rainforest Researchers, also from Tom Snyder). Some of these experiences rely on contrived situations that are quite realistic, whereas others rely on real data (such as the web-based Exploring the Environment, part of the Classroom of the Future project sponsored by the National Aeronautics and Space Administration).

Virtual Labs and Simulations

Software allows science activities impossible in the "real" world

Various software and Internet-based tools allow students to engage in lab-based activities that would be difficult or impossible in the regular classroom. For example, Cooties from GoKnow uses handheld technologies, such as Pocket PCs and Palm handhelds, to simulate the spread of a disease. There would be no way to perform this activity without technology. Similarly, chemistry labs that would otherwise be dangerous can be carried out safely on the computer. ChemDiscovery, featured in Figure 13.6, is one such simulation.

Students control variables

Further, computers can allow more control over the variables in an experiment than would be possible in the real world. One online example

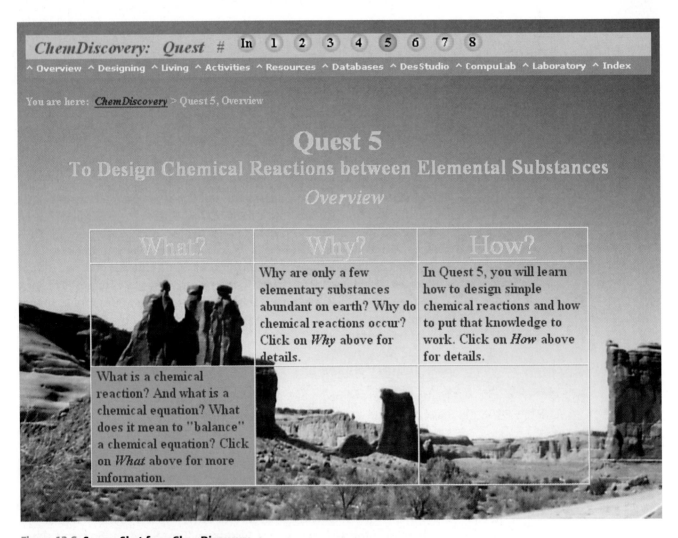

Figure 13.6 Screen Shot from ChemDiscovery
Source: ChemDiscovery Online DEMO! http://kendallhunt.com/index.cfm?PID=219&PGI=150)

Software that demonstrates otherwise-inaccessible phenomena

Software to introduce scientific processes

is Funderstanding's Roller Coaster simulation **(http://www.funderstanding.com/k12/coaster).** This simulation provides students with only a few of the variables that a roller coaster designer would attend to, but it provides enough hands-on experience for students to develop a meaningful understanding of how physics affects a roller coaster (see Figure 13.7).

Models and Demonstrations

Like virtual labs, models and demonstrations allow students to see things they otherwise would be unable to see. For example, Cells Alive! **(http://www.cellsalive.com)** provides 3-D animations of cellular-level phenomena. High schools don't have access to the equipment necessary to see these functions. Similarly, Measurement in Motion (from Learning in Motion, Inc.) allows students not only to see particular kinds of motions, but also to analyze those motions by overlaying measurement tools on video of the phenomena. By using these video explorations as models, students can gain a meaningful understanding of motion and its connection to data.

Science Software for Young Learners

Perhaps necessarily, science software for young learners concentrates more on developing scientific processes—the means of approaching problems—than on developing understandings of particular content. Thus many of the software products available for young learners focus on introducing students to such scientific activities as observation and

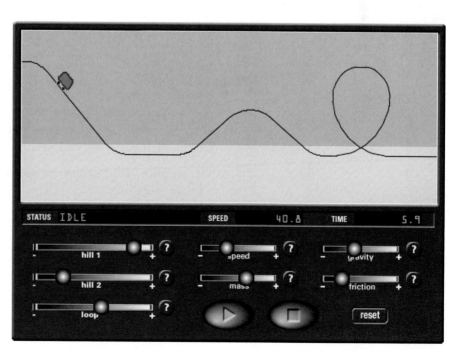

Figure 13.7 Screen Shot from the Funderstanding Roller Coaster

hypothesis generation. They provide interesting opportunities for students to explore phenomena but don't build an in-depth understanding of the content itself. Such titles for young learners include Sammy's Science House and Thinkin' Science, both available from Riverdeep software.

Many teachers have taught scientific processes with the aid of small calculators and probes, as described in the following "Technology in Action" feature.

Technology in Action

Using Calculators and Probes

One of the goals of school science is to engage students in authentic inquiry activities that familiarize them with scientific processes. Using Texas Instruments calculators with Vernier probes provides exactly this kind of opportunity. A **probe** in this sense is any device that measures a particular variable, such as temperature, voltage, or oxygen level. A special calculator (such as the Texas Instruments TI-73 Explorer, TI-83 Plus, or TI-84 Plus models) captures data from the probe. Students can then organize and display the data on the calculator, analyze it, and make inferences based on it. To connect a probe to the calculator, you use either a CBR (calculator-based ranger) or a CBL (calculator-based lab) unit. These units, shown in Figure 13.8, allow data to be converted to a format the calculators can work with.

Examples of calculator labs that a science or mathematics teacher can conduct include the following:

1. Use a voltage probe to test battery power over time. Is one brand of battery better than another?
2. Use a motion detector or CBR to determine whether different objects fall to the floor at different rates.
3. Use an oxygen probe to determine which water sample has the highest levels of dissolved oxygen and determine why.
4. Use pressure and motion sensors to determine what happens when a basketball has more or less air in it.

The websites for Vernier probes and Texas Instruments have many more lesson plan ideas.

Texas Instruments
   http://education.ti.com

Vernier
   http://www.vernier.com
   http://www.vernier.com/cmat
   http://www.vernier.com/calc/cbr.html
   http://www.vernier.com/mbl/cbl2.html
   http://www.eaieducation.com/cbl2-cbr-labpro-vernier-probes.html

Figure 13.8 Texas Instruments CBR (left) and CBL Unit
Source: http://education.ti.com/educationportal/sites/US/productDetail/us_cbr_2.html and http://education.ti.com/educationportal/sites/US/productDetail/us_cbl_2.html

■ Mathematics

The National Council of Teachers of Mathematics has explicitly included technology in its *Principles and Standards for School Mathematics* (NCTM, 2000). In the principles section, technology is described as "essential in teaching and learning mathematics; it influences the mathematics that is taught and enhances students' learning." Too often, computers are used in mathematics only for drill and practice or assessment, but they can create new mathematical experiences for students that allow them to understand the world differently and develop a deeper understanding of the mathematics they're learning and how it relates to real life. In this section we present a number of alternatives to simple drill and practice.

■■■ Skills Practice

It's challenging for preparing teachers to make sense of how the national standards are intended to impact classroom learning. The NCTM standards, for example, are concerned (in part) with students' development of basic skills. The standards reflect the idea that students should have

Math skills software that helps students learn why

Modeling Software in High-School Geometry

Online Study Center

To see modeling software in action, go to the Online Study Center and watch the HM Video Case **Using Technology to Promote Discovery Learning: A High School Geometry Lesson.** Notice how the software allows students to change angles inscribed within a circle and develop conjectures about what happens to the arcs defined by those angles. In these explorations the students are behaving like real mathematicians. What would the lesson be like if students didn't have access to the software? In the Bonus Videos, the teacher discusses some challenges of using technology and offers advice to new teachers.

opportunities to learn mathematics in meaningful ways—that is, to understand *why* 2 × 4 is 8, rather than just to know *that* 2 × 4 is 8. To this end, skills software should provide students with opportunities to try different answers, to see multiple representations, and to move beyond simple recall.

For example, in Ten Tricky Tiles from Sunburst (Figure 13.9), students are given ten tiles, each with a digit between 0 and 9. Students must use these tiles to solve a series of simple math problems. They can use each tile only once. This task requires not only a solid knowledge of basic math facts (addition, subtraction, multiplication, and division), but also some strategy and problem-solving skills. In other practice games, students are provided with multiple representations of a single concept; one example is Math Arena (Sunburst). Still others, such as The Learning Equation (CogniScience/Isacsoft), offer tutorial information to support students' learning.

▄▄ Modeling Software

Students manipulate geometric shapes, explore concepts

Mathematical modeling software allows students to create and manipulate either data sets or representations of their problems, so they can explore various features. For example, The Geometer's Sketchpad (Key Curriculum Press; see the following "Technology in Action" feature) is a widely used program that allows students to create and manipulate a

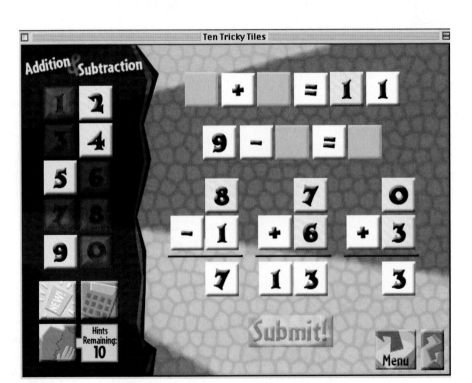

Figure 13.9 Screen Shot from Ten Tricky Tiles

variety of geometric shapes. These manipulations can range from simple explorations of the properties of shapes to more complex explorations of calculus concepts. Other software from this category allows students to work with fractions in ways that are impossible with paper (for example, Fraction Bars and Chopped Sticks) and to analyze data from their own data collection efforts (Fathom).

▄▄▄ Simulations

Most mathematics simulations engage students in a gamelike atmosphere in which they run some kind of business. Their task is generally to make good decisions that allow the business to make money. As with much of the other software discussed in this chapter, students' success in learning from the software depends on how the teacher structures the learning activity. For example, in Ice Cream Truck (Sunburst), students operate their own ice cream truck. They buy and sell products each day and set the prices. A number of variables in the game affect how successful they'll be. This can be an important activity that helps students practice basic math skills, gain a sense of simple economic principles, and develop some problem-solving strategies—or it can degenerate into just an entertaining game. The teacher has to structure the activity to focus on the learning goals students should meet.

Gamelike experiences for learning math

Technology in Action

Modeling with Computers

The Geometer's Sketchpad (GSP) is a powerful tool that helps people understand geometry in ways that paper and pencil can't. This is true in part because the software allows users to manipulate their construction, rather than create multiple constructions for a single investigation. As an example, imagine that students are exploring the relationship of the area of a triangle to the area of a rectangle.

> The problem: *A triangle lies within a rectangle. The triangle shares two vertices and one side with the rectangle. The triangle's third vertex is anywhere on the side opposite to the shared side.*
>
> *How does the area of the triangle compare with the area of the rectangle? Why do you think this relationship holds? (Wilson, Hannafin, & Ohme, 2006)*

Using GSP, we can construct a rectangle and the triangle inside it. Then we can use tools to measure the areas of the two figures and the ratio of those areas to each other. As shown in the three parts of Figure 13.10, the areas and the ratios of the two areas to each other stays constant regardless of where we move point E. This kind of tool allows students to see why there's a relationship and why it stays constant.

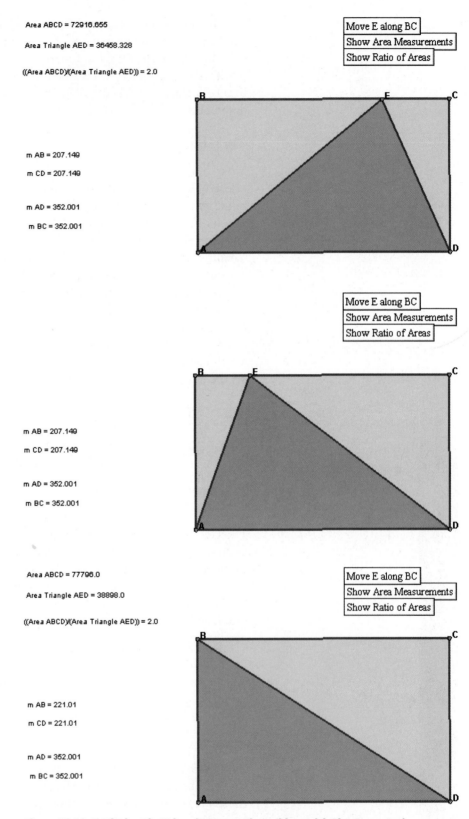

Figure 13.10 Exploring the Triangle-Rectangle Problem with The Geometer's Sketchpad

Figure 13.11 Screen Shot from Zoombinis Logical Journey

Problem-Solving Applications

Students solve a puzzle or problem

A few software titles focus more on helping students develop problem-solving skills than on developing further mathematical skills. These tools include titles such as Zoombinis Logical Journey (The Learning Company), a series of logic puzzles that students must solve in order to move to the next level. These puzzles, which become increasingly harder, pose different situations for the Zoombinis to figure out (see Figure 13.11).

A very different title, also in the problem-solving category, is the Math Mystery series from Tom Snyder. In this software, students are provided with a contextualized mathematics situation. They're responsible for determining what the problem is that they're trying to solve, what information is important for solving it, and what mathematical operations they'll need to use. This title also features both whole-class situations and individual student situations.

Calculation Tools

There are, of course, a number of technologies for the mathematics classroom that serve calculation purposes. Graphing Calculator (Pacific Tech) and ordinary spreadsheet software not only calculate but can be used for analysis and modeling as well. Other technologies, such as simple calculators, are more important for simple calculations.

Proper use of calculating tools

The use of these tools tends to be controversial, because teachers want their students to know basic facts before using technology. However, even before students have memorized their times tables or their simple addition facts, calculating tools can often be used to enhance math classes. Teachers need to consistently review their goals to determine whether these tools would add to the lesson or detract from it.

◼ Other Content Areas

This chapter has focused mainly on technology in the four key content areas, but there are plenty of ways technology can be used to enhance the fine arts and physical education courses as well.

▬ Physical Education

Learning about fitness

Software can help physical education (PE) teachers track student fitness, schedule games, and even support students in learning about anatomy related to sports and sports injuries. For example, a PE or health teacher can use a program like Personal Fitness: Looking Good Feeling Good or Cramer's PE Fit-N-Dex software to support students in tracking their own fitness. Similarly, a coach may find value in using Cramer's Sports Injuries 3-D software to help students learn about how injuries happen.

As a productivity tool, scheduling software, such as Splendid City or Team Scheduler, can make complex scheduling tasks easier. PE teachers may also find value in using calculators and probes to help students learn about motion.

▬ Music Education

Students learn music theory, create their own music

In music education, the software is very diverse. There are a number of titles aimed at helping students learn music theory concepts, do ear training exercises, and learn about instruments. These include Practice Musica and Auralia. Some software, such as Sibelius, aims to help students learn about instruments. Other titles support music educators and their students in creating music (for example, Garage Band, Finale, and Performer). These programs all have the benefit of being engaging and offering individualized support to students as they learn more about music. Notation software is also a critical tool for band directors as they modify arrangements of compositions for their own bands.

▬ Art Education

Students create images they couldn't make on paper

Art educators will find software that extends the kinds of things their students can create in the classroom. There are tessellation programs, such as KaleidoTile and KaleidoMania, which help connect math and art. There are also 3-D modeling and animation programs that allow students to create images that are impossible to make on paper. One of these, Cosmic Blobs, is made just for younger learners to create 3-D images and animations. Art teachers will also find a host of drawing and painting programs for various ages, such as KidPix for younger children and Illustrator for more expert users.

▬ Integrated Content Areas for Young Learners

Much of the software in the prekindergarten-to-second-grade range is hard to categorize within a single content area. Rather, many of the titles aim at supporting students' learning an array of skills that they'll need to be successful as they begin school. For example, To Market, To Market

(Learning in Motion), which centers on basic math skills, includes various integrated elements; students can learn sign language and make movies to communicate their mathematics learning. In Bailey's Book House (Riverdeep), learning focuses on vocabulary building, letter recognition, and symbols. In Knock Knock (Sunburst), learners develop basic literacy and note-taking skills, and learn about letter and sound alignment.

You can learn more about selecting software for the youngest learners at **http://www.netc.org/earlyconnections/preschool/software.html.**

Comprehensive Software Solutions

One popular tool currently available is comprehensive curriculum management software. These titles offer practice keyed to state standards in each of the content areas and provide management tools for teachers to gauge their students' learning. These tools often include tutorials and skills practice for students. Often the software uses appealing graphics and tasteful presentations to hold students' interest.

Some of these software packages provide evidence of students' learning with the software. However, these reports are often flawed, in that they show merely that students improved from the beginning to the end of the academic year. They don't consider that other forms of instruction took place as well.

The adoption of these tools is a district-level decision because they're expensive and wide ranging. However, you, as the teacher, will have the opportunity to determine when and whether these tools may be appropriate for your classroom. Remember to use your software evaluation skills and your learning goals to determine what role the software should play in your teaching. See the "Resources" at the end of this chapter for examples of comprehensive software packages.

SUMMARY

In this chapter we introduced some critical elements to think about as you consider whether to use software in your own instruction. We pointed out that you should always look for education rather than "edutainment" for your students, and we suggested that, in choosing software, you'll want to consider factors such as quality of the content, ease of use by students, and management aspects, such as record keeping and adaptability to different difficulty levels and instructional needs.

Through our descriptions of software in the content areas, we introduced the big ideas that software can be used to address and suggested some different kinds of software that you might use to meet your own instructional goals. Though there's no way to offer a truly comprehensive guide to the software that's available, we've provided an extensive listing of software titles that align with the major categories.

The main idea of this chapter is this: Evaluate software carefully before you use it. No one knows better than you whether a piece of software will support your students in learning the content skills and understandings that you've specified. With the high expectations now placed on students, there isn't enough time in the day to have them working with software that doesn't help them meet their goals.

RESOURCES

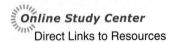
Online Study Center
Direct Links to Resources

OPEN-SOURCE TOOLS

Edubuntu
http://www.edubuntu.org
> An open source, Linux-based operating system with many educational tools built into it, ranging from drawing programs to the periodic table.

GIMP
http://gimp.org
> An open-source image-editing program.

Making Decisions About Open Source Software for K–12
http://www.netc.org/openoptions
> A website packed with information on whether using open-source software is a good idea for your school.

Mozilla Firefox
http://www.mozilla.com/firefox
> An open-source web browser.

OpenOffice
http://www.openoffice.org
> An open-source productivity suite.

SOFTWARE EVALUATION FORMS AND REVIEW SITES

Edutaining Kids
http://www.edutainingkids.com
> A site offering reviews of software, videos, books, toys, games, and music.

enGauge Resources: Classroom Resources
http://www.ncrel.org/engauge/resource/resource/index.html
> Reviews of a variety of classroom resources organized by discipline, as well as a Resource Evaluation Tool that includes a handy evaluation form.

ISTE NETS: Sample Software and Web Site Evaluation Forms
http://cnets.iste.org/teachers/web/t_form_software-eval.html
> An evaluation tool aligned with NETS standards.

Kathy Schrock's Software Evaluation Form
http://kathyschrock.net/1computer/page4.htm
> A simple software evaluation tool.

Learning Village: Guide to First Class Learning Software
http://www.learningvillage.com/html/guide.html
> Information on a variety of learning software.

Parents' Choice Foundation
http://www.parents-choice.org
> An organization dedicated to locating high-quality media for children.

Seven Steps to Responsible Software Selection
http://www.netc.org/software/eric_software.html
> A brief article about selecting software.

Software Evaluation: The Process of Evaluating Software and Its Effect on Learning
http://hagar.up.ac.za/catts/learner/eel/Conc/conceot.htm
> A website with information on software evaluation, as well as tools to support evaluation.

SuperKids Educational Software Review
http://www.superkids.com
> Software reviews of a wide variety of software.

SOCIAL STUDIES

Fact Resources

Brittanica
http://store.britannica.com
> A comprehensive online encyclopedia.

Carmen Sandiego Series
http://www.learningcompany.com
> A series of games designed to support learning about geography.

Facts On File
http://www.factsonfile.com
> An interactive database of historical facts, as well as curriculum ideas for the classroom.

Google Maps
http://maps.google.com
> An online resource of maps and satellite photos.

Grolier Multimedia Encyclopedia
http://go.grolier.com/orl/pages/gmefeatrs.htm
> A comprehensive interactive encyclopedia.

National Geographic TOPO! Map Software
http://maps.nationalgeographic.com/topo
> A resource of topographical maps.

Street Atlas USA
http://www.delorme.com/software.htm
> Atlas software.

Wikipedia
http://www.wikipedia.org
> A multimedia encyclopedia built using wiki technology, which allows anyone to add to the knowledge base.

World Book Encyclopedia
http://www.worldbook.com
> Another comprehensive interactive encyclopedia.

Decision-Making and Problem-Solving Software

Community Construction Kit
http://www.tomsnyder.com
> A simulation in which students in grades 2 through 6 create their own buildings and print them out to construct a paper version of a community.

Decisions, Decisions
http://www.tomsnyder.com
> Role-playing software for grades 5 through 10 that engages students in using evidence to learn about history from multiple perspectives.

The Finance Center
http://www.classroominc.org/products/simulations/finance.html
> A simulation for middle-school students that has students act as financial advisers to solve clients' problems.

The Oregon Trail
http://www.riverdeep.net
> A simulation in which students make real-life decisions as they move their characters along the Oregon Trail.

SimCity
http://simcity.ea.com
> A simulation that allows users to create cities.

SimCity Teacher's Guide
http://simcity3000unlimited.ea.com/us/guide/tips/teachers
> A guide to help teachers incorporate the SimCity game into their curriculum.

Organizational Resources

HyperHistory Online
http://www.hyperhistory.com/online_n2/History_n2/a.html
> An online timeline of historic events.

TimeLiner
http://www.tomsnyder.com
> K–12 software that supports students in organizing historical events into a timeline.

LANGUAGE ARTS

Reading Comprehension

Accelerated Reader
http://www.renlearn.com/ar/default.htm
> A system for teaching reading in which students read books, then take computerized comprehension exams to move on to more difficult materials.

Destination Reading
http://www.riverdeep.net
> A series of reading programs based on research about how students learn to read.

Reading for Meaning
http://www.tomsnyder.com
> A reading comprehension program for grades 3 through 8.

Scholastic Reading Inventory (SRI)
http://www.tomsnyder.com
> A tool for measuring student progress in reading and comprehension.

Thinking Reader
http://www.tomsnyder.com
> A comprehension program for struggling readers in grades 5 through 8.

General Reading Software and Interactive Books

The Book of Lulu
http://www.organa.com/lulu.html
> An interactive book about a princess named Lulu, available in eight languages.

The Dugout Collection
http://store.sunburst.com
> A reading and writing lab focused on stories.

High School Reading Comprehension Series
http://www.optimumlearning.com/prod_lang/lang_hsrcs.html
> A reading comprehension tool for high-school students.

Imagination Express Series
http://store.sunburst.com
> K–8 software to support story writing.

Mia's Reading Adventure: The Search for Grandma's Remedy
http://www.kutoka.com/_en/products.html
> An interactive book for ages five to nine that includes a story, 3-D graphics, and puzzles to be solved.

Mike Mulligan and His Steam Shovel
http://store.sunburst.com
> An interactive version of a popular book for young students.

Polar Express
http://store.sunburst.com
> An interactive version of the Caldecott Medal–winning story.

Reader's Quest
http://store.sunburst.com
> A reading workshop with interactive activities.

Reading Milestones
http://www.riverdeep.net
> A reading program for students with hearing impairments and other special reading needs, including second-language learners and those with learning disabilities.

Read On! Plus
http://store.sunburst.com
> A program that teaches students strategies for improving their reading.

SuperKids Educational Software Review: Interactive Book/Early Reading Software
http://www.superkids.com/aweb/pages/reviews/e_read/4/sw_sum1.shtml
A website offering reviews of reading software.

Phonics

Fonty
http://www.fontyonline.com
Software that teaches reading through phonics.

I Love Phonics
http://www.riverdeep.net
Software based on a seven-step model for learning to read with phonics.

Interactive Phonics Readers
http://www.tomsnyder.com
Independent phonics practice software.

Jump Start Learning System
http://www.jumpstart.com
An interactive program that focuses on skill building in reading and math.

Reader Rabbit Learn to Read with Phonics
http://www.riverdeep.net
A phonics-focused skill-building software package.

Spelling

Curious George Reads, Writes, and Spells
http://www.superkids.com/aweb/pages/reviews/spelling/1/cgrws/merge.shtml
A spelling practice program based on the Curious George character.

I Love Spelling
http://www.riverdeep.net
A practice program with spelling embedded in six different scenarios.

Stickybear's Spelling
http://www.optimumlearning.com/prod_lang/lang_spelling.htm
A spelling program with more than 3,000 words.

Tenth Planet: Consonant Blends and Digraphs
http://store.sunburst.com
A spelling program focused on consonant blends.

Grammar

Accelerated Grammar and Spelling
http://www.renlearn.com/ags
A system that measures student ability with a computer-based assessment and provides practice activities based on the results of the assessment.

Grammar Fitness
http://www.meritsoftware.com/software/grammar_fitness
An interactive grammar program focused on difficult grammar problems in grades 4 through 8.

Grammar for the Real World
http://store.sunburst.com
A program for grades 4 through 12 that engages students in an interesting scenario as it supports them in learning writing and grammar skills.

MiddleWare Grammar
http://www.optimumlearning.com/prod_lang/prod_lang_mware.html
A comprehensive, self-paced approach for supporting students in grades 3 through 9 in learning grammar.

Missing Links
http://store.sunburst.com
A series of grammar puzzles as a practice tool for grades 3 through 8.

Writing Support

The Amazing Writing Machine
http://www.riverdeep.net
A writing tool for grades 1 through 5 that engages students in learning to write stories using a five-step model.

FableVision Essay Express
http://www.educate-me.net
An interactive approach to teaching writing skills for a variety of formats.

iMovie
http://www.apple.com/ilife/imovie
Simple software for editing movies, free on Macintosh computers.

Inspiration
http://www.inspiration.com
Concept-mapping and graphic organizer software that can help support students' planning of writing projects.

Kaplan Writing and Vocabulary
http://www.superkids.com/aweb/pages/reviews/writing/1/kaplanWV/merge.shtml
A program covering grammar and writing skills for high-school students.

OmniOutliner
http://www.omnigroup.com/applications/omnioutliner
Software for outlining.

Storybook Weaver
http://www.riverdeep.net
A rich writing environment for young writers.

StyleWriter
http://www.writersupercenter.com/stylewriter
A program that builds students' skills in grammar by providing feedback on their writing.

Writeboard
http://writeboard.com
Web-based collaborative writing software that allows easy tracking of changes.

Write It Right
http://www.meritsoftware.com/software/write_it_right
Writing software focused on helping students identify their writing problems.

Writely
http://www.writely.com
Interactive, web-based collaborative writing software that works much like a word processor.

FOREIGN LANGUAGE AND ESL SOFTWARE

Resource Websites

Elementary Education: Foreign Language Resources
http://www.pitt.edu/~poole/eledforeign.html
A page of web links to a number of foreign language software titles and resources.

ESL: Games
http://iteslj.org/links/ESL/Games
Web-based games and links to software for reinforcing foreign language skills.

ESL.net: ESL Software for Public or Private Schools
http://www.esl.net/software_schools.html
A company that markets ESL software.

Foreign Language Home
http://www.foreignlanguagehome.com
A website with information on how to learn foreign languages, including games, such as Vokki, that assist in learning.

Practice and Games

Language Adventure
http://www.magictheatre.com/language.html
A CD-ROM–based mimicking approach to language learning for children; available for multiple languages.

Mia's Language Adventure: The Kidnap Caper!
http://www.kutoka.com/_en/mia_language.html
Introduces children to French or Spanish using a rich, story-based 3D environment.

Rosetta Stone
http://www.rosettastone.com
A software package available in twenty-nine languages that supports learning through an immersion-based approach.

Tell Me More Education
http://www.auralog.com/us/education_home.htm
Lessons on language and culture for ten different languages.

ESL Software for Practice

Core Reading and Vocabulary Development (ESL)
http://www.esl.net/core_reading.html
An English-learning package for ESL learners and students with low literacy levels.

Easy Writer
http://www.esl.net/easy_writer.html
ESL software and grammar help that teaches by having them correct others' errors.

ESLSoftware
http://www.eslsoftware.com
A suite of software for all aspects of English learning, from comprehension to writing.

Focus on Grammar Series
http://www.exceller.com/focus-on-grammar.html
English grammar practice through reading, writing, and listening.

IdioMagic
http://www.idiomagic.com
Software focused on supporting ESL learners in mastering idioms.

Pronunciation Power
http://www.esl.net/pronunciation_power.html
Focuses on pronunciation of American English.

Reading in the Workplace
http://www.esl.net/reading_in_the_workplace.html
Supports reading comprehension in workplace-related situations.

Speech Works
http://www.altaesl.com
A listen-record-compare approach to English pronunciation.

BLOGGING

The Educated Blogger: Using Weblogs to Promote Literacy in the Classroom
http://www.firstmonday.org/issues/issue9_6/huffaker
An online paper by David Huffaker that explores the use of weblogs in the classroom.

Educational Bloggers Network
http://www.ebn.weblogger.com
A blog with information on tools for and approaches to using blogging and other technologies in education.

ePals SchoolBlog
http://schoolblog.epals.com
An example of a safe blogging environment designed for teachers and students.

European Association for the Education of Adults: Educational Blogs
http://www.eaea.org/news.php?aid=7505&%20d=2005-11
Information on blogging in education and links to some of the primary blogging packages.

Livejournal
http://www.livejournal.com
One of the free online journal services. This one allows "private" posts that limit who can read them.

Why Weblogs Work in K–12 Education
http://jhh.blogs.com/gaetc
  A blog about blogging in K–12 classrooms, complete with links to examples.

SCIENCE

Digital Library for Earth System Education (DLESE)
http://www.dlese.org
  A large collection of lesson ideas, activities, Web-Quests, and more—all related to earth science.

National Science Digital Library
http://nsdl.org
  A compilation of high-quality educational resources for innovative teaching in science, technology, and mathematics.

Inquiry-Based and Problem-Solving Approaches

ChemDiscovery
http://www.kendallhunt.com
  Multimedia high-school chemistry curriculum organized around quests.

Exploring the Environment
http://www.cotf.edu/ete
  A rich, problem-based learning environment for high-school students, featuring real-world problems and resources to help students find solutions.

Rainforest Researchers
http://www.tomsnyder.com
  A middle-school science expedition in which students act as scientific team members in the rain forest. Appropriate for a one-computer classroom.

Science Court Explorations
http://www.tomsnyder.com
  Exploration-based science in which elementary- and middle-school students must examine evidence in a court case and conduct their own experiments.

Science Seekers
http://www.tomsnyder.com
  Supports middle-school students in applying science concepts to solve problems.

Variations in Life Science: Investigations
http://www.learn.motion.com/products/variations_inv
  Twenty-four high-school science investigations that engage students in analyzing captured data.

Virtual Labs and Simulations

Cooties
http://www.goknow.com/Products/Cooties
  A simulation for hand-held computers that engages students in understanding how viruses spread.

Funderstanding Roller Coaster
http://www.funderstanding.com/k12/coaster
  An online applet that allows students to apply basic physics knowledge to the construction of a roller coaster.

Online Science-athon
http://scithon.terc.edu
  Online lessons that require students to gather and analyze their own data, share their data in a worldwide database, and analyze data from that database.

Sidewalk Science Series
http://www.tomsnyder.com
  Hands-on and computer-based science for grades 2 through 4.

Smart Science Active Learning System
http://www.paracompusa.com/SmartScience/SmartScience.html
  A lab experience for students that is partially hands-on and partially virtual.

Models and Demonstrations

A.D.A.M. Essentials High School Suite
http://www.adam.com/Our_Products/School_and_Instruction/Educators/High_School/essentials.html
  A physiology program to support students in learning about humans.

Cells Alive!
http://www.cellsalive.com
  A series of animations to help students understand cellular-level physiology.

The Magic School Bus
http://place.scholastic.com/magicschoolbus/cdrom
  A series of science-related explorations for elementary students based on the adventures of Ms. Frizzle's science class.

Measurement in Motion
http://www.learn.motion.com/products/measurement
  Software for capturing motion and translating it to graphic form.

Motion Visualizer
http://www.albertiswindow.com
  Software allowing students to record and analyze motion.

Science Software for Young Learners

Sammy's Science House
http://www.riverdeep.net
  Seven modules for young learners aimed at introducing scientific thinking.

Thinkin' Science
http://www.riverdeep.net
  Engages K–2 students in solving scientific problems.

Texas Instruments Calculators with Vernier Probes

CBR/CBL Hardware and Probes from Vernier
http://www.vernier.com
http://www.vernier.com/calc/cbr.html
http://www.vernier.com/mbl/cbl2.html

http://www.eaieducation.com/
cbl2-cbr-labpro-vernier-probes.html

Sites with information on purchasing a wide variety of Vernier probes for measuring such things as temperature, motion, light, and pH.

Texas Instruments
http://education.ti.com

The education homepage for Texas Instruments, which makes many varieties of calculators.

MATHEMATICS

Skills Practice

Dimenxian
http://www.dimenxian.com

An engaging, interactive videogame for practicing algebra skills.

Equation Tile Teasers
http://store.sunburst.com

Problem-solving for middle-school students to practice their logical thinking.

Math Arena
http://store.sunburst.com

A series of practice games for grades 4 through 7.

Millie's Math House
http://www.riverdeep.net

A program for young math learners which introduces them to shapes, numbers, sizes, and more.

Piggy in Numberland
http://www.learninginmotion.com/products/
piggy_numberland/index.html

A series of games for very young (pre-K–1) math learners to develop basic counting and number skills.

Splish Splash Math
http://store.sunburst.com

Students in grades 1 through 3 can practice their computation in this logic-building game.

Ten Tricky Tiles
http://store.sunburst.com

Students in elementary, middle school, and beyond can develop mathematical knowledge while solving a series of seemingly simple problems.

Modeling Software

Fathom Dynamic Data Software
http://www.keypress.com/sketchpad

Software to support middle- and high-school students in data analysis.

Fraction Bars and Chopped Sticks
http://www.transparentmedia.com/downloads.php

Modeling software for exploring fraction concepts and computation.

The Geometer's Sketchpad
http://www.keypress.com/catalog/products/software/
Prod_GSP.html

Modeling software for exploring geometry, number, and algebra concepts.

Java MathWorlds
http://www.simcalc.umassd.edu/software/jmw

A part of the SimCalc Projects aimed at helping students understand the mathematics of motion.

Shape Up!
http://store.sunburst.com

A tool for exploring two- and three-dimensional shapes.

Tabletop, Tabletop 2, and Tabletop Jr.
http://www.terc.edu/work/618.html
http://www.terc.edu/work/190.html

Data analysis software for elementary- and middle-school students.

TinkerPlots Dynamic Data Exploration
http://www.keypress.com/tinkerplots

A robust graphing program for exploring algebraic relationships.

Simulations

Concert Tour Entrepreneur
http://store.sunburst.com

Students in grades 7 through 10 learn math by taking on the role of a band manager.

The Court Square Community Bank
http://www.classroominc.org/products/simulations/
cscb.html

In a simulation for developing real-world problem-solving skills, middle-school students act as a bank manager.

Hot Dog Stand: The Works
http://store.sunburst.com

Students in grades 5 through 12 learn about money and practice math by running their own small business, a hot dog stand.

Ice Cream Truck
http://store.sunburst.com

Elementary students learn about math and business by running an ice cream truck.

The Sports Network
http://www.classroominc.org/products/simulations/
sports.html

Middle- and high-school students learn about data analysis and problem solving as they manage a sports network.

Problem-Solving Applications

Math Mysteries
http://www.tomsnyder.com

A series of elementary-level mysteries that focus students on understanding problem solving. These are ideal for a one-computer classroom.

Zoombinis Logical Journey

http://www.terc.edu/work/423.html

A rich, complex, problem-solving environment for developing logic skills in students of all ages.

Calculation Tools

Excel

http://www.microsoft.com/Education/Excel.mspx

Popular spreadsheet software.

Graphing Calculator

http://www.pacifict.com

A robust graphing calculator program that uses standard equation formats.

Texas Instruments Calculators

http://education.ti.com

The education homepage for Texas Instruments, which makes calculators for students of all ages.

PHYSICAL EDUCATION

Cramer's PE Fit-N-Dex Software

http://www.onlinesports.com/pages/I,CR-135622.html

Software for assessing and tracking student fitness.

interact Health Studies

http://rols.ramesys.com/XSIQ-C38.aspx

Software for supporting secondary students in learning about health.

interact Secondary Physical Education

http://rols.ramesys.com/XSIQ-C38.aspx

Software for learning about aspects of physical education, including fitness, training, and fatigue.

Personal Fitness: Looking Good Feeling Good

http://www.kendallhunt.com

Software for high-school students to track their personal fitness.

Splendid City

http://www.splendidcity.net

Software for scheduling teams and events.

Sports Injuries 3-D Software

http://www.cramersportsmed.com

Informational physiology software about sports injuries.

Team Scheduler

http://www.empiresoftware.org/team-scheduler/index.html

Software for scheduling teams and events.

World of Sport Examined

http://www.aroga.com

A CD-ROM focused on the science of sports for grades 6 and up.

MUSIC EDUCATION

Theory and Music Fundamentals

Auralia

http://www.risingsoftware.com/auralia30

Ear-training software.

MiDisaurus

http://www.venturaes.com

Music-learning system for children ages four through eleven.

Music Ace Deluxe

http://www.harmonicvision.com/madfact.htm

Music lessons and games to teach theory, pitch, rhythm, and note reading.

Musition

http://www.sibelius.com/products/musition

Music theory training and testing for people of all ages.

Practica Musica

http://www.ars-nova.com/practica.html

Program to support beginners in learning music theory fundamentals.

Sibelius Instruments

http://www.sibelius.com/products/instruments

Information on instruments and arrangements.

Theory Games

http://www.alfred.com

Games to support young learners in developing their understanding of theory.

Music Composition and Notation

Band-in-a-Box

http://www.pgmusic.com

A MIDI-based composition tool.

Cakewalk Kinetic

http://www.cakewalk.com/Products/Kinetic

A tool for creating electronic music.

Digital Performer

http://www.motu.com/products/software/dp

A high-end tool for creating digital music.

Finale

http://www.finalemusic.com

Professional-level music notation tool.

GarageBand

http://www.apple.com/ilife/garageband

A user-friendly, simple MIDI composition tool.

LilyPond

http://www.lilypond.org/web

Music notation software.

MOTU Symphonic Instrument

http://www.motu.com/products/software/msi

A sound library.

Music Creator Pro

http://www.cakewalk.com/products/musiccreatorpro

Multitrack recording software.

NoteWorthy Software

http://www.noteworthysoftware.com

A music composition and notation processor.

Songworks II
http://www.ars-nova.com/songworks.html
A music composition program.

ART EDUCATION

Tessellations

Artlandia SymmetryWorks
http://www.artlandia.com
A plug-in for Adobe Illustrator that allows simple repetition of patterns.

KaleidoTile
http://www.geometrygames.org/KaleidoTile
Software allowing tessellations of 2-D and 3-D surfaces.

Kali
http://www.geometrygames.org/Kali
Software to support K–12 students in learning about tiling (tessellations).

Painting and Drawing Tools

Art Rage
http://www.ambientdesign.com/artrage.html
A digital painting program.

Drawing for Children
http://www.kidsdomain.com/down/pc/
drawingforchildren.html
A program to support children in learning to draw.

Kid Pix
http://www.riverdeep.net
A popular drawing tool for young students. For ideas for Kid Pix lessons, see **http://www.uvm.edu/~jmorris/kidpix.html**

LopArt
http://www.lopart.net
Software for drawing on your computer and sharing your drawings with others as postcards or in portfolios.

Shapari
http://www.kidsdomain.com/down/pc/shapari.html
A geometry-based program for building images with shapes, for ages four and up.

3-D Drawing and Animation

Art of Illusion
http://www.artofillusion.org
A free 3-D animation tool.

Blender
http://blender.org
Another free 3-D animation tool.

Cosmic Blobs
http://www.cosmicblobs.com
A 3-D package for kids.

Guides and Resources

Art Education
http://grove.ufl.edu/%7Erolandc/html/link_archives/
arted.html
A wide array of information about art for educators.

Guide to First Class Learning Software: Mini-Guides—Art and Graphic Software
http://www.learningvillage.com/html/mguideart.html
An overview of art and graphics software.

COMPREHENSIVE SYSTEMS

Classworks
http://www.classworks.com
Comprehensive individualized instruction for grades K–12.

CompassLearning Odyssey
http://www.compasslearning.com
Pre-K–12 comprehensive curriculum and assessment tool.

Orchard
http://www.orchardsoftware.com
Targeted instruction and assessment tool for all grades.

Waterford, SuccessMaker Enterprise, and KnowledgeBox
http://www.pearsondigital.com
Standards-based digital pre-K–12 curriculum.

SOFTWARE FOR YOUNG LEARNERS

Bailey's Book House
http://www.riverdeep.net
A software package for young learners focused on letter recognition, symbols, position words, and sentence building.

Knock Knock
http://store.sunburst.com
A software program for young learners that develops early literacy skills, introduces note-taking skills, and works on sound and letter relationships.

Selecting Software for Young Children
http://www.netc.org/earlyconnections/preschool/
software.html
Guidance for selecting software to support young learners.

To Market, To Market
http://www.learn.motion.com/products/market
A set of mathematics games to introduce young learners to number concepts.

Software Evaluation

Now that you've had a brief introduction to evaluating and selecting software for your content area, it's time to try out your software evaluation skills. Using the following form, evaluate at least three software packages that are appropriate for the grades and content area that you plan to teach.

SOFTWARE EVALUATION FORM

Title of Software: _____

Primary Subject Addressed: _____

For which grades does this software seem most appropriate? _____

OVERALL RATING (circle & explain briefly):   Recommend   Do not recommend

_____

_____

Overview Information

What educational goals does this software address? _____

_____

Brief description (tell about what the software is/does): _____

_____

Computer System Information

Platform: Windows version(s) _____   Mac versions(s) _____

Rate the Following

(5 = excellent, 4 = good, 3 = okay, 2 = weak, 1 = unacceptable)

Content of Software   *(Total Score: _____/55)*

___ Sufficient amount of content

___ Content is accurate and current/relevant

___ Free of gender, ethnic, racial bias

___ Feedback is given that promotes learning

___ Offers students opportunity to think at a higher level (more than memorizing or practicing)

___ Offers students an opportunity to engage in transferable learning (learn how to do things that will help them with other topics or in other subjects)

___ Is interactive

___ Provides opportunities for collaborative and independent learning

___ Offers a variety of challenge levels

___ Content educationally sound in design

___ Content presented in ways consistent with instructional approaches used in the classroom

Comments: _____

_____

Ease of Use (for student)   (Total Score _____/40)

___ Student can use program independently
___ Easy to navigate (clearly marked icons, etc.)
___ Written at an appropriate reading level
___ Feedback about mistakes is helpful
___ Directions are explicit
___ Help section is available
___ Help section is helpful
___ Seems engaging

Comments: _____

_____

Management Aspects   (Total Score _____/20)

___ Is it easy to keep individual student records?
___ Is it easy to set the difficulty level?
___ Does it augment the classroom learning in meaningful ways?
___ Is it appropriate for differentiating instruction?

Comments: _____

_____

Additional Information

What type of child would benefit most/least from this product? _____
Is this product most appropriate for (circle all that apply):

    Center work

    Whole-class instruction—teacher led

    Small group activity

    Individual student tutorial use

    Assessment

    Other _____

What did you like best about this software package? _____

_____

What did you like least about this software package? _____

_____

Questions for Reflection and Discussion

After you have completed the Software Evaluation Form for at least three software packages, address the following questions:

1. Did you find it useful to use the Software Evaluation Form?
   a. In what ways was it helpful?
   b. In what ways was it not helpful?
2. Would you feel comfortable recommending the purchase of one or more of the software packages based on their scores on this evaluation? Why or why not?

3. What changes would you make to the Software Evaluation Form before using it again?
4. What is the value in evaluating the software in this fashion rather than just reading the description on the box?

Meet the Standards

Online Study Center

Standards
The Online Study Center has additional resources on standards.

As shown in "Standards to Guide Your Preparation" at the beginning of this chapter, we've aligned the chapter with NETS standards focused on both content knowledge and learning skills. Take some time now to reflect on what you've learned so far and what else you need to do to meet these standards. Think about these questions:

▶ How might you, as a teacher, determine what software to use with your students? What are some of the criteria that you'd use? Where can you turn for help?
▶ How can you be sure the software you select is the best choice for your particular students?
▶ How might using software programs help you promote higher-order thinking?

Chapter 14

Emerging Technologies for Learning

ISTE NETS

Teachers

▶ Plan for the management of technology resources within the context of learning activities.

▶ Plan strategies to manage student learning in a technology-enhanced environment.

▶ Apply technology to develop students' higher-order skills and creativity.

Prospective Teachers

▶ Differentiate between appropriate and inappropriate uses of technology for teaching and learning while using electronic resources to design and implement learning activities.

▶ Use content-specific tools (e.g., software, simulation, environmental probes, graphing calculators, exploratory environments, Web tools) to support learning and research.

▶ Collaborate in constructing technology-enhanced models, preparing publications, and producing other creative works using productivity tools.

OTHER RELEVANT STANDARDS

Association for Educational Communications and Technology (2003)

Candidates in educational technology programs should be grounded in instructional systems design, which among other things includes:

▶ *Developing:* the process of authoring and producing the instructional materials.

▶ *Implementing:* actually using the materials and strategies in context.

267

ome of the most promising and most exciting technologies available for learning right now fall into the group we've labeled as "emerging technologies." These include a variety of video games, simulations, modeling tools, and virtual reality tools. The common thread among these tools is that they allow you and your students to experience phenomena in ways that are impossible or impractical in the "real" world. Though they work in a variety of ways, all of these emerging technologies permit highly interactive and immersive learning experiences.

For our purposes in this chapter, we divide emerging technologies into two basic types: video games and virtual reality. There are many reasons why people subdivide these categories, but we believe that the tools used in education align fairly well with one or the other of these two types. See Spotlight 14.1 for a list of other important terms.

SPOTLIGHT 14.1   A Lexicon of Emerging Technologies

Artificial intelligence. Though it has been popularized as robots' taking over the roles of humans, artificial intelligence (AI) is actually a form of computer programming that seeks to allow the computer to demonstrate "intelligence." Most commonly, AI is used to allow computers to react to particular situations in ways that humans might, as in video games. AI is also used to help create more robust interaction systems, as in some search engines and other programs.

Augmented reality. A setting that mixes virtual and real elements, so that the technology supplements the user's actual surroundings (see Figure 14.1). For example, by means of a hand-held device, a geology student in the field might see a map of the land and an overlay of additional information. Augmented reality is often used for armed forces training. It's also being used in education, as in the simulation game Environmental Detectives, which was developed at MIT **(see http://education.mit.edu/ar).**

CAVE (Cave Automatic Virtual Environment). A fully immersive virtual reality environment created through images projected on the walls of a cube-shaped room. (See Spotlight 14.5 later in this chapter.)

Digital manipulatives. **Digital manipulatives** are computerized versions of traditional manipulatives, such

Figure 14.1 Building a Class Project with Augmented Reality Technology

as Cuisenaire rods. These open-ended modeling tools allow the user to experiment in order to make sense of a concept; in this way, they provide a kind of microworld. (See **http://llk.media.mit.edu/papers/dig-manip** for a more detailed explanation.)

Gaming platform. A machine on which a video game can be played. These include video game consoles like Nintendo GameCube, PlayStation, and Xbox, as well as handheld platforms like PlayStation Portable (PSP) and Gameboy. Computers and the Internet are also video game platforms.

Haptic. Haptic refers to the sense of touch. In some virtual reality environments, high-tech gloves and special haptic tools can be used to give the user the impression that she is touching things in the virtual world.

Immersive. An immersive virtual reality environment is one in which the user feels entirely absorbed or surrounded. This effect is often achieved through a special helmet or a CAVE that helps the user imagine that she is actually "in" the virtual space.

Massive Multiplayer Online Role-Playing Game (MMORPG). Game that takes place on the Internet using a client software package. The player joins a group of people located throughout the world to complete a quest.

Microworld. A simulation program designed to allow the user to explain ideas, test assumptions, and explore concepts. **Microworlds** are often open ended and provide the user the ability to interact with a single concept (such as "force") in creative ways. Sometimes these are also called digital manipulatives. (For examples, see **http://www.umcs.maine.edu/~larry/microworlds/ microworld.html.**)

QuickTime VR (QTVR). A movie file format that allows photos to be "sewn together" to create 3-D movies. Essentially, QTVR allows panoramas to be used as 3-D environments.

Simulation. As you've seen earlier in this book, a simulation is a program that imitates a real system, device, or process. Simulations often engage the player in a real-life role and unfold in different ways based on the decisions the player makes. Simulations are widely used in professional development in fields where people would have great difficulty learning on the job. For example, pilots learn to fly in simulators before being allowed to fly real airplanes, and many doctors work with simulated patients before they work with real ones.

Video game. Any form of interactive game in which video (rather than, say, audio or text) provides the main stimuli. Video games range from shooting games to puzzle games to sports games.

Virtual reality. A simulated environment created by a computer, sometimes supplemented by other devices. Virtual realities can exist in a number of different forms; for example, users may simply "watch" the virtual experience, or they may use special gloves and displays that allow them to "touch" elements in the environment.

VRML and X3D. Computer languages that provide standard file formats for 3-D images on the World Wide Web. VRML stands for Virtual Reality Modeling Language, which has been in use for some time. VRML is now giving way to X3D, which incorporates the same type of coding used in XML (Extensible Markup Language).

Video Games

Video games provide students with the opportunity to solve problems, make decisions, and alter the outcomes of their efforts. Unlike edutainment games that provide a primarily drill-and-practice focus, the video games discussed here involve meaningful learning.

Uses for Video Games in Education

There's a growing body of research on the benefits of using video games for learning. The reasons range from motivational benefits (see Spotlight 14.2) to the ability of these media to engage students in complex activities that mimic the real world. Clearly, these tools are best used by students in hands-on settings rather than for demonstrations.

SPOTLIGHT 14.2   What Makes Video Games So Engaging?

Research on the use of technology-based games in education is an emerging field that builds from the basic understanding that kids like to play video games a lot. One of the goals of the research is to understand why video games are so compelling and to figure out how to build educational games that are equally engaging. The basic findings of the research are good food for thought for creating any instruction. Here are a few basic "rules" of video games that you'll be able to use anywhere in your instruction:

- There's always an answer, and there's always more than one way to get to that answer. Video games are fair, in that they never present a situation without an answer, but most are also very flexible in allowing gamers to find their own ways to solve the task at hand. Trial and error is okay, but too often school doesn't allow that kind of work.
- Nothing is impossible. Kids who play games have a sense that they can succeed at the game. School should be like that, too.
- Competition and collaboration are both healthy states. Both can and should be used. This is true online and in the classroom.
- There are clear rules. There are also clear consequences for violating the rules. The research suggests that even avid gamers shut down when they're confronted with arbitrary rules in the classroom.
- Games provide clear roles for players, and the players willingly take on those roles. Too often in traditional classroom activities, students don't take on authentic roles, such as researcher, writer, or historian.
- Effort is related to outcome. In the gaming world, playing more games generally makes kids better game players. Even students who don't work hard in the classroom will stay engaged with problems in their games for hours on end. This is the challenge for teachers: Engage students in ways that reward them for sticking with complex tasks.
- Games simulate consequences. Video games offer the player the opportunity to fail in ways that are congruent with failure in life. A flight simulation game ends when the plane crashes; a medical simulation ends when the patient is either treated or dies. Though such consequences are sometimes difficult to bring to the classroom, this kind of authenticity seems to help hold students' interest.

Source: Adapted from Simpson (2005) and Squire et al. (2005).

Linking games to other instructional activities

They can be used in combination with questioning and reflection activities to help students learn new content, or they can be used after content learning has taken place, as an application of learning. Video game simulations can also be used as a kind of authentic assessment that requires students to tie together pieces of information and apply them to complex situations.

As an example of a fairly simple video game for learning, consider a problem-solving simulation like The Green Mountain Paper Company, or GMPC **(http://www.classroominc.org).** In this simulation, students become the managers of a paper company and must collect information from employees, newspapers, and community members to make decisions that affect the company (see Figure 14.2). The GMPC simulation is divided into twelve episodes, with each episode requiring both a minor decision and a major decision. The decisions to be made range from where to hold the company picnic (a minor decision) to addressing a problem with the company's pollution levels (a major problem). Students receive feedback from stakeholders on the decisions they've made, and then they're asked to write about those decisions.

A game that simulates problem solving and decision making

The program provides feedback in the form of a bar chart showing how well the manager is doing in terms of environmental friendliness,

Figure 14.2 Screen from The Green Mountain Paper Company Some video games use simulations to immerse students in role playing. In this game, students make decisions based on information they collect from characters like the one shown here.

profitability, employee satisfaction, and community relations. In this way, each decision endures from one episode to the next, to create a final overall assessment of the students' work. Through the use of GMPC, students can learn about science, mathematics, and social studies, and also build their written communication skills. Because it was created as an educational product, GMPC is structured to be completed in one-hour chunks.

Creating a simulated city

In contrast to GMPC, SimCity (teacher's guide available at **http:// simcity3000unlimited.ea.com/us/guide/tips/teachers/index.phtml**) offers a far more complex simulation environment. This video game simulation allows users to create a city and watch it grow. Playing the role of the city's mayor, the user determines a wide variety of things ranging from zoning to taxes. The mayor gets advice from city advisers, as well as feedback from citizens. If the citizens aren't happy with a decision, there are often serious financial implications; for example, citizens may move out of the city. SimCity has been used in middle and high schools as well as colleges to simulate city planning and to help learners better understand local government issues. The game's publisher has developed many similar Sims games, like the one shown in Figure 14.3.

Kinds of Video Games

Hundreds of video games are available on the market today, but only a handful of them are useful in educational settings. The following sections describe some typical kinds of games and offer thoughts about their appropriateness for learning.

Figure 14.3 Screen from The Sims 2 Open For Business In this simulation game, students create and manage their own businesses.

First-Person Shooters

First-person shooting games are the stereotypical type of video game. The player's primary objective is to kill his or her opponents. These games are called "first-person" because the player sees the activity on screen in first person—as if she or he were present in that virtual world. Popular titles include Halo, Half-Life, Grand Theft Auto, and Doom. First-person shooters have limited educational value.

Simulations and Strategy Games

Simulations and strategy games are more complex than shooting games. Their goal is to complete a specified objective within a complex environment. These games range from business-oriented and training tools, such as flight simulators, to complex games like The Sims, in which the player is responsible for the entire life and happiness of a character. As a category, these are some of the most promising tools for educational use, from early elementary grades through the adult level. Titles frequently used in education include SimCity, Civilization III, Theme Park World, and The Sims. (See the "Resources" at the end of this chapter for websites related to these and other useful games mentioned in the text.)

Sports Games

In sports games, the player becomes a member of a particular team in a sport like hockey, basketball, or football. In addition to having fast reflexes, the player must make good strategic decisions to succeed in winning the game. There are certainly some educational uses for these games, particularly as they relate to sports training.

▤ Role-Playing Games

Role-playing games engage the player in a long-term quest situated in an unfolding story line. These games typically include a number of skill areas, ranging from problem solving to budgeting, and the character is given opportunities to develop particular skills over time. Some of these games may be appropriate for educational settings. Examples include EverQuest, Warcraft, and Neverwinter Nights.

▤ Puzzle Games

Tetris is one of the oldest and most enduring of the puzzle games for computers. Puzzle games typically rely on strategy, logic, pattern finding, or word completion. Once the puzzle is solved, a more difficult one often follows. Puzzle games are often used as tools in mathematics classrooms.

▪ Choosing Video Games for Learning

As with any other technology, video games are good only when they're used to meet appropriate goals. Without learning goals, video games become classroom babysitters, and students don't necessarily learn from them. For you as a teacher, a critical first step in selecting video games is to define your learning goals.

Next, you'll need to answer a variety of questions.

Questions to ask about video games

▶ Will the video game or simulation help your students meet the goals you've identified?

▶ What additional support will students need in order to make sense of what they're learning?

▶ How long will the learning take?

Scaffolding the gaming experience

Most likely you'll need to scaffold the gaming experience to help your students make sense of it. This may mean having the students keep a journal where they enter information about their game session, or it may mean creating worksheets that help students focus on particular aspects of the game. As with any good instruction, each gaming activity should end with a culminating discussion in which students have an opportunity to reflect on their learning and compare strategies.

In our own work with teachers, we've found that one of the hardest parts of using games in the classroom is helping students see what they should be learning. For example, in our work with elementary students, we use simulations that allow them to run a business by buying and selling a couple of items each day. The students buy and sell, and watch the scenes that unfold. Without intervention from the teacher, students won't necessarily watch for patterns in their selling or discover ways to become more strategic in their buying. Similarly, without supports, they won't identify which combinations of products lead to the highest profits or

SPOTLIGHT 14.3 — Video Game Authoring as a Learning Experience

One of the emerging areas for video games in the classroom is having students design their own video game or virtual environment. Research projects dating as far back as 1996 show that this is an effective and engaging way to help students learn particular content and to engage them in very authentic storytelling activities.

The process of designing the video game can be a multistage, complex activity that includes outlining a story, creating models or drawing characters, creating storyboards that show how the video game will flow, authoring the game to make it playable, and writing all the story elements that the game needs in order to make sense.

Clearly, the learning outcomes of a project like this can include content development, enhanced written and visual communication skills, and a lot of logic development. After all, to create good games, your students will have to think about different paths their story may take based on decisions the player makes. This is complex storytelling. Next, they'll have to use their logic skills to program the game. Even in a relatively simple authoring tool, such as HyperStudio, students will have to think carefully about how to make their game work once it's complete.

For more information on video game authoring as a learning project, check these resources:

Kafai, Y. B. (1998). Video Game Designs by Children: Consistency and Variability of Gender Differences. In J. Cassell & H. Jenkins (Eds.), *From Barbie to Mortal Kombat: Gender and Computer Games* (pp. 90–114). Boston, MA: MIT Press.

Robertson, J., & Good, J. (2005). Children's Narrative Development Through Computer Game Authoring. *TechTrends, 49*(5), 43–59.

which selling locations offer the best customers. However, by asking students to track this information using a paper-based register, the teacher can guide them to focus on the important information. Then the teacher can conduct discussions to help them reflect on the buying and selling patterns that they see.

When you become comfortable with using a careful selection of video games in your classroom and scaffolding the learning experience, you may even want to have your students design their own game, as described in Spotlight 14.3.

The Ethics of Video Games for Students

It's hard to imagine a conversation about video games that doesn't include someone complaining about the negative effects of such games on kids. After all, the goal of many video games is to kill as many of your opponents as possible. Some other video games include sexually explicit material, inappropriate language, and other material that makes using the games for educational purposes highly problematic.

Ways to protect students from negative experiences

Obviously you'll want to avoid the most offensive games. There are also several other ways to protect your students from potentially harmful video game experiences. The first is to select video games that are rated as being appropriate for your students. Like movies, all video games are rated when they're released. For young students, a rating of E (Everyone) or EC (Early Childhood) is safe; E10+ (Everyone 10 and Older) and T (Teen) are safe for older students. For more information on video game ratings, visit the Entertainment Software Rating Board website, at **http://www.esrb .org/esrbratings_guide.asp.**

Another way to protect your students is to engage them in a discussion about the issue of violence in video games. Using frameworks that help students understand the implications of violence and sort out the long-term effects of their activities can be a powerful way to protect them. For guidance on teaching about violence related to video games, see "Resources" at the end of this chapter.

A third way to protect students is to provide a discussion of video games in your school's Acceptable Use Policy (AUP) and expect them to adhere to it. AUPs provide a means of communication and a level of protection for teachers, students, and parents alike. Students are provided with clear language about how technology can be used in their school, and parents are provided with an opportunity to express concerns. Often, AUPs are limited to discussing issues of Internet use, but as software for gaming, simulations, and virtual reality becomes more widely available, it's worth expanding the language to cover a wider variety of activities.

Clearly, protecting your students from violence isn't a simple, one-time activity. Using a combination of the three approaches suggested here can lead not only to protecting students while they're in your classroom, but also to enabling them to make good choices for themselves once they've left your classroom.

Virtual Reality

This section assumes you have no experience with virtual reality (VR), Virtual Reality Modeling Language (VRML), or QuickTime Virtual Reality (QTVR) technologies. First, we discuss the potential uses of VR in local classrooms. Then we go into some specific examples and applications.

VR in Education: The Potential for Teaching and Learning

Briggs (1996) defines *virtual reality* as a computer-generated, 3-D simulation in which users can interact with and have the feel of immersion in another environment. Most commonly, students use VR to see things that they normally wouldn't see, such as distant galaxies or complexities of anatomy. History students can explore ancient historical sites or take a virtual tour of a present-day site that would be too expensive and time consuming to visit. English students can take a virtual tour of a Shakespearean playhouse. The possibilities for these uses are truly endless, and students experiencing a virtual environment may be more engaged than if they were simply reading a text or sitting in a classroom listening to an instructor. However, more advanced VR applications also allow students to create these environments, manipulate them, and interact with them—a truly immersive and interactive experience.

Students use VR to see what they otherwise couldn't

Until recently, developers of classroom technologies have found immersive educational environments too expensive to produce (Dunning, 1998). However, advances in VR techniques have now made it affordable and practical to implement these technologies in the classroom (Rodriguez, 2001). New software packages have lowered the costs and increased the usability, in part because desktop computers are now powerful enough to run complex VR programs.

Winn and Jackson (1999) advance several ideas about VR in educational environments.

Advantages of VR

▶ Virtual environments are safer than some real-world environments.
▶ VR allows a quasi-natural interaction with environments or objects.
▶ Virtual environments are very useful when they simulate concepts that aren't normally accessible to the senses.
▶ VR is especially effective when changes in 3-D perspectives increase learning.
▶ VR can support constructivist concepts of teaching and learning.
▶ VR helps situate education in a real-world context.
▶ VR can readily provide space for collaborative interactions between learners.

Ease of creating VR media

One exciting aspect of VR technology is that it's now reasonably easy to create VR media for teachers and students. Software packages presently available to develop VR include Blaxxun (**http://www.blaxxun. com)** and VR Worx (**http://www.vrtoolbox.com).** VR Worx is a comprehensive software package developed for photorealistic visualization of environments or objects. It's based on Apple's QTVR, which was one of the first VR authoring tools on the market for use on a personal computer. VR Toolbox, the publisher of VR Worx, has developed a complete package that includes everything needed to integrate QTVR into classroom curricula.

Nevertheless, in our own work with teachers learning to incorporate VR into their lessons, we've found several barriers to increased use of VR in the classroom.

1. Though there's a growing body of content, there are still many topics for which VR isn't readily available. This problem is best addressed by using the instructional model we present in this book. If you begin planning with your goals in mind, it will be much easier to identify those places where VR might enhance your curriculum; then you can search for appropriate VR applications.
2. For many teachers, the most common problem with using VR is lack of adequate projection devices. Projectors are very expensive, and many schools have only one or two to share among the teachers. Therefore, as with other technologies, planning is important. In this case, you'll need to plan far enough ahead to have access to the projector.
3. Teachers are often unsure where to start with VR. At its simplest level, VR is an effective tool for presentation and demonstration

of material, and in this respect it can be effective even in a one-computer classroom. VR can also be a valuable tool for assessments, because it allows students something visual to link to their explanations and understandings. Some VR sites allow teachers to create assessments that can be accessed either during class or after school, when the student has access to the Internet.

4. Teachers sometimes struggle to identify which programs are worthwhile for their needs. Once the teacher has found some promising VR content, she'll need to engage in a process like that used for selecting websites or software. Again, relying on the learning goals of the unit as a guide can help any teacher decide whether a program is appropriate.

◼ Photographic Immersive Imaging Techniques

One of the most common forms of VR is the interactive photographic process, sometimes termed *photographic immersive imaging*. This technology allows developers to "stitch together" images to create a photorealistic image of a place. Unlike other kinds of virtual reality, these photographic forms rely on real photos, rather than computer-generated images, to create the virtual environment. These images allow students to view and manipulate environments or objects from many viewpoints. By manipulating the image with the cursor, one may rotate an object and pan in and out, up and down, or left to right.

Panoramic movies

Panoramic movies, also known as object movies (see Figure 14.4), are one type of immersive imaging (Comer, 1999); several examples of these can be examined on the Web.

▶ The QuickTime VR gallery provides several unique examples of VR movies **(http://www.qtvr.com)**.

▶ An interesting site that shows how VR can be used to explore a facility is at the Harvard University website **(http://www.news.harvard.edu/tour/main.html)**. Here, approximately seventy-five QTVR movies take the visitor on a virtual tour of the Harvard campus.

▶ The Visual Human Project, supported by the U.S. National Library of Medicine, offers links to a number of VR applications on human anatomy.

▶ With a VR system developed at Penn State, architecture students can tour a building or house to fully understand constructional considerations and develop a comprehensive understanding of the interior makeup (see **http://www.architectureweek.com/2002/1023/tools_1-2.html)**.

These sites give you a taste of what VR can offer on a professional level. Most likely, though, you want to know how VR can help in your own classroom, right now. The following "Technology in Action" feature provides a dramatic demonstration. Also see Spotlight 14.4, which offers important information about preparing your web browser to work with VR sites.

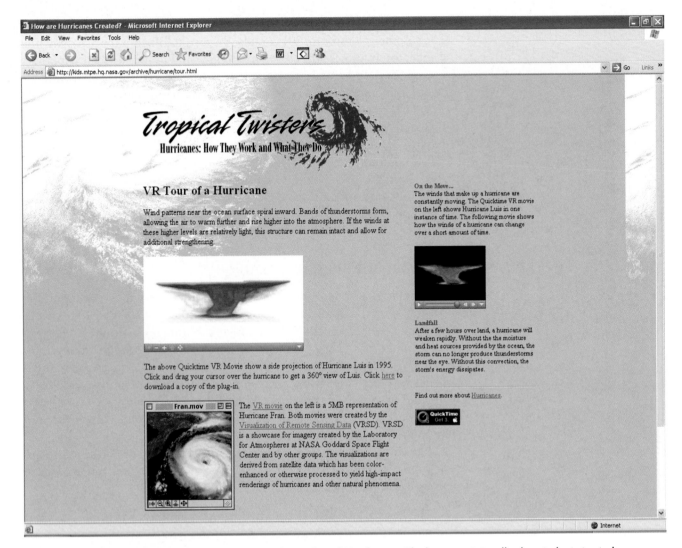

Figure 14.4 A NASA Web Page with Three Panoramic Movies of Hurricanes The images rotate, allowing students to study hurricanes in three dimensions and from a 360-degree perspective.

Technology in Action

A Sample Implementation of VR

As we mentioned in our chapter on guided learning activities, a fourth-grade teacher with over ten years' experience realized that his students every year were challenged in learning maps and legends.[1] The students didn't make the connection between the colors used in the legends and

[1]Lesson developed by Glyn Ellis of the Valdosta City School System in Valdosta, Georgia; see **http://www.teacherresourcebank.com/VRML/LessonPlans/MapsEllis/maps.htm.**

Figure 14.5 Screen from the Fourth-Grade VR Geography Unit Using a mouse and keyboard, students can rotate the image for different views of the landscape, seeing how a map represents real geographical features.

maps, and actual geographic characteristics of the earth. Up to this point, the teacher had been using traditional instructional materials, consisting of an old paper map with a color-coded legend. There were multiple discipline problems in his class, so keeping the students engaged was critical. The teacher had just one computer in the classroom, but it had a projection device, and he thought he might be able to use VR effectively.

By searching the Internet, he found several useful resources for teaching maps and legends. He settled on one VR site and developed a series of learning activities using the Technology and Learning Continuum Model (see Figure 14.5).

In setting his objectives, he decided that, by the end of the lesson, students should

▶ Know that a map represents an area of the earth's surface.
▶ Be able to use a map legend.

▶ Recognize terrain features from a map and mentally visualize them.
▶ Be able to navigate using a map.

Next, the teacher planned the initiating activity as follows:

1. Learners should first be shown a list of map characteristics.
   ▶ A map is a picture of a part of the earth's surface.
   ▶ Different maps show different types of information, such as
     —Boundaries.
     —Population.
     —Terrain features.
   ▶ Legends tell what colors and symbols on the map mean.
     a. Review basic characteristics of the map, as indicated on the page.
     b. Emphasize the legend. Each map has its own legend, and legends can all be different, so they must all be viewed when reading a given map.

2. Show the legend that's used on the website

   Blue: Water
   Dark green: Low land
   Dull green: Higher land areas
   Gray: Low mountains
   White: High mountain peaks

   Discuss the meaning of the different colors, then have students copy the information onto a sheet of paper that they can refer to while viewing the map.

3. Go to the map site at **http://www.edcenter.sdsu.edu/projects/vrml/ lod.wrl.** (*Suggestion:* This is best done by having the website already open behind the presentation pages. Simply minimize the presentation pages when ready to go to the map.)
   a. Review the colors on the map and discuss what each terrain feature represented would actually look like.
   b. Point out a spot in the valley at the northwest part of the map. Discuss the best way to get from this spot to the south end of the river at the edge of the map (down the valley, followed by a right turn at the river to the end). Also discuss the terrain along the trip, such as the need to take the left fork in the valley to avoid a dead end, low mountains off to the right, and high mountains to the left, as you travel down the river.

4. Press the left button on the map, which places you at the beginning point in the valley, as indicated above. Then make the trip down the valley and the river, as discussed with the class. Point out the features you expected to see.

5. Repeat and discuss as desired.

At later stages of the lesson, students view the website on their own and navigate the map. For assessment purposes, they could use the computer's Print Screen function to print materials demonstrating their knowledge of how features on the map were reflected in the legend.

SPOTLIGHT 14.4 — VR Browsers

A Web3D or VR browser is a piece of software that lets you view and navigate a 3-D scene, such as a file written in VRML format, on the Web. These browsers can be stand-alone programs, but more typically they're plug-ins for common web browsers, such as Netscape Communicator or Internet Explorer. A number of companies produce Web3D products.

- Blaxxun Contact (**http://www.blaxxun.com**; look for the free version)
- Cortona from ParallelGraphics (**http://www .parallelgraphics.com/products/cortona**)

- Cosmo Player from Platinum Technologies (**http://www .karmanaut.com/cosmo/player**)
- Multiple browsers and plug-ins from Web3D Consortium (**http://www.web3d.org/applications/tools/ viewers_and_browsers**)
- QuickTime Player for viewing QTVR files (**http://www.apple.com/quicktime/download**)

We recommend Blaxxun Contact because it's the most versatile VRML browser plug-in, accommodating the widest variety of VRML products.

■ Using Virtual Reality in Your Own Classroom

The fourth-grade lesson in maps and legends illustrates how useful VR can be, even for young students in a classroom with limited computer capabilities. Are you excited about the possibilities for your own classroom?

As mentioned earlier in this chapter, one of the biggest challenges you'll face in using virtual reality technologies is locating appropriate examples that will work with your computer setup. You can find many ready-made VR resources on the Web. The first step is to identify keywords in the lesson for which you're interested in using VR. With billions of web pages on the Internet, you'll get better search results by using, not just single words, but combinations of keywords.

Here's the search routine we recommend:

A method for finding VR resources

1. Identify the lesson you wish to convey using VR interaction. Remember to start with your learning goals, not with the VR.
2. Choose among keywords like *VR, VRML, virtual, virtual reality, virtual worlds, education, model, interactive, 3-D, K-12, K-5, middle grades,* or *secondary.* Use combinations of such terms plus a specific topic; for instance, search for *VRML history K-5; virtual reality language arts middle school; QTVR French history;* or *VRML Mars.*
3. Conduct the web search using your favorite search engine, such as Google, Yahoo! or Dogpile. Once you find a good virtual reality resource, bookmark it.
4. Remember to be flexible while you're searching. Don't get locked into a search for a specific VR item unless you *know* it exists. Instead, look for any interactive content that supports your lesson.

Creating Your Own VR Resources

As you learn about VR, you'll discover how easy it is to build VR objects and worlds. At some point, you may want to create your own virtual teaching tools. There are many books and online tutorials devoted to that topic. A list of some online resources and tutorials follows:

Online Study Center
Go online for direct links to these VR resources.

▶ *Lighthouse Interactive VRML Tutorial.* **http://sim.di.uminho.pt/ vrmltut.** The Lighthouse VRML tutorial is an interactive experience. To explore its full potential you'll need Netscape 6.0 or a higher version.
▶ *Creating an Interactive 3-D Product Using VRML.* **http://www .virtualrealms.com.au/vrml/tute01/tutorial.htm**
▶ *VRML Basics.* **http://philliphansel.com/cybertown/vrmlbasics .htm.** A very simple introductory lesson by Phillip Hansel.
▶ *Floppy's Web3D Guide.* **http://web3d.vapourtech.com**
▶ *Thyme's VRML Tutorial.* **http://www4.tpg.com.au/users/gperrett/ triangles**

Virtual Reality Learning Resource Sampler

To get you started with VRML and QTVR resources, here's a list of just a few of the sites available on the Web. (You'll need Blaxxon Contact 4.4 VRML and QuickTime browser plug-ins to view the content on this list!) Also see Spotlight 14.5 for information on CAVEs, an immersive type of virtual reality environment.

SPOTLIGHT 14.5   CAVEs

Cave automatic virtual environments (CAVEs) were originally developed by the military and other government agencies to provide realistic training. Likewise, the video gaming industry has been creating CAVEs and immersive VR environments that provide realistic environments. Users step into a CAVE, typically a room or semi-enclosed area (three walls, ceiling, and floor), donning apparel and apparatus connected directly to a computer system. (See Figure 14.6; for another good illustration, see **http://cave.ncsa.uiuc.edu/ about.html.)**

Apparel is often in the form of gloves that offer a sense of touch and resistance, as well as a means of input into the environment. Glasses and helmets are common, to provide "sight" in the virtual environment. Head movement is tracked as the user looks side to side, for example, and this input

automatically adjusts the display. Other apparatus may include tools, research equipment, or other implements the user would employ in the real environment.

CAVEs are especially effective for immersing people in dangerous environments, such as toxic waste cleanup or a nuclear reactor facility. CAVEs are being used in other interesting ways, such as physics data sets, atomic structure displays, and architectural displays. For example, data on atomic structures of metals are fed into powerful computers that generate visualizations from the information. A person with access to a CAVE can access the data set stored on the remote server, to actually walk through and experience the model, moving and manipulating it in the virtual environment. An interesting K–12 application for teaching earth science can be found

Figure 14.6 **A CAVE**

at http://esto.nasa.gov/conferences/estc2005/papers/a5p2.pdf.

For more information and links to specific CAVEs, see http://en.wikipedia.org/wiki/Cave_Automatic_Virtual_Environment.

Art

Alexander Calder Exhibition at the National Gallery of Art
http://www.nga.gov/exhibitions/caldwel.htm

Constantin Brancusi sculptures at the Philadelphia Museum of Art
http://www.narrativerooms.com/pogany/vr/index_a.html

Early Childhood Education

Build a Snowman
http://www.frontiernet.net/~imaging/build_a_snowman.html

Coloring.com (online coloring)
http://www.coloring.com

Literacy Center Education Network
http://www.literacycenter.net

Play a Piano
http://www.frontiernet.net/~imaging/play_a_piano.html

Earth and Space Science

CNN Hurricane Visualization
http://www.cnn.com/SPECIALS/multimedia/vrml/hurricane

CNN's Destination Mars
http://www.cnn.com/TECH/9706/pathfinder/index.html

Mars Pathfinder Models and Animations
http://mars.jpl.nasa.gov/MPF/vrml/vrml.html

NOVA Online: Mount Everest
http://www.pbs.org/wgbh/nova/everest

The Virtual Museum of Minerals and Molecules
http://www.soils.wisc.edu/virtual_museum/index.html

Geography/Social Studies

Don Bain's Virtual Reality Panoramas (geographic images)
http://www-geoimages.berkeley.edu/GeoImages/QTVR/QTVR.html

Explore the Taj Mahal
   http://www.taj-mahal.net

QTVRs of Japan, China, and Mongolia
   http://www.kiku.com/qtvr/index.html

QuickTime VRs of the Desert Southwest
   http://www.desertusa.com/qtvr/du_qtvr.html

Virtual Reality Panoramas of Philadelphia (presented by Spruance Elementary School)
   http://www.phillyvrtour.org/mainmenu.htm

VR Seattle (QTVR collection from Seattle and Washington)
   http://www.vrseattle.com

History and Archaeology

The Amistad (exploring a recreation of the notorious slave ship)
   http://www.thirteen.org/julyfourth/amistad.html

Ancient Scotland Tour
   http://www.stonepages.com/tour/images.html

Canada Hall Virtual Tour (Canadian history and settlement of North America)
   http://www.civilization.ca/hist/qtvr/caqtvr1e.html

Journey Through Tikal (ancient Mayan ruins)
   http://www.destination360.com/tikal/guide.htm

Kirkstall Abbey Ruins, Leeds, England
   http://www.vrleeds.co.uk/tours_kirkstall/abbey_main.html

NOVA Online Adventure: Pyramids
   http://www.pbs.org/wgbh/nova/pyramid/explore/khufuenter.html

PalenqueTour (exploration of an ancient Mayan city)
   http://www.palenquetour.com

Quarai Pueblo Mission Ruins
   http://virtualvisitor.com/vrpages/ruins5.html

Tour the Greenbrier Bunker (a secret underground bunker from the Cold War era)
   http://www.pbs.org/wgbh/amex/bomb/sfeature/bunker.html

Virtual Gettysburg: The Ultimate Battlefield Tour
   http://www.virtualgettysburg.com

Life Science

Bones of the Skull
   http://www.lib.uiowa.edu/commons/skullvr

Interactive Animated Atlas of Structure and Function
   http://www.bioanim.com

QTVR Anatomical Resource
   http://www.anatomy.wright.edu/QTVR/index.html

3-D Insects
   http://www.ento.vt.edu/~sharov/3d/3dinsect.html

Virtual Frog Dissection Kit
   http://www-itg.lbl.gov/vfrog

Mathematics

Java 3d Viewer: Faceted and Wireframe Objects (geometry)
   http://www.frontiernet.net/~imaging/java3dviewer.html

Zona Land: Education in Physics and Mathematics
   http://id.mind.net/~zona

SUMMARY

Emerging technologies, when used appropriately, can be a wonderful addition to the curriculum. They're particularly useful in allowing students to experience phenomena in ways not possible in the "real" world.

Video games are proving to be important tools for engaging students in learning and for helping learners understand complex environments. On the downside, they're also blamed for leading some children to violence. With proper planning and integration into your lesson planning, though, video games can provide positive learning experiences. You need to consider your lesson goals carefully and make sure students focus on what they're supposed to learn.

Virtual reality is no longer an expensive technology tool monopolized by government, corporations, or businesses. VR is a practical tool that can be integrated into education, for subjects ranging from history and English to advanced science. It can help even young students visualize complex concepts that they might otherwise struggle to learn.

RESOURCES

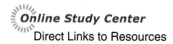
Online Study Center
Direct Links to Resources

DIGITAL MANIPULATIVES

Interactive Math Applets
http://highered.mcgraw-hill.com/sites/0072532947/student_view0/interactive_math_applets.html
> Several interactive puzzles and games that help students explore mathematical concepts.

Virtual Manipulatives
http://otec.uoregon.edu/virtual_manipulatives.htm
> An article on the uses of digital manipulatives.

VIDEO GAMES

Ethical Questions and Ratings

Entertainment Software Rating Board
http://www.esrb.org/esrbratings_guide.asp
> Ratings of individual games and an explanation of the rating codes.

Media Awareness Network: Video Games
http://www.media-awareness.ca/english/resources/educational/lessons/secondary/video_games/video_games_lesson.cfm
> A lesson for grades 7 through 9 on the issue of violence in video games.

National Issues Forums: Violent Kids
http://www.nifi.org/discussion_guides
> Use the site's search feature to find the discussion guide called "Violent Kids: Can We Change the Trend?"

Reality Bytes: Eight Myths About Video Games Debunked
http://www.pbs.org/kcts/videogamerevolution/impact/myths.html
> An essay by Henry Jenkins of MIT.

Specific Games

These are some of the more popular games that have educational uses.

Civilization III
http://www.civ3.com

The Green Mountain Paper Company
http://www.classroominc.org

SimCity
http://simcity.ea.com
Teacher's guide: http://simcity3000unlimited.ea.com/us/guide/tips/teachers

The Sims
http://thesims.ea.com

Theme Park World
http://www.themeparkworld.com

VIRTUAL REALITY

Teacher Resource Bank: Virtual Reality
http://www.teacherresourcebank.com/VRML
> A simple explanation of virtual reality, with a sample QTVR movie and links to other useful sites.

Thant's Animations Index
http://mambo.ucsc.edu/psl/thant/thant.html
> Links to sites with animations and VR.

Web3D Consortium
http://www.web3d.org
> Current news about X3D developments and a weblog devoted to the subject.

Educational Applications

Encyclopedia of Educational Technology: The Use of Virtual Reality in K–12 Education
http://coe.sdsu.edu/eet/Articles/vrk12/index.htm
> A short article, with illustrations, on the educational uses of VR.

HITLab Projects
http://www.hitl.washington.edu/projects
> Descriptions of a number of current projects involving virtual reality; a site sponsored by the Human Interface Technology Lab at the University of Washington.

Virtual Reality and Education Laboratory
http://vr.coe.ecu.edu/otherpgs.htm
> Links to VR sites categorized by subject.

VR Software Packages and Plug-ins

The following virtual reality programs run either separately or as plug-ins for your web browser.

Blaxxun
http://www.blaxxun.com

Cortona
http://www.parallelgraphics.com/products/cortona

Cosmo Player
http://www.karmanaut.com/cosmo/player

QuickTime
http://www.apple.com/quicktime

VR Worx
http://www.vrtoolbox.com

case
STUDY

Virtual Reality/Simulation

When Malcolm Dewey, a middle-school science teacher, learned that his school system had changed the content and process standards for the science curriculum, he began investigating ways he could change his classroom environment accordingly. In addition to curricular changes, his school had recently adopted a new technology initiative, and the administrators wanted the science department to pioneer their effort. Malcolm was selected as the department leader for identifying software and developing materials to be used in the coming school year.

Malcolm reviewed several pieces of commercial and open-source (free and publicly available) software. His primary goal was to identify software that wouldn't simply replicate traditional teaching techniques and activities, but would instead lead to dynamic learning opportunities and enhance students' learning. One type of software that Malcolm identified as particularly useful was virtual reality and simulation software. He found several free VR applications suitable for middle-school science, on such topics as insects, space, chemistry, physics, geography, and astronomy.

Over the summer Malcolm developed and led several training sessions to help his fellow science teachers learn the VR and simulation software. As a group they identified the software that best aligned with their state standards and shared ways they could use the software in their classrooms. One piece of software that Malcolm found extremely beneficial to his own teaching was Celestia **(http://www.shatters.net/celestia).** Celestia enhanced the learning environment he wanted to create because it allowed him to address science misconceptions that his students had about the solar system. The software also helped him to develop new activities integrating content from other domains and to explore the solar system in ways that were otherwise unavailable to him. Moreover, he was able to find tutorials and software add-ons through the Internet (for instance, at **http://www.celestiamotherlode.net/catalog/educational .php).** Here are overviews of two lessons that Malcolm developed using the VR software:

Lesson 1. Malcolm and the other teachers realized that one of their students' most common misconceptions about astronomy had to do with the phases of the moon. Students often thought that the moon's phases were caused by the earth's shadow on the moon. Malcolm decided to use the Celestia software to address this misconception.

Malcolm first demonstrated the software and the moon's phases to the entire class using a projector and computer (see Figure 14.7). Next, he provided the students with a guided tutorial. In the computer lab, students used the software themselves and replicated the demonstration. Malcolm also provided other activities as alternative ways to examine the moon's phases. Through these activities, Malcolm was able to demonstrate the moon's phases

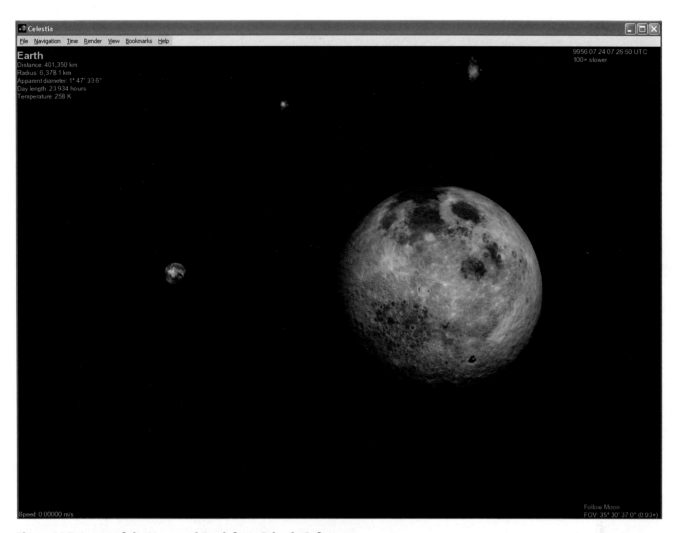

Figure 14.7 Image of the Moon and Earth from Celestia Software

and clearly show that they're caused, not by the earth's shadow, but by the angle the moon makes in relation to the earth and the sun. In addition, he was able to familiarize students with the software so that he could use it in future lessons.

Lesson 2. Malcolm also wanted to integrate mathematics into his lessons more effectively and illustrate the vast expanse of space. With Celestia, Malcolm had the students use their problem-solving skills to calculate the speeds of objects traveling between the earth and the moon. In addition, he asked them to estimate when each object would arrive at the earth. Using the speeds of known vehicles—such as automobile, 30 m/sec; space shuttle, 7.8 km/sec; Apollo 11, 11 km/sec; and New Horizons spacecraft, 21 km/sec—Malcolm set up each simulation on a separate computer (hiding the speed) and asked the students to record data points (distance and time) at 10-minute intervals. Using these data, the students calculated the speed of the object traveling toward the earth and generated an estimated time of arrival. The students also plotted the data points using line graphs.

Over the course of a year, Malcolm familiarized himself with several types of VR and simulation software, and began to integrate them seamlessly into his teaching. He found that using this software changed his classroom environment, in that he was better able to demonstrate and relate concepts that were difficult to teach through traditional methods. He was able to integrate other subjects, particularly mathematics, into his lessons, because the software provided data that were otherwise unavailable. This integration helped the students make connections between the subject matter and real-world applications. Overall, Malcolm and the other teachers in his department found VR and simulation software to be valuable additions to their middle-school classrooms.

Questions for Reflection and Discussion

1. How is technology helpful for student learning? How is it effective in learning specific concepts or addressing misconceptions?
2. When is it appropriate to integrate technology into your teaching? How did Malcolm make this decision?
3. What resources are available to help you find powerful resources that you can use in the classroom? How do you know if they're appropriate for your classroom?

Meet the Standards

Online Study Center

Standards
Go online for more resources relating to standards.

Reread "Standards to Guide Your Preparation" on the first page of this chapter. Notice that one of the NETS standards indicates that teachers should "apply technology to develop students' higher-order skills and creativity." Consider the wide array of emerging technologies discussed in this chapter. With such technologies, there are countless ways you could engage students with diverse backgrounds in critical thinking and the use of other higher-order skills.

Here's a challenge for you: Develop a culminating performance for a learning unit centered on specific learning standards and concepts known to challenge students. The choice of grade level and subject domain is yours. In particular,

▶ Choose one of the technologies introduced in this chapter to develop an activity that will demonstrate to your students, yourself, and other teachers that the students have overcome typical challenges; for instance, that they've learned difficult concepts or overcome misconceptions.

▶ Which concepts are you focusing on? Why do students have difficulty learning these concepts (or why are the misconceptions so deeply embedded)?

▶ Have your classmates participate in the activity and provide you with feedback. Did you accomplish your goals and objectives? What would you do differently next time?

Chapter 15

Integrating Technology for Diverse Learners

ISTE NETS

Teachers

▶ Use technology to support learner-centered strategies that address the diverse needs of students.

▶ Apply technology resources to enable and empower learners with diverse backgrounds, characteristics, and abilities.

OTHER RELEVANT STANDARDS

Council on Exceptional Children (2002)

Teachers should:

▶ Incorporate and implement instructional and assistive technology into the educational program.

▶ Provide a stimuli-rich indoor and outdoor environment that employs materials, media, and technology, including adaptive and assistive technology.

Association for Childhood Education International (2003)

Teacher candidates should:

▶ Create instructional opportunities that are adapted to diverse students.

▶ Know and understand how children differ in their development.

▶ Know how to seek assistance and guidance from specialists and other resources to address students' diverse learning needs.

Technology has long played an important role in removing barriers for students with disabilities. More recently, technology has come to the forefront in the movement to integrate all types of diverse learners into the educational mainstream. This movement focuses on using technology to provide equal educational opportunities for students of many different ethnic groups, linguistic backgrounds, and social and geographical circumstances (Englert & Zhoa, 2001; Zorfass, 2001). By removing barriers to learning, technology can provide an avenue for diverse learners to accomplish many difficult tasks independently. Let's begin by discussing the topic of multiculturalism as it relates to technology.

Multiculturalism

Multiculturalism is the perspective that different ethnic groups should preserve their own culture while interacting peacefully with the other cultures within a nation. This is in contrast to the older perspective of a country's being a "melting pot," which suggested that cultures ought to be mixed and combined and thus lose their identity. The world we live in is becoming more of a global village every day. Most likely, your classroom will have students from multiple ethnic groups, for some of whom English may be a second or third language. Clearly, it's important for all your students to be integrated fully into the learning experience and to interact well with one another.

Providing Equal Learning Opportunities for Students from Different Cultures

When you integrate technology into your teaching, one of your primary responsibilities is to make sure you're facilitating learning for every student, whatever his or her cultural and ethnic background. This often takes some thought and preparation. Much has been written about the "digital divide" that makes technological resources less available to some groups than to others. To the extent that such a divide exists among your students, you need to recognize it and overcome its challenges.

In any lesson involving technology, you'll typically have some students who jump right in, using the technology as if they were born to it. Others may hang back or experience difficulties, and if so, you need to determine whether their cultural background is an issue and provide extra guidance as needed. Used properly, technology should broaden the educational experience for all your students, not create additional divisions.

Consider the following principles (adapted from Gorski, 2006) as a foundation for your preparation and practice:

Principles for providing equal learning opportunities

▶ As you build your knowledge of computer-related technology, be prepared to facilitate learning for every individual student, no matter how culturally similar or different.

▶ Provide opportunities for students to engage technology in ways that produce socially and critically active and aware students.

▶ Use technology in ways that are student centered and inclusive of the voices and experiences of all the students.

▶ Take a more active role in reexamining *all* educational practices and materials, and how they affect students' learning: testing methods, teaching approaches, uses of technology, textbooks and other materials, and so on.

Building Appreciation of Other Cultures

Besides making sure that all students can participate fully in classroom learning experiences, you should provide opportunities for them to learn from one another about their differences and similarities. Your classroom is an important venue for developing the multicultural understandings that students need in order to participate in a diverse society (Gorski, 2006). Table 15.1 provides a list of commitments and actions focused on integrating multiculturalism in your classroom.

Using technology to extend multicultural experience

Using technology, especially telecommunications, you can also extend your students' multicultural experiences beyond their own classroom. With videoconferencing, e-mail, listservs, and online chat, students may interact with other students from different cultures, exchange ideas, and even participate in multicultural projects. Our chapter on communications tools discusses these kinds of activities in detail.

Table 15.1 Techniques for Approaching Diversity and Multiculturalism

Awareness	Commitment	Action
In publications and visual environment		
Evaluating instructional strategies, materials, and curricular resources for attention to diversity	Increasing diversity in instructional strategies, materials, and curricular resources, including technology, and reviewing topics and coverage in light of multiculturalism	Reflecting an inclusive and accepting environment in publications, displays, bulletin boards, websites, and public spaces
In student life		
Addressing use of harmful language or behavior when accessing websites or utilizing technology to communicate with others	Addressing concerns for equity and multiculturalism by establishing a code of conduct to include equity issues	Modeling appropriate behaviors for all students; empowering all students by creating a comfortable, inclusive culture for all students
In community celebrations		
Utilizing technology to help the class learn about and participate in traditional ethnic celebrations	Identifying and planning opportunities for student participation in celebrations through the use of technology (e.g., videoconferencing)	Providing activities and opportunities for multicultural celebrations as community-building events
In curriculum (the Banks Model)		
Adding to the curriculum units study on particular groups of people	Infusing the perspectives of different groups of people into the mainstream curriculum	Engaging students in WebQuests to inquire into the culture and celebrations of their own and other communities

Source: Adapted from Katz & Wishne (1997).

Remember, though, that, whenever students engage in online multicultural exchanges, their actions and words will be interpreted through the lens of the local cultures of other participants. Hence, the student participants should have some prior understanding of people from various cultures who are using the same systems. This knowledge and understanding of other cultures will help facilitate positive experiences for all participants.

The following "Technology in Action" feature discusses e-mail intercultural exchanges, which many teachers are using to expand their students' understanding of other cultures, and Spotlight 15.1 offers a number of resources on multiculturalism for you to explore.

Technology in Action

Using E-Mail for Multicultural Exchanges

Keypals, as we mentioned earlier in the book, are penpals who communicate by e-mail. This is an easy way to promote multicultural understanding by putting your students in direct contact with students from other cultures. A number of websites, such as ePALS Classroom Exchange (**http://www.epals.com**) and Intercultural E-mail Classroom Connections (**http://www.iecc.org**), have been set up to facilitate this process. Figure 15.1 offers an illustration. Of course, you can set up your own e-mail exchange independently if you know a teacher from another culture who wants to collaborate.

What will your students discuss with their keypals? Tanner (n.d.) suggests these possible topics:

▶ Books the students are reading
▶ What their school, city, and state are like
▶ Their favorite subject in school
▶ What they're studying right now in school
▶ What's special in their area, such as state parks, national parks, rivers, places of entertainment, and so on
▶ How many people are in their family
▶ Their favorite animal
▶ Their favorite sports team
▶ Their favorite TV show
▶ Hobbies

For the e-mail exchange to be a genuine learning experience, however, you don't want students' conversations to be random. Plan keypal exchanges the way you would any other learning unit, with an initiating activity, guided learning, and a culminating performance, and make sure your students have the necessary preparation. Do they know how to write an e-mail? Do they know what topics to discuss? Do they understand enough about their correspondents to avoid making inappropriate remarks? Clearly establish the goals of, rules for, schedule for, and means of assessing learning.

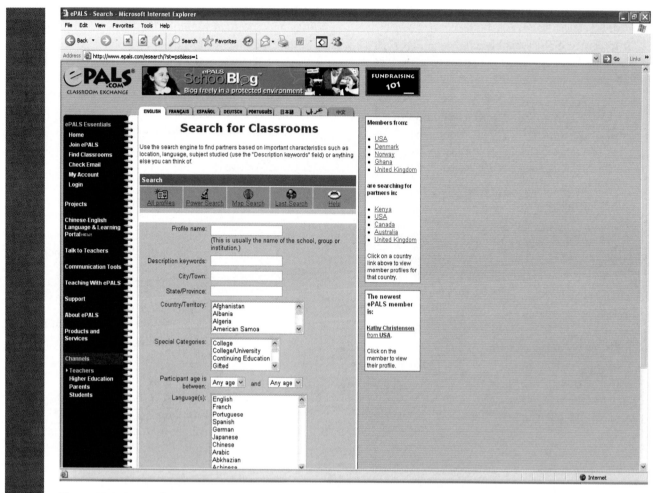

Figure 15.1 Screen from the ePALS Site Through websites like this one, students can find e-mail penpals in other cultures.

SPOTLIGHT 15.1

Online Resources on Multiculturalism

African American History & Heritage Site: Teacher Toolkit for Grades K–12

http://creativefolk.com/toolkit/home.html

Created by Lesley University graduate Gerri Gribi, this comprehensive site guides teachers in selection of web, print, and media resources for teaching African-American studies.

The Electric Gallery

http://www.egallery.com

Online art collections featuring art from Haiti and the Amazon, folk art from around the world, paintings reflective of jazz and blues, as well as prints, still lifes, urban landscapes and country roads, and contemporary art.

ePALS Classroom Exchange

http://www.epals.com

ePALS calls itself "the Internet's largest community of collaborative classrooms engaged in cross-cultural exchanges, project sharing, and language learning." It offers various ways of connecting students and classrooms worldwide.

Global Gang: Planet Teacher

http://www.globalgang.org.uk/planetteacher

Activities and lesson plans for exploring other countries and issues of global importance.

Global SchoolNet Online Expeditions
http://www.globalschoolnet.org/expeditions
Students follow a team of explorers who go to remote places and cultures to seek answers to intriguing questions.

Intercultural E-mail Classroom Connections (IECC)
http://www.iecc.org
IECC is a free service that helps teachers find "partner" schools to share intercultural e-mail exchanges.

Japanese-American Exhibit and Access Project: Camp Harmony
http://www.lib.washington.edu/exhibits/harmony
This site was developed by the University of Washington Libraries to give in-depth information on the internment camps into which Japanese Americans were forcibly moved during World War II. Includes background, first-person accounts, and images.

Kids' Space
http://www.kids-space.org
This organization aims to "break down cultural, religious, ethnic and racial barriers between children of the world by promoting cross-cultural collaboration in creative projects." The website offers ways for students to share stories, pictures, and music; to find e-mail penpals; and to set up their own web pages.

Multicultural Pavilion
http://www.edchange.org/multicultural
From the Curry School of Education at the University of Virginia comes this exceptional site featuring a Teacher's Corner, opportunities for dialogue, a multicultural song database, full-text papers and research documents in multicultural education, sets of data from social service agencies, and a checklist for evaluating multicultural websites.

National Association of Multicultural Education (NAME)
http://www.nameorg.org
NAME publishes the journal *Multicultural Perspectives*, a newsletter, and a variety of position papers on multicultural issues. The organization also hosts a listserv and sponsors an annual meeting. The aim is to bring together a wide variety of people with an interest in multicultural education.

NativeTech: Native American Technology and Art
http://www.nativetech.org
Dedicated to changing the perceptions of those who consider Native American art and technology "primitive," this site explores various areas of Native American art and technology, emphasizing the Eastern Woodlands region.

Scavenger Hunts for Kids
http://www.vickiblackwell.com/hunts.html
This site provides links to various online scavenger hunts, a number of which develop students' knowledge of other cultures. You may find ideas for creating your own scavenger hunt.

Sipapu: Chetro Ketl Great Kiva
http://sipapu.ucsb.edu/html/kiva.html
An interactive site that allows students to explore a model of the Great Kiva, in Chaco Canyon in northwestern New Mexico.

United States Holocaust Memorial Museum
http://www.ushmm.org
The Holocaust Museum site provides extensive information on the Holocaust, including a photograph collection, a searchable library database of the museum's holdings, a description of teaching about the Holocaust, and information on the museum and other related organizations.

Rural Challenges

Distance education

In addition to bridging cultural divides, computer-related technology and telecommunications systems have the capacity to overcome geographic barriers. Web interfaces, videoconference, video capture, and other technologies are increasing access for teachers and students, even in remote rural areas.

For example, **distance education,** also known as distance learning, uses technology to allow students to learn from teachers and other experts who aren't at the same physical site. In some cases the teacher may be hundreds or thousands of miles away. This process offers schools in remote locations the capacity to deliver more courses. Through an online audio or video link, two or more schools can even "share" a teacher.

SPOTLIGHT 15.2 — Resources on Technology Use in Rural Education

National Telecommunications Infrastructure Act (NTIA): Technology Opportunities Program (TOP)
   http://www.ntia.doc.gov/otiahome/top
   Includes a variety of reports, public statements, and links to project descriptions.

Northwest Regional Educational Laboratory: National Rural Education Resources
   http://www.nwrel.org/ruraled/nat_resources.html
   A substantial list of resources for learning about rural education and technology.

The Rural School and Community Trust
   http://www.ruraledu.org
   Website dedicated to connecting people to resources to improve learning in rural schools.

Students in remote areas of Australia, for example, have used amateur radio equipment to participate in classes. Recently, videoconferencing equipment has been distributed to these students' homes (many of which are more than fifty miles apart) to improve the quality of the interactions. Similarly, the Amateur Radio on the International Space Station (ARISS) program arranged for students in Italy and England to speak with International Space Station Commander Bill McArthur about his experience of living in space.

Many rural schools in the United States have used distance learning technologies to share teachers. Many schools can't afford a health teacher, for example, who would be teaching only one class, but an Internet video link allows a single health teacher to teach classes at several different rural schools. Similarly, advanced placement classes are rare in rural schools, but through videoconferencing or web-based virtual schools, enough schools can join together to make an advanced placement class financially feasible.

There have been some restrictions, however, on the spread of technology to rural schools. In addition to fiscal problems, teachers often aren't ready to make full use of distance education technologies. Teacher training, therefore, is crucial. If you intend to teach in a rural area, it's vital for you to be fully competent with technology that can bridge distances and give all students a chance to engage in challenging learning activities. Spotlight 15.2 offers resources for investigating ways to use technology in rural schools.

Integrating Technology for Learners with Disabilities

For learners with disabilities, technology can provide an avenue to accomplish many difficult tasks independently. Common areas of difficulty for learners with disabilities include organization and planning; reading, processing, and understanding language (print or electronic); writing and spelling; and expressing ideas through language.

The role of software

For decades, technology has offered hardware devices, such as hearing aids and Braille readers. Recently, however, software has played a much greater role. In fact, many learners with disabilities benefit from the same kinds of software as other students: word processors, spell checkers,

SPOTLIGHT 15.3   Universal Design

Universal design focuses on making resources accessible to everyone. You've probably noticed buildings that have been remodeled to accommodate people with disabilities. Adding a ramp to bypass steps at the front door would benefit people in wheelchairs; but universal design would mean redesigning the entrance to make the building easier for everyone to enter.

Similarly, in education we expect our teaching and learning resources to accommodate everyone's needs and not limit access to knowledge. There are many useful resources for universal design in educational settings. For further inquiry, see the following resources:

Universal Design Education Online
  http://www.udeducation.org
  A resource for ideas on teaching and learning with universal design.

Center for Applied Special Technology (CAST):
What Is Universal Design for Learning?
  http://www.cast.org/research/udl/index.html
  Provides a definition and many links to resources focused on universal design.

and the like. As for web resources, "no group is more likely to benefit from web-based education than people with disabilities. Learning over the web can minimize the impact [of a disability] by eliminating barriers. . . . It can make previously inaccessible classroom materials accessible" (Web-Based Education Commission, 2000).

In the following sections we talk about assistive technology, which is designed particularly for people with disabilities. Spotlight 15.3 explains the complementary concept of universal design, which refers to products and technology that make life easier for everyone, not just those with special needs.

■ What Is Assistive Technology?

According to the Individuals with Disabilities Education Improvement Act (IDEA, 2004), an **assistive technology** device is "any item, piece of equipment, or product system, whether acquired commercially off the shelf, modified, or customized, that is used to increase, maintain, or improve functional capabilities of a child with a disability." IDEA also defines the term *assistive technology service* as any service that directly assists an individual with a disability in the selection, acquisition, or use of an assistive technology device. Although assistive technology originally focused on helping children with more severe disabilities, the field now focuses on mild disabilities as well (Edyburn, 2003). Work on assistive technology has essentially merged with recent efforts to adapt technology so that all students have access to equal educational opportunities (Englert & Zhoa, 2001; Zorfass, 2001).

One way to think about assistive technologies is to divide them into three broad types: low-tech, medium-tech, and high-tech.

Three types of assistive technology

Figure 15.2 Pencil Grip, an Example of Low-Tech Assistive Technology

▶ *Low-tech* items can be made from simple materials and are typically nonelectronic. Examples include color transparencies, pencil grips (see Figure 15.2), slant

Figure 15.3 Electronic Spell Checker, an Example of Medium-Tech Assistive Technology

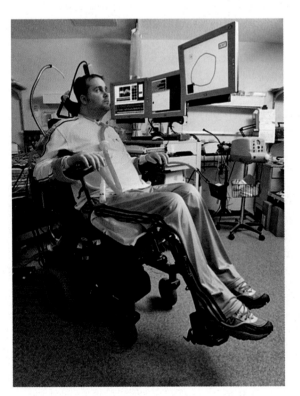

Figure 15.4 An Example of High-Tech Assistive Technology This man can control a computer and a robot by means of a sensor implanted in his brain.

boards (for holding papers and books at a convenient angle), changes in text or paper (boldface print, large print, underlining, raised lines), writing guides, dry erase boards, picture boards, and graphic organizers.

▶ *Medium-tech* devices include tape recorders for note taking, copy machines, electronic spell checkers (see Figure 15.3), beepers/buzzers, and portable word processors.

▶ *High-tech* devices frequently include computers, alternate-input keyboards, hand-held or talking calculators, FM amplification devices, speech synthesizers, and voice recognition software. Some ultra-high-tech devices are even implanted in or attached to the person's body (see Figure 15.4).

IDEA states that children with disabilities who are eligible for special education have a legal right to technology to assist them with learning. Each student must have an **individualized education program (IEP),** developed and monitored by a team composed of teachers, specialists, and the child's parents. The IEP team can and should determine whether assistive technology devices or services are required for a student to receive the most appropriate education in the "least restrictive" environment (one that best accommodates the needs of the student). These devices and services, if deemed

An Inclusive Classroom

A truly inclusive classroom is collaborative work for multiple people. All students need access to appropriate learning opportunities, and this takes people working together to design and implement ideas for activities.

Take a few minutes to watch the HM Video Case called **Inclusion: Grouping Strategies for Inclusive Classrooms,** available in the Online Study Center. In this video you'll see a real inclusive classroom and one teacher collaborating with others to create a supportive environment for all the students. Read the Viewing Questions before watching the video—they'll help guide your attention to critical events.

What other resources are available to support you in creating an inclusive environment? Can you think of ways you might use these resources in your own design and implementation of learning units?

necessary, should be written into the IEP plan for the student and should be made available both at home and at school if appropriate. Cost or lack of availability can't be used as excuses. This IDEA requirement that schools consider assistive technology is considered a giant step forward in making certain that all students receive what the law calls a "free appropriate public education" (Reed & Bowser, 2000).

Potential Benefits of Assistive Technology

There are many potential benefits for students who use assistive technologies, including access to parts of the general curriculum that may otherwise be unattainable. Assistive technology enables students to compensate for difficulties in various settings and to accomplish tasks more independently, within the least restrictive environment. In some cases, technology helps students complete tasks that they otherwise couldn't perform at all.

Examples of assistive technology's benefits

Think, for example, of a child with dyslexia who struggles to read printed words. Books on tape can allow this student to learn by listening. Similarly, voice recognition software can assist a student who struggles with writing. The software will recognize the student's spoken words and display them on the computer screen, helping the student develop written expression skills.

The following "Technology in Action" feature provides a sampling of ways to use specific types of assistive technology with your students.

Making Decisions About Assistive Technology

When you have a role in choosing assistive technology for children in your class, how should you make your decisions? Here are some thoughts to keep in mind.[1]

Thoughts to keep in mind

▶ *A piece of technology isn't for life.* Children outgrow assistive technology devices just like they outgrow their shoes; new technology comes along that may be a better fit for the child and the task he or she is trying to perform.
▶ *Actual device value doesn't always equal "use value."* An inexpensive device can be priceless when a child uses it successfully to perform a task. Conversely, an expensive device can be worthless if the child is unable to use it to perform the intended task.

[1] The materials in this section were developed under the direction of Dr. Martha Venn for a U.S. Department of Education Preparing Tomorrow's Teachers to Use Technology (PT3) Grant Project (#P342A000204), funded to principal investigators Drs. Art Recesso and Martha Venn while faculty at Valdosta State University (VSU). We also acknowledge the contributions of Dr. Karla Hull, VSU; Danny Smith, VSU; Kim Hartsel, Georgia Project of Assistive Technology; and Joy Zaballa. For additional resources developed by this project, see **http://coefaculty.valdosta.edu/spe/ATRB.**

Technology in Action

Assistive Technology in the Classroom

It's important to remember that assistive technology may include devices initially designed for purposes other than education. What counts is the technology's effectiveness in helping students learn.

Word processing programs. These programs can assist students with learning disabilities and other impairments by changing the writing process. They can eliminate handwriting problems, make proofreading easier, and make grammar and spelling less of an issue, so that the writer can concentrate more on the subject matter. In many cases they reduce the student's frustration and anxiety. Standard word processing programs include spell checkers, thesauruses, and auto-correction features, all of which are useful for students with disabilities.

More advanced programs incorporate word prediction functions that assist with spelling and word selection. When a student types part of a word, a menu of possible selections appears. For example, if a student types "fr" the list of choices would include "free," "from," "frog," and so on. This kind of software can also fill in complete words when the student types an abbreviation.

Optical character recognition and text-to-speech. A scanner with **optical character recognition (OCR)** software can take text from printed material and convert it to display in a word processor. This function can be combined with **text-to-speech software,** which reads the written material to the user. Devices that provide text-to-speech conversion are often called **screen readers.** Options, such as voice, rate of speech, highlighting, and screen display, may be individualized depending on the software and on student needs. Text can be read back a letter at a time or a word, line, sentence, paragraph, or screen at a time. This technology can be used by many students who are visually impaired or who display reading difficulties.

Augmentative communication. The term **augmentative communication** refers to either speech or writing that is enhanced by special tools or techniques. Augmentative devices include speech-enhancing devices, picture communication boards, talking switches (which play specific messages when the student activates them), and sign language. These devices give voices to students who otherwise would struggle with or be unable to communicate with language.

Students with severe cerebral palsy, for example, might use an augmentative communication device that can record their voice and provide an easy-to-use interface. Some such devices are quite small and portable; the DynaVox Dynamo shown in Figure 15.5 weighs less than two pounds and runs on batteries.

Figure 15.5 The DynaVox Dynamo, an Augmentative Communication Device

FM systems. A local wireless FM broadcast system, consisting of a microphone and transmitter for the speaker and a small radio receiver with headphones for the listener, can be beneficial to many students with hearing impairments. It can also help students with attention difficulties or learning disabilities. Such a system allows students to hear the teacher more clearly when she is delivering a lesson. They also help shut out distractions and enhance students' concentration.

Hand-held calculators. Hand-held calculators often prove helpful for students who have difficulty writing numbers in the correct order. Students with learning disabilities often have visual perception difficulties and can't process numeric information at the same pace as students without disabilities. It isn't that they don't or can't understand the information; they just process it more slowly. Hand-held calculators may enable these students to perform the same mathematical calculations with the same basic understanding and at the same pace as other students in the class.

▶ *A technology device doesn't by itself provide success.* Knowledgeable adults, other materials, and accessible and well-designed learning environments are required for successful use of a device.

▶ *Technology training should be reasonable and efficient.* If training requires weeks of learning and practice, it may not be worthwhile for a relatively small task.

▶ *Technology should enhance rather than alter the activity's intent.* Keep in mind the point of your instructional activity. Say, for example, that a child in your class is using a communication device for the purpose of joining in regular class lessons. But if the other children are distracted by the device rather than listening to the child using it, it may serve neither the child's purpose nor yours.

▶ *Technology should positively change the child's participation role.* A device should always increase, not decrease, a student's level of participation in the class.

SPOTLIGHT 15.4 — Questions to Ask When Considering Assistive Technology

1. To make for easier communication, does the child need
   - The ability to have speech output to say things?
   - To receive information in a multimedia fashion (pictures, animation, objects)?
   - Alternative choice-making systems?
2. For accomplishing self-care tasks, such as eating, toileting, and dressing, does the child need
   - Adaptive or alternative tools?
   - The ability to signal for help?
   - Alternative choice-making systems?
3. For easier mobility, does the child need
   - Alternative ways to move independently?
   - Outside supports for stability?
4. To grow intellectually, does the child need
   - Alternative choice-making systems?
   - Alternative ways to ask for, obtain, and organize information?
   - Alternative ways to share and organize information (show what he or she knows)?
   - Alternative ways to investigate and experiment with his or her environment (understanding cause and effect)?
5. In order to play like other children, does the child need
   - Adapted toys?
   - Adapted toy activation methods?
   - Outside supports for stability?
   - Alternative choice-making systems?
6. To get opportunities for socialization, does the child need
   - Alternative ways to communicate with peers during activities?
   - Outside supports for stability within typical positions for activities?
   - Alternative choice-making systems?

▶ *Technology in different hands and different situations brings different results.* One teacher may get a child to have a positive experience using the technology, but that same child may not respond in the same way with another adult in a different situation.

With these ideas in mind, see Spotlight 15.4 for some specific questions to ask when you're considering using assistive technology with a student in your class.

SUMMARY

Our classrooms reflect the diversity of our country and our local communities. Recent efforts to expand on the capacity that technology brings to the classroom involve using technology to ensure equal educational opportunities for all students. Technology helps you integrate all kinds of diverse learners into the educational mainstream. Technology can also broaden multicultural understanding by linking students from different cultures and even different countries. For rural students, techniques like online videoconferencing can provide access to new courses and distant teachers.

For your students with disabilities, you should become familiar with assistive technology, which includes any device that improves the student's functional capabilities. Even low-tech items like picture boards and pencil grips can make a substantial impact. Electronic devices, though they may seem more complicated, are often small, portable, and easy to use. In all such cases, your decision making in the design of technology-integrated learning activities can help remove barriers to students' learning. Remember that assistive technology is mandated by IDEA and will form part of the student's individualized education program.

The resources in this chapter give you a starting point for discovering and implementing a wide variety of meaningful ways to use technology for diverse learners.

RESOURCES

 **Online Study Center**
Direct Links to Resources

MULTICULTURALISM

ePALS Classroom Exchange
http://www.epals.com
A site that helps connect classrooms for cultural exchanges.

Intercultural E-mail Classroom Connections (IECC)
http://www.iecc.org
A service to help teachers identify partners in other cultures for classroom activities.

Kids' Space
http://www.kids-space.org
Promotes cross-cultural collaboration in creative projects.

Multicultural Pavilion
http://www.edchange.org/multicultural
Much information and many resources for multicultural education.

National Association of Multicultural Education (NAME)
http://www.nameorg.org
Offers various publications and a listserv.

RURAL AND DISTANCE EDUCATION

National Center for Education Statistics: Navigating Resources for Rural Schools
http://nces.ed.gov/surveys/ruraled
Data and resources from the U.S. Department of Education.

Northwest Regional Educational Laboratory: National Rural Education Resources
http://www.nwrel.org/ruraled/nat_resources.html
A page of links to resources on rural education.

The Rural School and Community Trust
http://www.ruraledu.org
An organization devoted to the improvement of rural schools.

ASSISTIVE TECHNOLOGY

The Access Center: Improving Outcomes for All Students K–8
http://www.k8accesscenter.org
A center devoted to technical assistance for students with disabilities.

The Alliance for Technology Access
http://www.ataccess.org
Offers a way to search for resources in specific categories.

Assistive Technology and Augmentative Communication
http://www.lburkhart.com/main.htm
Handy information provided by Linda J. Burkhart.

Assistive Technology Resource Bank
http://coefaculty.valdosta.edu/spe/ATRB
Helpful hints on selecting and using assistive technology.

Center for Applied Science Technology (CAST)
http://www.cast.org
An organization that works to improve learning opportunities for students with disabilities, through the principles of universal design.

Closing the Gap: Assistive Technology Resources for Children and Adults with Special Needs
http://www.closingthegap.com
Offers a directory of products and publications devoted to assistive technology.

DynaVox Dynamo
http://www.dynavoxsys.com
A hand-held augmentative communication device.

Journal of Special Education Technology
http://jset.unlv.edu
Online access to back issues of the journal.

LD Online
http://www.ldonline.org
A site with information on learning disabilities, including a section for education featuring articles on instructional strategies.

Learning Disabilities and Technology Literacy Project
http://www.cwu.edu/~setc/ldtech
A project focused on the use of technology for students with learning disabilities.

Lekotek of Georgia
http://www.lekotekga.org
This organization uses technology, among other tools, to support students with disabilities; it offers software bundles created by the staff.

National Center for Learning Disabilities
http://www.ncld.org
Offers *LD News*, a free online publication, and many other resources.

ReadPlease
http://www.readplease.com
Text-to-speech software.

Tools for Life
http://www.gatfl.org
An organization that aims to increase access to assistive technology devices and services.

University of Toronto Adaptive Technology Resource Centre
http://www.utoronto.ca/atrc
Online tutorials, papers, and a glossary of terms.

Videos of Integrating Assistive Technology into the Classroom
http://coefaculty.valdosta.edu/spe/ATRB/Video_Tips.htm
A library of videos from Valdosta State University in Georgia. Many of the videos demonstrate the use of particular assistive technology devices.

Wisconsin First Step: Toy Catalogue Listing for Children with Special Needs
http://www.nas.com/downsyn/toy.html
A list of toy manufacturers with brief descriptions of their products.

WordWeb
http://wordweb.info/free
A free electronic thesaurus and dictionary for Windows operating systems.

Planning Technology Integration for a Multicultural Setting

Suppose you've accepted a teaching position at the grade level and subject area you studied during teacher preparation. The school building is only three years old, serving a community that's growing fast. Characteristics of the student population are changing rapidly, as families from all over the country move to the surrounding areas for job opportunities.

The principal has invited you to school and given you access to the building and your classroom for the summer. This is a great opportunity to get your classroom organized and to become familiar with the building environment. You have a lot of work to do to prepare for the beginning of school. As you get settled, you receive a class roster for the first day of class. You see that your new classroom will have twenty-five students, about average for middle grades or high school. But it occurs to you that this list of names is the only information you have about your students. You've never been in the school while it's in session, and you're new to the community. You know that the area as a whole is becoming more culturally diverse, but you have little idea how that will affect your classroom.

Your new principal has made it clear that you'll be evaluated four times this year. From conversations with the principal and other teachers, you know you'll be expected to use technology in innovative ways. Furthermore, you're expected to attend to the needs of all your students. How will you prepare?

Questions for Reflection and Discussion

1. How can you learn more about your students, even before you've met them? What types of information can you look for? Where might you find helpful information about your students?
2. What impact will the diversity of the student population have on your teaching strategies and activities?
3. What supporting technology must be in place to support these activities?
4. How will your classroom learning activities differ if you have access to one computer, five computers, or a transportable laptop cart (with one computer for each student)?

Meet the Standards

Online Study Center
Standards
For more resources
on standards, visit the
Online Study Center.

In the "Standards to Guide Your Preparation" at the beginning of this chapter, notice the call to use technology to "enable and empower learners with diverse backgrounds" and to do so with "learner-centered strategies."

Remember what you read in our chapter on initiating activities, which are critical for grabbing students' attention, introducing the topics of the learning unit, and connecting the new material to students' prior knowledge. To help yourself meet the standards on teaching diverse students, design an initiating activity that engages students from a variety of backgrounds.

Here are some questions to guide you:

▶ How will you determine whether the activities are appropriate for all your learners?
▶ How will students with diverse cultural and socioeconomic backgrounds contribute to the knowledge-building activities?
▶ What resources are available to help you with your decision-making process?
▶ How will you use technology to help students connect their formal learning inside the classroom with their informal knowledge from outside the classroom?

Appendix A

Technology Planning and Decision Making

To implement new teaching practices integrated with technology, you'll need to do a fair amount of planning and decision making. Too often, the technology integration process begins with discussion and selection of the latest hardware or software. This approach does a disservice to both students and teachers, because there's no connection among learning, instruction, and the technology to be used in the classroom. A more appropriate approach is to determine your students' needs first, *then* select software and hardware. As we've emphasized throughout this book, the key to choosing the right technology for your classroom is to remain focused on the learners' needs.

This appendix offers some general resources for planning and then some guidelines for evaluating hardware that you or your school may want to acquire.

RESOURCES FOR TECHNOLOGY PLANNING

Here are three useful resources to consult whenever you find yourself engaged in planning the use or acquisition of educational technology:

National Center for Technology Planning
http://www.nctp.com
Intended as a clearinghouse for planning information, the center offers articles, a guidebook, and links to technology plans by states, districts, and individual schools.

North Central Regional Educational Laboratory: Developing a School or District Technology Plan
http://www.ncrel.org/sdrs/areas/issues/methods/technlgy/te300.htm
An informative discussion of technology planning, along with several illustrative cases.

North Central Regional Technology in Education Consortium: Guiding Questions for Technology Planning
http://www.ncrtec.org/capacity/guidewww/gqhome.htm
This site archives the "Guiding Questions" developed during a technology planning project funded by the U.S. Department of Education. The subjects include the "vision of learning" needed to drive the process, garnering public support for a technology plan, implementing the plan, and evaluating the plan's effects.

ACQUIRING AND EVALUATING HARDWARE

Our chapter on content-area tools discusses ways to evaluate software. But what about the hardware—the computers and other devices that you'll use to run the software? You may think you won't have much say about hardware, that you'll be limited to what the school makes available. Often, though, there's some room for choice, especially as you gain experience and input. In fact, you can sometimes acquire hardware by means of a small grant.

Grant Sources for Acquiring Hardware

A number of organizations are eager to help you acquire hardware to use in your classroom. A web search can help you identify small grant opportunities, ranging from a few hundred to a few thousand dollars, to teach your class in ways consistent with state and national standards. Here are some resources to get you started:

Beaumont Foundation of America
http://www.bmtfoundation.com/bfa/us/public/en/grants

Best Buy Te@Ch Program
http://communications.bestbuy.com/communityrelations/teach.asp

HP Technology for Teaching Grant Initiative
http://www.hp.com/hpinfo/grants/us/programs/tech_teaching/index.html

Kathy Schrock's Guide for Educators: Business Sources and Grants
http://school.discovery.com/schrockguide/business/grants.html

SchoolGrants
http://www.schoolgrants.org

Teachnology: Funding
http://www.teach-nology.com/teachers/funding

Technology Grant News: K–12 Grants
http://www.technologygrantnews.com/grant-index-by-type/k-12-grants.html

U.S. Department of Education's Office of Educational Technology
http://www.ed.gov (look under "Office of the Secretary")

If you need guidance for writing grant applications, see *Kathy Schrock's Guide* in the foregoing list. Other guidance can be found at

Learning to Teach with Technology Studio
http://ltts.org
Online course titled *Obtaining Hardware and Software: How Do I Write a Fundable Grant for Acquiring Technology in My School?*

Minnesota Council on Foundations: Writing a Successful Grant Proposal
http://www.mcf.org/mcf/grant/writing.htm

Scholastic.com Grant Seminar
http://teacher.scholastic.com/professional/grants/scholgrantseminar.htm

Scholastic.com: What Do Winning Proposals Have in Common?
http://teacher.scholastic.com/professional/grants/WinningProposals.htm

Considerations for Selecting Hardware

Planning for hardware needs is a longer-term process than planning for lessons, because identifying equipment needs and acquiring hardware are slow and expensive processes. Therefore, you should always plan from two perspectives: (1) What do I want to do with technology to help my students meet their learning goals? and (2) What can I do to meet the learning goals with the materials that are already available to me? Over time, you can acquire the hardware you want to enact (1), and in the meanwhile, you can work on making (2) a reality for your classroom.

When you're considering what hardware you need to conduct the learning activities you've developed, you can use the following questions to guide your thinking:

What Other Hardware Must the New Hardware Work with or Connect To?

Will the new hardware need to connect to existing equipment in your school or classroom? If so, this will dictate many of the specifications. For example, if you're purchasing a new computer for a lab of PCs (Windows-based machines), another PC would most likely be the best choice. Or if you're buying a printer or scanner for a lab of Macintoshes (computers that use Apple's operating system), the new equipment must be specifically compatible with Mac workstations.

Whenever you're considering peripherals, such as a scanner or an external drive, you need to make sure it's compatible with your computer. For example, you need to decide whether it will connect to your computer through a USB port or via FireWire. This is really important because different computers and peripherals offer different types of connectors.

What Are the Technical Requirements of the Software and of Other Technologies to Be Supported by the Hardware?

By the time hardware selection becomes an issue, other technologies have typically been chosen to support instruction and learning. Those technologies (such as software, learning systems, and projection devices) must be compatible with the hardware. For each such technology, review the manufacturer's list of requirements. In general, you should always try to have a better computer than the minimum specified by the technology you're going to use with it. This means that your new hardware should be faster and have more memory than the minimum required to run the software or peripheral you're connecting to it.

As you plan, consider what other technologies you might want to use with your new hardware. For example, is there older software that you want to use? Is there other equipment that must be supported? If so, you'll need to make sure that these items are also compatible with the new system. It's possible that your older software won't run on newer systems. This means that, when possible, you'll need to replace older versions of software at the same time you replace your hardware.

What Space Is Available for the Hardware?

When you're determining your equipment needs, you should also determine what kinds of desks, chairs, tables, and other work surfaces you'll need to make the workspace appropriate for your students. If you're seeking funds to purchase new equipment, find out whether the grant source will also buy furniture for the computer equipment.

As you consider space needs, remember that, for computer workstations, desks should be at least 30 inches deep (from wall to student) and 36 inches wide, to provide enough space for the equipment and work area. This space may be a little smaller if your students are using laptops or all-in-one computer systems like the Apple iMac. However, you'll want to ensure that there's enough room not only for the computers and the students, but also for books, notebooks, and other materials the students may use as they work. Also make sure computers will be stationed away from heating and air-conditioning units, and areas where the equipment could potentially come in contact with water.

Are Power Outlets Available for All of the Hardware?

If new equipment is being added, make sure the existing power outlets can handle the power needs of the new equipment. Don't assume that more power strips can be plugged into the wall. Ask your building maintenance person for help if you're unsure.

What Computer Platform Will be Used?

The least important, but most contentious, of decisions is the platform—should you use the Apple operating system, the Windows operating system, or a less user-friendly system, such as Linux or Unix? To resolve the decision of platform, consider the following:

▶ Determine which of your existing software titles you want to use on the new machine and research which platforms they run on.

▶ Determine whether there are other software titles you want to purchase in the next year or two and find out which platforms they run on.

▶ Determine which platforms are already in use in your school.

▶ Determine which platforms are supported by the school's technical support personnel.

▶ If workforce development is a concern, take into account that there are more PCs in the workplace than Macs. However, in graphic arts, multimedia development, music, and other arts-related fields, there are more Apple-based machines, and in certain programming environments, there are sometimes more Unix- and Linux-based machines than either Apple- or Windows-based.

For more information on each of these systems, check out the following resources:

Apple Computer Education
http://www.apple.com/education

Edubuntu: Linux for Young Human Beings
http://www.edubuntu.org

Linux for Education
http://www.ceap.wcu.edu/houghton/EDELCompEduc/Ch1/linux.html

Microsoft in Education
http://www.microsoft.com/education

Appendix B

Resources for Growing Your Knowledge and Practice

As we discuss in our chapter "Technology for Decision Making and Growth," self-assessment and observation of others will help you develop a more concrete understanding of your own and your students' needs. Once you've had a chance to observe an experienced teacher, you may want to locate more information to support your thinking about technology integration. In this appendix we focus on a number of teaching- and technology-centered resources available to you.

TEACHING-CENTERED RESOURCES

In our work with preservice teachers, we've consistently heard them express an understanding of the technology integration standards. However, they've also been frustrated because they don't know what these standards look like in practice. A number of resources can help you see what it means to integrate technology effectively.

One freely available resource is from the U.S. Department of Education. For several years, the department has run a program called Preparing Tomorrow's Teachers to Use Technology (PT3). This grant-based program has funded a number of projects aimed at helping you, a preservice teacher, integrate technology in your classroom. Several of these projects include the use of videos to demonstrate key ideas. You can browse the projects through the PT3 website at **http://pt3.org.** Table B.1 provides a list of some other freely available online video resources that demonstrate school reform and technology integration.

Observing practices through predeveloped videos is different from field observation. High-quality videos have been purposely collected, concretely aligned with standards and known teacher needs, and put through a quality assurance review process. The main advantage of using prepackaged videos is that the perspective and focus are already clearly defined for you. You can watch the video knowing what you'll see—often, live footage of a classroom

Table B.1 Online Video Resources for Technology Integration

Sponsor	Project Name	URL
Apple Computer, Inc.	Apple Learning Interchange	**http://ali.apple.com**
Arizona State University	Technology Based Learning and Research	**http://tblr.ed.asu.edu/pt3**
California State University, Bakersfield	Project TNT	**http://www.projecttnt.com**
Rutgers University	Physics Teaching Technology Resource	**http://paer.rutgers.edu/PT3**
SOUNDPRINT Media Center, Inc.	Video Classroom	**http://www.videoclassroom.org**
University of Northern Iowa	InTime: Integrating New Technologies into the Methods of Education	**http://www.intime.uni.edu**

of real kids using technology. Although some of the videos are "canned" (pre-planned and staged for quality control), they're still helpful in demonstrating ideas for using technology in the classroom.

Some of the sites listed in Table B.1 provide a rubric for guiding your analysis of the practice. This rubric is often aligned with ISTE technology integration standards and can provide you with a kind of lens for thinking about the practice you see in those videos. With these resources, you not only become familiar with the standards as expectations of how to integrate technology, you also get to see the standards being met through real classroom practice.

Digital Libraries

A digital library is any online system that labels and categorizes artifacts (such as classroom materials) to improve the upload, storage, and retrieval of these resources. Using search engines, you may find a large number of resources, but digital libraries are able to sift through resources and collect those that cross a threshold of quality and meet a critical need for teachers or students. Digital libraries also organize resources in ways that you're most likely to need—such as by domain, by topic, or by guiding questions.

Materials in digital libraries come in a variety of formats, usually designed for easy access—such as PDF files, which you can open with the free Adobe Acrobat Reader. Furthermore, digital libraries code every resource with a labeling system that's common among all of the systems. This means that a user in one digital library has access to materials from a number of other libraries as well. If you're looking for resources on teaching music, for example, a digital library can assist you by searching and finding a lesson plan on one site and an audio clip on another and then providing both resources in a single web interface.

Several national digital libraries are being developed with the support of federal granting agencies, including the National Science Foundation (NSF) and the U.S. Department of Education, as well as state educational agencies. The following examples of digital libraries provide teacher and student resources for classroom learning. Their names indicate the kinds of resources that you'll find there.

> *Digital Library for Earth System Education*
> http://dlese.org
>
> *Gender and Science Digital Library*
> http://eecgsdl.edc.org
>
> *International Children's Digital Library*
> http://www.icdlbooks.org
>
> *Michigan Teacher Network*
> http://mtn.merit.edu
>
> *The National Science Digital Library*
> http://nsdl.org

Learning Communities

Teaching-centered learning communities provide a way for you to communicate with others in your profession. Through a learning community you can reach out to people who are just beginning teacher preparation or career professional teachers with a lot of experience.

Talking with peers and faculty, you can get connected with a learning community in your area. The group may meet in person or connect to online discussions through e-mail, discussion boards, or chat rooms. One resource for learning more about the history and philosophical underpinnings of learning communities is available at **http://www.creatinglearningcommunities.org.** This site even offers a free online book describing how to create your own learning community. Notice the site's links to existing learning communities. These links may help you find the right community for yourself.

Each learning community is different, based on design principles chosen by those who founded the community. Communities often use specific approaches to engage members in productive activities. Some communities, for example, use Critical Friends Group protocols, which guide the processes of looking closely at teaching and opening channels of communication about participants' experiences. (See **http://www.harmonyschool.org/nsrf/faq.html** for a description of Critical Friends Groups.) When looking for a learning community, it's imperative to find one whose structure and processes suit your needs—one that keeps you engaged in productive ways.

TECHNOLOGY-CENTERED RESOURCES

Teaching-centered resources provide you with ideas about good teaching and what it looks like. Technology-centered resources, in contrast, focus more on the functionality of the tool or application.

In some cases you can benefit from a technology resource that has nothing to do with education. A tutorial about how to develop a spreadsheet, for example, is applicable to any user, whether teacher or accountant. The extent to which you can use the technology for teaching and learning is left to you and experts in the domain to determine.

There are, however, a number of resources aimed specifically at helping teachers learn about technology that's useful in the classroom. Here are three such helpful sites:

> *Internet4Classrooms*
> http://www.internet4classrooms.com
>
> *Microsoft Product and Technology Tutorials*
> http://www.microsoft.com/Education/Tutorials.mspx
>
> *Special Needs Opportunity Windows: Adaptive Technology Tutorial Resources*
> http://snow.utoronto.ca/technology/tutorials

Regional Labs

For a number of years, the U.S. Department of Education's Institute of Education Sciences has funded ten regional educational laboratories. Each regional lab provides information, products, services, and resources valuable to educators in all fifty states and territories. Because of a new funding cycle, some names and locations have shifted, but most of the earlier material continues to be available while new programs are being developed. The following sites in particular offer important material on educational technology:

> *Edvantia (Appalachia Educational Laboratory)*
> http://www.edvantia.org
>
> *Midwestern Regional Educational Laboratory*
> http://www.learningpt.org
> This includes material from the former North Central Regional Educational Laboratory.

Professional Organizations

Just as there are professional organizations for the various disciplines and content areas (see **http://teacherpathfinder.org/ProfDev/proforganiz.html),** there are also professional organizations dedicated to the integration of technology in education. These technology-focused organizations provide many free online resources for teachers. They also publish both research journals and journals for teachers with ideas for technology integration.

The following list includes three such organizations and their primary publications and conferences. The International Society for Technology in Education (ISTE) is clearly focused on K–12 needs, whereas AECT and AACE/SITE are focused primarily on a higher-education audience.

International Society for Technology in Education (ISTE)
http://www.iste.org

Journal of Computing in Teacher Education (JCTE), a peer-reviewed publication focused on training and certification issues
Journal of Research on Technology in Education (JRTE), a peer-reviewed research journal on educational computing
Learning & Leading with Technology (L&L), a practitioner magazine providing ideas about how to use technology in classrooms
National Educational Computing Conference (NECC), a large national conference focusing on classroom uses of technology

Association for Educational Communications and Technology (AECT)
http://www.aect.org

Educational Technology Research & Development (ETR&D), a peer-reviewed journal focusing on the research and development of educational technology
TechTrends, a practitioner magazine focusing on the application of educational technology for teaching and learning
AECT Conference, an annual international conference to communicate the different ways in which educational technology is being used

Association for the Advancement of Computing in Education (AACE), which supports the Society for Information Technology & Teacher Education (SITE)
http://www.aace.org
http://site.aace.org

Contemporary Issues in Technology & Teacher Education (CITE), an electronic journal that often includes multimedia demonstrations of information technology
Journal of Technology and Teacher Education (JTATE), a peer-reviewed journal focusing on the use of technology in teacher education

For other educational technology organizations, check the listing at **http://www.educational-software-directory.net/organizations.html.**

Glossary

acceptable use policy (AUP) Policy established by a school or district to define how students are allowed to use the Internet.

assessment Measurement of what someone has learned. Teachers use a wide range of assessment methods, including tests and quizzes, informal observation, and student projects.

assistive technology Any device or service that increases the capabilities of people with disabilities.

asynchronous communication Communication in which a message is sent at one time and received at some later time, as with e-mail.

augmentative communication Speech or writing enhanced by special tools or techniques, such as by an electronic communication board.

augmented reality Setting in which technology adds information to the learner's actual surroundings. For example, students might use a headset or hand-held computer to enhance their experiences with a museum exhibit.

behaviorism Theory, developed by B. F. Skinner and others, that people learn through a series of reinforcements, whether positive or negative.

blog (short for "weblog") An online journal in which a user posts chronological, up-to-date events. A blog is kept in chronological order and is generally topical—relating to a single person, group, cause, or theme.

Bloom's taxonomy Classification scheme, developed by Benjamin Bloom, that organizes learning into levels according to the sophistication of mental effort necessary to meet a given goal. Bloom identified six levels, ranging from Knowledge (the lowest level) to Evaluation (the highest level).

bulletin board See *discussion board.*

cognitive information-processing theory A theory of learning that views the mind as an information processing device in which information can filed away and retrieved. Learning is characterized by moving information from short-term memory to long-term memory.

concept map Diagram that connects pieces of information in a way that shows the relationships among them; visual representation of the links between ideas.

concept-mapping tool Tool (usually software) for creating concept maps.

constructivism A set of learning theories that asserts that each person creates their own understandings through experiences with information and/or people. Learning occurs as the learner integrates new understandings into their existing ideas about the content or context.

content analysis Review of the content knowledge that students should learn in a given lesson—a useful step in writing objectives for the lesson. Content analysis often begins with review of the standards for the appropriate grade and content area.

content standard Standard that defines a set of concepts that students should have learned by a particular point in their learning career.

cooperative learning Teaching strategy in which small groups of learners (often at different ability levels) engage in a variety of activities together.

culminating performance Final stage of the learning continuum, in which students complete specified tasks to display their new knowledge and understanding.

demonstration Description or explanation of information or a process. Teachers are using demonstration techniques when they show the class examples or experiments.

development tool Tool that helps students develop their own projects and presentations. Typically includes software for creating and editing images, preparing web pages, and constructing multimedia projects.

diagnostic assessment See *preassessment.*

digital manipulative Computerized version of a traditional manipulative, such as Cuisenaire rods.

discussion Examination of information by argument, comment, or debate. Typically, a teacher frames questions around a topic being covered in class and asks students to discuss possible answers.

discussion board Site on the Internet (or other network) that allows people to communicate with others using simple text messages; also known as a *bulletin board* or *message board.*

distance education Process of using technology to allow students to learn from teachers and other experts who are not at the same physical site.

electronic whiteboard Interactive, whiteboardlike surface that allows teacher and students to point at items and even draw on the board with a special stylus. Work on the board can also be captured and saved for later analysis.

Evidence Based Decision Support (EBDS) Method of assessing how one's lessons work in practice and increasing understanding of teaching. With EBDS, the teacher collects evidence in the classroom (such as videotapes of teaching and samples of student work) and then evaluates that evidence systematically.

exit standard Expected outcome by the time a student graduates from high school.

facilitation Approach to teaching in which the teacher acts as a guide rather than as a mere deliverer of content. Students are encouraged to take control of their own learning process.

FireWire Interface standard offering high-speed communication between an external device and a personal computer; widely used for transferring video from digital camcorders.

formative assessment Assessment conducted during a learning unit to help the teacher gauge how students are progressing.

guided learning In the learning continuum, a transitional stage between the initiating learning activity and the culminating performance. Students are "guided" through the application and refinement of the knowledge and skills that were introduced in the initiating activity.

hand-held computer Small computer that allows students to capture data, write, or type (with a separate keyboard), calculate, and engage with a variety of special software packages developed for educational purposes; also known as a *personal digital assistant (PDA)*.

hypertext Text that links to something else—for instance, a phrase on a web page that takes the user to another page when the user clicks on it with the mouse.

Hypertext Markup Language (HTML) Coding used on web pages to tell the web browser how to display the content.

immersive technology Technology that immerses or envelops the student in a virtual environment for learning. One example is a flight simulator that mimics the experience of flying a plane.

individualized education program (IEP) Written educational plan required for each student covered by the Individuals with Disabilities Education Act. It is developed and monitored by a team of teachers, specialists, and the child's parents. Among other aspects of the student's needs, the IEP identifies assistive technology devices and services that must be provided.

informal learning environment (ILE) Setting or organization, outside of formal schooling, whose mission includes learning and development. Examples include after-school clubs, museums, and summer camps.

initiating activity Activity that introduces students to what they will be doing in the learning unit.

inquiry Active investigation into *why* and *how*. See also *inquiry-based learning*.

inquiry-based learning Approach in which students learn by exploring one or more essential questions. By engaging in research and other activities to answer the questions, students develop a meaningful understanding of concepts and practices.

instructional game Entertaining activity that helps students gain knowledge and skills through active participation. When such games use computer technology, they are often called *edutainment*.

Internet protocol camera Type of video camcorder designed to connect directly to an Ethernet wall jack. Using the Internet or another network, it can deliver video from remote locations to a designated monitor or server.

keypal Penpal who communicates by e-mail.

K-W-L chart Three-column chart in which students list what they already **K**now, what they **W**ant to know, and, at the end of the lesson, what they have **L**earned.

learner-centered environment Environment that attempts to meet the known conditions under which people learn.

Learner-Centered Psychological Principles Fourteen principles established by the American Psychological Association that focus on helping the learner create meaningful, coherent representations of knowledge.

learning community Group of educators who get together regularly, either in person or online, to discuss issues and practices. Often the members want to improve both their own skills and the overall education offered in their schools.

learning environment Space or spaces where learners interact with tools, materials, and resources. Broadly, it is the entire context in which learning is established and supported.

learning in *situ* See *situated learning*.

listserv Computerized mailing list that allows a message to be sent simultaneously to everyone on the list.

mastery Way of thinking about learning that assumes that a student who has mastered a topic, idea, or concept is able to demonstrate that knowledge at least a certain portion of the time. Mastery in a particular lesson might be defined, for instance, as completing the assigned task correctly 80 percent of the time.

meaningful learning Students' active development of deep understanding of complex concepts that are central to the learning domain and relevant to their everyday life.

message board See *discussion board*.

metacognition Learners' understanding of their own thinking and learning processes.

microworld Simulation program designed to allow the user to explain ideas, test assumptions, and explore concepts.

modeling (instructional) Approach in which the teacher deliberately practices a process to show others how to use it.

modeling (technological) Creating a representation of an object, concept, or process to help learners understand it. For instance, mathematics software can create interactive visual models that illustrate fractions.

multiculturalism Perspective that different ethnic groups should preserve their own culture while interacting peacefully with the other cultures of the nation.

multimedia Communication format (usually created by computer) that combines at least two different types of media, such as text, sound, still images, and video.

multiple intelligences Theory, developed by Howard Gardner, that people have at least nine different kinds of intelligence (such as visual/spatial intelligence, verbal intelligence, and bodily/kinesthetic intelligence) as opposed to one general intelligence. The implication is that instructional activities should be designed for various kinds of intelligence, so that students with different learning preferences can all benefit.

National Educational Technology Standards (NETS) Standards for technology integration developed by the International Society for Technology in Education (ISTE). There are NETS for students, teachers, and administrators.

nonimmersive technology Technology that does not transport the learner to a virtual "place" but does simulate another environment.

objective Statement that explains what a student will know or be able to do as a result of a learning activity.

optical character recognition (OCR) Process of using software to scan printed material and convert the text to display in a word processor.

PDF (Portable Document Format) Common format for print documents stored for Internet use; allows the user to see the document with all the original formatting intact.

performance assessment Way of measuring learning by assigning an authentic task to a learner—that is, a task that represents or closely models an activity the student might undertake in real life.

performance standard Standard that attempts to make content expectations clear by defining how students should demonstrate their proficiency in the skills and knowledge framed by content standards.

personal digital assistant (PDA) See *hand-held computer*.

preassessment Assessment that takes place before learning begins—for instance, at the beginning of a learning unit or before crucial transition points during the unit—allowing the teacher to discover what students already know and to structure the lesson accordingly. Also known as *diagnostic assessment*.

presentation Introduction, offering, delivering, and exhibition of information. Presentation is a common method for teachers at the beginning of a learning unit.

probe Device for measuring a particular variable, such as temperature, voltage, or oxygen level. Electronic probes can download their information into a computer or special calculator.

problem-based learning Approach in which students learn by working to find a solution to a problem that is complex and tied to the real world.

problem solving Process of attempting to resolve a matter involving doubt, uncertainty, or difficulty.

process standard Standard that defines skills and ways of thinking that are important to a discipline.

productivity tool Tool that supports people in doing tasks that would otherwise have to be done in a different, usually more laborious, way. In educational settings, productivity tools include such computer applications as word processors, spreadsheets, databases, presentation software, and concept-mapping software.

programmed instruction Behaviorist instructional approach developed by B. F. Skinner, in which teaching machines allowed learners to go through a body of information in a prescribed order, moving on to new material once they have mastered the previous material. Often considered the forerunner of many educational technologies.

reflection activity Activity that gives students an opportunity to stop and think about what they have learned. By conveying their current understanding, they solidify it and highlight areas where things are not yet making sense.

rubric Scoring scale for assessing students' performance on a particular task, such as an essay, project, or test. Rubrics are often shared with the students (or even created in collaboration with the class) so that students know exactly how their work is being measured.

scaffolding Supports put into place to help a learner make appropriate sense of learning and to make a complex task do-able. For example, in designing a roller coaster, there are hundreds of considerations to be made, ranging from the height of the hills to the materials used. To scaffold a learning environment so that students can design a roller coaster, a teacher may choose to have students consider only height, speed, gravity, and force. As students learn more, scaffolds are slowly withdrawn.

schema (plural: schemata) The brain's structure for organizing knowledge. We have schemata for concepts, skills, and other things we encounter in life.

screen reader Text-to-speech device that reads a computer display aloud.

server Computer that deals with information requests from other computers. For instance, when one accesses a web page, a web server sends the files for that page to one's own computer for viewing.

simulation Imitation of a process, knowledge, or skill to be learned. In computer applications, a simulation is a program that provides a realistic facsimile of an environment that students could not access in real life.

situated learning Learning that takes place in a realistic environment, one that closely replicates the setting in which the learning will eventually be applied; also known as *learning in* situ.

streaming media Continuous video or audio content that can be accessed on a computer.

summative assessment Assessment that occurs at the end of a project or learning unit to measure whether students have met the objectives.

synchronous communication Communication that occurs instantaneously, in "real time," as in online chat sessions.

teacher-as-facilitator See *facilitation*.

Technology and Learning Continuum Model Model for developing a technology-integrated learning unit. It divides the learning continuum into three stages—initiating activity, guided learning, and culminating performance—and conceives of the instructional design process as comprising objectives, instructional strategies, choice of possible technologies, and assessment.

technology-based learning environment Environment that engages students in learning through computer applications. Any noncomputer activities draw from and build on the computer activities.

technology-enhanced learning environment Environment that uses computers and related technology to augment the teaching and learning activities of the classroom. These are less dependent on computers than are technology-based learning environments.

telementoring Process of pairing a student with a mentor to explore a particular topic via email.

text-to-speech software Programs that read written material to the user.

universal serial bus (USB) Interface standard for connecting devices, such as key drives and digital cameras, to a computer. Usually multiple such devices can be connected simultaneously.

videoconferencing Audio and video communication in real time among multiple people in multiple remote locations. A simple videoconferencing system can be set up with small webcams, an Internet link, and free computer software.

video club Gathering in which several teachers review and discuss video clips of their own teaching in order to improve their practice.

video ethogram Video footage of animal behavior combined with coding to describe what is seen in the video.

video game Game played on a computer or other gaming platform. Better video games provide students with the opportunity to solve problems, make decisions, and alter the outcomes of their efforts.

virtual reality Simulation of three-dimensional, real-life environments through computers and other technology.

Virtual Reality Modeling Language (VRML) Computer language used for virtual reality environments, which allows developers to create graphical representations and screens where students can interact with objects and even with other characters.

webcam Any camera (usually video rather than still) that supplies images for transmission via a website.

weblog See *blog*.

WebQuest Inquiry-based instructional approach in which students use web resources to accomplish a defined task. Usually the challenge itself is presented to students by means of a web page, and then they are guided to appropriate web-based sources of information.

Web3D Shorthand for three-dimensional virtual reality modeling on the World Wide Web, such as environments created with Virtual Reality Modeling Language.

References

APA Work Group of the Board of Educational Affairs. (1997). *Learner-centered psychological principles: A framework for school reform and redesign* (rev. ed.). Washington, DC: American Psychological Association. Retrieved November 27, 2006, from www.apa.org/ed/lcp2/lcp14.html

Association for Childhood Education International. (2003). *Elementary education standards—Summary.* Retrieved November 27, 2006, from http://www.ncate.org/ProgramStandards/ACEI/ACEIstandards.doc

Association for Educational Communications and Technology. (2000). *Standards for the accreditation of school media specialist and educational technology specialist programs.* R. Earle (Ed.). Retrieved November 27, 2006, from http://www.ncate.org/ProgramStandards/AECT/AECTstandardsREV2005.doc

Association for Educational Communications and Technology. (2003). *Educational Communications and Technology Programs Standards for NCATE.* Retrieved November 27, 2006, from http://ncate.org/public/programStandards.asp?ch=4

Barab, S. A., Hay, K. E., Barnett, M., & Keating, T. (2000). Virtual solar system project: Building understanding through model building. *Journal of Research in Science Teaching, 37*(7), 719–756.

Becker, H. J. (2000, Sept.–Oct.). Pedagogical motivations for student computer use that lead to student engagement. *Educational Technology, 40*(5), 5–17.

Bennett, D., & Hawkins, J. (1992). Alternative assessment and technology. ERIC Digest. Adapted from an article in *News from the Center for Children and Technology and the Center for Technology in Education, 1*(3).

Bielefelt, T. (2001, Summer). Technology in teacher education: A closer look. *Journal of Technology in Teacher Education, 17*(4).

Black, P., & Wiliam, D. (1998a). Assessment and classroom learning. *Assessment in Education, 5,* 7–74.

Black, P., & Wiliam, D. (1998b). Inside the black box: Raising standards through classroom assessment. *Phi Delta Kappan, 80,* 139–148.

Bloom, B. S., Englehart, M. B., Furst, E. J., Hill, W. H., & Krathwohl, D. R. (Eds.). (1956). *Taxonomy of educational objectives: The classification of educational goals. Handbook I: Cognitive domain.* New York: McKay.

Boston, C. (2002). The concept of formative assessment. *Practical Assessment, Research & Evaluation, 8*(9). Retrieved November 27, 2006, from http://PAREonline.net/getvn.asp?v=8&n=9

Briggs, J. C. (1996). The promise of virtual reality. *The Futurist, 30*(5), 13–18.

Brooks, J. G., & Brooks, M. G. (1999). *In search of understanding: The case for constructivist classrooms* (rev. ed.). Alexandria, VA: Association for Supervision and Curriculum Development.

Clements, D. H., & Meredith, J. S. (1995). *Tumbling tetronimoes.* White Plains, NY: Dale Seymour Publications.

Colorado Model Standards for Mathematics. (1995). *Grades K–4.* Retrieved November 27, 2006, from http://www.achievementtech.com/files/CO_Math2.pdf

Comer, S. D. (1999). Immersive imaging technology: VR for the web in academia. *Syllabus, 13*(1), 22–26.

Council for Exceptional Children. (2002). *NCATE/CEC program standards (2002): Programs for the preparation of special education teachers.* Retrieved November 27, 2006, from http://www.ncate.org/ProgramStandards/CEC/CECStandards.doc

Dede, C. (2005). *Profile.* Christopher Dede's web page, Harvard Graduate School of Education. Retrieved November 27, 2006, from http://www.gse.harvard.edu/~dedech/

Dunning, J. (1998). Virtual reality-learning by immersion. *Technos, 7*(2), 11–13.

Edyburn, D. (2003). Reading difficulties in the general education classroom: A taxonomy of text modification strategies. *Closing the Gap, 21*(6), 1, 10–13, 30.

Englert, C. S., & Zhao, Y. (2001). The construction of knowledge in a collaborative community: Reflections on three projects. In J. Woodward & L. Cuban (Eds.), *Technology, curriculum and professional development: Adapting schools to meet the needs of students with disabilities* (pp. 187–202). Thousand Oaks, CA: Corwin Press, Inc.

Exline, Joe. (2003). *Science as inquiry: Operational definition.* Networking for Leadership, Inquiry and Systemic Thinking (NLIST). Retrieved November 27, 2006, http://www.nlistinquiryscience.com/documents/definition.htm

Gardner, H. (1999). *Intelligence reframed: Multiple intelligences for the 21st century.* New York: Basic Books.

Gorski, P. C. (2006). A working definition of multicultural education. *Multicultural Pavilion* [Electronic version]. Retrieved November 27, 2006, from http://www.edchange.org/multicultural/initial.html

Hannafin, M. J., Hill, J. R., & McCarthy, J. E. (2000). Designing resource-based learning and performance support systems. In D. A. Wiley (Ed.), *The instructional use of learning objects*. Bloomington, IN: Agency for Instructional Technology.

Hasselbring T., et al. (2000). *Literature review: Technology to support teacher development.* Retrieved November 29, 2006, from http://www.ericsp.org/pages/dogest/EdTechPrep.htm

Henseler, J. (2006). *No limits rollercoaster simulation.* Retrieved November 27, 2006, from http://www.nolimitscoaster.com/

Improving America's Schools Act. (1994). Revision of the Elementary and Secondary Education Act of 1965. Retrieved November 27, 2006, from http://www.ed.gov/legislation/ESEA/index.html

IDEA: Individuals with Disabilities Education Improvement Act. (2004). Retrieved November 27, 2006, from http://www.ed.gov/policy/speced/guid/idea/idea2004.html

International Reading Association. (2003). *Standards for reading professionals.* Newark, DE: Author. Retrieved November 27, 2006, from http://www.reading.org/resources/issues/reports/professional_standards.html

International Society for Technology in Education. (2000). *Profile for technology-literate teachers—Professional preparation performance profiles.* Washington, DC: Author. Retrieved November 27, 2006, from http://cnets.iste.org/teachers/t_profile-pro.html

International Society for Technology in Education. (2006). *National educational technology standards for teachers: Educational technology standards and performance indicators for all teachers.* Retrieved November 27, 2006, from http://cnets.iste.org/teachers/t_stands.html

Jonassen, D. H. (2000). *Computers as mindtools for schools: Engaging critical thinking* (2nd ed.). Columbus, OH: Merrill/Prentice Hall.

Jonassen, D. H., & Kwon, H. I. (2001). Communication patterns in computer-mediated vs. face-to-face group problem solving. *Educational Technology: Research and Development, 49*(10), 35–52.

Katz, L. L., & Wishne, B. (1997). *Building multicultural schools.* Independent Schools Association of the Central States (ISACS) Pamphlet. ISACS Midwest Diversity Committee. Available: http://www.misf.org

Kulieke, M., Bakker, J., Collins, C., Fennimore, T., Fine, C., Herman, J., Jones, B. F., Raack, L., & Tinzmann, M. B. (1990). *Why should assessment be based on a vision of learning?* Oak Brook, IL: North Central Regional Educational Laboratory.

Lehigh University. (2002). *Conductivity (Protocols for Pasco probes).* (LEO and SERVIT Group.) Retrieved November 27, 2006, from http://www.leo.lehigh.edu/envirosci/watershed/wq/wqtools/conductivity.html

Marzano, R., Pickering, D. J., & McTighe, J. (1993). *Assessing student outcomes: Performance assessment using the dimensions of learning model.* Alexandria, VA: Association for Supervision and Curriculum Development.

McDonald, J. P., & Naso, J. (1986, May). *Teacher as learner: The impact of technology.* Unpublished paper, Educational Technology Center, Harvard Graduate School of Education.

McKenzie, J. (2000, September). Beyond edutainment and technotainment. *From Now On: The Educational Technology Journal, 10*(1). Retrieved November 27, 2006, from http://www.fno.org/sept00/eliterate.html

Means, B. (2000). Technology in America's schools: Before and after Y2K. In R. Brandt (Ed.), *ASCD yearbook 2000.* Alexandria, VA: Association for Supervision and Curriculum Development.

Means, B., & Olsen, K. (1995). *Technology's role within constructivist classrooms.* Paper presented at the Annual Meeting of the American Educational Research Association. San Francisco.

Mills, M., Pea, R. D., Rosen, J., & Hoffert, E. (2003, July). Stanford Center for Innovations in Learning Case Study: DIVER (Digital Interactive Video Exploration and Reflection). *Post-Linear Video: Editing, Transcoding, and Distribution* (ACM SIGGRAPH Course Notes). Presented at ACM SIGGRAPH, San Diego, CA.

National Association for the Education of Young Children. (2006). *NAEYC early childhood program standards.* Retrieved November 27, 2006, from http://www.naeyc.org/accreditation/standards/

National Board for Professional Teaching Standards. (2002). *NBPTS early and middle childhood literacy: Reading-language arts standards for teachers of students ages 3–12.* Retrieved November 27, 2006, from http://www.nbpts.org/the_standards/standards_by_cert?ID=23&x=44&y=9

National Board for Professional Teaching Standards. (2006). *Five core propositions.* Retrieved November 27, 2006, from http://www.nbpts.org/

National Center for Education Statistics. (2001). *The nation's report card: Mathematics 2000.* NCES 2001-517. Washington, DC: Author, U.S. Department of Education.

National Center for Education Statistics. (2002a). *The nation's report card: Geography 2001.* NCES 2002-484. Washington, DC: Author, U.S. Department of Education.

National Center for Education Statistics. (2002b). *The nation's report card: U.S. History 2001.* NCES 2002-483. Washington, DC: Author, U.S. Department of Education.

National Center for Education Statistics. (2003). *The nation's report card: Science 2000.* NCES 2003-453. Washington, DC: Author, U.S. Department of Education.

National Commission on Excellence in Education. (1983). *A nation at risk.* Washington, DC: U.S. Government

Printing Office. Retrieved November 28, 2006, from http://www.ed.gov/pubs/NatAtRisk/index.html

National Council for Accreditation of Teacher Education. (2002). *Professional standards for the accreditation of schools and colleges of education: 2002 edition.* Retrieved November 28, 2006, from http://www.ncate.org/documents/unit_stnds_2002.pdf

National Council for the Social Studies. (2004). *Standards for the preparation of social studies teachers* (Vol. 1). Retrieved November 28, 2006, from http://www.socialstudies.org/standards/teachers/

National Council of Teachers of English. (1996). *Standards for the English Language Arts.* Urbana, IL: Author & Newark, DE: International Reading Association.

National Council of Teachers of English. (2003). *NCTE/NCATE program standards: Program for initial preparation of teachers of secondary English language arts, Grades 7–12.* Retrieved November 28, 2006, from http://www.ncte.org/library/files/Programs/Teacher_Prep/RevisionApprovedStandards904.pdf

National Council of Teachers of Mathematics (NCTM). (1989). *Curriculum and evaluation standards for school mathematics.* Reston, VA.

National Council of Teachers of Mathematics (NCTM). (2000). *Principles and standards of school mathematics.* Reston, VA: Author.

National Geographic Society. (2001). *National Geographic Xpeditions: Geography standards.* Retrieved November 28, 2006, from http://www.nationalgeographic.com/xpeditions/standards/04/index.html

National Research Council. (1996). *National science education standards.* Washington, DC: National Academies Press.

National Research Council. (2000). *How people learn: Brain, mind, experience, and school* (expanded ed.). Washington, DC: National Academies Press.

National Science Teachers Association. (2003). *Standards for science teacher preparation.* Retrieved November 28, 2006, from http://www.nsta.org/main/pdfs/NSTAstandards2003.pdf

NCLB. (2001). *No Child Left Behind Act of 2001* (Public Law 107-110). Retrieved November 28, 2006, from http://www.ed.gov/nclb/landing.jhtml

Nelson, R. (2004). Behavioral study: Methods. *The Shrimp-Goby Chronicles.* Retrieved November 28, 2006, from http://explorebiodiversity.com/Hawaii/Shrimp-goby/Psilogobius/studies/Behavioral/Methods.htm

Newby, T., Stepich, D., Lehman, J., & Russell, J. (2006). *Educational technology for teaching and learning* (3rd ed). Upper Saddle River, NJ: Prentice Hall.

Office of Technology Assessment. (1995). *Teachers and technology: Making the connection.* (Report Summary OTA-EHR-616). Washington, DC: U.S. Government Printing Office.

Papert, S. (1980). *Mindstorms: Children, computers, and powerful ideas.* New York: Basic Books.

Pea, R., Mills, M., Rosen, J., Dauber, K., Effelsberg, W., & Hoffert. E. (2004, Jan–March). The DIVER™ Project: Interactive digital video repurposing. *IEEE Multimedia, 11*(1), 54–61.

Reed, P., & Bowser, G. (2000). *Assistive technology pointers for parents.* Winchester, OR: Coalition for Assistive Technology in Oregon.

R*TEC Teachers. (2005). *What is a WebQuest?* Retrieved November 28, 2006, from http://www.4teachers.org/intech/webquest.jsp

Rodriguez, A. (2001). The virtual reality skeleton project. *The Journal, 29*(1), 64–71.

Rozaitis, B., & Baepler, P. (2005). *Active learning with PowerPoint: Using PowerPoint to facilitate classroom assessment techniques.* Center for Teaching and Learning Services, University of Minnesota. Retrieved December 6, 2005, from http://www1.umn.edu/ohr/teachlearn/tutorials/powerpoint/assessment.html

The Secretary's Commission on Achieving Necessary Skills. (1991). *What work requires of schools: A SCANS report for America 2000.* Washington, DC: U.S. Department of Labor.

Sherin, M. G., & Han, S. (2004). Teacher learning in the context of a video club. *Teaching and Teacher Education, 20,* 163–183.

Sherin, M. G., & van Es, E. A. (2005). Using video to support teachers' ability to notice classroom interactions. *Journal of Technology and Teacher Education, 13*(3), 475–491.

Simpson, E. S. (2005). Evolution in the classroom: What teachers need to know about the video game generation. *TechTrends, 49*(5), 17–22.

Soloway, E., Jackson, S., Klein, J., Quintana, C., Reed, J., Spitulnik, J., Stratford, S., Studer, S., Jul, S., Eng, J., & Scala, N. (1996, April 14–18). Learning theory in practice: Case studies of learner-centered design. In M. J. Tauber, V. Bellotti, R. Jeffries, J. D. Mackinlay, & J. Nielsen (Eds.), *Proceedings of the ACM CHI 96 Human Factors in Computing Systems Conference* (pp. 189–196). New York: ACM Press.

Squire, K., Giovanetto, L., Devane, B., & Durga, S. (2005). From users to designers: Building a self-organizing game-based learning environment. *TechTrends, 49*(5), 34–42.

Tanner, L. (n.d.). *Distance learning, keypals: Fun with keypals.* Retrieved November 28, 2006, from http://www.uen.org/utahlink/activities/view_activity.cgi?activity_id=8103

Teachers Development Group. (2005). *Teacher reflection tool.* Portland, OR: Author.

Valencia, S. (1990). A portfolio approach to classroom reading assessment: The whys, whats and hows. *The Reading Teacher, 43,* 338–342.

Valencia, S., Heibert, E., & Afflerbach, P. (1994). *Authentic reading assessment: Practices and possibilities.* Newark, DE: International Reading Association.

Web-based Education Commission. (2000). *The power of the Internet for learning: Moving from promise to practice.* Retrieved November 28, 2006, from http://www.hpcnet.org/upload/wbec/reports/WBECReport.pdf

Whalley, J. (2004). *Teaching interactively with electronic whiteboards.* Retrieved November 28, 2006, from http://ferl.becta.org.uk/display.cfm?resID=8224

White, B. Y., & Frederiksen, J. R. (1998). Inquiry, modeling, and metacognition: Making science accessible to all students. *Cognition and Instruction, 16*(1), 3–18.

Wiggins, G., & McTighe, J. (2000). *Understanding by design: Study guide.* Alexandria, VA: Association for Supervision and Curriculum Development.

Wiggins, G., & McTighe, J. (2001). *Understanding by design.* Upper Saddle River, NJ: Merrill/Prentice Hall.

Wilson, J., Hannafin, M., & Ohme, P. (2006). *Triangle inside a rectangle.* Retrieved November 28, 2006, from http://intermath.coe.uga.edu/topics/geometry/triangle/r07.htm

Winn, W. D., & Jackson, R. (1999). Fourteen propositions about educational uses of virtual reality. *Educational Technology, 39*(4), 5–14.

Zorfass, J. (2001). Sustaining a curriculum innovation: Cases to make it happen! In J. Woodward & L. Cuban (Eds.), *Technology, curriculum and professional development: Adapting schools to meet the needs of students with disabilities* (pp. 87–114). Thousand Oaks, CA. Corwin.

Credits

ISTE NETS (pp. 3, 16, 35, 55, 73, 92, 110, 128, 143, 171, 192, 209, 231, 267, and 289): Adapted and reprinted with permission from National Education Technology Standards for Teachers: Preparing Teachers to Use Technology. © 2002, ISTE ® (International Society for Technology in Education), iste@iste.org, www.iste.org. All rights reserved. Permission does not constitute an endorsement by ISTE.

Chapter 1: p. 10 Courtesy of Seymour Papert. **p. 10** Courtesy of Chris Dede. **p. 11** Courtesy of Michael Hannafin. **p. 12** Courtesy of Marcia Linn. **p. 12** Courtesy of David Jonassen.

Chapter 2: p. 20 *Spotlight 2.1* American Psychological Association (1997). *Learner-Centered Psychological Principles.* Available online at http://www.apa.org/ed/lcp2/lcp14.html. Copyright © 1997 by the American Psychological Association, adapted with permission. This document is in the process of being revised and updated by an APA task force using a broad range of current psychological research. **p. 26** *Figure 2.1* Created by Qi Li.

Chapter 3: p. 37 *Figure 3.1* Used by permission of Behavior.org. **p. 43** *Spotlight 3.3* From www.cotf.edu. Reprinted by permission of Classroom of the Future, Center for Educational Technologies, Wheeling Jesuit University. **p. 54** *Figure 3.5* Supported by NSF, reprinted by permission of the TELS Center.

Chapter 4: p. 67 *Figure 4.1* Reprinted with permission from NCTM Principles and Standards for School Mathematics by National Council of Teachers of Mathematics. **p. 68** *Figure 4.2* Used by permission of Shodor Education Foundation, Inc. **p. 69** *Figure 4.3* Used by permission of National Library of Virtual Manipulatives, Copyrighted by Utah State University, with partial support from the National Science Foundation.

Chapter 5: p. 79 *Spotlight 5.3* Huitt, W. (2004). Bloom et al.'s taxonomy of the cognitive domain. Educational Psychology Interactive. Valdosta, GA: Valdosta State University. Used by permission. **p. 83** *Figure 5.5* Nelson, R. (2004). "Ethogram of Snapping Shrimp" Hawaiian Shrimp-Goby. Behavioral Study: Methods, The Shrimp-Goby chronicles. Retrieved July 1, 2006. Used by permission of Rob Nelson, www.ExploreBiodiversity.com

Chapter 6: p. 100 *Figure 6.3* Louie Psihoyos/GettyImages.

Chapter 7: p. 120 *Figure 7.2 Source:* http://www.teachersresroucebank.com/vrml/lessonplans/mapsellis/maps.html **p. 121** *Figure 7.3* Copyright © 2000 Landis Bennett,

360Geographics. www.360geographics.com. Reprinted with permission. **p. 124** *Figure 7.4* Used by permission of EnchantedLearning.com. **p. 125** *Figure 7.5* Used by permission of National Library of Virtual Manipulatives, Copyrighted by Utah State University, with partial support from the National Science Foundation. **p. 125** *Figure 7.6* From Intermath.coe.uga. Reprinted by permission of James W. Wilson, Math Education Department, University of Georgia.

Chapter 8: pp. 132–133 *Spotlight 8.1* Adapted from "Misunderstood Minds: Attention Responses," www.pbs.org/wgbh/misunderstoodminds/attentionstrats.html **p. 133** *Figure 8.1* Reprinted by permission of National Geographic Society. **p. 137** *Figure 8.3* Used by permission of Blackboard Inc.

Chapter 9: p. 150 *Figure 9.1* Created by Qi Li. **p. 151** *Figure 9.2* Created by Qi Li. **p. 151** *Figure 9.3* Created by Qi Li. **p. 153** *Figure 9.4 Source:* John Whalley, "Teaching Interactively with Electronic Whiteboards," http://ferl.becta.org.uk/display.cfm?resID=8224 **p. 155** *Figure 9.5* Created by Qi Li.

Chapter 10: pp. 180–181 *Figure 10.6* The FileMaker K–12 Starter Kit screenshot used in this publication is used with permission of FileMaker, Inc. FileMaker is a trademark of FileMaker, Inc., registered in the U.S. and other countries.

Chapter 11: p. 194 *Figure 11.1* Created by Chandra Orrill. **p. 198** *Figure 11.2* Reprinted by permission of Madison County Schools, Richmond, KY. **p. 199** *Figure 11.3* Reprinted by permission of Davison Community Schools, Davison, MI. **p. 200** *Figure 11.4* Used by permission of Bernie Dodge, PhD, San Diego State University. **pp. 201–202** *Figure 11.5* Reprinted by permission of ThinkQuest, Oracle Education Foundation. **p. 204** *Figure 11.6* Used by permission of Elaine Fitzgerald. **p. 205** *Figure 11.7* Copyright © Exploratorium, www.exploratorium.edu. Reprinted by permission.

Chapter 12: p. 210 *Spotlight 12.1* Jansen, Erin. "NetLingo The Internet Dictionary." 1994. http://www.netlingo.com. **p. 212** *Figure 12.1* From Knowledge Forum, see www.knowledgeforum.com for further information. Used by permission of Learning in Motion. **p. 213** *Figure 12.2* From Knowledge Forum, see www.knowledgeforum.com for further information. Used by permission of Learning in Motion. **p. 214** *Figure 12.3* From Knowledge Forum, see www.knowledgeforum.com for further information. Used by permission of Learning in Motion. **p. 220** *Figure 12.4 Source:* http://viz.globe.gov/viz-bin. Used by permission.

Index